IFFERENCE,
NATION

POINT/COUNTERPOINT

Philosophers Debate Contemporary Issues
Series Editors: James P. Sterba and Rosemarie Tong

This new series provides a philosophical angle to debates currently raging in academic and larger circles. Each book is a short volume (around 200 pages) in which two or more prominent philosophers debate different sides of an issue. For more information contact Professor Sterba, Department of Philosophy, University of Notre Dame, Notre Dame, IN 46566, or Professor Tong, Department of Philosophy, Davidson College, Davidson, NC 28036.

DISABILITY, DIFFERENCE, DISCRIMINATION

Perspectives on Justice in Bioethics and Public Policy

Anita Silvers, David Wasserman,
and Mary B. Mahowald

Afterword by Lawrence C. Becker

ROWMAN & LITTLEFIELD PUBLISHERS, INC.
Lanham • Boulder • New York • Oxford

ROWMAN & LITTLEFIELD PUBLISHERS, INC.

Published in the United States of America
by Rowman & Littlefield Publishers, Inc.
4720 Boston Way, Lanham, Maryland 20706

12 Hid's Copse Road
Cumnor Hill, Oxford OX2 9JJ, England

British Library Cataloguing in Publication Information Available

Library of Congress Cataloging-in-Publication Data

Silvers, Anita.
    Disability, difference, discrimination : perspectives on justice
in bioethics and public policy / Anita Silvers, David Wasserman, and
Mary B. Mahowald.
        p.   cm.—(Point/counterpoint)
    Includes bibliographical references and index.
    ISBN 0-8476-9222-1 (cloth : alk. paper).—ISBN 0-8476-9223-X
(paper : alk. paper)
    1. Physically handicapped—United States.   2. Discrimination
against the handicapped—United States.   3. Social justice—United States.
I. Wasserman, David, 1953–   .   II. Mahowald, Mary Briody.   III. Title.
IV. Series.
HV3023.A3S55   1998
362.4'0973—dc21   98-38036
                                                                              CIP

Printed in the United States of America

∞ ™ The paper used in this publication meets the minimum requirements of
American National Standard for Information Sciences—Permanence of Paper for
Printed Library Materials, ANSI Z39.48–1984.

Contents

Acknowledgments

The authors all wish to thank Janet Kourany, James Sterba, and Rosemarie Tong for their support for this project; Richard Arneson for his challenging comments; and Maureen MacGrogan for superb editorial guidance.

Anita Silvers expresses her gratitude to her wonderful colleagues—Larry Becker, Mary Mahowald, and David Wasserman—for making the creation of this volume a stimulating and pleasurable experience. Anita Silvers also thanks Leslie Francis, Mary Rorty, and Iris Marion Young for their encouragement of philosophical work on disability; Rosamond Rhodes, whose invitation in 1973 to speak at Mount Sinai Medical School about disability rights opened an intellectual door; Barbara Koenig and Hank Greely of the Stanford Center for Biomedical Ethics for the opportunity to participate in the Center's activities and address cutting-edge issues in bioethics and public policy from a disability perspective; Colin Barnes, Mairian Corker, Vic Finkelstein, Mark Priestly, and Tom Shakespeare for their enlightening comments (on the disability research Internet list) about the differences between American and British approaches to justice for people with disabilities; Els Maeckelberghe of Groningen University and Marian Verhey of Erasmus University for their stimulating and challenging questions; Dean Nancy McDermid and Cathy Grans of San Francisco State University for much help and thousands of kindnesses; Judy Kertész, Sandy Nelson, and Darra Wilcox for their patience and skill in conducting research and helping with manuscript preparation; and her San Francisco State University colleagues Don Brown and Ned Fielden for their solidarity in the pursuit of equality for people with disabilities.

David Wasserman would like to thank Jerome Bickenbach for extensive, insightful comments on the first draft of his chapter/section and Arthur Evenchik and Robert Wachbroit for valuable advice on his responses.

Mary Mahowald appreciates support from the American Council of Learned Societies and the Creighton University Center for Health Policy and Ethics and from the University of Chicago for leave to work on this book and related projects. She thanks Susan Wendell for reading an earlier draft.

Introduction

On the day I completed my contribution to this volume, a faculty colleague and I sat soaked by rain outside the local grocery store, waiting until some pedestrian, happening by, was willing to walk in, find the manager, and convince him to unpadlock the only entrance to the store wide enough to admit our wheelchairs. The manager's reason for chaining it shut? Other shoppers were using it to push shopping carts out to the parking lot, and sometimes farther. Their transgressions cost the business time and money to retrieve or replace the carts. For the manager, stranding a few wheelchair-using shoppers in the rain seemed a small price for protecting his property.

My colleague saw our situation with the fresh indignation of someone who, physically carefree for most of his life, now finds the thoughtlessness of the driver who knocked him off his bicycle and into a wheelchair reimposed on him daily by a thoughtless society. Later he wrote to me: "The aspect of these situations that pushes me over the edge is how someone else's problem (in this case, shopping cart migration) becomes my problem (cannot enter). As you well know, we accept countless humiliations and repudiations daily and learn to ignore most of them, but then something like this happens. Folks wonder why wheelchair types like us care if we can't get into a store. What is wrong with these people? This is America, which at least pays lip service to issues of equality."

Although my colleague and I have led very different lives, possess different talents, and seek to satisfy different tastes, we share a special reality imposed on us because we use wheelchairs. This volume engages with that reality by exploring how justice can address the social exclusion we experience in common with the fifty million other Americans who have disabilities.

Anita Silvers

1

Because their difference from other people is inescapable and can be concealed—if at all—only at formidable cost to their energy and self-esteem, the existence of people with serious disabilities tests the comprehensiveness of theories of social justice. For what we expect a just society to place within everyone's reach, and how far we think every citizen's reach should extend, is shaped by the commonplaces of our corporeal and intellectual functioning. How we function constructs not only the objects of our ambition but also how we express and collectivize our interests in them.

Traditional democratic morality privileges the perspectives fashioned by familiar ways of functioning, thereby magnifying "normal" bodily and intellectual performances into standards against which the disabled shrink so as to become invisible. Traditional political morality thus has adopted a discourse in which disability, in virtue of the functional limitations it represents, is easily supposed to alter people so profoundly as to render them "naturally" and irredeemably unequal. As a result, many traditional democratic accounts of justice have failed to embrace people with disabilities and so have not advanced them, while many others have immobilized the disabled in a suffocating embrace. One aim of the essays in this volume is to consider how the theories of some leading contemporary philosophies of social justice situate people with disabilities. Another is to propose how they should be situated in a comprehensive theory of social justice.

Whether we invoke justice in responding to disability, and how we do so, affects those individuals, from neonates to the fragile elderly, who are identified as being disabled, as well as their families and acquaintances. Another group with interests in this matter consists of people who someday will be disabled. If nothing else, prudence recommends that members of both groups invest in an understanding of disability compatible with maintaining their self-respect and self-esteem.

Nor should we forget those individuals, not themselves disabled, whose interests engage with the interests of disabled people. So, for example, feminist scholarship approaches the topic of disability with concern about the responsibilities of caring for people with disabilities and about the importance of liberating women from narrow and oppressive caregiving roles. More generally, a robust analysis of justice cannot avoid considering whether people without disabilities have a fair interest in eliminating disability so as to free up otherwise encumbered resources.

If so, is justice served better by restoring or rehabilitating those who are disabled or instead by removing the social barriers that make disability burdensome to the disabled and nondisabled alike? Moreover, is justice furthered by preventing disability? If so, does justice obligate us to keep existing people from becoming disabled? And if this is the case, do the grounds that impel us to protect existing nondisabled people against becoming disabled make it similarly just to keep people who are disabled from existing? Some philosophers have argued just so, insisting that in view of their suffering it would be better if people with certain disabilities did not exist.

Classical liberal thought has not regarded serious corporeal or intellectual impairment as merely accidental to a person's moral status. Nor have individuals' disabilities been considered negligible in deciding whether they deserve a full array of opportunities for social participation. Furthermore, whatever their personal accomplishments, people who are impaired bear the burden of membership in what traditionally has been viewed as a "weak" class, one defined as requiring heightened protection because its members are feeble or incompetent. Insofar as they are defined as being helpless, they have been exempted from contributing to, but also preempted from profiting from, the collective good. That is, their being disabled has been taken to justify a drastic reduction in their opportunities and also in their obligations.

What philosophy usually has considered important about people with disabilities is their difference. For, in searching for limiting cases, philosophers have turned to prototypical portrayals of disability for illumination. For example, considering whether the congenitally blind understand color terms is used to delineate the role direct observation plays in understanding. Asking whether profoundly impaired neonates should live tests how much we value life itself, as distinct from what individuals accomplish in life. And questioning why we favor severely intellectually compromised people over clever animals suggests where we locate the value of being human.

But limiting cases do not center significance; they lie at its edges. The philosophical practice of prototyping people who are physically, sensorily, or cognitively impaired and presenting them as limiting cases cannot help but marginalize them. The philosophers who introduce these examples do so to drive their philosophical inquiries, not to represent life with a disability. Yet whatever their intentions, by repeatedly describing the extremities, and almost never the routine, of living with a disability, philosophical practice depicts living this way as a fringe existence.

In this regard, the public sphere is in advance of philosophy in acknowledging a larger role for people with disabilities. For from the civic point of view, a profound transformation in our consciousness of citizens with disabilities has been gathering momentum for the past thirty years. Drastic policy alterations and shifts of expectations now regularly affect the lives of the fifty million Americans identified by the U.S. census as "disabled." The 1990 Americans with Disabilities Act marks a significant evolution of the status of citizens with disabilities by advancing them beyond confinement to a class subject(ed) to special treatment and by joining them with other minorities as classes explicitly designated to command equal treatment.

Nevertheless, it would be misleading to suppose that people with serious physical, sensory, and cognitive impairments have enjoyed a seamless, transparent, and unproblematic transition from exclusion to equality. Even though inferior or unfavorable treatment based on an individual's disability is more often challenged today than formerly, perplexing questions remain about whether to equalize people who appear to be in deficit in respect to customary modes and typical levels of functioning. If so, in what does their equality consist? And do obligations to compensate them rest with nondisabled people who are not responsible for anyone's being impaired? As people with disabilities become more visible in the community and more vocal in their claims, this last matter occasions increasing discord.

Must a just society equalize people because of (rather than despite) their disabilities? Anita Silvers argues that the inequality visited upon persons with disabilities is rooted in social practices that bar them from demonstrating their competence. Neglecting to offer people with physical, sensory, or cognitive impairments access to the opportunities we think it just that other citizens enjoy usually has been defended by conceptualizing them as limited and deficient. The disabled furthermore are categorized as having "special" needs. The consequent apprehensiveness about their being demanding and burdensome results in practices that avoid their presence rather than seek it out. To illustrate the impact of such practices, Silvers quotes the writings of people with disabilities who describe the socially imposed isolation that characterizes their lives.

To assume that the "problem" of disability should be addressed distributively exacerbates such stereotyping, Silvers argues. Distributive approaches take disability to be the product of profound natural inequalities in corporeal and intellectual functioning. Distributive discourses discuss the disabled primarily in terms of whether their deficits warrant their receiving extraordinary allocations of resources. Distributive considerations thus naturalize the identification of disability with neediness. In doing so, they define disability as a condition that defies equalizing. Distributing resources more generously to the disabled than to others thus cannot reconfigure the circumstances that dim their prospects, for doing so sustains rather than shatters interpersonal practice unfair to, because dismissive of, them.

Silvers urges that the social isolation of people with disabilities be diminished, and their equality furthered, by remedying the externally imposed obstructions to their social access rather than by correcting their personal flaws and failings. Her theory echoes the revolutionizing theory of the 1990 Americans with Disabilities Act (ADA)—namely, the view that not extraordinary resources but, instead, social access equal to other people's is needed to affirm the public value of the lives of people with disabilities. The ADA, she says, promotes a momentous evolution of the status of citizens with disabilities by advancing them beyond confinement to a class subject(ed) to special treatment and by joining them with other minorities as classes explicitly designated to command equal treatment.

She recommends assessing the justice of traditional practices by considering whether they are in denial about, and consequently deny, the full social participation of people with physical, sensory, or cognitive impairment. The idea is to reveal and correct the social deprivation that past attempts to collectivize them as a weak class have visited upon the disabled. Practices fashioned in the belief that disability is a good reason to disqualify people from access to civic and commercial goods require the strictest scrutiny. Considering the fairness of the historical assumptions about disability that shape our social practice will indicate what compensation justice demands for the class of people with disabilities. But this does not mean that personal compensation is owed to the class's members.

Because readers may be unfamiliar with our current disability system and unaware of the perspectives of people with disabilities, Silvers includes illustrations from the history of disability policy and observations voiced by people with disabilities. This material also provides a context for the two essays that follow hers.

In contrast to Silvers, Wasserman argues that a just social response to disabilities must encompass distributive concerns and that it can do so without treating people with impairments as defective or incompetent. At the same time, he acknowledges that recent theories of distributive justice have tended to distort the significance of impairments by treating them as natural inequalities that a just society has some obligation to correct or compensate for. Seen in these terms, people with impairments have a claim to special assistance because they fall below the line for full participation in a society's cooperative scheme; such assistance typically takes the form of resources set aside from the general distribution to fix impairments or compensate the impaired.

Wasserman argues that this response is manifestly inadequate, reflecting an oversimplified view of disabilities as internal deficits. Because the disadvantages associated with impairments largely arise from the interaction between the impaired individual and her physical and social environment, justice requires modifications of the environment as well as, or instead of, corrective or compensatory measures. The issue is not one of compensating for natural inequalities but of accommodating a wide variety of needs, interests, capacities, and ends with limited resources; it is a general problem of distributive justice, not a special problem of disability.

Wasserman then considers approaches that view justice for people with impairments primarily or exclusively in terms of the redress of discrimination and the reconstruction of the social environment. While the recognition that disabilities are socially constructed has served as an important corrective to theories of justice that treat disabilities as natural inequalities, that recognition does not obviate the need for an adequate theory of distributive justice. In shaping the environment, no less than in distributing goods and services, we inevitably face difficult trade-offs among the interests of different people, trade-offs that cannot be adjudicated by an injunction against discrimination or a demand for equal access. Unless we wish to make these trade-offs on an ad hoc basis, we require a more comprehensive theory of justice.

Wasserman concludes that such a theory faces two formidable challenges. First, it must assess the fairness of a cooperative scheme with a metric of well-being that takes account of what people can do with the resources they have, while respecting the multiplicity of ways in which people can do well. But what is the appropriate metric? Should we strive to ensure that every citizen has the opportunity to select from a replete array of possible life plans? Must we guarantee that each is able to exercise at least the primary abilities? Should each be offered the embrace of a welcoming culture or subculture?

Second, a theory of justice must decide how much inequality on its chosen metric is acceptable. It must address perennial questions about the morality of "leveling down" to achieve equality, about the priority of the worst-off, and about the moral significance of numbers in conflicts over scarce resources or incompatible designs.

For Mahowald, justice for people with disabilities is neither formal nor distributive but instead a dialectical process mediating among various standpoints irreducible to one another. It involves recognition of differences and the inequities associated with them, along with efforts to reduce such inequities through therapeutic or social measures. The notion of equality that underlies Mahowald's view entails attribution of equal value to different individuals. Practical implementation of this view requires participation of nondominant individuals in the determination of social priorities. She proposes an egalitarian version of feminist standpoint theory as the rationale for assigning a privileged position to this participation.

While particularly concerned with justice for women, an egalitarian feminist standpoint also demands justice for other nondominant individuals and groups. Further, it demands attention to differences that occur within nondominant groups. In this context, differences relevant to disabilities are considered, including their cause or etiology, time of onset, duration, severity, type of impairment, and visibility to others. Mahowald also examines differences with regard to the caregiving role, which is often associated with gender inequity.

Egalitarian feminism, for Mahowald, focuses on material equality, recognizing that this sometimes entails constraints on the liberty of those who would otherwise acquire inequitable material advantage. Addressing the potential tension between feminist concerns for women's self-determination and advocacy for persons with disabilities, she argues that the two are compatible so long as the woman's choice—for instance, about whether to carry or terminate a fetus who may be disabled—remains uninfluenced by the fact of the disability. Such a criterion preempts, or at least reduces, the possibility that women's exercise of autonomy may contribute to the material disadvantage of people with disabilities.

A just social policy consistent with an egalitarian feminist standpoint is one that mediates between the interests and needs of those who are disabled, their caregivers, and others, attributing equal value to each. Mahowald's conclusion returns us to the question of compensation. Who is harmed by the current disability system, who should be compensated, what are the permissible personal and social costs of compensation, and who should bear them? Does the system mitigate inequalities or prolong them? Although some of their views about disability are compatible, the authors represented in this volume are not in agreement about the answers to these questions. In this regard, they reflect the discord that disability policy increasingly occasions in the larger society.

Finally, Lawrence Becker adds another perspective in an afterword, commenting, "[M]y own experience in living with a significant physical disability since my early teens . . . has been that when my own 'disability issues' are framed either in terms of love or in terms of justice, in the long run things do not go very well for anyone concerned." Becker goes on to propose that disability issues are both clarified and more readily resolved if they are treated as coordination problems. He offers a brief exploration of this idea, drawing upon the theory of strategic action coupled with consideration of norms of reciprocity.

Several themes central to the philosophical consideration of disability run through these essays. Among these are dependence, independence, and interdependence; equality and difference; normalcy and deviancy; biological and social, or natural and artificial, (dis)advantage; (the loss of) intrinsic or instrumental value; fairness in allocating benefits and burdens; Kantian concerns for human dignity and utilitarian concerns for aggregate welfare; and assessments of quality of life and the requisites for human flourishing.

However, an important matter that is often addressed in the initial stages of theorizing about disability is not fully discussed in any of the essays. This is the matter of nomenclature, about which much discussion and almost as much discord exists. At the heart of the problem is the desire to employ non–value-laden or neutral terminology, language that does not dispose those who talk about disability to adopt one rather than another of the competing models of disablement.

Take, for example, the connection between impairment and disability. The variety of ways in which impairment is distinguished from disability (and, for that matter, disability from handicap) still confuses scholarship in this field. In the currently prevailing nomenclature, impairment is a physical or mental anomaly. When impairments occasion substantial limitations in major life activities, they are disabling. However, while some writers use *impairment* to refer to a biological condition (such as a missing limb) and *disablement* to refer to any functional limitation occasioned by such a condition, other writers treat functional limitations (such as dyslexia or dyscalculia) as impairments that are disabilities whenever they impede major life activities. Another way of making the distinction is to conceptu alize impairment as pertaining to individuals' anomalous physical, sensory, or cognitive performances, whereas disablement characterizes the way in which their environment reduces such individuals' functionality. Examples of all these uses of the nomenclature, and of other uses as well, will be found in the scholars' comments quoted by the authors of this volume.

Because walking, seeing, and hearing are performances crucial to major life activities, impairments that substantially limit them usually are considered disabilities. But from some perspectives, the inability to walk, see, or hear does not signal that a person is impaired. Those who are at home in Deaf culture, for instance, communicate with each other so effectively that they consider themselves at no loss and therefore as unimpaired. Moreover, not every impairment imposes disablement. On the other hand, disablement can occur without impairment; sometimes merely being regarded as impaired can disable a person.

The "disabled" names the class of individuals whose apparently anomalous physical, sensory, or cognitive performances are the occasion of diminished functionality. But, as a class, the "disabled" is not coextensive with the class of those who are impaired. Parenthetically, the World Health Organization is revising its International Categorization of Impairment, Disability, and Handicap by replacing "disability" with "limited activity" and "handicap" with "limited social participation." The revision reframes impairment as pertaining to biological systems rather than, as in the earlier version, to organs, but it retains reference to supposed biological norms as the standard against which individuals are judged to be impaired.[1]

Furthermore, there is no uniformity of preference among those who continue to use the expression "disabled," especially in the context of emancipatory writing on the subject. British disability activists speak of "disabled people" to emphasize that disablement is the social process of preventing individuals with certain characteristics from being respected and rewarded as ordinary persons are. American disability activists speak

---

1. For these texts, see the World Health Organization Web page at URL // www.who.ch/Welcome.html/.

of "people with disabilities" to emphasize that disablement does not reduce the essential inner person, however much it oppresses the contingent
social person. In both countries reference to "the disabled" is vexed by a
felt conflict between rejecting the stereotyping that relegates individuals
with very different types of impairments to a single inferior class and reap-
ing the political benefits of collectivizing people with very different types
of impairments into a significant political force.[2]

Given the complexity of the conceptual relationship between impairment and disablement, and the controversy about the lexical relationship
between disability and persons, the authors of this volume's essays have
not essayed either to analyze or to stipulate proper usage. Each has tried
to be lucid in her or his own usage. Generally, "people with disabilities"
refers to collections of individuals who have a condition commonly considered to be a physical, sensory, or cognitive impairment; "disabled people" to collections of individuals who are subjected to the social process
of disablement; while "the disabled" signals an assertion about the class
of people with disabilities rather than about each individual included in
the class of such individuals. "The disabled" thus is the subject of sen-
tences that assign collective rather than personal attributes. The authors
also have tried to be clear about how, within the framework of each essay,
the connection between impairment and disablement is being conceived.
Nevertheless, given the absence of a broader standard regarding terminology, attention to how these terms are being used, especially by the many
different writers quoted in the volume, is advisable to avoid confusion.

Finally, much of the work contained in this book has been enriched by
insights coming from the newly emerging area of disability studies, so a
few words describing this academic field are in order. Analyzing disability
as a category of oppression was initiated during the 1970s by crossovers
from radical philosophy to the disability movement in Britain. Subsequently, American disability activists adopted the model because it both
illuminated how they experienced their restrictions and gave a direction to
social reform.[3]

---

2. Vic Finkelstein, *Attitudes and Disabled People* (New York: World Rehabilitation Fund, 1980) and private E-mail correspondence from Vic Finkelstein, 6 December 1996.

3. See, for instance, Mark Priestley, "Commonality and Difference in the Movement: An 'Association of Blind Asians' in Leeds," *Disability and Society* 10, no. 2
(1995): 157–69; Tom Shakespeare, "Disability, Identity and Difference" in *Ex-*

Disability studies has attempted to integrate lines of thought drawn from Georg Hegel, Karl Marx, and Michel Foucault with the classical liberalism of the American civil rights movement. Although in Britain disability studies scholarship has been dominated by sociologists and other social scientists, literary and historical cultural studies have been afforded somewhat more prominence than sociology as the field has developed in the United States. But it is the divergence in public policy, not in academic setting, in the two nations that makes the most important difference in how disability studies has evolved.

In Britain the reconceptualization of disability has emerged from academic study to inform public policy. In the United States, on the other hand, it is reconceptualized public policy that draws scholarly attention to a more profound understanding of the theoretical dimensions of disability. We should not underestimate the influence of the 1990 Americans with Disabilities Act on how academics in the United States are coming to theorize the just treatment of corporeal and cognitive difference.

This volume illustrates the new law's impact on what we think, both personally and socially, about disability. The essays that comprise it take very different positions about how justice for people with disabilities may best be secured. Nevertheless, all reflect the conceptualizations introduced and the social climate induced by the Americans with Disabilities Act. As a result, all the essays discuss disability in fresh terms as they argue about how it challenges philosophical commonplaces.

---

ploring the Divide: Illness and Disability, ed. Colin Barnes and Geoff Mercer (Leeds, U.K.: Disability Press, 1996), 94–113; and Sharon Barnartt, "Disability Culture or Disability Consciousness?" *Journal of Disability Policy Studies* 7, no. 2 (1996): 2–19.

1

Formal Justice

Anita Silvers

A person is someone who can be a citizen, that is, a fully cooperating member of society over a complete life . . . for our purposes . . . I leave aside permanent physical disabilities . . . so severe as to prevent persons from being normal and fully cooperating members of society in the usual sense.[1]—John Rawls

Faruk Sabanovic, 21, who was felled by a sniper on a street in central Sarajevo last year, must now use a wheelchair. "It's strange," said Mr. Sabanovic, a paraplegic who slaloms along the rutted sidewalks or down the streets, going about his business in his Quickie, a state-of-the-art, lightweight wheelchair. "I was walking normally like anybody else. A few days after I was wounded, I was meeting the same people, and they treated me differently. There's something in people's minds that makes them think because we are in wheelchairs we are weird."[2]—*New York Times*, 1 August 1996

Introduction: Access to Equality

For most of this century, and in earlier times as well, the drawn curtains of invalid rooms, rest homes, hospitals for incurables, sheltered workshops, asylums, and almshouses concealed most disability from the public view.

---

1. John Rawls, "Justice as Fairness: Political Not Metaphysical," *Philosophy and Public Affairs* 14 (1985): 233.
2. Jane Perlez, "Bitter Burden on Sarajevo: Invalids of War: A City with a Legacy of Tolerance Finds It Hard to Help the War Wounded," *New York Times*, 1 August 1996, A5.

That was an era when American courts sometimes barred children with physical disabilities from school to avoid the other pupils becoming depressed. For a similar reason, maimed, mutilated, or otherwise deformed individuals were banned from public thoroughfares in some municipalities.

Over the past thirty years, however, people with disabilities increasingly have advanced their claims to equality in civic and commercial life. Disability accordingly has become a visible presence in the public sphere. That there is a growing public commitment to acknowledge individuals with disabilities is suggested by the growing expression of a previously unheard of interest in making the built and manufactured environment accessible to their inclusion.

The blue-and-white wheelchair symbol that marks doors, rest rooms, parking, and other facilities as usable by people with disabilities has become a familiar sight in public places. For deaf viewers, every television set sold since July 1993 has to have the capacity to display captioned text to make visible what speakers say, and most television programs (but not commercials and public service announcements) produced after January 1998 have to be captioned. E-mail and relay telephone operators facilitate commercial communication between hearing people and deaf people. Watches, calculators, computers, and even cars now talk to their users using descendants of adaptive voice output devices originally designed to give visually impaired people audio access to text. Similarly, speech recognition devices originally developed to assist data entry by persons with limited manual ability now are in common use by a much broader population. Consumers can choose from among more than a dozen software programs that permit them to dictate to computers. And many other kinds of machines have been made to perform to the sound of their master's voice.

But as the adaptive tools people with disabilities use become more familiar and their existence consequently less easy to disregard, the challenge their differences pose for a democratic society is increasingly troubling. The centuries during which these differences were defined as inferiorities cannot easily be overcome. It thus becomes pressing to consider whether justice requires only that the presence of people with disabilities be acknowledged, or whether, in a just society, they must be equalized as well.

Disability: A Democratic Dilemma

If equality should be conferred upon people with disabilities, in what does their equality consist? Democratic morality inveterately condemns artificial inequalities stemming from social arrangements, particularly if individuals are unwarrantedly penalized because they are identified with an unfairly disparaged group. In contrast, the democratic point of view does not likewise uniformly reject natural inequalities occasioned by individual disparities of talent, industriousness, or luck.

This leaves us with two crucial questions about the equality of people with disabilities. First, we must decide whether the disadvantages characteristically associated with those differences we identify as physical, sensory, or cognitive impairments are artificial or natural. Second, we must come to terms with whether we are morally or politically obligated to mitigate or rectify the specific kind(s) of disadvantage occasioned by those sorts of differences—that is, whether we are required to equalize people because of their disabilities.

There are answers to these questions that present familiar profiles because they have been so important in elevating other subordinated groups. The emancipatory arguments that improved the social participation of women and people of color are illustrative. As the twentieth century began, the inferior status and attenuated social participation of women and people of color were portrayed as being natural consequences of their differences in talent and character.

For instance, as George Fredrickson observes, "Blacks . . . were regarded for centuries as inherently unassimilable because . . . subhuman."[3] And Rosalind Miles comments on a similar phenomenon, the biologization of the rationale for women's oppression: "Women's imputed physical and mental frailty . . . became the grounds for refusing her any civil or legal rights, indeed any change from the 'state of nature' in which she dwelt."[4] Now, as the twentieth century ends, political morality attributes these same disadvantages to misuses of power that promote social arrangements artificially biased against women and people of color. The harmful results of such bias call for compensation; its institutional residue is condemned as overdue for change.

Are the disadvantages of being disabled similarly traceable to being inequitably treated merely because of being different from the dominant class? Or should the disadvantage that results when illness, injury, or ge-

---

3. George Fredrickson, "America's Caste System: Will It Change?" *New York Review of Books* 44, no. 16 (23 October 1997): 68.

4. Rosalind Miles, *A Women's History of the World* (London: Joseph, 1988), 187.

netic inheritance reduces physical or cognitive performance below the common level of proficiency be written off as the natural outcome of bad luck or of unhealthy or irresponsible lifestyles? With our immense medical, technological, and manufacturing proficiency, there is a growing probability that individuals made dysfunctional by infection, trauma, or deleterious genes need not remain so if appropriate social arrangements are in place to address their deficits. At least in this sense, then, when disadvantage attendant on disability goes unremedied, its persistence is a social rather than a biological phenomenon.

There are three familiar social strategies for addressing the dysfunction associated with disability:

1. We provide medical treatment and rehabilitation that restores people's functionality.
2. We manufacture adaptive equipment such as talking computers and power wheelchairs that assists people's functionality.
3. We alter the environment to make it more functional for people who cannot see, hear, walk, or execute other familiar performances.

Of course, the fact that we can equalize people with physical, sensory, and cognitive impairments by enhancing their functionality, and that our medical and mechanical skills permit us to do so with more facility than ever before, does not entail that we are obligated to do so. Nevertheless, our increasing proficiency in securing functional success for people despite their physical, sensory, or cognitive impairment makes the prospect of equalizing them ever more feasible. So clarifying whether justice obligates us to do so becomes more urgent than it was when relatively little in the lives of such people could be improved.

The initial step in pursuing this discussion is to ask whether just principles of material distribution may reference physical, sensory, or cognitive anomalies and, if so, whether they should do so. That is, should individuals' physical, sensory, or cognitive anomalies be taken to authorize increases of material opportunity allocated for the purpose of repairing them or rectifying their impact? Or instead should such anomalies serve as justificatory reasons for the practical exclusion of some individuals from material opportunity? One other option also presents itself, namely, that material principles and the practices that express them should be constructed to be neutral in respect to whether persons are normal or impaired.

Conflict about Competence

In this regard, people with disabilities encounter a deep-seated cultural ambivalence concerning the roles considered appropriate for them. The result is to obscure what should count for equalizing them. So one of the goals of this essay is to clarify the discussion about what obligations democratic morality imposes on a liberal society in respect to its disabled members.

I shall argue that justice requires us to act affirmatively by enlarging the artificially depressed social opportunities available to people with physical, sensory, and cognitive impairments. But I shall be cautionary about any approach to doing so that directly compensates individuals with disabilities for their disadvantages. However praiseworthy, the generous distribution of resources cannot reconfigure the circumstances that dim their prospects. Distributing benefits to individuals with disabilities does not address the bias that isolates them. The disadvantage imposed by biased practice is best addressed by reforming that practice itself.

Nondisabled readers may be unaware of, and consequently never have questioned, the presuppositions of our current disability system or reflected on the far-reaching impact of its operative conceptualizations. In fact, they may know nothing about how this system works or have not imagined how it not only pervades the experiences of people with disabilities but also influences what other people think of them. Consequently, I will interject more illustrative narrative than philosophers are accustomed to finding in work conducted in the discipline. By interpolating cases and commentary about life as a person with a disability into my argument, I aim to offer readers a disability perspective on the current system.

Sociologist Gary Albrecht believes that the current disability system is driven by two conflicting values.[5] One is the self-regarding virtue of working, and the other is the other-regarding value of sustaining people who are not working. In Western society, he says, individuals earn their place in society through their work—indeed, are identified with their work.[6] Employment, then, is a personal or individual value. On the other hand, there is a social need to acknowledge the fundamental value of human life,

---

5. Gary Albrecht, *The Disability Business: Rehabilitation in America* (London: Sage, 1992), 134.
6. Albrecht, *Disability Business*, 119.

which requires maintaining a safety net to supply a minimum level of support to those unable to sustain a productive employment identity.

"Disability," Albrecht comments, "is a relative concept based on work and need values negotiated in specific social situations."[7] All too often though, as Albrecht also observes, the situation in which such negotiations take place pits an individual worker pursuing a personal interest in retaining her employment identity against a system that identifies impairment with weakness and the inability to be productive. Eliding impairment with incompetence, a conceptual move executed all too easily on such occasions, forestalls sustaining individuals with disabilities in the workplace.

The case of Pauline Horvath is illustrative. In its outline, it is a story many people with disabilities recognize as theirs. Evident in Horvath's history is the intolerance they have experienced in attempting to maintain their productive identity in the workplace.

When Horvath was hired by the U.S. Navy for a clerical position, a wheelchair ramp was installed to give her access to the office. Horvath worked successfully for six years. In 1988, however, a new supervisor refused to let her use the chair in the office area, saying, "It's my office and I do not want a wheelchair in it." Proclaiming that no one should have to hear about or see any of that "handicapped stuff" in a work environment, the supervisor required Horvath to conceal her wheelchair in a closet during work hours and prohibited her from using a desktop in-box (she had to cross the room to get each piece of work) and a speakerphone (her severe rheumatoid arthritis made raising the receiver to her ear very painful).

As her doctors had warned, Horvath's arthritic hips became so damaged that she had to have them replaced; during her recovery from surgery, the Navy fired her, claiming she was not able to execute the essential duties of her job.[8] Although the Navy's internal investigation determined that

---

7. Albrecht, *Disability Business*, 119.

8. Disability discrimination law protects individuals from supervisors who construe requests for accommodation to a disability as demands for privilege that challenge managerial authority. See Thayer C. Scott, "Disabled Woman, Alameda Depot Settle Bias Suit: 9 Years of Torment at Naval Station," *San Francisco Chronicle*, 27 November 1997, A25. Here the supervisor incorrectly assimilated adaptive aids like wheelchairs and speakerphones (when used to permit an individual with an unusual body to perform the essential duties of a job) to the office furniture ordinarily used or not used according to a manager's preference.

Horvath had been discriminated against, the Navy continued to defend her supervisor's right to determine the mode she used to execute the work. Horvath sued and settled for $300,000; other actions she filed are pending.

Philosopher-attorney Jerome Bickenbach echoes Albrecht's point when he observes how public policy is driven by conflicting convictions about whether people with disabilities should be expected to work:

> In Canada, as in most industrial nations, the greatest portion of funding allo-cated for disablement policy is devoted to programs that give people with disabilities a ticket out of the labour market. But a considerable portion of what is left over is spent trying to induce this same population to become employed.[9]

This ambivalence about whether people with disabilities should assume ordinary roles or be confined to specially protected ones pervades the culture. Supervisors fear that they will be required to assume the burden of protecting people with disabilities in the workplace, and the parents of children with disabilities fear that their children will forfeit protection if they enter the workplace. Writing as the mother of a daughter with a disability, but plainly not as a woman with a disability herself, feminist Barbara Hillyer argues in *Feminism and Disability* that to have a disability is to be dependent: "Basic to working out relationships among women in connection with disability are social expectations about dependence and independence. For the disabled person, the problem is how to cope with being dependent."[10]

Hillyer continues with a story about "a paraplegic woman . . . who insisted on building her own house without the aid of a contractor or other able-bodied help. No one questioned the possibly inappropriate or excessive quality of her 'independence.' "[11] The "paraplegic woman" completed the project successfully, but her competence is of negligible interest to the author. What is instead of paramount importance to Hillyer is the disagreeableness or threat of the "paraplegic woman's" having

---

9. Jerome Bickenbach, *Physical Disability and Social Policy* (Toronto: University of Toronto Press, 1993), 121.

10. Barbara Hillyer, *Feminism and Disability* (Norman: University of Oklahoma Press, 1993), 10.

11. Hillyer, *Feminism and Disability*, 11.

stepped beyond her properly dependent role. Hillyer perceives such an act as disturbingly excessive. Her own reactions inadvertently show that disabled people's problems about "how to cope with being dependent" are not only or always about needing others' care.

Hillyer is convinced that women with disabilities must accept their limitations by absenting themselves from roles not traditional for the disabled. Reviewing *Feminism and Disability*, Karen Hirsch writes, "In Barbara Hillyer's world all caregivers are women, and a woman is either a caregiver or she is disabled and needs care to be provided for her. Thus, there is no place for the experiences of disabled women."[12] As Hillyer makes evident by the nature of her admonitions, for a person with a disability, coping with being dependent is often a matter of absorbing condemnation for assuming roles that one can perform competently but that are considered inappropriate or excessive because they are executed without others' help.

I admit to finding Hillyer's example particularly irksome because I am a paraplegic woman who remodeled my house without the aid of a contractor. But the point to be made here is far more general: people with disabilities find themselves enmeshed in a paternalistic culture in which their successful engagement in commonplace enterprises that support their flourishing is felt by (some) others to be threatening. Why do persons with disabilities face disapproval, even intimidation, for aspiring to normal independence and ordinary social participation?

Philosopher Allen Buchanan's account is enlightening here. Buchanan supposes that the nondisabled people who flourish under our current system have an interest in promoting the most productive practices in which they themselves can participate effectively. While "some compromises with efficiency are required in the name of equal opportunity for those with disabilities . . . ," Buchanan writes, "the interests of employers (and workers who do not have disabilities) are also legitimate."[13] In so remarking, Buchanan takes the interests of people with and without disabilities to be pitted against each other. Bioethicist Norman Daniels makes a similar

---

12. Karen Hirsch, "Raising Our Voices: Perspectives on the Book *Feminism and Disability*," *Resourceful Woman* (a newsletter published by the Health Resource Center for Women with Disabilities, Rehabilitation Institute of Chicago) 3, no. 1 (Winter 1994): 3.

13. Allen Buchanan, "Choosing Who Will Be Disabled: Genetic Intervention and the Morality of Inclusion," *Social Philosophy and Policy* 13, no. 2 (Summer 1996): 42.

assumption about the costliness of inclusion of people with disabilities by supposing that, in both the employment and the health care arenas, opportunity for them compromises efficiency for everyone else:

> A commitment to equality of opportunity leads us to accept somewhat greater costs to protect the range of opportunity of those who are most impaired. . . . The loss of efficiency here . . . is a reasonable [response] to the demand of equality of opportunity. We go an extra distance to bring those whose opportunities are most impaired or threatened as close to normal functioning as we can. Of course, health care settings are not competitive in the same way job competition is. . . . Still, it is instructive to see that a commitment to equality of opportunity in the health care setting has an analogue to reasonable [response] in the employment setting.[14]

As the extent to which even devout and resolute egalitarian thinking is influenced by assumptions such as those adopted by Daniels and Buchanan—namely, the belief that it is in the nature of disability to compromise efficiency—becomes evident, we are made aware of how the disability system contains this threatened cost. For allocating public support for people with disabilities preempts their compromising productivity by trying to participate in economic, social, and cultural activities. Far from protecting weak and vulnerable individuals, such a system serves nondisabled employers and workers. It promotes dependence to keep the disabled segregated and so prevent them from jeopardizing maximization of output or otherwise impeding the achievement that seems otherwise to be possible for the nondisabled majority.

We should recognize that both public and private special services programs for people with disabilities are aimed at individuals whose participation is feared to disrupt the efficiency of our ordinary transactions. If wheelchair users ride paratransit rather than regular buses, for example, nondisabled bus riders and drivers are not inconvenienced by the need to lower and raise wheelchair lifts to board some passengers, nor need transit companies install such lifts in their buses and try to train their drivers to use them.

To take another example, with the advent of special schools and special education programs, children whose type of impairment would not pre-

---

14. Norman Daniels, "Mental Disabilities, Equal Opportunity, and the ADA," in *Mental Disorder, Work Disability and the Law*, ed. Richard Bonnie and John McNahan (Chicago: University of Chicago Press, 1997), 286.

viously have kept them out of school were diverted from mainstream education to fill segregated classrooms. Writer Stephen Kuusisto describes
how this force was exerted:

> My mother must fight with the local district to gain my admission to an
> ordinary first-grade classroom. I am a legally blind child, and it is the era of
> Kennedy. It will be another thirty years before people with disabilities are
> guaranteed their civil rights. . . . [M]y mother decides to enroll me in public
> school instead of an institution and finds both consternation and disapproval
> from school and staff officials.[15]

Kuusisto relates how a blind social worker was sent to argue with his
mother:

> That argument has never ended for me: on that day over thirty-six years ago,
> both were approximately correct. The social worker says I am too blind for
> the public schools of the day. My mother counters that I won't have the same
> kind of social experience at a blind institution. "Those places teach kids how
> to cane chairs," she says. The blind woman insists I won't learn braille in a
> public school, won't learn to use a white cane.[16]

To create segregated facilities is to develop a cadre of professional staff
whose interests, like those of the social worker in Kuusisto's story, lie in
recruiting a population sufficient to maintain their organizations. That
such professionals often encourage the dependency of their "clients" on
special services is well recognized in the disability literature.[17]

Thus, there is a dimension of disability policy that evokes the larger
societal debate about the extent to which a homogeneous, as opposed to
a diverse, culture is an orderly and thereby efficient one. The more diverse
are the tastes, values, backgrounds—and bodies and minds—of those who
are active in the commercial and civic spheres, the more our having to
be flexible and open-minded in response to their diversity threatens the
orderliness secured by the normal or conventional practices of a homogeneous population. Throughout our subsequent discussion, the reader
should keep in mind how disruptive disability can be of current practice,

---

15. Stephen Kuusisto, *Planet of the Blind* (New York: Dial, 1998), 12–13.
16. Kuusisto, *Planet of the Blind*, 14.
17. Michael Oliver, *Disablement: A Sociological Approach* (New York: St. Martin's, 1990), passim.

and how profound the changes in it would have to be to facilitate the fully embracing inclusion of people with disabilities. Even the dialogical practices so critical to forming reciprocal moral bonds are not comfortably deployed to engage individuals who do not speak fluently, make eye contact, or respond as convention demands.

Broadening the access people with disabilities are given to social participation means profoundly transforming some dimensions of the core conventions that regulate our interpersonal transactions. At a minimum, doing so calls for revising conventional behaviors like handshaking, making eye contact, and talking when engaging with individuals who cannot execute these performances. But for many—perhaps the majority—of nondisabled people, even altering expectations of how others will behave is intimidating; refashioning their own habits of movement and communication is too disturbing a challenge to accept. Rather than broadening the social participation of people with disabilities by reducing their isolation, theoretical egalitarians who are unprepared to alter interpersonal conventions turn to distributive schemes that compensate people with disabilities for their isolation but continue them in it. For it is less distressing to minimize the occasions when conventional practice must sustain exchanges between nondisabled and disabled individuals than to be compelled to change it.

Segregation

A segregated system is sometimes thought to be more responsive to the "special" needs of people who cannot see, hear, move, think, or perform other activities as well as most. But segregation has drawbacks. Segregated facilities and special programs are often not as efficacious in providing ordinary services as facilities and programs with similar objectives that serve the broad public, especially when the population being segregated is a powerless one.

Of course, some separate educational facilities for children who are deaf or blind offer important training in special adaptive techniques such as using a cane for mobility, effective instruction using appropriate formats or modes such as signing (in American Sign Language) rather than speech, and, in addition, excellent opportunities to learn subject matter. Too often, however, becoming qualified to teach in special education settings substitutes acquiring information about disabilities for mastering the academic subject matter youngsters with disabilities, like all others, should learn from their teachers. Sociologist and disability studies scholar Mike Oliver comments, "There is no doubt that the medical hegemony in special education has hardly been challenged."[18] For this reason, children with disabilities who have been in segregated schooling tend to be less well prepared than other children to exercise the skills and display the knowledge of basic subjects such as English, math, and science.

Separate "paratransit" systems manifest similar problems in respect to the level and quality of service. These van systems almost never maintain full schedules or routes, nor do they provide on-demand service for tourists and other users unable to schedule days or weeks in advance. Furthermore, these systems tend to be so unreliable, even when booked in advance, that people cannot use them to get to jobs. Nor do they have the capacity to serve all who have to use them. Because special paratransit services are notoriously oversubscribed, individuals with disabilities must compete against each other for transportation.

Until recently, cab companies have viewed accessible transportation as a market reserved for paratransit, which is subsidized at the public expense. Consequently, wheelchair users have had little alternative to paratransit and therefore have had only compromised access to the lifestyle that "on-demand" urban transportation supports. Now, however, municipalities, especially those in "sunshine" localities courting "elderly" tourists and emigration by retirees, have created accessible taxi service through a variety of low-cost methods, such as offering scarce taxi medallions on a preferential basis to whichever of the competing taxi proprietors agree to equip a percentage of their vehicles with fold-out manual ramps.

There are, then, three devastating problems with imagining that treating people with disabilities justly means creating programs to serve their "special needs." First, to calm fears about compromising the efficiency with which nondisabled people enjoy ordinary public services, segregated systems isolate people with disabilities. Paratransit systems, special education classrooms, and exemptions from paying certain fees because a facility is not fully accessible to those with disabilities are examples where programs are created on the supposition that people with disabilities need

---

18. Michael Oliver, "Disability and Dependency: A Creation of Industrialized Societies?" in *Disability and Dependency*, ed. Len Barton (London: Falmer, 1989), 15.

special services (as some undoubtedly do), but the existence of special services then is made an excuse, or worse, for denying all who are disabled access to ordinary public services.

What has been less often noticed about segregated systems of special services is that they place the interests of individuals with disabilities in competition with one another for access to whatever resources nondis-abled people are willing to allocate to the disabled. Unlike competition for other kinds of goods, however, there is no suggestion that contests between people with disabilities for disability benefits stimulate achieve-ment or productivity. So, second, systems whose structures foment such competition are unredeemingly damaging. To illustrate, the Swedish *boen-deservice* system provides centralized attendant service in semi-institutional settings for seriously disabled people. To try to gain a competitive edge over other residents so as to obtain a higher priority for their personal care, residents vie with each other to develop personalities that are non-offensive and appealing to the staff.[19]

Third, to be viable, schemes that sequester disabled people by providing special services and benefits must distinguish reasonably accurately be-tween individuals whom restorative, rehabilitative, or adaptive measures can make capable of effectively contributing to production and those whom neither medical treatment nor accessible environments can keep from impeding it. Otherwise, the productive people whose work supports the system will perceive it as draining rather than fortifying productivity and also as unjust because it offers some otherwise able people a ticket out of the workplace. But, as Jerry Mashaw, chair of the Disability Policy Panel of the National Academy of Social Insurance, comments, efforts to apply such distinctions must abandon the traditional procedural controls associ-ated with just decision making because "adopted wholesale, these forms would be, to say the least, dysfunctional." So, Mashaw concludes, any program that relies on making such eligibility decisions about who is so impaired as to deserve services and support "cannot escape giving the im-pression . . . that its . . . processes . . . are a form of second-class justice."[20]

Furthermore, eligibility decision processes that incorrectly purport to

---

19. Gerben DeJong, *Independent Living & Disability Policy in the Netherlands: Three Models of Residential Care and Independent Living* (New York: World Reha-bilitation Fund, 1984).

20. Jerry Mashaw, *Bureaucratic Justice: Managing Social Security Disability Claims* (New Haven: Yale University Press, 1983), 197.

separate out just the truly incompetent run the risk of arbitrarily limiting anomalous but competent people. By stipulating which impairments constitute sufficient conditions for needing care, the benefits eligibility process a priori identifies having those impairments with being incompetent. We should not underestimate the invidiousness of criteria that falsely purport to have found the line between competence and incompetence when it is simply separation they serve. In this regard, the discourse of twentieth-century disability resembles earlier discourses on race. Kwame Anthony Appiah cautions, "Remember always why the intellectual incapacity . . . of blacks is invoked . . . as part of a catalog of differences, which, when taken together, make it certain that blacks and whites cannot live together as equal citizens."[21] A similar purpose is served by the catalog of impairments or dysfunctions that carry entitlement to disability benefits.

Institutionalization

The system of removing people from the workplace because they are impaired took hold in the United States after the Civil War. The history of mental retardation, as related by James Trent in *Inventing the Feeble Mind*, follows a pattern common to other disabilities as well.[22] Before 1820, cognitively impaired people stayed with their families or were placed with neighbors; they often did simple but necessary work in the household or on the farm.

During the next forty years, however, institutions meant to train these individuals so that they could be more productive sprung up, supported by charitable donations and government funds. Beginning in the period after the Civil War, facilities created to improve the life skill proficiency and productivity of cognitively impaired people and return them to work in the community were transmogrified into custodial institutions. Several contributing factors intersected to promote the change.

First, the superintendents were physicians, more accustomed to diagnosing patients as either curable or incurable and assigning them to the community or the sick room accordingly.[23] Second, waves of immigrants

---

21. Kwame Anthony Appiah and Amy Gutmann, *Color Conscious: The Political Morality of Race* (Princeton: Princeton University Press, 1996), 48.

22. James Trent, *Inventing the Feeble Mind: A History of Mental Retardation in the United States* (Berkeley: University of California Press, 1994).

23. Angela Licia Carlson, "Mindful Subjects: Classification and Cognitive Disability," Ph.D. diss., Toronto: University of Toronto, 1998.

needed work so jobs in the community became scarcer, and the disabled competed for work with other groups when they returned home from the training schools. Because the training schools could command both public and private funding, they accumulated the resources to expand into custodial institutions. As populations became urbanized and their work industrialized, caring for an impaired family member interfered with wage earning. The factory did not have the same tolerance for cognitively compromised individuals as the farm. Public and private support to expand the training facilities into permanent custodial institutions was solicited in the name of sheltering the disabled, relieving the community of the burden of caring for them, and protecting the community from individuals who were too damaged to conduct themselves with proper moral constraint.

To become even more financially viable, these "homes" vigorously recruited less impaired inmates who, once they were institutionalized, were put to work caring for the most seriously dysfunctional. During World War II, when other help could not be found, "institutional officials were reluctant to release 'better worker patients.' " So, when a new young superintendent had inmates at the Iowa Home for Feeble-Minded Children tested in the early 1950s, he found more than fifty testing higher than some of the employees, with normal IQs ranging to at least 120. These individuals had been institutionalized because their anomalies were disturbing. For example, one had been institutionalized as a child nearly sixty years earlier because of his peculiar eye rolling.[24]

---

24. Trent, *Inventing the Feeble Mind*, chaps. 1–4, 230, 253, 298. Also see "Mpho ya Modimo—A Gift from God: Perspectives on 'Attitudes' toward Disabled Persons," in which Benedicte Ingstad describes how institutionalization in Africa similarly debilitated the productivity of a cognitively disabled individual. In the case she reports, the individual was institutionalized at age eight at the behest of rehabilitation professionals. After repeated requests while he grew to adulthood, the family was able to bring him home, but only on condition that he be locked up. He was unable to communicate and often was violent. However, over the years they were unable to maintain his incarceration. As he was less and less restrained, he acquired communication skills, began to perform work around the house— sweeping and chopping—and eventually, he took up life as a goatherd. This was the kind of work people with cognitive impairments often performed in the United States prior to the institutionalization movement. *Disability and Culture*, ed. Benedicte Ingstadt and Susan Reynolds Whyte (Berkeley: University of California Press, 1995), 246–66.

The United States allocates large sums of public money to care for a subset of the disabled population, that part not in the workforce. There is unending contention about (re)drawing the eligibility line for these programs. For example, in the 1970s disability programs became available for individuals without severe impairment whose other characteristics (poor education, few skills) made it difficult to find employment. The rate of participation in these programs shot up at a rate surpassed only by that in the Netherlands. As Leo Aarts, Richard Burkhauser, and Philip DeJong explain:

> The 1980 Amendments to the United States Social Security Act . . . led to significant reductions in the disability . . . population in the midst of the deepest American recession since the Great Depression. But this retrenchment was accomplished by a review process that could not survive the political firestorm it generated.[25]

To illustrate the costs of serving those who do get benefits, in 1991 the state of New York estimated an $8 billion expenditure on special services such as paratransit for people with disabilities and older citizens.[26] Curiously, although the rate of dependence on government programs has increased for the general population of individuals who are impaired, at present only about a third of working age (twenty-two to sixty-four years) individuals with severe disabilities—which means individuals completely unable to execute major functions like walking, hearing, or seeing—receive government benefits support such as Social Security, Disability Income, and Medicaid. Further, according to gerontologist Raymond Coward, the rich can afford to buy the home care they need, and the poor qualify for Medicaid, which provides such care. "It is the middle class that gets squeezed the most," he observes.[27]

More than 12.6 million Americans benefit from one of two disability programs. The first, Social Security Disability Income (SSDI), began in 1950, some fifteen years after Social Security for the aged was started, as a

---

25. Leo Aarts, Richard Burkhauser, and Philip DeJong, "Introduction and Overview," in *Curing the Dutch Disease: An International Perspective on Disability Policy Reform*, ed. Leo Aarts, Richard Burkhauser and Philip DeJong (Aldershot: Avebury, 1996), 8–9.

26. Albrecht, *Disability Business*, 135, 160.

27. Sara Rimer, "Families Bear a Bigger Share of Caring for the Frail Elderly," *New York Times*, 8 June 1998, A17.

New Deal program to provide for disabled workers, their spouses, and children—if the workers had paid into the Social Security trust funds. The second program, Supplemental Security Income (SSI), was added in 1974 to help disabled adults and children who had not paid into Social Security. SSI benefits are drawn directly from the federal budget. By 1998, payments to SSDI and SSI beneficiaries totaled $75 billion, not including the cost of administering the programs.[28] While the numbers of individuals over sixty-five receiving Supplemental Security Income and Medicaid dropped during the period from 1975 to 1994, the number of working-age adults and children with disabilities receiving benefits more than doubled; this population increased from 42 percent to two-thirds of the recipients.[29] From 1992 to 1998, SSDI costs increased by 45 percent and SSI costs by 25 percent. From 1990 to 1996, the number of children receiving SSI benefits increased from 340,000 to one million.[30]

Individuals elicit large expenditures of public funds not just because they are disabled but because they manifest certain kinds of impairments. For instance, a *New York Times* series described the move of a self-mutilating youth of "low normal" intelligence from hospital to community care. Physicians cannot isolate a physical cause of his tearing at his own skin, but he has been institutionalized since his childhood. In this case, the needed resources were allocated and the individual given priority over others waiting in institutions for community placements to prove "the notion that anyone, no matter how overwhelmingly needy, can live independently," which "has become an article of faith advanced by most professionals who work with the handicapped."[31] The article describing the case is titled "Patient's Quest for Normal Life, at a Price," for the annual cost to have him live outside an institution, in an apartment of his own in the community, is nearly a quarter of a million dollars, most of which pays his caregivers and their supervisors. This is, however, less than the annual cost of institutionalizing him, and he is happier outside the institution.

---

28. Christopher Ruddy, "SS Disability Programs: New Forms of Welfare?" *Pittsburgh Tribune-Review*, 31 May 1998.

29. Edward Berkowitz and Richard Berkhauser, "A United States Perspective on Disability Programs," in *Curing the Dutch Disease*.

30. Ruddy, "SS Disability Programs."

31. N. R. Kleinfield, "Patient's Quest for Normal Life, at a Price," *New York Times*, 22 June 1997, A15.

The Cost of Impairment

The standard approach to whether such large distributions of public resources to single individuals are just is to debate who should have first call on funds available for people with disabilities and who should not be eligible for them at all. Rarely, however, are discussions about eligibility for disability benefits informed by examining the various reasons that might impel a democratic society to allocate resources to people because they have physical, sensory, or cognitive impairments. We do not seem to have articulated a democratic theory of disability that delineates the equality to which people with such differences can justifiably lay claim.

Neither the interpretations nor the implications of our intuitions about this matter have been systematically explored. Philosophical accounts of equality often accept the claim that, in a fair distributive system, disabled people—for instance, persons who cannot walk—would be compensated—for example, with extraordinary medical treatment or a mechanical means of mobilizing—even if doing so means that they are allocated more resources than (some) other persons. To illustrate, Amartya Sen famously maintains that unequal allocations of resources are intuitively correct if they equalize individuals' capabilities for primary functionings, the performances that are fundamental to attaining a positive quality of life. So he finds nothing objectionable in allocating more resources to a needy cripple to buy a wheelchair than are given to needy able-bodied individuals who can attain that same degree of mobility with no extraordinary allocation of resources. Sen adds that this superior allocation of resources is required even if the impaired individual is so forbearing or selfless as to believe herself as well off as others—that is, as equal to them—regardless of her physical deficits.[32]

The intuition that the resources of society should be tapped to obtain a wheelchair for a citizen who cannot walk, even if the allocation is greater than that afforded other citizens to support their needs, is well attended to in the philosophical literature about equality. But what the intuition does and does not show about the justice of unequal distributions is not so well understood. It is one thing to accept that there are circumstances in which allocating an unequally large amount of resources to those who

---

32. Amartya K. Sen, "Equality of What?" in *The Tanner Lectures on Human Values*, ed. S. McMurrin (Cambridge: Cambridge University Press, 1980), 217.

are more than usually disadvantaged is neither to privilege them nor to be unfair to everyone else. However, we should not conflate the permissibility of an unequally large allocation with the obligation to allocate greater than usual amounts of resources.

For not merely an intuition but a convincing theoretical justification is needed to require allocating greater than equal public resources away from one group of people to benefit a different group. Our feelings about the goodness of acting charitably to the disabled may cloak and thereby obscure this point in the shame of ignoring the neediness of the disabled. Why should we need to call on theory to impel us to help out whomever we regard as undeservingly unfortunate? The importance of theory should quickly become obvious to whoever thinks her intuitions suffice if she is called on to decide whether mobility-impaired people deserve greater allocations because they need wheelchairs than blind people deserve for guide dogs or deaf people for sign language interpreters. Who is more unfortunate? Who is more deserving? What do these questions mean, and are they the right questions to ask? If we commit ourselves to relieving whatever neediness disability incurs, we appear to require a powerful distributive theory, one capable of determining who among us deserves compensatory resources and how great a disparity in allocations may be tolerated without privileging individuals in virtue of their being perceived as needy.

Richard Arneson thinks that "a theory of distributive justice could legitimately recommend special compensation for individuals who are burdened with physical handicaps such as the lack of usable arms and legs."[33] But, while Sen thinks there is an objective standard with reference to which citizens should agree that satisfying an expensive preference for normal vision contributes more to an objectively good life than satisfying an expensive taste for champagne, Arneson thinks such claims appeal to an illusory perfectionism. The claim that we can identify and rank objective goods rests, he complains, "upon a large promissory note that contemporary moral theory has not redeemed and that may ultimately prove unredeemable."[34]

The standard response to Arneson's objection is exemplified in the following discussion by the bioethicist and legal scholar Dena S. Davis of a

---

33. Richard Arneson, "Liberalism, Distributive Subjectivism, and Equal Opportunity for Welfare," *Philosophy and Public Affairs*, 184.
34. Arneson, "Liberalism, Distributive Subjectivism," 193.

situation she labels a "genetic dilemma": "Deeply committed to the principle of giving clients value-free information . . . , most counselors nonetheless make certain assumptions about health and disability—for example, that it is preferable to be a hearing person rather than a deaf person."[35]

Genetic counseling thus assumes the very kind of ranking Arneson dismisses. Counseling practice leaves no room for doubt that, regardless of other circumstances, it is better to be hearing than deaf. Davis continues:

> Thus, counselors typically talk of the "risk" of having a child with a particular genetic condition . . . parents with certain disabilities who seek help in trying to assure that they will have a child who shares their disability . . . are understandably troubling to genetic counselors.[36]

The Deaf (the uppercase *D* indicates that the individual is a sign language speaker who is culturally Deaf as well as physically deaf) parents who wish their children to be Deaf clearly do not agree that being hearing is better than being deaf. They say their deafness does not make them incomplete. They seek socializing and communication, just like hearing people, and they fulfill this aim in the company of other Deaf people as satisfactorily as hearing people do among their own kind. *New York Times* writer Natalie Angier comments: "several subcultures have arisen—of people who were born deaf, or achondroplastic or intersexual—who do not want to be regarded as handicapped and do not want to be 'repaired.' "[37]

While Deaf people do not consider themselves impaired, there are disability advocates who not only embrace being impaired but also claim that their preference for being in this state overrides the nondisabled society's conviction that it is preferable to repair them. A *New York Times* article, "Disability Culture: Eager to Bite the Hands That Would Feed Them," describes promoters of the disability culture (mostly individuals with mobility or manual deficits) as preferring impaired bodies to "normal" ones. They "castigate Christopher Reeve for his campaign for a cure for spinal injury, saying it is unrealistic and offensive to people who have learned to

---

35. Dena Davis, "Genetic Dilemmas and the Child's Right to an Open Future," *The Hastings Center Report* 7, no. 2 (March–April 1997): 7.

36. Davis, "Genetic Dilemmas," 7.

37. Natalie Angier, "Joined for Life, and Living to the Full," *New York Times*, 23 December 1997, B15.

live with their disabilities and indeed thrive on them," and they urge that resources are more justly allocated to adaptive living needs (personal attendants, SSDI benefits, adaptive equipment) than to medical treatment meant to restore impaired people to "normal."[38] Thus, they construct an emancipatory discourse, but one that promotes a view of liberation primarily in terms of satisfying certain individuals' needs.

To see, walk, or hear undoubtedly has value. The question is, what kind of value? Is the value of performing such activities so special that being unable to do so calls for extraordinary compensation? Arneson argues that there is no essential difference between a visually impaired individual's expensive preference for, let us say, normal eyesight (the expense here is the cost of medical treatment or rehabilitation) and other expensive preferences like "champagne" tastes. Some expensive tastes are as involuntary as impaired vision, he suggests.

There are, however, contingencies that assign the former preference more weight in fair allocation schemes. For instance, if throughout their lives, people typically prefer to have normal eyesight, but the preference for champagne waxes and wanes, it is likely that allocating resources for eyesight is a better bet for generating welfare over a lifetime. And it also may seem more likely that people's claims to prefer normal eyesight are more reliably true about them than (some) other claims they make about their preferences. This makes the extent to which fulfilling preference is satisfying, and the degree to which such persistent preferences normally are satisfied, the measure of systematically equitable treatment.[39]

But this still leaves unclear which otherwise unfulfillable preferences should be the basis for extraordinary compensation. For it is our failure to imagine how profoundly, but legitimately, serious impairment can alter preferences that induces us to consider, as Arneson suggests we do, the typically persistent preferences of people who are not impaired to be a reliable standard. On the one hand, Arneson is right to advise us to clarify why not seeing, hearing, or walking detracts from a good life before we agree that there is an objective reason that these deficits should command prodigious compensation in the form of unusually large allocations of resources. On the other hand, despite the efforts of both Arneson and dis-

---

38. D. Martin, "Disability Culture: Eager to Bite the Hands That Would Feed Them," *New York Times*, 1 June 1997, 1.
39. Arneson, "Liberalism, Distributive Subjectivism," 186.

ability culture advocates to persuade us of the point, it is odd to think of people's wanting to see or walk or hear in terms of their merely preferring to do so.

To summarize, whether we take the measure of equality to be demonstrating equivalent capability for basic functionings or achieving equivalent success in satisfying persistent preferences, the question of whether the normal mode or typical kind should be the standard is inescapable. To address this issue, we must ask whether being in the physical, sensory, or cognitive minority—that is, being anomalous or atypical in one or more of these respects—is naturally disadvantageous or whether it is merely made to be so artificially by unjust social arrangements. In exploring this distinction, we should consider the nature of discrimination against people with physical, sensory, or cognitive impairments and assess various corrective strategies if their exclusion from social participation is unfair. Subsequently, we can explore whether being just to people with disabilities involves compensating them, and, if so, for what deprivations compensation is due. By learning this, we will better understand what claims to equality people with disabilities can plausibly advance.

In the course of developing an account of justice for people with disabilities, I will argue that attempts to equalize individuals with disabilities by distributing extraordinary resources to them in virtue of their impairments are self-defeating. I will show these policies to be so *contingently* in that the distributive schemes devised to implement them isolate rather than integrate their putative beneficiaries. I will show they are so *systematically* because the inherent elasticity of eligibility criteria for the benefits provided by such schemes invite insupportable expansions of the class of beneficiaries. And I will show that they are so *conceptually* because to explain why policies allocating special benefits to the disabled are justified inescapably is to cast them as exceptionally needy and thereby as being in deficit compared with other people.

This last point bears some preliminary expansion. Any policy to allocate unequally generous resources to a subset of the population requires construction of the class of those eligible for benefits and concomitantly demands the conceptualization of criteria that identify the individuals in the eligible class as deserving of the benefits. To construe the disabled as a class deserving of and eligible for such benefits is to warrant each member of the class of eligibles as deserving of them. Individual members of the class of eligibles must be uniform in possessing the character in virtue of which the benefits are allocated. For to construct the class of eligibles so it is no more than probable that its members are deserving beneficiaries unfairly risks transferring resources from nonneedy ineligibles to equally nonneedy eligibles.

Schemes to allocate extraordinary resources to the class of the disabled thereby cannot help but construct the class's members as being uniformly needy. I will present considerations—examples drawn from several disciplines, analyses of cases and of concepts, as well as arguments—to challenge this construction. Furthermore, I will contend, to so construct disability nourishes the exclusionary practices that isolate people with disabilities, curtail their opportunities, and, ultimately, drive them into the very state of neediness purported to have warranted the initial construction of their neediness. To understand these connections is to comprehend why distributive policies that target the disabled seem too facilely self-justifying.

For these reasons I do not agree that treating people with disabilities justly consists in extraordinary distributions made in virtue of disability. However, it is important not to confuse the type of policy I reject with another very different and important policy, namely, the commitment of resources to correct the disadvantaging outcomes of exclusionary past practice. It is appropriate—indeed, it is requisite—to allocate exceptional resources to rectify the lingering results of the biased past. Yet a third policy stance—redistributing by broadening responsibility for the care of the subset of individuals with disabilities who are truly needy rather than merely constructed as being so—should also be differentiated; here policy is concerned not with justice for the disabled but instead with justice for those nondisabled individuals for whom the responsibility of caring for a disabled person is unfairly burdensome.

Invisibility and Exclusion

The 1992 U.S. Census found that almost fifty million individuals—about one in six—are disabled, meaning they report having some physical or mental impairment that limits their performance of one or more major life activity. This count has increased by more than a third from the thirty-seven million enumerated in the 1987 U.S. Census. About half of the fifty million are severely disabled, a 1995 census study found. Twenty-six million Americans—that is, one in ten—are "completely unable to perform a functional activity such as seeing, hearing, talking, walking, climbing stairs and so on."[40] Of these, 5.1 million use an assistive device such as crutches to walk, and an additional 1.8 million use wheelchairs.

This is a substantial number of citizens. Yet, their attempts at social participation are so extensively disallowed that, for most Americans, working side by side with a severely disabled person counts as extraordinary, while engaging in an intimate social relationship with such a person is unimaginable. Although 82 percent of working-age nondisabled persons are in the workforce, for instance, only 26 percent of working-age people with disabilities are.[41] This is despite the fact that impairment alone clearly does not prevent productivity. The achievement of persons with impairments shows that deafness bars neither the composing (Ludwig Beethoven) nor professional performing of music (Evelyn Glennie); visual impairments do not prohibit outstanding scientific careers (Gerrit Vermaaj); and although some individuals with mobility impairments are classified as unfit for work and expected not to do so, others with virtually identical impairments have thrived in most sorts of work, including the presidency of the United States (Franklin D. Roosevelt).

Given the size of the population involved, the devaluation of people with disabilities is an acute social problem. It is also an increasingly urgent problem. Roughly 40 percent, or ten million individuals, of those with severe disabilities are aged over sixty-five years.[42] Because the number of people in this age group is expected to increase greatly, there will be more individuals who experience some lesser or greater degree of impairment in performing activities—seeing, hearing, talking, walking, cognizing—that normally are central to functioning and flourishing. The growing magnitude of the number of people who are at risk makes it especially important to assess why being in a state of deficit in regard to one or more of these performances invites, and has even been thought to justify, social exclusion.

---

40. Chronicle Staff Report, "1 in 10 Americans Disabled, Study Says," *San Francisco Chronicle*, 17 September 1997, A10.

41. Chronicle Staff Report, "1 in 10," A10.

42. Unless otherwise noted, the statistical data on the population of people with disabilities cited here is to be found in John M. McNeil, "Americans with Disabilities 1994—Text," *Household Economic Studies, Current Population Report*, P70-61, at //www.census.gov/hhs/www/disable/sipp/disab9495/asc9495.html.

Let us begin considering how being disabled limits an individual. Jenny Morris was a mother, a winning politician, an activist buoyed on the rising tide of a flourishing feminist movement. Others valued her presence and thought her life worth living, even envied her. But, at age thirty-three, Jenny Morris tumbled off a wall at the bottom of her garden and injured her lower spine so that she lost the ability to walk.[43]

Morris retained all her political knowledge and skills, her relation with her child, her disposition to fight for social justice. Very little about her that had been of social value changed after the fall—certainly not the skills and knowledge she had demonstrated. Yet, hers was a social as well as a physical fall, for in the eyes of others, she found, her life no longer seemed worth living in virtue of her disability.

Disability commonly attenuates personal relationships. Disability researchers Lamb and Layzell comment:

> There is an unspoken taboo about relationships and disabled people. Disabled people's sexual and emotional needs are rarely included in any . . . representation in everyday life. . . . This reinforces the public's attitudes and expectations toward disabled people as seeing them as "sick and sexless" rather than as participating in full sexual and family relationships.[44]

Women with disabilities are especially devalued. Fully one quarter of all married women who become disabled eventually are separated or divorced, nearly twice the rate for similarly situated nondisabled women and for disabled men. Even their friends and relatives have trouble envisioning women with disabilities as functional wives and mothers.[45] In a study of how physically disabled young women in Sweden who have been the lifelong recipients of personal, parental and medical care nevertheless seek their identity in traditional female caregiving roles, disability scholar Karin Barron comments:

> Social life is organized around sex/gender and we generally behave consistently with the sex we were "given" at birth.[46] . . . [R]ejecting the traditional

---

43. Jenny Morris, *Pride against Prejudice* (Philadelphia: New Society Publishers, 1991), chap. 1 passim.
44. Brian Lamb and Susan Layzell, *Disabled in Britain: A World Apart* (London: SCOPE, 1994), 21.
45. William J. Hanna and Elizabeth Rogovsky, "Women with Disabilities: Two Handicaps Plus," *Disability, Handicap & Society* 6, no. 1 (1991): 55–56.
46. Karin Barron, "The Bumpy Road to Womanhood," *Disability & Society* 12, no. 2 (Spring 1997): 224.

subservient role of "the disabled"[47] . . . the mothering role [has] been described as a means of becoming "equal" for women, [and] disabled women may thus strive for this role . . . [but] this is not the traditional role of disabled women [who] have traditionally been denied the role of homemakers and mothers.[48]

Barbara Hillyer exhibits how women without disabilities sometimes are threatened by disabled women who aspire to normal women's roles. As unfolded chapter by chapter in her aforementioned book, Hillyer struggles with disability in the person of her cognitively impaired adopted daughter, who does not acknowledge her limitations and ignores her mother's assessment of them.

> Jennifer as she is, a woman with very serious limitations . . . Jennifer spends a lot of time being upset by what she fears is her inability to meet others' expectations, an anxiety that comes to a crisis when she perceives (rightly) that I do not want her to get married and have children.[49] Her need to separate from me, the one who interprets her world to her and to others, was in a sense self-destructive, as separation would leave her unprotected.[50]

That those without disabilities have an obligation to care for the disabled is a commonplace. But in condemning her daughter for trying to disconnect from her (and, as we saw earlier, in berating the paraplegic woman for doing her own construction work), Hillyer introduces the thought that people with disabilities owe it to others to accept their care. In his 1997 Carus Lectures, Alasdair MacIntyre indicates how this could be imagined to be so. A community's virtue depends, he suggests, on how ill and disabled people are cared for in it.[51]

But societies cannot be virtuous under this scheme absent there being needy people to receive care. We can see this constraint operating in Hillyer's family: if Jennifer's current identity is constituted by her mother's interpreting her world, Jennifer's disconnecting from her mother inhibits the latter's avenue for manifesting virtue. But we have a duty to facilitate,

---

47. Barron, "The Bumpy Road," 223.
48. Barron, "The Bumpy Road," 234.
49. Hillyer, *Feminism and Disability*, 247.
50. Hillyer, *Feminism and Disability*, 13.
51. Alasdair MacIntyre, *Rational Dependent Animals: Why Human Beings Need the Virtues* (Chicago: Open Court, forthcoming).

not impede, others' progressing along paths of virtue. Within this framework of values, then, Jennifer arguably has a duty to support her mother by depending on her. It is in this sense that Hillyer and her daughter are interdependent.

Parenthetically, it is a different sense that feminist theory rightfully emphasizes when urging, as some feminists do, that we all are interdependent. For autonomy, as it is sometimes portrayed, is an abstracted idealization. To be self-determining does not require being aloof from and unaffected by our relations with other people. Even Thomas Hobbes, that unreconstructable individualist, does not recommend the solitary life; it is by associating with others that life becomes longer and more civilized, he famously argues.

In this regard, it might be supposed that people with disabilities are pioneers of interdependence because they, more than most people, have had to acknowledge needing others' help. But the role to which Hillyer aspires to assign her daughter is no model for facilitating flourishing. Although interdependence is often thought to enhance connectedness, promoting it can prove as isolating in reality for people with disabilities as communitarians suppose their theoretical autonomy condemns them to be. The reason is that relating to others mediated by their perception of one's neediness is a distancing, not a bonding or integrating, experience.

Devaluation

Political scientist and disability studies scholar Harlan Hahn describes the isolation of being devalued in terms deeply familiar to people with disabilities, yet opaque in some ways to persons not of this class:

> [O]ne of the most unpleasant features of the lifestyles of . . . disabled individuals . . . is the pervasive sense of physical and social isolation produced not only by the restrictions of the built environment but also by the aversive reactions of the nondisabled that often consign them to the role of distant friends or even mascots rather than to a more intimate status as peers, competitors, or mates.[52] . . . [F]ew nondisabled individuals would tolerate the curtailment of individual options that become part of the daily experience of people with disabilities.[53]

---

52. Harlan Hahn, "Civil Rights for Disabled Americans," in *Images of the Disabled, Disabling Images*, ed. A. Gartner and T. Joe (New York: Praeger, 1987), 198.

53. Hahn, "Civil Rights for Disabled Americans," 193.

Roles marked by isolation, lack of social support and social networks, low social esteem and a concomitant feeling of powerlessness, and roleless-ness or purposelessness are the kind social scientists warn against perpetu-ating because the individuals assigned to them are highly exposed to psy-chosocial risk. It is furthermore probable that whoever has to live this way will suffer adverse psychosocial effects. For example, Richard Wilkinson's research reveals that "inequality itself, irrespective of material standards, has adverse effects. . . . [P]erceptions of inequality translate into psycho-logical feelings of lack of security [and] lower self-esteem."[54] Accustomed to believe that people with disabilities are treated as a specially protected class, few nondisabled people fully comprehend the degree to which the insecurity and abandonment Hahn describes pervade the everyday lives people with disabilities, regardless of their achievements. We should keep in mind that no equalizing proposal is adequate if it fails to reduce the psychosocial hazards disabled people now endure.

Transitioning from the class of able-bodied people to the class of the disabled, Jenny Morris was shaken to find people without disabilities shun-ning her new standpoint. Morris's loss was much more global than the ability to walk. Although her capacity for social function remained intact, her previous social identity seemed to have vanished.

She comments:

> Disabled people—men and women—have little opportunity to portray our own experiences within the general culture, or within . . . political move-ments. Our experience is isolated. . . . This lack of a voice, of the representa-tion of our subjective reality, means that it is difficult for non-disabled [peo-ple] to incorporate our reality into their research and their theories, unless it is in terms of the way the non-disabled world sees us.[55]

To be isolated and ignored just because she could no longer walk, a capac-ity with little direct connection to her previous achievements, shocked Morris, as it has so many other newly disabled people. This was especially so because those for whom she had become nonviable adhered to the same Marxist and feminist theories, and engaged in the same social activism, that she herself embraced prior to her transition from the dominant class

---

54. Adam Swift, "Equality Matters," *Times Literary Supplement*, no. 4959, 17 April 1998, 29.

55. Morris, *Pride against Prejudice*, 8.

of walking persons to that marginalized class of individuals who are dismissed from social participation by virtue of their being characterized as defective. She discovered that her peers—the Marxist and feminist champions of social justice with whom she previously identified ardently—had no interest in extending their theories to reflect the life of the kind of person she had become—that is, a nonwalking person.

Morris came to recognize, and to be threatened by, the bias that accords the lives of people with disabilities so little value. In an essay called "Tyrannies of Perfection," she cites three examples of public policies that evidence the low regard in which disabled people's lives are held. These are (1) American court rulings that it is entirely rational for a person with a serious physical impairment to choose to die,[56] (2) British legislation excepting pregnancies diagnosed as likely to result in children with disabilities from a prohibition against terminating past twenty-four weeks, and (3) the 1939 German decree authorizing physicians to accord a mercy death to impaired persons who could not be cured. About this last example, Morris reminds us, from 1939 to 1941 two hundred thousand physically and mentally impaired children and adults were judged to have "lives unworthy of life" and were killed "out of pity for the victim and out of a desire to free the family and loved ones from a lifetime of needless sacrifice," to quote one of the physicians who signed their death warrants.

Implementation of this program corrupted the moral climate and facilitated subsequent stages of the Holocaust. Morris concludes, "The explicit motivation for these three occurrences is the notion that physical and intellectual impairment inevitably means a life which is not worth living."[57] The kind of attack the Nazis made on the half million Aryan individuals with disabilities was not unique to Germany. As late the 1930s, more than

---

56. Morris refers to the case of Kenneth Bergstedt, one of four usually cited by disability activists to make this point. The other cases are those of David Rivlin, Larry McAfee, and Elizabeth Bouvia. All quadriplegics, all petitioned the courts for permission to remove life-sustaining mechanisms (respirators in the cases of the three men, artificial feeding in Bouvia's case). In all four cases, the courts adhered to the line of argument taken by the U.S. Supreme Court in Cruzan and Casey, namely that individuals have the right to refuse invasive treatment even if it is life sustaining. Bergstedt and Rivlin then had their ventilators turned off and died, McAfee did not, and Bouvia initiated but then abandoned an attempt to die by starvation.

57. Jenny Morris, "Tyrannies of Perfection," *The New Internationalist*, 1 July 1992: 16.

half the states in this country had laws on the books encouraging sterilization of people with disabilities, usually those with developmental disabilities including epilepsy, but also those who were blind or deaf, because
they were viewed as so burdensome as to be not worth reproducing or as
so incompetent as to be unqualified for parenting. In the United States,
California had sterilized more people than the rest of the states combined
by 1930. Daniel Kevles remarks that California's "eugenic sterilization law
helped inspire the Nazi measure, which was passed in 1933."[58]

In Western Europe, such practices existed well past the half-century
mark. Recently, the world has learned that sterilization programs, to reduce the number of children who might require extraordinary support,
accompanied the post–World War II expansion of generous social service
policies in Scandinavia and the Netherlands. Kevles reports:

> The experts raised the spectre of social "degeneration," insisting that "fee-
> ble-minded" people—to use the broad-brush term then commonly applied
> to persons believed to be mentally retarded—were responsible for a wide
> range of social problems and were proliferating at a rate that threatened social
> resources and stability. Feeble-minded women were held to be driven by a
> heedless sexuality, the product of biologically grounded flaws in their moral
> character[59]. . . . With the onset of worldwide economic depression in 1929
> . . . sterilization acquired broad support, not primarily on eugenic grounds
> . . . but on economic ones, raising the prospect of reducing the cost of institu-
> tional care and poor relief.[60]

Bioethicist Leon Kass suggests that attitudes similar to those that distress Morris are to be found in current health care practice:

> [W]e know that persons afflicted with certain diseases will never be capable
> of living the full life of a human being . . . so a child or fetus with . . . Down's
> (sic) syndrome,[61] will never be truly human. . . . There is no reason to keep
> them alive. This standard, I would suggest, is the one which most physicians
> and genetic counselors appeal to in their hearts, no matter what they say or
> do. . . . Why else would they have developed genetic counseling?[62]

---

58. Daniel Kevles, "Grounds for Breeding: The Amazing Persistence of Eugenics in Europe and North America," *Times Literary Supplement*, no. 4944 (January
2, 1998), 3.

59. Kevles, "Grounds for Breeding," 3.

60. Kevles, "Grounds for Breeding," 4.

61. The correct name of this condition is Down Syndrome.

62. Leon Kass, "Implications of the Human Right to Life," in *Intervention
and Reflection: Basic Issues in Medical Ethics*, ed. Ronald Munson (Belmont:
Wadsworth, 1983), 400.

New York Times writer Natalie Angier reports on another manifestation of the viewpoint Morris and Kass identify: "surgeons say that their techniques are better than ever, and they can effectively correct many physical defects early enough that children will grow up never knowing they were outliers to begin with."[63] In the same article, bioethicist Alan Fleischman is quoted as saying, "I'm concerned that as more abnormal children are prevented through abortion and testing, we'll be less tolerant of abnormality. We'll blame families if they knew there would be an abnormal child but chose not to abort."[64]

Today, the conviction that society repudiates the lives of people who are disabled is widespread and widely discussed. Columnist Debra J. Saunders claims that parents who kill children with disabilities are treated more leniently by the criminal justice system than those who kill children without disabilities.[65] And former Equal Employment Opportunities Commission Chairman Evan Kemp writes in an article in the *Washington Post* entitled "Could You Please Die Now?" that, in the campaign to ration health care, the medical profession's pessimism about the level of quality of life possible for people with disabilities will induce physicians to facilitate such persons' deaths.[66] In the Supreme Court's 26 June 1997 decision on physician-assisted suicide, Chief Justice Rehnquist echoed this concern by expressing the Court's conviction that the state must intervene to protect the lives of people with disabilities from physicians who do not appreciate the intrinsic value of life, for "the state's interest . . . goes beyond protecting the vulnerable from coercion; it extends to protecting disabled and terminally ill people."[67]

Fear

Morris believes that fear fuels these hostile reactions. But what is there about disabled people to frighten the strong and healthy individuals who dominate society? She hypothesizes:

63. Angier, "Joined for Life," B15.

64. Angier, "Joined for Life," B15.

65. Debra J. Saunders, "Children Who Deserve to Die," *San Francisco Examiner*, 23 September 1997, A21.

66. Evan Kemp, "Could You Please Die Now?" *Washington Post*, 5 January 1997.

67. *Washington et al. v. Glucksberg*, 1997 WL 348094. See also *Vacco v. Quill*, 1997 WL 348037.

Our disability frightens people. They don't want to think this is something
which could happen to them. So we become separated from common humanity; [we are] treated as . . . alien. Having put up clear barriers between us
and them, nondisabled people further hide their fear and discomfort by turn-
ing us into objects of pity, comforting themselves by their own kindness and
generosity.[68]

Morris is not alone in believing the presence of people who are disabled
threatens nondisabled people by representing the ever-present possibility
of becoming disabled. In *Justice and the Politics of Difference*, political
philosopher Iris Young offers a similar analysis of why people with disabilities are denied equitable social participation. Young supposes that the
process of abjection, wherein we experience as permeable the boundaries
that heretofore have seemed to separate us from people we think of as
inferior to ourselves, accounts for why people with disabilities are isolated:

I cannot deny that the old person will be myself, but that means my death,
so I avert my gaze from the old person, or treat her as a child, and want to
leave her presence as soon as possible. My relationship to disabled people has
a similar structure. The only difference between myself and the wheel-chair
bound person is my good luck. Encounter with the disabled person again
produces the ambiguity of recognizing that the person whom I project as so
different, so other, is nevertheless like me.[69]

But it is improbable that nondisabled people first identify with, but then
repress their resemblance to, people with disabilities. The evidence is that
they never identify with them at all. Unlike old age, the prospect of disability is not envisioned as a wind blowing from our futures. Each of us ex-
pects, barring early fatal accident or illness, to become an old person. But
by no means is identification, whether prospective or immediate, with
those whose lives are limited by disability a similarly commonplace expectation. Despite the frequency with which disabling accidents or illnesses
occur, when disability comes upon us, it is surprising and shocking.

We prepare for, rather than insure against, old age. In contrast, we indemnify ourselves against the risk of disability because this is prudent, as
we insure against fire, flood, and earthquake, imagining while we do that

---

68. Morris, *Pride against Prejudice*, 192.
69. Iris Marion Young, *Justice and the Politics of Difference* (Princeton:
Princeton University Press, 1990), 147.

we will not become the victims who need to collect. Each of us anticipates experiencing the burdens of aging, but it is other people, not ourselves, whom we expect to suffer the misfortune of becoming disabled. While no more than time separates the young from the old, much more than luck distances the able-bodied from the disabled. Compassion, which differs from pity because it precludes denying that one's own possibilities and vulnerabilities are similar to the sufferer's, vanishes into the resulting chasm.

To explicate her proposal that fears about their own morbidity lead the able-bodied to devalue the disabled, Young appeals to my own discussion of the Oregon Health Plan. This plan reduced priority for health care for procedures likely to leave patients with residual disability. State officials justified the policy as reflecting the public's views about what people wished to be insured for.[70] As I explained it:

> This ranking was arrived at through a telephone survey of able-bodied individuals who surmised, for example, that they would rather be dead than confined to a wheelchair. (Parenthetically, such morbid counterfactual speculation by the able-bodied often is utilized in public policy contexts to justify exclusion of people with disabilities from many parts of life.)[71]

I also observe that those surveyed

> apparently surmised that they would rather be dead than confined to a wheelchair. . . . [T]his survey was used to impose somebody else's suicidal fantasies on disabled individuals, thereby diminishing their access to health care, and, as well, withholding from them recognition as equally important moral beings.[72]

Young takes me to suggest (her words), "When asked to put themselves in the position of a person in a wheelchair, [able-bodied people] do not

---

70. Ronald Dworkin, "Will Clinton's Plan Be Fair?" *New York Review of Books*, 13 January 1994, 20–25.

71. Anita Silvers, "Reconciling Equality to Difference: Caring (f)or Justice for People with Disabilities," in *Hypatia, Special Issue on Feminist Ethics and Social Policy*, ed. Patrice DiQuinzo and Iris Marion Young, 10, no. 1 (Winter 1995): 30–55.

72. Silvers, "Caring (f)or Justice."

imagine the point of view of others; rather, they project onto those others their own fears and fantasies about themselves."[73]

Young is right in understanding me to hold that the lives of people with disabilities are opaque to the nondisabled in a way that interferes with the latter's being able to understand accurately what it is like to be in the former's place. (I remain undecided as to whether this opacity is an experiential correlate of the difference between freely functioning and functioning with severe physical or cognitive limitations, or whether it is instead correlated with the difference in the social positions to which nondisabled and disabled are assigned.) Of course, I fault myself if my earlier analysis suggested to Young that those surveyed in Oregon tried to project themselves into the typical wheelchair user's point of view. Rather, in saying they imposed their suicidal fantasies on disabled individuals, I meant to convey that they imposed a principle they believed wheelchair users should accept by fantasizing that they themselves would act upon it were they in a similar position. Notice that judging how others should act by supposing that one would oneself act consistently with such judgment were one in the others' place does not require supposing that one would share the actual feelings of those others. Indeed, judging others to be acting inappropriately often involves believing that, were one situated as they are, one would have more admirable feelings than they do.

While the explicit protests of groups of wheelchair users left no doubt as to their desires for equitable treatment, they failed to sway the Oregon officials. Only the federal government's imposition of the principles of the Americans with Disabilities Act (ADA), which prohibits disadvantageous treatment of people by reason of their disability, impelled Oregon to override the preferences of the able-bodied and change its rankings. How might disabled and able-bodied Oregonians have come to agree about the allocation of health care, though asymmetrically socially positioned in respect to one another? Young recommends:

> I can listen to a person in a wheelchair explain her feelings . . . or frustrations. Her descriptions will point out aspects of her situation that I would not have thought of. . . . I can even spend a day living in a wheelchair in order better to understand the difficulties and social position of a person in a wheelchair.[74]

73. Iris Marion Young, "Asymmetrical Reciprocity: On Moral Respect, Wonder, and Enlarged Thought," *Constellations* 3, no. 3 (1997): 344.
74. Young, "Asymmetrical Reciprocity," 355.

But it is improbable that someone who can easily rise and walk away from a wheelchair or strip off a blindfold is sufficiently skilled in the techniques of functioning with a physical impairment to comprehend the full potential of living such a life. Absent having acquired the skills of living and working with a disability, those participating in such simulations will despair of the difficulties, instead of appreciating the achievements and the promise, of living with a disability. What seems unachievable to someone temporarily trying out life without walking or seeing or hearing is often routinely accomplished by someone expert in that kind of life. Moreover, to focus on the difficulties of people living in wheelchairs invites precisely the perspective of which Jenny Morris complains—namely, the identification of individuals with a group whose lives are defined in terms of or distinguished by reference to their limitations.

Adopting an approach not unlike Young's, moral philosopher Lawrence Blum[75] advises that it is not by reasoning about their equality but rather by feeling about their situations as they do themselves that we can conduct ourselves morally toward people with disabilities. Blum's diagnosis grows from his conviction that logic-driven judgment stumbles where agents must behave ethically to persons less advantaged than themselves. Rather than trying to judge neutrally—that is, by constructing judgments that endeavor to be from no point of view—advantageously positioned agents should respond so sensitively that their perceptions of the particularities of any situation validate the perspective of whoever may be victimized by it.

Blum thinks the perspectives of better- and worse-positioned agents may be so polarized by both contested concepts and divisive affects as to be experientially inaccessible to each other. Nevertheless, he is convinced that interpersonal moral understanding can be achieved in these cases if we give up trying to homogenize the different perspectives and, instead, engage with uninviting perspectives simply by acknowledging them. To illustrate, he considers a case of a disabled worker, debilitated by distress and treated unfeelingly by a supervisor who refuses to adjust to his impairment.

Blum describes a supervisor, Theresa, who accepts her company's legal obligation under federal law to accommodate to the disability of an employee, Julio, but who

---

75. Lawrence Blum, "Moral Perception and Particularity," *Ethics* (July 1991): 701–25.

offers Julio less than he needs and is entitled to. . . . It is not that Theresa fails entirely to see Julio as "disabled" and as "in pain," but she does fail fully to grasp what this means for him and fails fully to take in or acknowledge that pain. . . . Theresa is failing to perceive or acknowledge something morally significant—namely, Julio's physical pain and his distress at the impact of his condition on his work situation.[76]

In Blum's view, it is natural to recognize the reality of others' pains, even if one cannot imagine having them. Other people's pain is invisible only to the morally blinded. Like Young, Blum attributes Theresa's impaired moral vision to emotional blockage against certain threatening aspects of reality. That is, advantaged persons are supposed to dread beholding damaged persons out of fear that they in future might themselves become impaired.[77] Because the worker's debilitating despair is real, Blum adds, it is only the supervisor's impaired perception that blocks her from accepting the pained person's estimation of the incapacitating impact of his pain and his assessment of what she owes him in regard of it. But is this so?

I do not think it can be so, for to condemn the supervisor's moral proficiency in this way has some bizarre implications. First, although Blum condemns Theresa for offering Julio less than he needs and is entitled to, he seems to focus her deficiency on her failure to validate Julio's suffering. For in respect to what Julio is entitled to, both Title I of the ADA and its predecessor, Section 503 of the Rehabilitation Act, provide that she need offer only what is required for him to do his job, as long as the cost of accommodation is not unreasonable when compared with the employer's entire budget. Legally, Theresa surely does not owe Julio all that he needs. Moreover, even on the most indulgent needs-based model of moral and social justice, we cannot assure everyone of what they need, since satisfying some needs may prevent satisfying others. This suggests that the needs of whoever is disadvantaged constitute no clearer a standard of just interactions between superiors and their inferiors than the needs of whoever is advantaged do.

Second, however, Blum privileges Julio's judgment over Theresa's on the ground that the former, rather than the latter, has the veridical point of view regarding the reality of the debilitation attendant on his impair-

---

76. Blum, "Moral Perception," 704–5.
77. Blum, "Moral Perception," 718.

ment. Blum thus seems to think Theresa owes forbearance to Julio to compensate for his position's being opaque to her. But a common experience in learning how to be functional if impaired is to reject, when looking backward, one's initial debilitating panic and abdication, in a way not dissimilar to how Theresa distances Julio's affliction. This process is recounted again and again in anecdotal and autobiographical material authored by persons with disabilities.

On Blum's account, which for this reason cannot be right, persons reconciled to their impairments thus would be guilty of moral insensitivity to themselves. But it is odd to think that impaired persons' earlier despairing states are opaque to or not understandable by their later, more hopeful selves. And it is absurd to explain that people who distance themselves from and devalue their initial reaction to becoming disabled do so because they now are more threatened by disability than they were originally. And if not so for them, then why so for people without disabilities?

So far we have seen how problematic it is to attribute the social exclusion of people with disabilities to fearful feelings they invoke in other people. To summarize, save for the explanation that people without disabilities take the disabled as omens of their own feared future, the notion that individuals characterized as weak and vulnerable are threatening to unimpaired, vigorous people can be dismissed as far-fetched. Nor does this affective account of their exclusion appear to offer a promising platform for building a more embracing moral position, for our predictive and precautionary practices do not suggest that people identify themselves, however uneasily, with a future in which they are disabled. Not displaced fear but rather a commonplace cognitive mistake—namely, the failure to weigh realistically the likelihood that in the future one might suffer undeservingly—degrades the compassion with which the nondisabled might otherwise engage individuals with disabilities into distancing pity.

Yet for some there will be such a future, one for which the invisibility and unthinkability of disability renders them enormously unprepared. The following story is by no means singular:

When Herman and Annette Adelson moved to the . . . retirement community 20 years ago, they were happy to pay extra for a condominium on the second floor. . . . There were no elevators, but who needed elevators? . . . But that was another life, when the Adelsons were in their 60's. Today those same stairs—14 concrete steps—loom as an insurmountable obstacle. Now Mrs. Adelson, who is 83, has severe rheumatism [and] can negotiate the stairs only painfully, going down backward with the help of her 85-year-old husband. And she does so only once a week. . . . [The secretary of the Florida Department of Elderly Affairs] said: "There is no money for elevators. What do you do? Do you . . . call out the National Guard to move these people up and down the steps? We didn't think ahead."[78]

Marginalization

In broad outline, this could also be the story of the seventeen-year-old athlete who injures his spine in an automobile accident, of the thirty-year-old businesswoman whose accelerating hearing loss now leaves her virtually deaf, or the fifty-five-year-old scholar whose retinopathy finally blurs his vision irremediably. Most adults who become disabled are outraged and dismayed by the extent to which the hostility of the constructed environment magnifies their social dysfunction well beyond any limits inherent in their physical dysfunction. Yet nondisabled people are not ignorant of how the environment excludes those who are impaired. It is inescapable that placing even a single step in front of a door bars people in wheelchairs, tacking a notice on a bulletin board disregards vision-impaired people, and playing recorded announcements fails to inform people who are deaf. For the most part, nondisabled people appear sincerely to regret these profoundly marginalizing outcomes, yet they do little to avoid them.

The conflicted response of the nondisabled—including the earlier selves of people who become disabled—to disablement thus confounds the claims of people with disabilities to enjoy respect from other people, and it sometimes defeats their efforts to maintain self-respect as well. This pervasive ambivalence also obscures the basis on which support from the nondisabled for the disabled should be forthcoming. Why is deploring, yet accepting, social arrangements that exclude individuals with physical, sensory, or cognitive impairments so commonplace?

Ambivalence about people with disabilities, marked by a complex interplay of approving and diminishing judgments, suffuses our culture. A 1991 Louis Harris and Associates survey, "Public Attitudes toward People with Disabilities,"[79] is illustrative. Asked to describe what they felt about

---

78. Sara Rimer, "New Needs for Retirement Complexes' Oldest: New Needs for Retirement Communities in Trying to Serve the 'Oldest Old,' " *New York Times,* 23 March 1998, A1, A14.

79. Kevin Hopkins, "Public Attitudes toward People with Disabilities," *Willing to Act* (Washington, D.C.: National Organization on Disability), September 1991, 7.

the disabled, 92 percent of the respondents said that they admired people with disabilities, while 74 percent pitied them. Even assuming that the 8 percent who do not feel admiration all are pitying, far more than half of the respondents seem to experience a clash of feelings, contemplating people with disabilities both with approbation and with despair. "Sentiments . . . about persons who are disabled tend to be ambivalent rather than unambiguously hostile or friendly," psychologists Irwin Katz, R. Glen Hass, and Joan Bailey found.[80]

Katz, Hass, and Bailey[81] also discovered how such ambivalence circumscribes the roles people with disabilities can comfortably assume. In this study, subjects were paid to complete a survey administered by an individual who in some sequences was not disabled but in others used a wheelchair. In some administrations, the surveyor was pleasant, efficient, and upbeat; in others, defeated, ineffective, and complaining. After the subjects completed the survey, a second individual arrived to explain that the first person had made a mistake in giving instructions and to ask the subjects to donate their time by redoing the survey. The hypothesis was that subjects in sequences in which the surveyor was pleasant would be more cooperative.

Unexpectedly, subjects in the pleasant sequence were three times as likely to help the nondisabled surveyor as the disabled one, but in the complaining sequences they were equally biased in the other direction— that is, in favor of helping the disabled surveyor. In other words, personal qualities usually thought of as being socially desirable were advantageous in securing cooperation for nondisabled individuals but were disadvantageous in securing cooperation for disabled individuals. The researchers hypothesize that nondisabled people reject people with disabilities when they seem to behave unsuitably by not limiting their aspirations and achievements—for instance, by assuming the role of a researcher. Nondisabled people "devaluate the unfortunate person because he or she ought to suffer but does not," they propose.[82]

In his important 1992 essay "Disability, Handicap, and the Environment," philosopher Ron Amundson makes a similar observation about

---

80. Irwin Katz, R. Glenn Hass, and Joan Bailey, "Attitudinal Ambivalence and Behavior toward People with Disabilities," in *Attitudes toward Persons with Disabilities*, ed. Harold Yuker (New York: Springer, 1988), 56.
81. Katz, Hass, and Bailey, "Attitudinal Ambivalence," 51–53.
82. Katz, Hass, and Bailey, "Attitudinal Ambivalence," 53.

how the expectations of the nondisabled majority limit the disabled minority: "One interesting correlation is that ablebodied people are often offended by disabled people who appear satisfied or happy with their condition. A mood of regret and sadness is socially expected."[83]

Sociologist and disability studies scholar Mike Oliver urges that the exclusion of people with disabilities is more usefully ascribed to specifically oppressive practices that debar them from productive social roles than to their inspiring the terror of becoming disabled in the dominant group who are not.[84] The latter kind of explanation "sees the problem as being located within the minds of able-bodied people, whether individually (prejudice) or collectively, through the manifestation of hostile social attitudes and the enactment of social policies based on the tragic view of disability," he says.[85] In contrast, the former account sees the problem as located within the institutionalized practices of society.[86] Oliver argues that, just as the discrimination against women and people of color fueled by sexism and racism persists if remedies focus on revising negative attitudes rather than on reforming the institutions that empower such attitudes, so the remedy for disablism lies in changing the behavioral practice constitutive of a disablist society.[87]

In 1987, Robert Funk, at the time director of the Disability Rights Education and Defense Fund (DREDF), an organization often described as "the national legal arm of the [U.S.] disability rights movement," and later to become chief of staff of the U.S. Equal Employment Opportunities Commission,[88] identified the restriction of their roles as the focus of discrimination against people with disabilities:

> People with disabilities have historically been treated as objects of pity—individuals who are incapable and neither expected nor willing to . . . contribute to organized society. . . . This social construct has been supported by

83. Ron Amundson, "Disability, Handicap, and the Environment," *Journal of Social Philosophy* 23, no. 1, 114, 118.

84. Michael Oliver, *The Politics of Disablement* (London: St. Martin's, 1990), 79.

85. Oliver, *Politics of Disablement*, 82.

86. Oliver, *Politics of Disablement*, 83.

87. Oliver, *Politics of Disablement*, 83.

88. Robert Funk, "Disability Rights: From Caste to Class in the Context of Civil Rights," in *Images of the Disabled, Disabling Images*, ed. A. Gartner and T. Joe (New York: Praeger, 1987), 7–30.

national welfare policies . . . charitable programs . . . , and rehabilitation services. . . . This has resulted in discriminatory programs, policies, and laws designed to deny disabled people's participation in organized society. These discriminatory policies and practices affect all classes of disabled people in virtually every aspect of their lives.[89]

Funk's innovative analysis contributed significantly to the legal theory that informs the ADA. Arguing that the limitations of Americans with physical, sensory, and cognitive impairments are mainly the product of discrimination, Funk shows that their liberation falls squarely within the American civil rights tradition. His analysis also suggests that to understand both disability and our moral and political obligations with respect to it, we must consider who is disabled and the social history of how they came to be so.

What Is a Disability?

Cultures commonly create social roles that are imagined to be especially suited to people with a particular impairment. For instance, in Western Europe, groups like the guilds of the blind joined together to hire guides, work at certain crafts, and visit the sick, but these organizations declined with the rise of a factory economy. Guilds of blind musicians and fortune-tellers survived for many further centuries in China; and in Japan guilds of blind acupuncturists and of masseurs who often doubled as money lenders flourished from the seventeenth century onward. (That these assignments are the product of social assignment rather than of natural aptitudes becomes evident when we notice that, in Japan, blind individuals are limited in virtue of their impairment to "body work" occupations such as massage therapy and acupuncture, while, in virtue of their impairment, blind individuals in the United States traditionally are barred from the same line of work.) Members of these organizations were offered preferential opportunities to practice their professions, much as in the United States today food concessions in state buildings often are reserved for lease by blind vendors. In the United States, deaf men traditionally worked in print shops, and blind men tuned pianos and repaired watches (during World

---

89. Funk, "From Caste to Class," 9.

War II, the latter were in high demand to assemble delicate military instruments).

The idea that individuals with physical, sensory, and cognitive impairments together form a class of "the disabled" is an invention of the current century. In earlier times, classification was in terms of physical, sensory, or cognitive condition. Persons were described as crippled or deaf or blind or mad or feebleminded, but only in the first part of this century was the term *disabled* introduced to characterize and collectivize them. In contemporary Western culture, to be disabled is to be disadvantaged regardless of how much success one achieves individually. That is because costs are extracted if one is seen as a member of a poorly regarded group. Being identified with a "weak" class invites oppression. This is the generic implication of "disability."

Today, being physically, sensorily, or cognitively impaired is virtually identified with disability, so much so that persons in very different conditions, with very different degrees of physical or cognitive limitation and quite disparate levels of socially significant achievement, are all referred to as "disabled." Regardless of their personal attainments, individuals identified with this class suffer from a paternalism similar to that which women once endured. This presumption of incompetence is the burden of membership in what is viewed as a "weak" class incapable of the performances required for full social participation.

Some misfortunes we bring on ourselves; others are visited upon us. The agency that impels events belonging to the latter category is sometimes a natural one, perhaps an illness or an accident. But, often, it is social rather than natural agency that is at fault. Thus, for instance, an unfortunate illness or accident sometimes is unpreventable; on the other hand, the illness may result from negligent, indifferent, corrupt, or cruel social arrangements. Are people disabled by illness or accident to be pitied because they are nature's hostages or because they are society's victims? This question reprises our initial queries about the nature of the disadvantage so inveterately associated with disability. Is it fundamentally a natural consequence of illness or accident that damages the body, the senses, or the mind? Or instead is it an artificial effect imposed by a social organization that is unfavorable to individuals who have become different from other people as the result of inheritance, illness, or injury? The conceptual frame that emerges as we answer this question will suggest whether compensatory justice is integral to equalizing individuals with disabilities and, if so, how so. Specifically, reconceptualizing disability will indicate whether the disadvantage occasioned by it will best give way to procedural or to distributive applications of justice.

In its original usage, a disability is a limitation suffered by individuals because they belong to a class regarded as incompetent to exercise at least some of the rights people normally enjoy. It is, then, construed to be an incapacity that disqualifies individuals from protected equality of participation under the law. Children, for instance, are disabled in respect to entering into contracts, purchasing alcoholic beverages, and protecting their privacy. To abrogate the bans that racist disparagement of their civic and commercial competence constructed against them, African Americans embraced juridical strategies to establish that color should not likewise be a disability under the law, disqualifying some individuals from the right to use public facilities.

In a similar vein, the status of women in Western democracies prior to the twentieth century illustrates the perils of being identified with a devalued and consequently disabled group. The culture supposed, and the law specified, that being a woman be accounted a disability. Consequently, women were disabled from voting, owning property, and retaining custody of their own children because they were imagined to be too biologically fragile and emotional, and thus too dependent, to bear the responsibility of doing so. Feminist emancipatory politics explicitly pursued legislation to eliminate such "women's disabilities." For instance, the Women's Disabilities Bill debated in the English Parliament in the 1870s addressed women's rights rather than their physical or cognitive condition. What should be kept in mind, however, is how the widespread deprecation of the strength of females' character and constitution provoked their being perceived as a "weak" and thereby an inferior class. This perception figured crucially in rationalizing their inferior and unfavorable legal treatment.[90]

As disability is now identified almost exclusively in ordinary language with being physically, sensorily, or cognitively impaired, individuals so categorized have until very recently been regarded as so naturally inferior as to be ineligible to be equally protected by the law. Their impairments have defeated their appeals to rights, so to speak. Either they have been denied

---

90. Rosalind Miles, *A Women's History of the World* (London: Joseph, 1988), 187.

rights others possess because law or tradition deems them incompetent, or else their impairments have barred them from meaningful exercise of the rights others appeal to freely.

Thus, saying that someone has a disability has had the force of discharging the duty to offer that individual normal protection, and respect. Over the last three-quarters of a century, progressive U.S. legislation and judicial decisions challenged racial segregation and gender oppression by affirming that differences in race and sex do not coincide with natural differences of ability or talent. Increasingly during this period, differences in race and sex were dismissed as justifying privileges or disadvantages in protection under the law or in opportunities for social participation. But in this same period of improving racial and gender justice, being physically, sensorily, or cognitively impaired continued to defeat claims to education, to work, to purchase insurance, and otherwise to engage in transactions central to making the lives of citizens more worth living. These social limitations were attributed to the impaired individuals' weakness or other personal flaws or shortcomings, not to biased social practice. To understand why this conceptualization persisted unchallenged throughout most of the era in which claims about the naturalness of other nondominant groups' inferior status were vigorously protested, we should turn to how our discourse traditionally has modeled disability.

The Moral Model of Disability

In almost all places and among most people, individuals with certain physical or intellectual anomalies are assumed to be, by the very nature of their condition, inferior. There is, of course, no global uniformity in how anomalies are reputed. Worldwide, the atypical condition that provokes most alarm is to be the product of a multiple birth, perhaps because having twin babies is seriously disruptive, especially in subsistence societies. Multiple births endanger the mother and challenge inheritance traditions. In some cultures, multiples are thought to battle each other for the single available soul.[91] To be the second of twin births in cultures with this belief

---

91. Benedicte Ingstadt and Susan Reynolds Whyte, eds. *Disability and Culture* (Berkeley: University of California Press, 1995), 11. In this same volume, see also Ida Nicolaisen, "Persons and Nonpersons: Disability and Personhood among the Punan Bah of Central Borneo," 38–55, 44.

is so serious a disability as to invite termination of the neonate at birth unless it can be adopted by a very distantly located family. Nevertheless, there are other cultures in which twins who survive enjoy a socially superior status.

The classical historian Robert Garland adduces other such variations in the valuation of human anomalies:

> In New Guinea albinos are regarded as holy, while in Senegal they are considered to be ominous. . . . [T]he Bayaka reverence their blind but deride their deaf, the deaf members of an Amazonian tribe experience no social stigma because of the ability of the whole tribe to communicate in sign language.[92]

What is true of the Amazon tribe Garland cites was also the case on the island of Martha's Vineyard, which had a large deaf population and where, until well into the twentieth century, almost everyone, hearing or not, was able to converse in Sign.[93]

Nevertheless, the disadvantage associated with having a disability typically has been attributed to the flaws, failings, or inferiorities of anomalous individuals or else to those with whom they are closely associated. From antiquity the traditional explanation for their disadvantage has supposed that there is some moral flaw, not necessarily theirs but perhaps that of their progenitors, for which failing they must suffer. For instance, the Greek god Hephaistos had deformed feet because his mother, Hera, defied her husband, Zeus, by conceiving a child without intercourse.[94] Oedipus, also born with deformed feet, brings his blindness on himself, but his precipitating actions resemble Hera's in that he also challenges the limitations of his station by attempting to defy the life plan designed for him. Garland tells us:

> Racial as well as individual deformity was interpreted as a punishment for what might loosely be described as the pagan equivalent to the doctrine of Original Sin. Ailian, for instance, alleges that when the Lokrians ceased to submit maidens as tribute to the goddess Athena, their wives were afflicted

---

92. Robert Garland, *The Eye of the Beholder: Deformity and Disability in the Graeco-Roman World* (Ithaca: Cornell University Press, 1995), 3.
93. Nora Groce, *Everyone Spoke Sign Language Here: Hereditary Deafness on Martha's Vineyard* (Cambridge: Harvard University Press, 1985).
94. Garland, *Eye of the Beholder*, 62.

with a disease which caused them to bear "crippled and monstrous children."[95]

Among the Songye of Zaire, some kinds of anomalies make people "bad" and others make them "faulty." Dwarfism and albinism make children bad. They are thought to be in contact with the supernatural and are expected to die soon. On the other hand, deformities of limbs from such causes as polio make for faulty people who have no clear social status; they are neither superior, as twins are in this society, nor inferior. "Much more attention is given to interpreting the fault. The issue is tackled by the family in a search for the cause, a process in which the person with the fault may be left out completely. In this view, the fault is only a symptom of something more important."[96]

The moral model of disability directs philosophical reflection to the question of responsibility. Thus, in the *Protagoras*,[97] Plato remarks that others' helpful intervention is appropriate only if a disabling condition is self-induced. If nature or luck enfeeble somebody and thereby place him at a disadvantage, there is no point in interfering in the hope of initiating a change. Aristotle[98] tells us that blindness, when due to factors beyond a person's control, properly evokes pity, but it is shameful when caused by condemnable conduct such as excessive drinking.

On the moral model of disability, disadvantage is the deserved consequence of impairment because impairment itself is likely to have been earned, if not by the individual who suffered it, then by some ancestor who failed to be sufficiently solicitous of his descendant's welfare. For the Greeks, disability is the due of flawed individuals. However, at least from the time of early sixth-century Athens, disabled war veterans were maintained at public expense. And, by Aristotle's time, men whose means fell below a specified line and who were too incapacitated to work received daily public payments through a treasurer elected by lot.[99] Thus, from antiquity, the idea has been maintained that disability invites compensation.

95. Garland, *Eye of the Beholder*, 60–61.
96. Patrick Devlieger, "Why Disability? The Cultural Understanding of Physical Disability in an African Society," in *Disability and Culture*, 94–105, 96.
97. 323d
98. Aristotle, *Nichomachean Ethics* 3, 1114a, 25–28.
99. Garland, *Eye of the Beholder*, 35–37.

Some impairments—blindness, for instance—were supposed capable of transfiguring an individual as a kind of compensation. For instance, because the highest kind of knowledge transcends visual perception instead of being constituted by it, blindness was often portrayed as enhancing an individual's skill in comprehending refined or hidden meaning.[100] (Much later, this theme would reappear in early detective stories featuring blind sleuths whose powers of ratiocination were not deflected by the appearances of false clues created by the criminal.)

Garland observes that in antiquity impairment was associated with lack of self-discipline and abandonment of other-regarding virtues.[101] Thus the compensatory powers conferred by impairment could be as dangerous to others as repudiation by others is to individuals with disabilities. Garland remarks on a scene in *Oedipus Rex* in which Oedipus taunts Tiresias, charging him with having vision to look to his own advantage but none to put in the service of others. Tiresias retaliates by revealing more than he should about Oedipus's lineage, thus provoking the unfolding of Thebes' tragic events.

The Medical Model of Disability

In the modern era, the progressive approach to justifying the disadvantage visited on physically, sensorily, or cognitively impaired individuals substitutes a physiological or mental deficit for the moral flaw blamed by antiquity. This medical model fixes on reducing the numbers of people with disabilities by preventative or curative medical technology. Despite its scientific associations, the medical model resembles the earlier moral model in its assignment of responsibility, for impaired individuals' deficits often are attributed either to their own inadequate health practices or to their bad genes—that is, once more to their own or their ancestors' failings. For instance, Dr. Samuel Gridley Howe, superintendent of a nineteenth-century asylum, comments, "The moral to be drawn from the existence of the individual idiot is this—he, or his parents, have so far violated the natural laws, so far marred the beautiful organism of the body, that it is an unfit instrument for the manifestation of the powers of the soul." Howe offered five causes for cognitive impairment: inferior physical condi-

---

100. Garland, *Eye of the Beholder*, 34.
101. Garland, *Eye of the Beholder*, 29.

tion, intemperance, self-abuse, intermarriage of relatives, and failed attempts to terminate pregnancies.[102]

Bickenbach points out that the medical model introduces the possibility of separating the diagnosis of disability from the assessment of personal blame:

> [T]he most significant contribution of the practice of medicine to the normative component of disablement theory was its clinical insistence upon etiological neutrality. . . . A patient is a patient, whether the impairments are self-caused or the result of an accident, an epidemic, or the intentional actions of others. . . . Pain, suffering and incapacitation are bad things that should be avoided if possible and those who help to make this happen are providing an important and valuable service.[103]

But, as Bickenbach's subsequent analysis reveals, traces of its predecessor—that is, the moral model—bias the medical model so that disability continues to be enmeshed in contexts that invite condemnatory judgments. Bickenbach observes:

> [G]iven our conviction that science and technology can always meet the challenge posed by a threat to human life and health, people with disabilities—especially those who are chronically ill or dying—come to represent the failure of biomedicines' mastery over the human body. . . . [F]ailures must be explained away, and their embodiments hidden. One all too familiar way of doing both of these things is to attribute the failure to the victim and to blame, fear, and eventually physically isolate the victim.[104]

Initially, the medical model promised to resolve a difficulty which has been increasingly pressing from at least the time of the Athenian democracy's commitment to support certain individuals with disabilities. This is the problem of distinguishing those who are genuinely unable to be productive from those who do not wish to be so. Athens' Council annually reviewed the condition of individuals who claimed to be eligible for disability benefits. In addition, to discourage fraudulent claimants, Garland reports, " 'anyone who wished' was free to challenge a claimant's entitle-

---

102. Marvin Rosen, Gerald Clark, and Marvin Kivitz, eds., *The History of Mental Retardation: Collected Papers Vol. I* (Baltimore, Md.: University Park Press, 1975), 35.

103. Bickenbach, *Physical Disability*, 91–92.

104. Bickenbach, *Physical Disability*, 82.

ment to public support by prosecuting him in a court of law."[105] In *The Disabled State*, Deborah Stone traces the long history of similar attempts, including the recurring efforts to gatekeep U.S. workers' compensation and Social Security disability benefits eligibility. Although physicians initially were reluctant to accept this gatekeeping role, the second half of this century has seen significant medical involvement in attempts to delineate disability definitively to produce eligibility criteria for public and private disability insurance and social welfare schemes.[106]

However, both the enormous amount of current litigation over who should be receiving benefits and the rapid growth of U.S. disability rolls (and those of many other Western nations) during the 1980s (when many kinds of diminished or inappropriate performances were medicalized) suggest the indeterminateness of medical evidence of disability. For it is the perception of compromised competence—not impairment per se—that occasions the allocation of public resources to compensate for disability. And there is a notorious paucity of correlation between the kind and degree of an individual's physiological impairment—the damage to nerve, muscle, vessel, organ, or other tissues—and that individual's success, or lack of it, in accomplishing physical, daily living, and higher-order functions.

As Stone correctly points out, we still have a relatively poor understanding of the connection between medically identifiable impairments and the kinds of functional limitations that are the target of compensatory public policies.[107] For example, individuals with identical prelingual hearing losses vary markedly in their ability to lip-read and speak. Similarly, individuals with apparently identical muscular or nerve impairments differ in whether they can grasp, lift, stand, and walk. There is a vast range of print-intensive occupations in which some people with dyslexia succeed while others fail, and this was equally the case prior to the medicalization and treatment of learning disabilities. Although acclaimed as a vehicle for focusing efforts to preserve and protect people with disabilities, the medical model of disability has failed to stimulate the development of adequate methods for distinguishing who is made dysfunctional by physical, sen-

---

105. Garland, *Eye of the Beholder*, 35–37.
106. Cited in Bickenbach, *Physical Disability*, 75–76.
107. Deborah Stone, *The Disabled State* (Philadelphia: Temple University Press, 1984), 116–17, 128.

sory, or cognitive impairment from who is not. Consequently, millions of dollars are expended in processing claims for benefits; more money is spent by claimants to hire experts to prepare and pursue their claims and by program administrators to investigate fraudulent claims.

Another difficulty with the medical model, which takes disability's diminishing of opportunity to originate in individuals' natural—namely, their biological—shortcomings, is its inattention to the crucial role obstructive environments play in dysfunctionality. For the supportiveness, adaptability, and accessibility of the environment can have an enormous effect on whether impairment limits function. Let me illustrate from bioethicist Dan Brock's discussion about containing high-cost but low-benefit treatments.

Brock appeals to one of the familiar quality-of-life scales used in the health care field for determining treatment priorities.[108] Of almost equal weight on this scale are the patient's mode of physical activity, which means the mode the individual employs to perform major life functions, and the patient's level of activity, which means the scope of social opportunity available given the individual's mode of functioning. Using a wheelchair is rated as more limiting than not walking as far or fast as others, despite radical differences in the types of complex undertakings these different modes of mobility impact. That is, whereas wheelchair users are usually limited in the types of sites they can access but not in the speed at which and distance from where they travel to those sites, compromised walkers can climb into many more types of sites but only those they have the time and stamina to reach. That quality-of-life scales abstract from complex differences between modes of performance itself reveals that they are more responsive to the mere fact of an individual's being limited than to how functionally devastating or benign the limit might be.

We should distrust the reliability of any scale of well-being that purports to measure life's quality by comparing modes of performance without considering the facts of their effectiveness. After all, in everyday life mechanically aided functioning is not thought to be inferior to unassisted activity. Far from it, engineered assistance has been the instrument of the improved living standards we have pursued and attained throughout the century. To illustrate, using a car to go from place to place is not deprecated as the

---

108. Dan Brock, *Life and Death* (Cambridge: Cambridge University Press, 1993), 346.

crutch of defective hikers. So it cannot simply be categorically assumed that using mechanical assistance to perform a life's activity lowers the quality of that life. Consequently, we should discount any scale that arbitrarily ranks the relative effectiveness of different modes of performing any function, and equally any scale that illegitimately naturalizes such rankings by stipulating that mechanically assisted performance must be inferior.

While the scale's physical activity category is focused on individual performance, the limitations addressed by the mobility category cannot escape being relativized to the environment. The rankings on the scale for this category are specified in terms of certain transactions with the built environment, such as whether someone can get into a car or use public transportation. Notice, however, that in each such case the question of successful performance is as much a question about the availability of appropriately designed vehicles as about the patient's proficiency. To give just one example, if two-door sedans are available, an individual with a folding wheelchair can drive independently, pulling the chair into the car behind the driver's seat. But the design of four-door cars precludes this maneuver. Consequently, the rarity of the once common two-door automobile has attenuated the mobility of many wheelchair users who can get into a two-door car but not a four-door car by folding their wheelchairs. How, then, to assess their quality of life in a culture in which automobile styles fluctuate so rapidly?

In general, we should mistrust any summative process that treats variable elements as fixed and thus disregards the contexts to which they are relativized. The degree to which either personal or environmental limitations result in social limitations—that is, prevent an individual from normal social achievement such as having a family and earning a living—is the outcome of complex interactions between the individual's limits and the limits of her environment. This is why it is so difficult not only to predict the degree to which but also to comprehend the process whereby physical dysfunction leads to social dysfunction. This is also why it is misleading to assume that the misfortune of disablement must be due to natural rather than social agency.

Marginalizing by Medicalizing

Nevertheless, the identification of physical, sensory, or cognitive deficit with anomalous modes of performance, and the subsequent equation of anomaly with dysfunction and then with diminished quality of life, take on the character of a mantra within the context of the medical model. Reduction of the ability to perform in so-called normal modes and at so-called normal levels must be cured or compensated for on the medical model because physical, cognitive, and emotional functioning in the common or familiar way is supposed to be required for a life to have the usual quality. So, despite continuing to equate disability with individuals' failures or flaws, the medical model does differ from the moral model by recommending a different approach to compensating for the infelicities or inconvenience of atypical functioning—namely, by abating these through curative or rehabilitative therapies.

The bioethicist Norman Daniels puts it this way: "The basic idea is that . . . diseases (I here include deformities and disabilities that result from trauma) are deviations from the natural functional organization of a typical member of a species." If an individual does not maintain "normal species functioning," Daniels insists, her ability to achieve whatever choice she makes of goals and tasks (and consequently to be happy) will be diminished. He thinks the needs picked out by reference to normal species functioning are objectively and constantly important because they meet this high-order interest persons have in maintaining a normal range of opportunities.[109]

"Life plans we are otherwise suited for and have a reasonable expectation of finding satisfying or happiness-producing are rendered unreasonable by impairments of normal functioning," he says. Moreover, "if people have a higher-order interest in preserving . . . opportunity . . . , then they will have a pressing interest in maintaining normal species functioning by establishing institutions—such as health care systems—that do just that."[110] Daniels's prescription is quite clear: because the functioning that typifies a species seems so expressive of its nature, species-typical functioning appears to be a self-justifying standard, nature's way of deducing how we ought to conduct ourselves given what kind of creature we are.

Thus, interventions that normalize seem to Daniels to command a natural warrant. Normal functioning appears as a firm and impersonal, yet

---

109. Norman Daniels, "Justice and Health Care" in *Health Care Ethics: An Introduction*, ed. Donald Van DeVeer and Tom Regan (Philadelphia: Temple University Press, 1987), 302.

110. Daniels, *Justice and Health Care*, 302.

compelling, standard. It is a clear standard as well, he supposes, because to determine what mode and level of functioning is normal, we need only observe the natural functional organization of human beings. This task, he says "falls to the biomedical sciences . . . since claims about the design of the species and its fitness to meeting biological goals underlie at least some of the relevant functional ascriptions."[111]

Further, what could be a more naturally modest expectation of individuals than the prospect of functioning as their species typically does? So all individuals equally might be thought to have a natural stake in social arrangements designed to prevent or repair anomalous conditions that interfere with species-typical functioning. Concomitantly, relatively few individuals would have an interest in preserving or promoting any specific functional anomaly or singularity. So again it seems as if the broadest-based public support very naturally will go to social arrangements that reduce whatever anomalies or singularities hinder adherence to the species-typical functional standard.

By no means, however, should it be supposed that a policy of restoring impaired individuals so that they function typically for the species is the natural correlate of an objective biological principle. For one thing, biology tends to eliminate dysfunctional individuals, not to repair them. Furthermore, nature does not issue an imperative to normalize individuals by altering them so that they perform in the most familiar way. As philosopher Alexander Rosenberg points out, modern biology suggests that there is no "base-line repertoire of abilities common to normal agents" that is adaptive for the organism.[112]

That there are average, common, or typical modes and levels of human performances does not make these the normal or natural modes and levels for humankind.[113] Normalizing individuals by imposing the standard of species-typical functioning may itself disadvantage rather than preserve and protect any population that already has been made vulnerable because its members do not function in the normal, typical, or customary way. A policy of normalizing can worsen the position or otherwise oppress the very individuals whose quality of life it purports to improve.

---

111. Daniels, *Justice and Health Care*, 302.

112. Alexander Rosenberg, "The Political Philosophy of Biological Endowments, *Social Philosophy and Policy* 5, no. 1 (1986): 5.

113. Eliot Sober, "Evolution, Population Thinking, and Essentialism," *Philosophy of Science* 47 (1980): 350–83.

Nevertheless, for people without disabilities who are convinced there is a democratic imperative to restore people with impairments to the average or common level of functioning, the existence of incurables may be perceived as a frustrating failure of justice. For if democratic policy drives toward securing equality through restoring personal functioning, then to achieve equality medically is, ultimately, to eliminate or circumvent impairment. But many persons with disabilities cannot be fully or even significantly restored or rehabilitated. For individuals with disabilities, something troubling thus attaches to assigning an egalitarian purpose to the provision of health care, as Daniels does. For such a policy has the effect of freeing society from the company of the disabled, who either will be cured, and consequently no longer be disabled, or else will be sequestered from society for the purpose of their continued medical treatment.

Brock speaks to the coercive potential of medicalizing people's departures from typical or customary functioning: "Generally it is when we have noticed an adverse effect or change in our normal functional capacity that we contact health care professionals and begin the process which can result in our being labeled as sick or diseased."[114]

In my view, Brock accurately describes the impact of medicalized discourse. Designating an anomaly, difference, or change in one's customary functioning as sick, diseased, or a defect or deviance in health is potentially coercive.[115] It consequently is completely understandable that he, along

---

114. Dan Brock, "The Human Genome Project and Human Identity," in *Genes and Human Self-Knowledge: Historical and Philosophical Reflections on Modern Genetics,* ed. Robert Weir, Susan Lawrence, and Evan Fales (Ames: University of Iowa Press, 1994), 29.

115. Medicalizing anomalous biological states took hold in the nineteenth century and quickly became enormously persuasive. The conduct-altering principles spawned by this process influenced practice well beyond the scope of the evidence accrued in their favor. For instance, in the late nineteenth century, Clark University undertook the largest study of children conducted until that time. Generalizing from poor samples and amateurs' observations of the subjects in them, researchers concluded that being an only child "was a disease in itself." They shored up their conclusion with the claim that animals that typically began life in multiple births—pigs and partridges, for instance—were more teachable—that is, developed more quickly and were more tractable—than singletons such as cows and eagles. So compelling was the stereotypical figure of the solitary and putatively spoiled and selfish single child that "the prejudice retains much of its power today," even though there is overwhelming evidence (the first solid study was published in 1928) that the nineteenth-century claims are false. Today, the only-

with many others, worries about how advances in genetic testing for anomalous inherited traits may prove detrimental to individuals found to have these traits:

> [P]eople who feel healthy and who as yet suffer no functional impairment will increasingly be labeled as unhealthy or diseased. . . . For many people, this labeling will undermine their sense of themselves as healthy, well-functioning individuals and will have serious adverse effects both on their conceptions of themselves and the quality of their lives.[116]

Notice that this outcome is equally likely to be the case regardless of the penetrance of the relevant genes. That is, an individual who possesses a troublesome gene would be adversely labeled as "unhealthy" regardless of whether its presence guarantees its expression, as in Huntington's disease, or whether its presence simply increases to some extent the probability that an illness will develop, as the alleles correlated with breast cancer appear to do. It seems, then, that it is not necessarily malfunctioning itself but merely being regarded or labeled by medical practice as having a liability to malfunction that impairs an individual's sense of self in a manner so dire as to reduce the quality of the person's life.

Medicalizing's Horrible History

Thus, both the actual and the prospective anomalies labeled as impairments damaged putatively impaired people's self-regard by depreciating how other people regard them. That is, as Brock insightfully describes the social process, putatively impaired people's self-regarding tolerance of themselves is superseded by other people's other-regarding disparagement of them until the anomalous individuals become socially incapacitated. History suggests that concerns about the coercive potential of equating difference with defectiveness by medicalizing it are not exaggerated. For instance, feminist bioethicist Susan Sherwin describes how medicalizing their differences contributed to women's disabilities:

---

child stigma still coerces parents; providing a sibling is one of the most common reasons parents give for having a second child. Bill McKibben, "What Only-Child Syndrome?" *New York Times Magazine*, 3 May 1998, 48.

116. Brock, "Human Genome," 29.

The mid-nineteenth century brought . . . a new medical interest . . . to establish menstruation as disability that demands rest and withdrawal from ordinary activities. . . . By the end of the century physicians were in the forefront of the campaign to . . . restrict women's participation. . . . The prevailing . . . attitude was that menstruation created invalids out of women and made them particularly unfit. . . . [N]o thought was given . . . to adapting the demands of the universities or the workplace to these supposed special needs of women.[117]

To understand this process of disability discrimination more thoroughly, it will be useful to look more carefully at a historical example to appreciate the social consequences of an anomaly's being naturalized by being designated a biological defect. In the late nineteenth century, educators of the deaf divided into two camps, one that passionately supported and one that vehemently opposed educating deaf children in the language of manual signs. Each charged the other with protracting the dysfunctionality of deaf people and consequently with unfairly constricting their opportunity. At the heart of this debate lay another divide—namely, an unbridgeable chasm that separated two very different beliefs about the relationship between biology and opportunity.

As Douglas Baynton writes in *Forbidden Signs: American Culture and the Campaign against Sign Language*, "The real battle [over sign language] was fought on a . . . rarefied plane, encompassing such questions as the larger purposes of education in a democratic and industrializing society . . . and the locus and character of cultural authority in America. Indeed, occupying a central place in the fight was a late-nineteenth century debate over the nature of nature itself."[118]

That deaf individuals talk by means of manual signs has been familiar to us from antiquity. As Plato writes in the *Cratyllus*, suppose we had neither voice nor tongue yet wished to communicate with one another. Should we not, like the deaf and dumb, make signs with our hands, head, and other parts of the body?[119]

In this vein, the early part of the nineteenth century saw the establishment of sign language schools as a mode of equalizing deaf people's access

117. Susan Sherwin, *No Longer Patient* (Philadelphia: Temple University Press, 1992), 182.

118. Douglas Baynton, *Forbidden Signs: American Culture and the Campaign against Sign Language* (Chicago: University of Chicago Press, 1996), 107.

119. 422e

to the Word, understood to be the conveyance of that moral and religious knowledge that is the goal of human imagination, intelligence, and understanding. Because signing was thought to rely on natural symbols that were self-interpreting, Sign was believed to engage the intelligence directly and lucidly and to stimulate the moral sense. It therefore was the instrument to repair deaf people's dysfunction and permit them to develop to greatest perfection. America followed Europe in becoming fascinated by signing. Teachers were imported to systematize and disseminate the gestural communication used by the deaf in this country.

Manualists considered deaf people to be a singular class, distanced from the transient fashions of speech and therefore less corruptible, out of the ordinary, remarkable, unique. Citing such eighteenth-century sources as Daniel Defoe and Denis Diderot, Lennard Davis writes in *Enforcing Normalcy: Disability, Deafness and the Body* that, for different reasons and in different respects, both the blind and the deaf often were thought to exhibit certain heightened and purer sensibilities than the ordinary person, although "deafness was more fundamentally about the existence and function of language."[120] Far from being roleless, deaf people were assigned a special place in the eighteenth- and early-nineteenth-century imagination.

But, as Baynton observes, "by the late nineteenth century, naturalness as an ideal was being challenged and eventually was not merely defeated but colonized by the competing ideal of 'normality.' "[121] For one thing, naturalness had lost its status as a trait independent of and superior to the artifice, convention, and craft characteristic of social organization. "This intellectual and indeed moral shift in American culture was crucial to the reversal in attitudes toward sign language and the deaf community," Baynton adds.[122]

An 1884 speech by oralist Alexander Graham Bell shows how naturalizing the preferred behaviors of the dominant class propelled a program of normalizing, where this meant conforming the behaviors of deaf children to those of the hearing majority: "I think we should aim to be as natural as we can. I think we should get accustomed to treat our deaf children as if they could hear. . . . We should try ourselves to forget that they are deaf.

---

120. Lennard Davis, *Enforcing Normalcy: Disability, Deafness and the Body* (London: Verso, 1995), 53, 57–59.
121. Baynton, *Forbidden Signs*, 110.
122. Baynton, *Forbidden Signs*, 110.

We should teach them to forget that they are deaf. We should . . . avoid anything that would mark them out as different from others."[123]

By 1899 we find the president of Amherst College, John Tyler, prefiguring Norman Daniels by folding the mantle of science around normalizing practices. Tyler assured a convention of oralists that America would "never have a scientific system of education until we have one based on . . . the grand foundation of biological history. . . . [T]he search for the . . . goal of education compels us to study man's origin and development." Such scientifically based or biologized education would maintain the functional strategies that seemed to place speech higher on the scale of evolutionary development than the expressive gestures of lower primates. It became a moral and social obligation to increase the opportunities of both deaf signers and gesticulating foreigners by repairing them, a duty that a scientific system of educating them in the language and communication behaviors of the dominant class could discharge.[124]

It is important to understand that the fundamental division here is between competing ideas of what organizes a well-ordered society. The eighteenth century's ideal of individualized moral perfection had given way to an ideal of communal or social participation by people who functioned dialogically in common in the public sphere. Where once language's highest function had been to engage individuals with ideas understood as transcendent sources of right belief and right conduct, now its most important use was to engage people with one another in productive commercial and civic interaction.

Arguing against the idea that deaf people could flourish with a language of their own, an oralist insisted, "To go through life as one of a peculiar class is the sum of human misery. No other misfortune is comparable to this."[125] This thought typifies the shift of priorities from personal to social improvement and the correlated elevation of the importance of collective over idiosyncratic individualistic identities. This urge to create fair opportunity by leveling the players rather than the playing field thus is a theme that has come more and more to dominate American egalitarianism over the past hundred years.[126]

---

123. Baynton, *Forbidden Signs*, 136.
124. Baynton, *Forbidden Signs*, 302.
125. Baynton, *Forbidden Signs*, 145.
126. Daniels usually is seen as following Rawls in setting equality of opportunity as the egalitarian goal. However, his emphasis on normal functioning as the

Normalizing is played out in both medical and educational programs that intervene to repair or restore or revise members of nondominant groups. As in the manualist/oralist controversy of the last century, this theme presents difficulty for individuals who see the policy of normalizing as reducing rather than improving their meaningful opportunities. Needless to say, that educating the deaf was, very early, assumed to be a social obligation deserving of public or charitable funds exacerbated this danger to the status and success of deaf people.

In being presented with arguments for normalizing deaf children, the public was invited to decide to which group of contenders the management of "deaf schools" would be awarded. As deaf people were not permitted in almost all hearing schools, the policy of normalizing them by insisting that they speak, not sign, rewarded oralists with jobs in state schools for the deaf, but from the 1880s to the 1980s it severely reduced teaching jobs and other opportunities for deaf people. By allocating resources to practices intended to normalize deaf people, public policy imposed a conception of the good under which they did not flourish.

Interventions that reduce rather than expand already limited functionality surely extract too high a price. Such is the history of oralism in the education of the deaf. Baynton reminds us, "Oralism meant that many deaf people had access only to limited or simplified language during the crucial early years of language development." For fear they would fall back to communicating in a more convenient but abnormal way, deaf children often were not taught to write unless they had mastered intelligible speaking.[127]

This practice has a deleterious impact that remains to this day, for it left a legacy of reduced literacy in the deaf community. Some commentators mistake this residue of the historical oppression of deaf people for a natural deficit. Thus, Dena S. Davis argues that it is preferable to be hearing than to be deaf because deaf children have a much more limited range of life plan options than hearing children do. "Deaf parents wishing to have Deaf children are an example of families . . . shaping . . . a radically narrow range of choices available to the child when she grows up."[128]

---

operative condition for equal opportunity takes him closer to Amartya Sen's competing proposal that it is more meaningful to level people's capabilities than their opportunities.

127. Baynton, *Forbidden Signs*, 151.

128. Dena Davis, "Genetic Dilemmas and the Child's Right to an Open Future," *The Hastings Center Report* 27, no. 2 (March–April 1997): 7.

One of the factors that narrows deaf children's opportunities, Davis asserts, is the likelihood that their reading and writing will be deficient. She appears unaware that their history of being deprived of effective education, not their deficit of natural talent, explains why many deaf people do not write English well. Rancorous disagreement about the best approach to introduce prelingual deaf children to language remains a legacy of the century-old debate about how and to whom deaf people should communicate. As a result, many deaf children's opportunities are narrowed far beyond what needs to be. This being the case, it seems social repair, rather than rehabilitative treatment, is the appropriate vehicle for securing deaf children's prospects for a more open and opportunity filled future.

"Oralism failed," Baynton concludes, "and sign language survived, because deaf people themselves chose not to relinquish the autonomous cultural space that their community and language made possible."[129] That is, for many people who cannot be made to hear, the opportunity of communicating fully within a limited group appears to be more satisfying, more equalizing, and more meaningful than the opportunity of communicating in a limited way with the larger community. This is not to say that all deaf and hard of hearing people make this choice but merely to point out how the alternative to normalizing profoundly deaf people is not a limitation of function but instead is a limitation in the segment of the social environment in which one attempts to function. To be made normal, at least in this case, thus appears to be about refashioning which groups an impaired individual socializes with rather than about restoring the individual to a naturally desirable biological standard. Kwame Anthony Appiah points out that conceptualizing race in a manner that invites racism is an artifact of nineteenth-century efforts to establish the homogeneity of certain populations, for instance, those encompassed by the politically drawn borders of the new nation-states.[130] Baynton tells a similar story about conceptualizing deafness in a manner that invites policies for "normalizing" people who are deaf.

The conceptualization of "language" that denied manual signing the status of being a language is a nineteenth-century artifact developed to

---

129. Baynton, *Forbidden Signs*, 151.
130. Kwame Anthony Appiah and Amy Gutmann, *Color Conscious: The Political Morality of Race* (Princeton, N.J.: Princeton University Press, 1996), 52–64.

homogenize communication and so facilitate the civic and commercial transactions of the emerging urban society. Signing's defect lay not in its power to signify but rather in its requirement for face-to-face contact, a characteristic considered retrograde in an era when an enhanced ability to communicate over distances facilitated commerce. It is no accident that Alexander Graham Bell, the inventor of that urban business lifeline, the telephone, spearheaded the oralist movement. For deaf people could not be permitted to weigh in and tip the balance in regard to whether tele-typed text or telephoned speech would be the primary vehicle of commercial communication. Nor is it likely to be mere happenstance that an integrated community of deaf and hearing individuals who used Sign was able to persist in Martha's Vineyard well into the twentieth century; rather, their manual culture was lost along with the rural character when the area became commercialized. Furthermore, it is revealing that we converse comfortably about whether Microsoft's corporate culture differs from Apple's, yet make Deaf people struggle to prove they have a culture.

The lessons available in the historical record should guide us as we seek effective approaches to equalizing people with disabilities. We have seen that normalizing programs are imposed to adjust anomalous individuals to environments suited not to them but to the dominant social class. These programs were pressed forward and significant resources deployed in their support, regardless of how they themselves contributed to the incapacitation of their subjects. Even if it was easier or less expensive, more effective or more humane to adjust their environments to these individuals, such an alternative to renovating supposedly defective people attracted little favorable thought and not an inconsiderable amount of opposition, except for proposals to create segregated situations, institutions that could be suited to individuals with disabilities because they separated them from the general public.

Normalizing equalizes opportunity only to the extent to which people can be maintained in or restored to the image of the dominant group. But we should recognize that the dominant group's fashions of functioning are not the product of any biological mandate or evolutionary triumph, nor are they naturally endowed to be optimally effective and efficient. Rather, members of this group impose on others a social or communal situation that best suits themselves, regardless of whether it is the most productive option for everyone. This being the case, we can see that the main ingredient of being (perceived as) normal lies in being in social situations that suit one—that is, in a social environment arranged for and accustomed to people like oneself. Thus, while in favorable situations normalizing can equalize individuals who are different by changing them, programmatic normalization—the equalizing strategy promoted by the medical model of disability—lends itself to oppression because it validates and further imposes the dominant social group's preferences and biases.

The Social Model of Disability

The medical model treats the built and arranged environment as an invariable to which humans have no choice but to adjust. But it clearly is human to manipulate and alter our environment. We, through our social processes, fashion the built environment, which can be hostile or welcoming in respect to specific impairments. We, or at least the preeminent ones among us, also influence what features are possessed by the dominant cooperative scheme that structures communication, allocation of resources, and the other transactional processes of our social environment.

The medical model assumes that disabilities are, fundamentally, deficits of natural assets rather than of social assets. How our democratic political morality inclines us to deal with disability turns on whether we persist in this view. For if disability is due to the disadvantageous arrangement of social assets that should be equitably accessible to everyone alike, social reform is at least as appropriate a vehicle as personal renovation for discharging any obligation we may have to equalize people with disabilities. To see whether disablement is primarily a natural or a social phenomenon, we should pursue the question of what binds it so tightly to disadvantage.

From the standpoint of persons mobilizing in wheelchairs, disablement is experienced not as the absence of walking but as the absence of access to bathrooms, theaters, transportation, the workplace, medical services, and educational programs—all those opportunities most other citizens expect to access. If the majority of people, instead of just a few, wheeled rather than walked, graceful spiral ramps instead of jarringly angular staircases would connect lower to upper floors of buildings. Were vision-impaired individuals dominant, information would not be conveyed in a format accessible only to the sighted. Tactile and aural modes of recording information would be used as frequently as printed texts. Suppose most were deaf? Closed captioning would be open and would have been the standard for television manufacture in the United States long before 1 July

1993.[131] People with schizophrenia now are thought to be individuals with physiological impairments "that make them especially vulnerable to emotional stress . . . often from dealing with other people [that] can . . . spiral down into psychosis."[132] Were the concern to maintain such individuals' productivity paramount, we would promote practices to reduce anxiety in interpersonal transactions instead of accepting—indeed, even admiring—the behavior of those who place stress on others while avoiding it themselves.

Often the functional deficits customarily associated with disability are neither more nor less than an alterable cultural artifact. The social model of disability transforms the notion of "handicapping condition" from a state of a minority of people, which disadvantages them in society, to a state of society, which disadvantages a minority of people. The social model traces the source of this minority's disadvantage to a hostile environment and treats the dysfunction attendant on (certain kinds of) impairment as artificial and remediable, not natural and immutable. It transfigures individuals with disabilities from patients into persons with rights, which, when acknowledged, should eliminate the social disadvantages that are attendant upon their being a minority. Their environment is inimical to them because, in respect to almost all social venues and institutions, people with disabilities are neither numerous nor noticeable.

The ADA, the 1990 landmark civil rights legislation that delineates disability discrimination, is thoroughly grounded in the belief that disability is socially constructed. The analysis of disability that this legislation reflects merges a line of thought drawn from Hegel, Marx, and Foucault with the classical liberalism of the American civil rights movement. Disability activist and scholar James Charlton identifies prominent strands of thought found in contemporary disability theory as drawn from these sources; he also shows how applications of the views of Sandra Bartky, Frantz Fanon, Antonio Gramsci, Nancy Hartsock, and Jean-Paul Sartre illuminate various aspects of disability.[133] Problematizing disability this way emerged

---

131. The 1990 Television Decoder Circuitry Act established the principle that for-profit makers of components required for public broadcasting have a responsibility to include deaf and hard-of-hearing citizens in the market segment they serve.

132. Denise Grady, "Studies of Schizophrenia Indicate Psychotherapy," *New York Times*, 20 January 1998, B17.

133. James Charlton, *Nothing about Us without Us* (Berkeley: University of

nearly two decades ago as a result of crossovers from radical philosophy to the disability movement in Britain. Subsequently, American disability activists adopted the model because it illuminated and gave a direction to social reform.[134]

The model explains the isolation of people with disabilities not as the unavoidable outcome of impairment but rather as the correctable product of how such individuals interact with stigmatizing social values and debilitating social arrangements. In creating the ADA, Congress found that

> historically, society has tended to isolate and segregate individuals with disabilities. . . . [I]ndividuals with disabilities are a discrete and insular minority who have been . . . subjected to a history of purposeful unequal treatment, and relegated to a position of political powerlessness in our society . . . resulting from . . . assumptions not truly indicative of the . . . ability of such individuals to participate in, and contribute to society.[135]

The thrust of this view is that disability is not a "natural kind," nor is the disadvantage attendant on it an immutable fact of nature. None of this is to deny that, in the main, disablement correlates with anomalous, nonideal, or troubling biological conditions. But once it is recognized that no biological mandate or evolutionary endorsement warrants the dominant group's fashions of functioning as being optimally effective or efficient, we can see that the main ingredient of being (perceived as) normal lies in being in social situations that suit one—that is, in a social environment accustomed to people like oneself.

Disability Is Not Illness

The social model of disability disconnects our conceptualization of disability from illness and pain so as to ensure that no judgment about the lives of people with disabilities is distorted by uncritical assumptions about their suffering. A proposal by bioethicist Franklin G. Miller, writing in *The*

California Press, 1998), 27, 28, 31, 40, 49, 55, 74–77, 115, 121, 155–56, 161–62, 170.

134. Vic Finkelstein, *Attitudes and Disabled People* (New York: World Rehabilitation Fund, 1980) and private E-mail correspondence. See also Funk, "From Caste to Class."

135. Public Law 101–336, Americans with Disabilities Act of 1990, Section 2 (7).

Hastings Center Report, illustrates the importance of this distinction. Miller proposes that the professional integrity of genetic counselors, who are health care professionals, requires them to help hearing parents avoid having deaf offspring. However, he thinks that same integrity is corrupted if they help deaf parents avoid having hearing offspring.[136] Both courses of action are mandated because, Miller thinks, hearing children are healthy but deaf children cannot conceivably be so. Consequently, he sees health care professionals as simply pursuing their obligation to foster health by promoting the birth of hearing but not equally of deaf children. Contrary to Miller's view, though, it is odd to describe a strong and flourishing baby as in ill health just because the child is born deaf. Noticing this point suggests that important distinctions are ignored, and significant policy decisions stipulated rather than justified, when having a physical, sensory, or cognitive impairment is conflated with being ill.

We may begin to address this point by noticing how ordinary language marks the difference between illness and disability. We speak of suffering an illness but of having or living with a disability. We cannot be both well and ill at the same time, but we can be both perfectly well and yet disabled, as are the competitive field and track contestants in the Para-Olympics, or the former Miss America Heather Whitestone, or John Hockenberry, the paraplegic reporter who covered the Gulf War for National Public Radio. Ron Amundson insists forcefully on preserving this distinction between illness and disability.[137] I expand on his arguments here.

First, persons with paradigmatic disabilities—paraplegia, blindness, deafness, and others—neither require nor are improved by medical treatment, differentiating them from people suffering from illnesses. When we are ill, we take medication to relieve pain, discomfort, weakness, loss of appetite, but there are no medications for disability. This observation furnishes further reason to think that the remedy for the "disability problem" lies in social reform, not in biochemical intervention.

Second, the distinction can be sharpened by noticing what shifts when illness (or accident) eventuates in disability. Although illness is traceable to specific physiological sites, its effects are diffused and so are manifested not just in the pathology of the site but in such sequelae as pain, discom-

136. Miller, Frank G., "Letter," *The Hastings Center Report* 27, no. 5 (September/October 1997): 5.

137. Amundson, *Disability, Handicap*.

fort, weakness, lassitude, absence of appetite, and disorientation. Illness interferes with performances not associated with or originating at the diseased or injured site(s), and this global debilitation invites the individual who is ill to assume the sick role.

Disabilities, on the other hand, rarely involve any such diffused manifestations; rather, disabilities (or more precisely the impairments that occasion them) are associated with delimited corporeal sites and identified in terms of the performances characteristic of those bodily areas. Thus, for example, we associate blindness with the mechanisms of the eyes or brain. We describe someone who is blind as being visually disabled, meaning he is unable to engage in performances that necessitate vision (although he may successfully execute functions such as reading that are typically performed by seeing, by adopting alternative performance modes). Or we call the group of people who cannot manipulate text (because they cannot see it, cannot interpret it, or cannot hold the pages or papers on which it is inscribed) "print disabled." In contrast to the specificity of functional limitation that characterizes disability, an individual who is ill usually is more globally incapacitated.

None of this is to deny that illness can be the preceding or chronic cause of disability (although traumatic accident is equally a cause of disability). As Susan Wendell points out, people often are disabled as the result of chronic illnesses such as diabetes that cause a variety of impairments such as loss of limbs and blindness.[138] And the hostility of the environments people with disabilities must endure sometimes causes them to become ill. For instance, an environmental defect such as the absence of wheelchair accessible bathrooms increases bladder and kidney disease in paraplegics, who are barred from the physiological benefit of relieving themselves, a need that typical building designs accommodate for the general public but not for them. It is informative to investigate how diseases contribute to disabilities, and there is reason to think that being disabled in a hostile environment increases one's exposure to becoming diseased. All of this suggests that disability may be linked empirically to illness but should not be identified with it.

For, as Amundson points out, the "sick" role is a kind of social stepping

---

138. Susan Wendell, *The Rejected Body: Feminist Philosophical Reflections on Disability* (London: Routledge, 1996), 20.

or stopping out that is inappropriate for someone with no illness but only a disability: "[T]he 'sick role' . . . relieves a person of normal responsibilities, but carries other obligations with it. The sick person is expected to . . . regard his or her condition as undesirable."[139] Amundson is not the only writer who recognizes the social disadvantage that being identified as sick or associated with illness imposes on those who are not ill, who need no recovery period, and who are harmed rather than benefited by disruption of or distancing from everyday responsibility.

Brock, among many others, warns that increased knowledge of genetics will identify more people who are at risk for future illness. As we come to understand genetic structures accurately enough to identify the potentially anomalous modes and levels of functioning consequent on an individual's genetic inheritance, more of us will find ourselves devalued by our own futures. Although performing splendidly at the time, we will be marginalized because we are at greater genetic risk than other people of certain kinds of deteriorating function. So, for instance, those at increased risk of Alzheimer's disease would be rejected as mates by whoever fears future service as a spousal caretaker, while employers desiring to keep medical insurance costs down would not hire individuals genetically disposed to develop various kinds of cancer. Merely being connected to prospective illness will damage their well-being and self-esteem by eroding their image of themselves as, in Brock's words, "well-functioning individuals," and so they "will have serious adverse effects both on their conceptions of themselves and the quality of their lives."[140]

Wendell fears that "some of the initial opposition in disability rights groups to including people with illnesses in the category of people with disabilities may have come from an understandable desire to avoid the additional stigma of illness."[141] To meet Wendell's concern, the distinction between disability and illness, as I limn it, acknowledges that disability often is a sequela of illness and also that illness, especially chronic illness, can itself be disabling. Thus, being ill is not a defeating condition of being disabled. So there is no justification for excluding people from being identified as disabled because they are ill. Nevertheless, being ill, even chroni-

---

139. Amundson, *Disability, Handicap*, 114, 118.

140. Dan Brock, "The Human Genome Project and Human Identity," in *Genes and Human Self-Knowledge*, 24.

141. Wendell, *Rejected Body*, 21.

cally ill, is neither a necessary condition nor decisive evidence that an individual has a disability.

Disability as Difference

In "The Politics of Disability," Joseph Stubbins suggests that the substance of disablement is to be found in the outcomes of processes rather than in the persons who are subjected to the processes: "The essence of disability is the social and economic consequences of being different from the majority."[142] What are the mechanisms that characterize such disabling processes? Disability discrimination cases such as *Cook v. State of Rhode Island*[143] and *Pushkin v. Regents of the University of Colorado*,[144] both of which address actions that predate the ADA, exemplify how disadvantageous social and economic outcomes are visited upon individuals simply in virtue of their physical deviation from the majority of people.

In 1988 Cook applied to fill a vacant state position as an institutional attendant, a job in which she had eight years of previous experience with a spotless work record. Both parties agreed that she had passed the routine preemployment physical but was denied the job because she was morbidly obese. Cook sued under the Rehabilitation Act, with which the employer (Rhode Island's Department of Mental Health, Retardation, and Hospitals [MHRH]) was required to comply. Cook claimed, and a jury agreed, that she had been subjected to disability discrimination.

The employer (MHRH) appealed, claiming that morbid obesity is not a disability and so Cook could not seek redress under the Rehabilitation Act. Because Cook did not have a disability, MHRH argued, she could not be the victim of disability discrimination. In confirming the lower court, the appellate level decision noted, "In a society that all too often confuses 'slim' with 'beautiful' or 'good', morbid obesity can present formidable barriers to employment. When, as here, the barriers transgress federal law, those who erect and seek to preserve them must suffer the consequences."[145]

---

142. Joseph Stubbins, "The Politics of Disability" in *Attitudes toward Persons with Disabilities*, ed. Harold Yuker (New York: Springer, 1988), 24.

143. 10 F.3d 17 (1st Cir. 1993).

144. 658 F.2d 1372 (10th Cir. 1981).

145. Ruth Colker, *The Law of Disability Discrimination: Cases and Materials* (Cincinnati, Ohio: Anderson, 1995), 48.

We should not overlook the court's clear message—namely, that disablement is not produced by the plaintiff's condition but rather by the character of the conduct to which the plaintiff was subjected. But what, precisely, constitutes the transgression referenced here? How did MHRH create barriers that made employment inaccessible in virtue of disability if neither Cook's person nor her performance was impaired?

To understand how MHRH's repudiation of Cook transgressed federal law, it is useful to review how "disability" or "handicap" has been understood in antidiscrimination law since the early 1970s. Originally,[146] the Rehabilitation Act defined the "handicapped" people it benefited as "Any individual who (A) has a physical or mental disability which for such individual constitutes or results in a substantial handicap to employment and (B) can reasonably be expected to benefit in terms of employability from vocational rehabilitation services." In 1974 the act was amended to define a person with a disability as someone who satisfies the following disjunctive test: (1) has a physical or mental impairment, (2) has a record of such a physical or mental impairment, or (3) is regarded as having such a physical or mental impairment.[147]

To better grasp the purpose of the definition, we should note that in *School Board of Nassau County v. Arline*,[148] Justice Brennan, writing for the majority, cites both congressional intent and the Department of Education's regulations to the effect that cosmetic disfigurement is a disability because the fears and prejudices of other people irrationally limit disfigured individuals' opportunities for social participation. In *Arline* Justice Brennan wrote:

> Congress was as concerned about the effect of an impairment on others as it was about its effect on the individual . . . The Senate Report provides as an example of a person who would be covered . . . "a person with some kind of visible physical impairment, which in fact does not substantially limit that person's functioning."[149] Such an impairment might not diminish a person's physical or mental capabilities, but could nevertheless substantially limit that person's ability to work as a result of the negative reactions of others to the impairment.[150]

---

146. Public Law No. 93–112, 7(6), 87 Stat. 355, 362 (1973).
147. Rehabilitation Act Amendments of 1974, PL 93–516, 88 Stat. 1617. See also Colker, *The Law of Disability Discrimination*, 30, 67.
148. 480 U.S. 273 (1987).
149. Senate Report n. 93—1297: 64.
150. Colker, *The Law of Disability Discrimination*, 27.

In 1990, the ADA reiterated the amended Rehabilitation Act's test (substituting "disability" for "handicap") for identifying who is protected against the hostility of built or arranged environments that exclude them from opportunities they are otherwise competent to pursue. Although Cook could not sue under the ADA (which became law two years after she was refused employment), interpretive guidance from the regulations implementing the ADA was applied at the appellate level to establish that "the Rehabilitation Act seeks not only to aid the disabled," but also 'to eliminate discrimination on the basis of handicap.' "[151] The appellate court pointed out that because the employer theorized Cook's physical state as foreclosing "a broad range of options in the health care industry" (despite her demonstrated ability to execute the essential tasks of such jobs), "detached jurors reasonably could have found that this pessimistic assessment of plaintiff's capabilities demonstrated that appellant regarded" Cook as satisfying one or another prong of the disjunctive definition of disability.[152] In other words, that Cook deserved protection against disability discrimination is demonstrated simply by the fact that MHRH rejected her on the basis of a theory that falsely equated her physical condition with incompetence.

More than a decade earlier, another appellate ruling had established that falsely theorizing incompetence on the basis of an individual's physical or mental condition is the substance of disability discrimination. In *Pushkin v. Regents of the University of Colorado*,[153] the appellate court affirmed the district court's finding that Pushkin had been denied admission to a psychiatric residency solely because he was confined to a wheelchair by multiple sclerosis. The prevailing psychiatric theory of the time considered mental disorders to be the result of emotions displaced by various psychological defensive mechanisms. That severe disability causes feelings that characteristically are suppressed and displaced was a theoretical assumption from which it seemed to follow that anyone who used a wheelchair was thereby likely to be emotionally damaged and consequently unqualified to be a psychiatrist. Guided by prevailing theory, and influenced as well by mistaken beliefs about the impact of multiple sclerosis, the senior psychiatrists who interviewed Pushkin all found him unqualified.

---

151. 45 C.F.R. 84.1
152. Colker, *The Law of Disability Discrimination*, 47.
153. 658 F.2d 1372 (10th Cir. 1981).

As quoted in the appellate decision, the opinions of the senior psychiatrists had so little to do with documentable objective fact as to be laughable. One claimed that Pushkin was unqualified to be admitted to the residency because the work would make him unhappy. Another psychiatrist gave primacy to his personal subjectivity, feeling that he himself could "never meet Dr. Pushkin head on" and that "there was some organicity here that impaired Dr. Pushkin being able to engage with him." Exhibiting considerable ignorance of medical fact, the same physician insisted that "there is some delirium" when a person has MS. The third psychiatrist also privileged his own subjectivity, rejecting Pushkin because his condition "elicits strong feelings in people" and because "I had a sense he is very angry underneath."[154]

The bias with which those who judged Pushkin thought about him is flagrant here. The senior psychiatrists displaced their own discomfort about disability onto Pushkin. Then they objectified their personal reactions by disguising them as conclusions warranted by psychoanalytic theory. Of course, psychoanalytic theory is famously circular about whether emotional problems cause, or are caused by, physical ones. The appellate court called special attention to the flawed reasoning the admissions committee displayed in using speculative theory about disability to predict what Pushkin was capable of, and in permitting speculative claims about the class of people with disabilities to trump the facts about Pushkin's competence. The appellate court concluded that the interviewers' rejection of Pushkin rested on "psychologic theory" that was "weak and inadequate." Apart from their biased theorizing, Pushkin's evaluators appeared to have no defense for describing him as flawed. Furthermore, they permitted their theory to supplant the facts. For, contra their theoretical conclusion, the appellate record documents that Pushkin's two former supervisors, one a psychiatrist at the Menninger Foundation and the other a senior psychiatrist at the University of Colorado, found him to have normal emotional responses and good relationships with patients. The appellate record demonstrates that the reasons the interviewers found Pushkin to be unqualified because of his handicap were based on "incorrect assumptions" or "inadequate factual grounds" regarding his physical condition.[155]

---

154. Colker, *The Law of Disability Discrimination*, 76–77.
155. Colker, *The Law of Disability Discrimination*, 79.

The physical capabilities of Pushkin and Cook were different. Pushkin was physically limited in his ability to perform the usual activities of daily life. Despite her weight, Cook was not. How, then, could both be disabled, let alone similarly so? Their commonality lies in their being subjected to false and biased theories simply because their bodies were anomalous. On the basis of these theories, they were denied access to roles for which their talents suited them. Extrapolating from their cases, we can see that the class protected by U.S. disability discrimination law is not to be sheltered because it is weak and vulnerable. Rather, it is to be shielded from the disadvantageous consequences of false theorizing about how being different from the majority means being incompetent to execute the usual social roles.[156]

Parenthetically, this review of case law indicates why Norman Daniels's seemingly generous interpretation of the ADA's reasonable accommodation requirement is dangerously misleading. Daniels declares that "in some cases, employers may be obliged to ignore modest decrements in relevant talents and skills, decrements that would have been grounds for replacing a nondisabled worker."[157] But there is neither Equal Employment Opportunity Commission regulation implementing the ADA, nor case law to sustain Daniels's account.[158] (Case law does suggest that employers may be required to alter their method of assessing productivity. For instance, if the total output of a team of production line workers with

---

156. A 1997 New York State Court of Appeals decision iterates this thesis, though with a different outcome. Here, the court decided that individuals denied employment because they were two to ten pounds over the company's weight limit had not been regarded as disabled and so had not been subjected to disability discrimination. "[W]eight, in and of itself, does not constitute a disability," the ruling said. Unlike "gross obesity," the plaintiffs' physical condition did not invite rejection for employment because of prevailing misconceptions about the (in)competency of individuals in such condition. (Somini Sengupta, "Airline Wins a Bias Suit about Weight of Personnel," *New York Times*, 18 December 1997, A22.)

157. Daniels, "Mental Disabilities," 281.

158. I speculate that Daniels also may not have noticed that the ADA understands disability very differently from earlier legislation that addresses disability in the workplace. Workers' compensation regulations, for instance, mandate that a worker's impairment be assessed in relation to her preinjury mode and level of functioning at her existing job. In this context, employers sometimes prefer to discharge their obligation to injured employees who cannot regain preinjury levels of productivity by continuing their employment rather than paying out disability or retirement benefits.

disabilities is as great as the total output of an identical number of individual workers, individual team members may not be penalized for low personal productivity even if, separately, each is significantly less efficient than the average nondisabled worker. In such a case, working as a team to achieve the requisite productivity is understood to be a reasonable accommodation to the disabled individuals' disabilities.) Misinterpretations such as Daniels's mistakenly elide disability with deficits in talents and skills and so fuel the misconception that increasing the social participation of people with disabilities must threaten standards and inflate costs. Of course, because Daniels's conceptualization of disability is embedded in his theory of health care resource allocation and his understanding of reasonable accommodation based on an analogy with medical treatment, he cannot help but see disablement as a state of individual deprivation crying out for repair.[159]

(Why) Is Disability Bad?

A key difference in how the social and medical models of disability have developed in the context of U.S. law lies in how each model responds to the misalignment between individuals and social practice. As we have seen, the medical model proposes to solve the problem by realigning (eligible) individuals, while on the social model it is society that should be reshaped. Which approach is more profound?

Disability discrimination case law suggests that those social mechanisms whereby limitation is imposed on people because of their physical, sensory, and cognitive impairments contain biased theoretical components that distort the impact of impairment. Such discriminatory theorizing takes impairment to be inescapably negative, so that whoever is impaired must thereby be in deficit, incompetent, and suffering and needy. Thus, the solution seems to lie in reshaping social practice to eliminate flawed theorizing by disconnecting disability from misleading presumptions and mistaken explanations of its badness. In the sections that follow, we first will consider whether to be disabled is definitively or intrinsically bad; next, whether to be disabled is inherently bad in virtue of being a state of suffering, neediness, or dependence; and, finally, whether to be disabled is in-

---

159. Daniels, "Mental Disabilities," 286.

strumentally bad. If none of these commonplace equations appears defensible, there will be a strong case for reform of social theory and practice along the lines recommended by the social model of disability.

Stipulating Badness

Why do we think disability must be bad? One reason is its presumed etiology, namely, that it is assumed to be a condition resulting from individuals' physical, sensory, or cognitive deficiencies (i.e., their impairments). By definition, an impairment may be an absence, deletion, omission, reduction, or diminution. Also by definition, an impairment may be a weakness, insufficiency, inadequacy, or loss. The difference between these two meanings of impairment is not as widely acknowledged as it should be.

Nothing definitive about value is predetermined by characterizing a condition as a reduction or absence. But to characterize a condition as a weakness or loss prematurely closes by definition what should be an open question about value. It might be thought that we can resolve this problem, and other biases that infect our discourse, by substituting neutral terms such as *difference* for weighted terms such as *impairment*. This is not so, for the problem does not lie in how we name various conditions but instead is much more deeply embedded within discursive practice.

Our discourse is shaped by a dialectical convention that precludes talking about impairment as if it is acceptable or even unexceptional. As we saw earlier in the section on "The Cost of Impairment," it is the practice in genetic counseling to treat the increased probability of the birth of a child with an impairment as an adverse future event—that is, to call it a risk. This stipulation places prospective parents on the defensive if they do not display reservations about having such a child.[160] They must justify continuing a pregnancy that may result in a child with an impairment, but are not equally required by the discourse to defend a pregnancy with no such prognosis. Consequently, even the prospect of impairment entering their lives places extra discursive demands on them.

The stipulation by genetic counselors that deafness is to be counted as a risk and therefore as bad is by no means unique. The discourse of the wider culture lays a special burden of proving the value of their presence

---

160. Davis, *Genetic Dilemmas*, 7.

and participation on people with disabilities. This feature of the general discourse influences how philosophy treats disability. That having a physical, sensory, or cognitive impairment disrupts assumptions about the value and power of being human has made the trope of disability especially attractive to philosophers searching for limiting cases to delineate conceptual boundaries. So, for example, asking whether profoundly impaired neonates should live tests how much we value life itself, as distinct from what individuals accomplish in life. And questioning why we favor severely intellectually compromised people over clever animals suggests where we locate the value of being human.

Another illustration of how philosophy turns to disability as the locus of limitation is found in the exchange of letters between philosophers Bryan Magee and Martin Milligan, published under the title *On Blindness*. Magee initiated the conversation to explore how much someone like Milligan, blind nearly from birth and with no memory of seeing, can understand the meaning of visual language and what is conveyed by visual experience. Milligan describes himself as an empiricist who does not count being able to see as essential to empirical knowledge, although he readily acknowledges it to be very useful indeed.

Throughout the correspondence, Magee insists that blindness is a significant epistemic deficit, despite Milligan's arguments that he fully understands most of what is involved in, or the product of, visual judgment. Milligan's thoughtful response to Magee's intransigence is worth quoting at length:

> You seem to have found my claims that born-blind people can understand, at the very least, a major part of the meaning of visual terms, and that many sighted people grossly exaggerate the importance of sight, somewhat exasperating in their presumption.[161] . . . [B]ecause the sense of which they make overwhelmingly the greatest use is sight, these sighted people just cannot imagine how blind people can manage without it.[162] . . . [W]hereas most sighted people will have known few if any blind people, and (if any) will often not have known them very well, born-blind people will usually have known a lot of other blind people, including blind people who have had sight, and also a lot of sighted people, and will have known some of both groups very

---

161. Bryan Magee and Martin Milligan, *On Blindness* (Oxford: Oxford University Press, 1995), 42.
162. Magee and Milligan, *On Blindness*, 43.

well . . . [B]lind people are apt to know a good deal more about sight and sighted people than the latter can know about blindness and blind people.[163]

Nevertheless, Magee remains unconvinced about the gap between what blind and sighted people can do. He insists that whoever considers blindness a difference rather than a handicap is "refusing to face the reality of his situation."[164] But, it turns out, Magee makes this assessment to support a philosophical conclusion—namely, that "many if not most human beings do exactly the same thing, systematically but in another way, in that we construct a total conception of our situation out of the input we consequently have and then proceed as if what this leaves out cannot really make all that much difference."[165] In other words, Magee relies on his mainly sighted readers' prejudice that, regardless of the force of testimony and the strength of arguments to the contrary, blind people must be missing some very crucial knowledge to propel the debatable proposition that all people "register only a fraction of what there is and . . . are unable even to conceptualize most of the rest."[166]

What is most telling about this discussion is its rhetorical structure. Despite the elegant argument Milligan offers (quoted earlier) as to the comparative expertise of blind and sighted people, both Magee and Milligan appear to assume that Milligan must bear the burden of convincing others that blind people do not suffer significant epistemic deficits rather than Magee's having to prove that they do so. Thus Magee uses the trope of blindness to suggest that if such an intelligent and well-educated philosopher as Milligan can be so badly deluded about his epistemic competence, so can we all be in denial about the limitations of our knowledge.

There is a grave inequity in the heaviness of the burden of proof imposed on those who approach being disabled nonjudgmentally compared with the light burden of proof placed on those who think that being deaf or blind or crippled is intrinsically bad. We have already noted how the latter must defend themselves. The conversation between Magee and Milligan illustrates our practice of expecting the notions of the sighted about blindness and sightedness to trump the testimony of the blind about both blindness and sightedness even though, as Milligan argues, people

---

163. Magee and Milligan, *On Blindness*, 49.
164. Magee and Milligan, *On Blindness*, 99.
165. Magee and Milligan, *On Blindness*, 99.
166. Magee and Milligan, *On Blindness*, 100.

who are blind have a more comprehensive and inclusive standpoint on much of what is at issue than people who are sighted.

But ask for some convincing reason to think that not hearing, seeing, or walking is intrinsically bad, and a relatively weak response will be forthcoming. We usually suppose that, because listening, seeing, walking, intelligence, and other such performances are central to our daily lives, the sheer exercise of the faculties that support them must gratify us. Based on this assumption, a case is often made that sight, hearing, mobility, and complex cognition are good in themselves, and, consequently, their loss constitutes a deprivation of intrinsically valuable experiences.

Intrinsic Badness

Things have intrinsic value when we esteem them for themselves or, more precisely, for the character of direct experiences of them. It might seem to follow, then, that the absence of intrinsically valuable experiences must be deleterious, injurious, or disadvantageous. But this inference is incorrect. Indeed, missing one kind of experience can enhance the quality of the remaining kinds.

Deafness does not enhance sight, nor blindness hearing, any more than paraplegia builds up the shoulders and arms. What deafness does do, however, is invite increased attentiveness to looking, as blindness does to listening, and as pushing a wheelchair or swinging on crutches does to the use of one's arms. So, Milligan observes, "because sight is in modern conditions so much more efficient than the other senses, sighted people have got into the habit of disregarding a lot of the information the other senses provide, or can provide."[167] Looking or listening, or manually manipulating, with greater skill increases the intrinsic worth of these experiences. Consequently, blindness, deafness, paraplegia, or other impairments of major faculties are not necessarily the occasion of a net loss in experiences of intrinsic worth, although each may rule out or limit a particular mode of intrinsically worthy experience.

The phenomenon the eighteenth-century philosopher David Hume made much of—namely, that the intrinsic value of experiences of art increases as perceivers acquire the skill of intense viewing—indicates the strategic importance of adept focusing. The proficient art viewer is the individ-

---

167. Magee and Milligan, *On Blindness*, 44–45.

ual knowledgeable enough to resist distraction. The gratified art viewer is the person who experiences the relevant aesthetically valuable features and is completely unaware of other characteristics the artwork displays. Thus, the qualified art viewer attends to the painting's colors and shapes but is completely oblivious whether the frame is pine or oak or walnut. Attending to the frame instead of being blind to it undoubtedly would increase the diversity of the viewer's perceptions but equally undoubtedly would intrude upon the viewer's aesthetic experience.

Moreover, consider those paradigms of intrinsically valuable objects, works of art themselves. While it could be a great advantage to own the *Mona Lisa* or *Starry Night* or the *Guernica*, it cannot be a disadvantage not to possess them, for to insist that every person but the possessor of such unique objects is disadvantaged is to exaggerate the deficiency of their condition. Of course, if I once owned the painting or visited its museum location regularly, its absence would be a loss, though not necessarily a disadvantage. In the same vein, someone who once enjoyed exercising a major faculty now lacking has suffered a loss. But neither the person who, impaired from childhood, has never exercised that faculty nor the person who never enjoyed exercising that faculty need experience a similar loss if deprived of the faculty. Nor need the absence of the faculty be experienced as a disadvantage except to an individual who once relied on exercising it to his advantage and has not acquired the skill of furthering his advantage otherwise.

The most familiar argument that goes to construing impairment as being necessarily bad is about the hardship of not being able to enjoy music or sunsets or skiing. For those who enjoy music, deafness seems an intolerable deprivation. For those who enjoy skiing, paraplegia seems the same. But many people who could enjoy these pleasures pass them up. Yet, unlike people who cannot hear or see or walk, people who can enjoy the pleasures of engaging in these performances are not expected to defend the quality of their lives when they choose not to pursue these pleasures. In view of this, it is odd to deem their absence disadvantageous to those who cannot enjoy them but indifferent to those who can but do not enjoy them. Only if, and to the degree, that others bereft of the pleasures of paintings or concerts or skiing are pitied should people with visual or hearing or mobility impairments be pitied for missing these pleasures.

Therefore, if disadvantage is tightly tied to impairment, its source does not seem to lie in the loss of something of intrinsic value. This is not to deny that seeing well, hearing well, and moving well possess intrinsic value and are crucial components of more complex activities having intrinsic value. Rather, it is to notice that, although the experience of engaging in these activities can be (but is not always) intrinsically good, not engaging in them is not intrinsically bad.

Nor does this analysis suggest that impairments are not, or should not be, experienced as a loss by those who become disabled, especially later in life. That becoming impaired is experienced as a loss is to be expected, for seeing, hearing, walking, and complex thinking are central and common-place in how most people carry out their lives. Consequently, the elimination of such performances is likely to disrupt the core of how one lives one's life and to inspire grieving, just as losing any other crucial life plan component, a child or spouse, an opportunity or a possession, would do. But what contributes badness here is neither objective impairment nor any disability it occasions but rather the subjective enduring of disruption and loss. And, of course, it is these feelings that a social environment hostile to impairment exacerbates.

Disability and Suffering

The social model does not deny that to have a disability is to be at heightened risk of suffering. But it gives first consideration in attributing this liability to the hostile environment that rebuffs the disabled individual when she tries to live under the conditions it imposes. Whether suffering is thought to originate within or, instead, beyond the suffering person makes an important difference in the significance assigned to it.

Feminist bioethicist Laura Purdy represents thinkers who urge us not to bring into the world children who will suffer in virtue of being disabled. This is not, she insists, a policy driven by bias against people with disabilities but rather one informed by concern for such children who, she thinks, are naturally vulnerable to pain and limitation. Their liability in this regard is, she explains, "caused not by . . . consciousness of having failed to live up to some artificial social value but by . . . intrinsic pain or limitation."[168]

As we have seen, however, there is no reason to think that suffering pain, or any other characteristic of illness, is an inherent feature of impair-

---

168. Laura Purdy, *Reproducing Persons: Issues in Feminist Bioethics* (Ithaca, N.Y.: Cornell University Press, 1996), 56–57.

ment. Furthermore, while any impairment may preclude some activities, limitations need not have a deleterious impact on well-being. Not every limitation is a loss. It is tendentious to claim that of two individuals, one whose physical condition makes it difficult to ski but who has never wanted to ski, while the other is physically able to ski but equally does not want to ski, the latter must be better off than the former because the former cannot do what she does not want to do, while the latter simply does not do what she does not want to.

Nor are activities necessarily of greater value if realized from choice rather than performed out of necessity. Surely, the activity of killing other human beings is not made better by being executed freely rather than out of some external or internal compulsion. Furthermore, having no limitations and, consequently, too many opportunities can itself initiate suffering. Uncertainty about which road to take, and regret about roads not taken, are familiar life spoilers. How much better to be focused successfully on a few fulfilling options than to be torn with indecision by many glittering ones. Because one has only one life to plan, the ultimate difference between having begun with a single or several equally satisfying life plan opportunities may be negligible. What is at least as important to well-being as having many options is whether parents can educate their children to be capable of overcoming disadvantageous circumstance where the range and kind of options available are not ideally desirable.

Purdy joins such writers as Norman Daniels, Allen Buchanan, Dan Brock, and Dena Davis in portraying disabilities as thwarting life plans that otherwise might be selected (or else might not be). All view any such source of limitation as being intrinsically bad. In this regard, Purdy writes:

> And it is not only major disability that can cause misery: I have both observed and felt it in connections that might well be dismissed as minor by those who are not experiencing them. In my own case, for example, my inability to see adequately at a crucial period in my development as a dancer was in part responsible for the failure to progress enough to make a career worthwhile. Yet that was a goal toward which I had worked since I was a small child and for which both I and my parents had made major sacrifices.[169]

Here, I think, Purdy wrongly attributes intrinsic badness to what is merely a contingent source of badness. I do not challenge the badness of her

---

169. Purdy, *Reproducing Persons*, 60.

experience, yet surely she would have suffered equally badly had her desired development been thwarted by absence of sufficient talent, lack of money, an unfashionable body type, racial prejudice, or the infamous politics of the dance world. Any one of these conditions could have put Purdy at equal risk of the suffering to which her anomalous vision exposed her.

Which of these sources of possible suffering is it so pressing to nullify as to recommend as the means of doing so the prevention of the lives of possible sufferers? Surely, it is excessive to oppose bringing individuals into the world just because they will be physically awkward or socially unastute, poor, well endowed, or individuals of color, all of whom risk having more limited opportunities in the dance world than Purdy. It is the unfairness of suffering, rather than the simple consequence of suffering, that calls for moral intervention.

We should recognize that the extent to which limitation causes suffering depends on each person's tastes. Purdy seems to think that because "neither immense human caring nor the most sophisticated gadgetry will restore freedom of movement to the paraplegic, for example, even were every conceivable aid available . . . the disease or disability itself would remain and be itself the cause of limit or pain."[170] But just as Purdy's bad experience of her limitations as a dancer must be respected, so must the feeling of many thousands of mobility-limited individuals who do not experience their inability to dance as a source of limitation or pain. (Most of us mobility-limited individuals never think about professional dancing. However, those who wish to dance, supposing they are talented, can pursue opportunities with the increasingly well-known dance companies that mix wheeling and walking dancers.)

Finally and importantly, to "open" a child's future is not just to offer more life plan options. The future is likely to close down quickly for a child whose upbringing does not instill the fundamentals of worthy character and principled conduct. At least as important as giving one's child many options is to teach him, by example and direct experience as well as principle, to make good choices in a world where not everything is possible. To do so is surely to facilitate rather than to compromise the child's future personal well-being. Nor need a reduction in options reduce a child's prospect of flourishing in principle. If it did, all parents proposing

---

170. Purdy, *Reproducing Persons*, 60.

to have children in disadvantageous circumstances should in principle be discouraged lest they diminish their child's future flourishing.

   What we have seen so far is that the suffering we would avoid by preventing children with disabilities from coming into the world is not the consequence of being impaired but rather reflects the anguish of those who cannot bear to bear culturally repudiated offspring. Here, the social model of disability usefully reminds us that it is not the individual but the environment that is defective. The more a society oppresses certain classes of people, the more pressing may be our moral obligation to defend the procreation of the class's members against its enemies. We magnify oppression if we permit flawed social arrangements to cause us to be overcome with despair and to depreciate the lives of people just because they suffer from being oppressed. Consequently, in contrast to the medical model of disability, the social model directs us to address the suffering of people with disabilities by eliminating or reforming the external circumstances that contribute to it rather than by eliminating or revising the people themselves.

   So far we have reviewed some reasons to prefer the social model of disability to the medical model. First we considered how the medical model is flawed. We saw that by its very nature, the medical model must distinguish between normal and deviant individuals so as to locate those who are candidates for repair. However, the way this line typically is drawn does not capture the difference between being functional and dysfunctional. Moreover, what does seem to be reflected in the medical model's conceptualization of being normal is the virtually arbitrary designation of the dominant class's mode and level of functioning as the standard.

   Second, we saw that, in contrast to the medical model, the social model of disability accords with how many people with disabilities experience their own situation. Recognizing how hostile environments, not personal deficits, disable people whose physical, sensory, or cognitive states are different from those of the dominant class is central to having a disability perspective. Disability studies scholar Liz Crow describes the moment that she realized the explanatory power of the social model: "[T]he social model of disability . . . gave me an understanding of my life . . . what I had always known, deep down, was confirmed. . . . It wasn't my body that was responsible for all my difficulties, it was external factors, the barriers constructed by the society in which I live."[171]

---

171. Liz Crow, "Including All Our Lives: Renewing the Social Model of Dis-

Third, we saw the important difference between the medical and social models as being the dissimilarity of how they characterize and approach relieving the suffering experienced by people on account of their disabilities. Integral to the medical model is the assumption that to be impaired is to suffer. The medical model thus decrees that such individuals need to be fixed—that is, returned to normal.

Consequently, policy influenced by the medical model directs resources to developing and purchasing restorative and rehabilitative treatments. Doing so exacerbates the depreciation of those who cannot be restored, labeling them as failures, and authorizing their being at greater psychosocial risk than would be permitted for so-called normal people. Because it exaggerates rather than eliminates the probability that being impaired exposes people to isolation, loss of purpose, depreciation, and powerlessness, conceptual frameworks that assume the medical model do not offer an avenue for equalizing people with disabilities.

The social model, in contrast, urges the rectification of disabled people's suffering by diminishing the hostility they experience in the environment. This analysis echoes the liberatory accounts that have furthered our understanding of what social justice means for other marginalized groups, especially women and people of color. But before we explore what the social model suggests about equalizing people with disabilities, we need to be sure we do not import elements of the medical model that would adulterate the discussion.

Neediness

Doubts may remain about whether the social model is realistic about how bad it is to have a disability. Milligan writes:

> [B]lindness is a "difference" . . . disadvantaging in . . . a wide range of frequently encountered circumstances. . . . Although many of the handicapping effects of blindness arise from the fact that blind people live in a world overwhelmingly populated by sighted people, and shaped by them for their own convenience, I would say that blindness would still be a serious handicap even if we blind people constituted the overwhelming majority of the world's population, and could arrange things to suit ourselves, and could subject the remaining sighted people to our will.[172]

---

ability," in *Exploring the Divide: Illness and Disability*, ed. Colin Barnes and Geoff Mercer (Leeds: Disability Press, 1996), 55.

172. Magee and Milligan, *On Blindness*, 38.

We have seen that impairment does not entail suffering. Nevertheless, it might be argued, impairment is widely disadvantaging, and to be at a disadvantage is to be especially vulnerable to suffering.

In this vein, Purdy cites with approval the views of disability activists Adrienne Asch and Marsha Saxton to the effect that, while not *necessarily* miserable, people with disabilities are *contingently* miserable because the distributive system fails to offer them entitlement to sufficient resources. Thus, to be disabled is to be needy, an intrinsically bad albeit defeasible condition. Purdy comments:

> One of the clearest and most powerful messages to come from both Asch and Saxton is that much suffering of disabled persons arises not from their disabilities but [because] . . . the United States is . . . an uncaring society that . . . tolerates a great deal of preventable misery on the part of those who must depend more than others on community resources.[173]

But to embrace this account is virtually to decree that people with disabilities experience deprivation and therefore must suffer.

For the account presumes that persons with disabilities are entitled to medical care, medical equipment, home health care, housekeeper support, and income support sufficient to raise them to the basic capability level enjoyed by nondisabled people. Once the assumption is accepted, of course, it follows that any disabled individual who does not enjoy basic capabilities thereby must be in a state of unrelieved neediness. The claim, notice, is neither that people with disabilities now unfairly receive less than others, nor that it is fair to offer them more than others receive, but rather the stronger claim that they suffer unless they receive more public resources than others do. Although this last claim falls short of equating being disabled with suffering, it does conceptualize disability as a definitively needy state of being, one that calls for extraordinary community effort to deflect suffering. However, there is reason to refrain from connecting disability with neediness this way, for the practical consequence of doing so is to amplify rather than relieve suffering.

We should notice, first, that many people with disabilities now assume the ordinary responsibilities of citizens, meet normal performance standards, and flourish, with no more or very little more than the ordinary resources, supposing only that they are offered equitable access to the

---

173. Purdy, *Reproducing Persons*, 55.

community benefits all other citizens enjoy. Furthermore, because social arrangements do not now support people who have physical, sensory, or cognitive impairments as generously as those who do not, it is no better than speculative to think they would still need to make special call on community resources if they enjoyed equitable access to ordinary community benefits. We cannot know for how many the pervasive exclusion in their lives has so reduced their opportunities as to render them artificially dependent when they need not be so, or at least has made them much more dependent than they need be. Clearly, working and living conditions first must be revised to provide equal access before the real dependence or neediness of people with disabilities can fairly be assessed. Pending evidence obtained under less biased conditions than presently obtain, we should avoid assuming that unusual suffering, let alone definitive neediness, characterizes the disabled other than as the price exacted from them by exclusionary practices.

Second, the virtue of such caution is urged by Elizabeth Spelman in *Fruits of Sorrow: Framing Our Attention to Suffering*: "Claims of . . . human suffering can do as much to reinforce claims of superiority and inferiority as they can to undermine them."[174] Spelman's warning recommends our being circumspect in advocating for extraordinary distributions for people with disabilities. Broadly, community resources are allocated unusually generously either to compensate or to privilege the recipients. Furthermore, compensation is bestowed either to repair previous societal wrongs or else to elevate individuals from an inferior condition of neither their own nor of society's making. Those to whom reparation is due are in no way more dependent on community resources than those who bear the liability; they simply are owed more by the community than individuals to whom there is no debt.

Purdy, however, analyzes the preventable misery of people with disabilities as occasioned by their extraordinary neediness in that, as she says, they "depend more than others on community resources." So her account distinguishes the disabled as being in an inferior condition because their claim to more than usual community support is based, as she sees it, on their being more than usually dependent on it. This portrayal designates them as a weak group who, like children, require special protection.

---

174. Elizabeth Spelman, *Fruits of Sorrow: Framing Our Attention to Suffering* (Boston: Beacon, 1997), 9.

Robert Veatch theorizes in a similar vein. He thinks that "the ethical conclusion to which the egalitarian assumptions drive us" would be that "the mentally and physically handicapped . . . have a first claim of justice on society for the use of common resources to compensate for their handicaps . . . to provide actual services that could restore as much as possible the abilities of which the losers in the natural lottery have been deprived."[175]

But, third, against their position there is the practical consideration that to direct extraordinary resources to people on account of their being extraordinarily needy invites more suffering because it induces more need. As we saw earlier, the disability system is designed on the premise that disability causes immoderate need. It addresses this demand by putting people with disabilities in competition with each other for resources, so some will have to suffer for others to be satisfied. Moreover, such programs inflate demand, so as to outstrip the available resources. Especially where disability benefits are generous, more people attempt to be declared eligible under existing criteria, and those who are denied often press for expansion of the criteria. The result cannot be other than to divert disability program resources, in virtue of the increased demand for them, away from those who initially were deemed to be in need, rendering them more needy than originally.

In addition, those who remain outside the system or support it rather than are supported by it view it as privileging whenever it elevates recipients to levels of well-being beyond the reach of everyone alike. While considering what features are required to make the disability system an instrument of justice, Veatch concludes "justice in dealing with the handicapped requires that resources be channeled into in-kind medical and educational services" rather than discretionary funds so that "persons would not end up with radically unequal outcomes."[176] But this provision invites a complaint that determining how recipients use resources allocated to them to promote their equality defeats their ability to self-determine, which should be one of the benefits of being acknowledged to be equal.

Veatch's response is to propose that "many in a position to be compensated are not competent, rational decision-makers,"[177] meaning that for

---

175. Robert Veatch, *The Foundation of Justice: Why the Retarded and the Rest of Us Have Claims to Equality* (Oxford: Oxford University Press, 1986), 140–41.
176. Veatch, *Foundation of Justice*, 143.
177. Veatch, *Foundation of Justice*, 142.

them liberty is not an achievable component of equality. His solution illustrates how compensatory systems predicated on the extraordinary neediness of people with disabilities must theorize their recipients as being in persistent deficit. Doing so seems to be a systematic requirement of schemes that allocate unequally generously to some recipients, for to be viewed as just they must provide reassurance of their beneficiaries' inability to be privileged by the resources they are given.

Fourth, in addition to the insecurity attendant on depending more than others do on community resources, there are other serious drawbacks to being assigned a dependent's role. A social system focused on protecting those seen as deficient too readily lends itself to harming the putatively dependent by requiring them to accept lesser-quality care than they could administer to themselves. For a dependent stance is advantageous only if genuine—that is, if the putative dependent is truly incompetent. So in a system in which caring for is the primary way able-bodied relate to disabled, it becomes socially incumbent upon the latter to profess incompetence even where they are more competent than the former.[178] It was not too long ago, recall, when women were expected to dissemble this way to men.

More generally, we should be mindful that welfarism—the belief that virtue is determined above all by how much one contributes to the well-being of (other) people—is inherently paternalistic because it authorizes distribution of benefits in conflict, as well as in concert, with the recipients' wills. Feminist ethicist Joan Tronto reminds us of the power imbalance inherent whenever caregiving becomes institutionalized:

> [C]aregivers may well come to see themselves as more capable of assessing the needs of care receivers than are the care receivers themselves. . . . The only solution I see is to insist that care needs to be connected to a theory of justice and to be relentlessly democratic. . . . What would make care democratic is its focus on needs, and on the balance between caregivers and care receivers.[179]

How such a democratic balance could obtain under these circumstances remains obscure, especially when Tronto frames this thought with the ex-

---

178. Robert Scott, *The Making of Blind Men: A Study of Adult Socialization* (New York: Russell Sage Foundation, 1969).

179. Joan Tronto, *Moral Boundaries* (London: Routledge, 1993), 170–71.

pectation that those debarred from assuming the caregiver's role are necessarily needy and often less expert and competent.

Tronto sometimes seems to think that the solution lies in reconfiguring the relative valuation of dependency and autonomy so as to elevate the value of dependency and to replace interests with needs as the central consideration in political deliberation. But political rearrangements meant to make dependence more desirable neither resolve the inherent power imbalance between caregiver and care receiver nor relieve its potential as a source of repression. In some personal relations, the reality of this imbalance may be benign. But when depersonalized, abstracted from, and theorized into a vehicle for just treatment, being cared for cannot help but be a perilous prototypical role.

Modeling social organization on being cared for and caring thus appears to make compliant behavior a mandate for persons with disabilities. For them, submissiveness remains the price of good treatment. In a framework of moral relations in which some must make themselves vulnerable so that others can be worthy of their trust—that is, in paternalistic systems, in which those viewed as incompetent are coerced into compliance "for their own good"—people with disabilities are typecast as subordinate.

This is the assignment that, as we saw earlier, so restricts the social participation of people with disabilities, elevating their exposure to psychosocial risk. We can comprehend why this is so by noting that even helping relationships that are voluntary are asymmetrically so. Help givers choose how they are willing to help, but help takers cannot choose how they will be helped, for in choosing to reject proffered help one withdraws oneself from being helped as well as from being in a helping relationship.[180]

To relate to others primarily by being helped by them, then, implies subordinating one's choices to one's caretakers, at least insofar as one remains in the state of being helped. Jenny Morris writes:

> [I]t is the loss of reciprocity which brings about inequality within a relationship—and disabled and older people are very vulnerable within the unequal relationships which they commonly experience with the non-disabled world. Very little attention has been paid to disabled and older people's experience of physical and emotional abuse within caring relationships. . . . Research needs to examine what makes "caring for" in a "caring about" relationship

---

180. Anita Silvers, "Reconciling Equality to Difference: Caring (f)or Justice for People with Disabilities," *Hypatia* 10, no. 1 (Winter 1995): 30–55.

possible in a way which meets the interests of both parties. Many disabled people have clearly identified that "caring for" in a "caring about" relationship cannot work unless there is real choice based on real alternatives."[181]

As Tronto observes, "in focusing on the preservation of existing relationships, the perspective of care has a conservative quality."[182] In sum, as Alison Jaggar reminds us, "despite the virtue of care thinking, its emphasis on the quality of individual relations seems to preclude its addressing the structural oppositions between the interests of social groups that make caring difficult . . . between members of these groups."[183]

(Inter)Dependence

Nothing argued so far suggests that caring and being cared for are necessarily repressive, for bonds of affection encourage mutual helping, and bonds of respect support reciprocal helping. Nor have I argued that people with disabilities neither need nor should be given help from others, anymore than I would argue that their disadvantaged social position warrants their being exempted from helping others. However, Wendell fears that, because our culture values self-reliance over interdependence, whoever needs help from others will be deprecated and dismissed unless we press to make being dependent itself a valued—and presumably sought-after—state.[184]

This proposal rests on Wendell's (and others') exaggeration of how we disregard dependence, I think. Even the most unsociable among us relies on the products or the good offices, if not the charity, of others. We are so dependent on others for the transactions of ordinary life that it would be unrealistic to dismiss interdependence. Nor, in approving of self-reliance, does our culture celebrate solitariness. Far from it, we are such admirers of connectedness that it is commonplace to pity the disabled because of their isolation.

Annette Baier observes that "equality of power and interdependency is

---

181. Morris, *Pride against Prejudice*, 163–64.

182. Joan Tronto, "Beyond Gender Difference to a Theory of Care," *Signs* 12, no. 4 (Summer 1987): 660.

183. Alison Jaggar, "Caring as a Feminist Practice of Moral Reason," in *Justice and Care*, ed. Virginia Held (Boulder, Colo.: Westview, 1995).

184. Wendell, *The Rejected Body*, 144–51.

rare and hard to recognize."[185] This being so, assuaging Wendell's worry involves something more than simply valuing interdependence over self-reliance. We must first get clearer about what is being claimed in the name of interdependence, so as better to grasp the relevance of (in)equalities of (inter)dependence to (in)equalities of power.

Arguably, the construction of personal identity is a sphere in which interdependence exercises significant influence. Charles Taylor notes that we develop our identities transactionally through socially interactive engagement with others. And Kwame Anthony Appiah observes:

> Collective identities . . . provide what we might call scripts . . . that people . . . can use in shaping their life plans. . . . This is not just a point about modern Westerners: cross-culturally it matters . . . that . . . lives have a certain narrative unity . . . in the way appropriate by the standards made available in my culture to a person of my identity.[186]

However, it is just this socialized dimension of personal identity—namely, the dependence on others' conceptualization of one's self—that places identities at psychosocial risk when they fall away from the available cultural standards. The compulsion of nonimpaired individuals to dismiss the disabled as being in an unthinkable state explains why disability experience is opaque to the nondisabled. But persons who are impaired are no better than nonimpaired individuals in putting themselves in the places of those with other impairments or even those who have similar impairments but who are dysfunctional to a markedly greater degree. This is because, when an individual's situation is thought of as unbearable or otherwise appalling, others are forestalled from joining in that person's standpoint, even vicariously.

Moreover, performing major life functions such as moving one's body, hearing, seeing, interpreting, and inferring are such intimate elements of the fabric of our experience that one cannot accurately imagine how to live otherwise. For what we view as within our reach in the world around us—and thereby what we take as the objects of our ambition—is directly a product of the scope of our functioning. The inability to envision what

---

185. Annette Baier, "The Need for More Than Justice" in *Science, Morality, and Feminist Theory,* ed. Marsha Hanen and Kai Neilson (Calgary: University of Calgary Press, 1987), 53.

186. Appiah and Gutmann, *Color Conscious,* 97.

one's ambitions or desires would be if one were much more limited in capability is not merely a matter of the degree to which one's own experience of impairment fails to approximate that of people with disabilities. Sometimes vast differences in functioning are occasioned by relatively small differences in impairment, while at other times relatively severe impairments are only minimally dysfunctional. There is no fixed proportional relation between the two, nor can one insightfully project from one's own normal experience to a much more restricted version of one's life. Wendell makes this fact about becoming impaired very clear in her narrative of her own disabling illness.

Being physically, sensorily, or cognitively impaired thus can render a person experientially inaccessible to others' understanding and, in the case of progressive impairment, to one's own earlier self as well. Being so impedes interpersonal relations and consequently disturbs the transactional process that is a component of the impaired person's self-identification. This suggests that Kant's assessment of heteronomy as riskier than autonomy be brought to bear in assessing the value of interdependence to people with disabilities. That is, the heteronomous individual makes herself more dependent than need be on how others think of her. How they do is likely to be alien and even antagonistic because of the opacity of experiences mediated by a serious impairment. That those whose experience strikes us as impenetrable are marginalized because they are "other" than we is attendant upon, rather than intruded into, the interdependent character of self-identification.

Once again, we see that interdependence masks dependence but cannot overcome it. Interdependence itself creates, rather than mitigates, inequalities of power because it is so thoroughly and detrimentally heteronomous. For what appears to be called for by those promoting the theoretical significance of interdependence is a moral economy that privileges neediness by endorsing its claims against collective resources. But such a scheme must supply plausible grounds for determining who is better and who worse off, so as to decide whose assets to transform into common assets and whom to supply from common assets. So we must turn back to considering the nature of the disadvantage imposed by disability.

Instrumental Badness

Close examination has disclosed the weaknesses of the claim that anchors the medical model—namely, the contention that because impairment is intrinsically bad, or culminates in extreme neediness or dependence that is intrinsically bad, whoever is physically, sensorily, or cognitively impaired should be indemnified for his heightened suffering. What we have learned is that, although disadvantage is tightly tied to disability, the connection does not lie in the inherent inferiority of life with a disability. Even if we reject such construals, however, it seems reasonable to prefer not to be impaired.

The alternative explanation for curbing impairment is that it preempts instrumental value. To pursue this thought is to try to understand how being impaired interferes with achieving important outcomes, especially important social outcomes. In "Choosing Who Will Be Disabled," Allen Buchanan suggests how impairments compromise instrumentality.

> [I]ndividuals can benefit from learning to cope with disabilities. Nevertheless, disabilities, as such, are undesirable. They are undesirable—for those who have them—because they interfere with opportunities for performing significant tasks and for full participation in valued social interactions. It is therefore a mistake to say that disabilities are not undesirable or that they are not necessarily a disadvantage to those who have them.[187]

Why does Buchanan imagine it to be *necessarily* a mistake to deny the disadvantageousness of disability? Notice first that he does not mistakenly conflate disability with impairment. For Buchanan, physical or psychological impairments are functional defects (as opposed to cosmetic or aesthetic ones), but not every such deficit is a disability. Every functional defect constitutes an inability, but only some result in disabilities,[188] which are those inabilities that interfere vitally with the performance of a range of socially significant tasks.

Although an impairment may be innocuous in the current social context, being impaired increases the risk of being functionally defective should a shift in the environment obtain. For instance, we do not usually imagine color blindness to be a disability. Nevertheless, how it could become so is easily imaginable. We need only suppose the majority of individuals to prefer color coding to other forms of labeling, and suppose as

---

187. Allen Buchanan, "Choosing Who Will Be Disabled: Genetic Intervention and the Morality of Inclusion," *Social Philosophy and Policy* 13, no. 2 (Summer 1996): 38.

188. Buchanan, "Choosing Who," 37–38.

well the success of aggressive commercial enterprises that market to this preference, thereby vastly increasing the importance of discriminating red from green and so on to being productive. Given the possibility of such a scenario's actually unfolding, it cannot be other than preferable to distinguish colors rather than be color-blind if all else were equal. But as all other things are rarely equal, the weakness of the preference for seeing colors, as well as the cost it is reasonable to pay to satisfy it, may render it of negligible importance for the purposes of personal or public policy.

On Buchanan's understanding of "disability," adaptive technology that restores functioning may transfigure a disability into a mere inability just in case it is available to and adopted by a sufficient proportion of the population. For example, reading glasses keep most hyperopics (farsighted people) from being print disabled. And the rapidly improving computer dictation programs will markedly reduce the dysfunctional aspects of hand and arm impairments. Of course, to understand the implications of Buchanan's usage is to see that, if speech input replaces rather than supplements keyboard input in computer usage, individuals with speech difficulties would become more disabled by the self-same environmental change that reduces the disability of manually impaired individuals.

As Buchanan uses "disability," an individual whose impairment is invariable may be more, then less, then once again more disabled as the environment shifts. When disability is put in these terms, manualists can be understood to be accusing oralists of disabling deaf people by eroding their opportunity to learn Sign and consequently to grasp the fundamentals of language at an appropriately early age. Similarly, oralists countercharge that, in disregarding the importance of developing usable speech, manualists disable deaf people by eroding their opportunity to interact with the majority population.

Because Buchanan rightly understands disability to be "a mismatch between the individual's abilities and the demands of a range of tasks," he notices that the two approaches to avoiding disability are "changing the individual or changing the social environment that defines the task."[189] A key to the difference between these lies in who should bear the responsibility of remedying those misalignments between individual and social practice that are so dysfunctional they become disabilities. Both prolific and unproductive people with disabilities repeatedly identify environmental

---

189. Buchanan, "Choosing Who," 39.

factors as critical to their success or failure in achieving social participation. There are countless illustrations of environmental failures: the shop aisles blocked with unshelved goods (inaccessible to wheelchairs), the meeting moved to another room with only a notice in print stuck to the door (inaccessible to visually impaired individuals), business conducted in a dark and noisy restaurant (inaccessible to lipreading), or the refusal of bus drivers to call off destinations for print-disabled people (illegal under federal law but currently requiring city-by-city litigation to enforce).

Political Disadvantage

Such gratuitous impediments make people with disabilities feel as if their flourishing is held hostage to the satisfaction of other peoples' gratifications and whims purely because they are a nondominant minority. In an environment that discriminates against them, their differences are so instrumentally disadvantageous as to be disabilities. This perception argues for politicizing the theorizing promoted by the social model of disability.

Modeling an emancipatory approach for people with physical, sensory, and cognitive impairments on successful efforts by other minorities suggests that their functional limitations vary with the degree to which the political environment recognizes and respects the differences of the minority of individuals who are impaired. It is because they are a minority, which has been commodified by being made nonproductive, that their caretakers have an interest in keeping them apart from ordinary society and in obscuring their potential competence. To improve their functionality, this application of the social model recommends, people with disabilities should employ the same organizational strategies other minorities have used to adjust the social environment to accommodate their differences.

During the past half century, the political movement to secure greater social participation for the disabled minority has grown vigorously. Political organization by people with disabilities is far from novel. For from antiquity and in quite diverse cultural settings, from the medieval guilds of the blind to the organizations formed by injured veterans following every war, where impaired individuals have fashioned a positive group identity, they have improved their socioeconomic condition.

Speaking very generally and glossing over national differences, the last few decades have advanced the class of persons with severe physical, sensory, or cognitive limitations so they enjoy an unprecedented (for this class) degree of opportunity to participate in society—in work, in education, in public and family life. Their success is manifested variously: for instance, in the increasing availability of curb ramps and ramped taxis, the appearance of televised subtitle captions to translate aural into visual communication, or the tightening of software-purchasing standards to ensure that graphical user interfaces do not keep digitized information from the voice-output computer programs relied on by visually impaired individuals.

Nevertheless, there are questions not only about whether people with disabilities can be, but whether they should be permitted to be, numerous and noticeable enough to contrive the adoption of cooperative social schemes that allow them to exercise their talents so as to be productive. Why they need to influence the dominant cooperative scheme's practical infrastructure is illustrated by the effects the marketing of Microsoft Windows had on the employment of individuals who are blind.[190]

When DOS was the predominant computer operating system, many blind and visually impaired people, using devices for reading the screen text aloud, embarked on careers that depended on the use of computer applications. Computers opened new avenues of productivity for people in this group. But the Microsoft Windows program that succeeded DOS substituted screen icons or graphics for the lines of text that could be read aloud by voice output devices. Microsoft, claiming that business necessity demanded secrecy, refused to reveal the computer codes for Windows to the specialized companies that developed voice output software. Microsoft marketed Windows so aggressively that more and more applications required Windows to operate. The result was that more and more blind and visually impaired individuals suddenly found themselves unable to perform the computer tasks essential to their jobs.

From their point of view, the fault lay not in their inability to see, as they had been sufficiently talented and diligent to perform their jobs before the advent of Windows. Rather, their problem grew out of a dominant social scheme that allowed the sighted majority's mild preference for pictures

---

190. John Perry first drew my attention to this important issue. I am indebted also to the disability E-mail list information on this subject provided by Gregg Vanderheiden, Jamal Mazrui, Scott Luebking, and Norman Coombs to the disabled community.

over text to outweigh the blind minority's urgent need for text rather than pictures. How this crisis for blind citizens was at least temporarily resolved is an edifying exercise in political morality.

Declaring that civic interests were better served by preserving the employment of blind citizens than by contributing to the general public's infatuation with icons, the state of Massachusetts's government, long a leader in integrating blind citizens into the workforce, announced that it would not purchase any new Microsoft products unless Windows 95 was rolled out with accessibility to screen readers. As a result, Microsoft agreed to build compatibility for adaptive devices into versions of Windows 95. This case offers an important insight into whether the claims that issue from our different needs in respect to the social and physical environment are competitive with each other. To retain a generation of talented blind people in the workplace by maintaining their access to computing extracted no cost in respect to other people's productivity.

To pursue this point, it is useful to consider Buchanan's view in more detail. The dominant institutional infrastructure for productive interaction determines who will and who will not be disabled, Buchanan explains. This is because the dominant cooperative scheme sets the demands that social participants must satisfy. To illustrate, Buchanan characterizes the rules of contract bridge as being so complicated as to disable young children from playing it. To include children in our games, we must select simpler ones; adults who desire a challenge must make a sacrifice to play with children.[191] Similar sacrifices may be the price of interacting with the disabled who, like children, are considered to be a "weak" or incompetent class: "[P]articipation by 'disabled' individuals can cause discoordination, and can reduce the benefits which the 'abled' might otherwise obtain from the form of interaction in question."[192]

While those disabled by a dominant cooperative scheme have an interest in reforming it so as to permit themselves to thrive, those who flourish under it have an interest in maintaining the most productive practices in which they themselves can participate effectively. "For this reason," Buchanan insists, "we must reject the disabilities rights advocates' slogan that we should 'change society, not individuals.' "[193] While "some compro-

---

191. Buchanan, "Choosing Who," 40.
192. Buchanan, "Choosing Who," 41.
193. Buchanan, "Choosing Who," 45.

mises with efficiency are required in the name of equal opportunity for those with disabilities . . . the interests of employers (and workers who do not have disabilities) are also legitimate."[194]

But it is oversimplified to think that what is in contention between those who seek inclusion for the disabled and those who would exclude them is efficiency, or the maintaining of an optimally productive system. There is no reason to accept, nor does analysis of the Windows case support, the supposition that the practices of the dominant cooperative scheme are maximally efficient or productive just because they are dominant. Power promotes some individuals' interests and sacrifices others' interests regardless of which are more productive and despite the possibility that both interests can be satisfied without sacrificing productivity.

Buchanan's view to the contrary, what was at issue in the Windows case was not whether to sacrifice productivity in order to maintain untalented visually impaired workers in employment. For in this case, the visually impaired minority's interest in being productive and society's interest in enhancing productivity coincided. Weighing against this interest in productivity was the dominant class's preference to click on pictures rather than words, which hardly increases productivity. Also weighing against measures to design screen readers to operate in a Windows environment was Microsoft's proprietary interest in hiding its codes, a concern driven by the desire for competitive advantage rather than a devotion to the collective enhancement of productivity.

Parenthetically, hindsight reveals Microsoft's concerns for secrecy to have been an overreaction, for an easily developed system protected their rights even after they began to make their software accessible to other software developers' screen-reading programs. Furthermore, in terms of social productivity, the cost of Microsoft's miscalculation about the importance of secrecy was very high. First, there was the human cost, the termination of needed employment for blind and visually impaired individuals; second, the waste of the years of education and training they had consumed; third, the denial of educational opportunity to blind students when new versions of computer-assisted instructional software operated only under Windows; and, fourth, the price of adding text tags for screen readers to subsequent versions of software that could have been made accessible during their original development at much less expense.

---

194. Buchanan, "Choosing Who," 42.

The Windows case suggests that Buchanan is overreacting in supposing that differences in their abilities place groups in conflict with one another in respect to the choice of a dominant cooperative scheme congruent with their interests. Buchanan supposes that those with disabilities have an interest in changes to make participation more inclusive, even at the expense of lowering productivity. On the other hand, he assumes, those not disabled have an interest in changes to make participation more productive, even at the expense of diminishing inclusiveness: "[T]he problem of justice is this . . . : Satisfying the interest in inclusion imposes costs on those who could benefit from a more demanding scheme; satisfying the maximizing interest imposes costs on those who would be excluded from effective participation in it."[195] However, to portray the interests of the nondisabled and the disabled as pitted against each other in this way does not fairly represent the issue.

First, it appears to disregard alternatives to the current dominant scheme on which the nondisabled are no less productive and the disabled become more productive. The Windows case demonstrates the potential for such happy solutions, for no one else has suffered in the course of making Windows at least partially accessible to visually impaired people. Furthermore, by comparing individuals with impairments who try to produce within the currently dominant cooperative scheme with small children trying to play contract bridge, Buchanan misleadingly suggests that individuals with disabilities are less competent than other people, a perspective that manifests the chronic influence of the medical model. In contrast, the social model makes clear that working and living conditions first must be revised to provide equal access before the potential for productivity of workers with and without disabilities can be fairly assessed. Without evidence obtained under less biased conditions than presently obtain, we should avoid assuming that it is characteristic of the former, when employed, to be less productive than the latter.

Second, the fact of our social interdependence becomes an important consideration here. For Buchanan's portrayal of competing interests overlooks how we contribute to each others' productivity, as well as the ways in which serving one person's interests may further others' interests as well. Buchanan speaks as if whether each solitary worker performs efficiently is the sole factor in increasing or reducing productivity. But factors

---

195. Buchanan, "Choosing Who," 42.

other than efficiency also affect productivity, and among these is the well-being of potentially contributing fellow humans.

Inclusion has its cost in lowered productivity, Buchanan worries, not noticing that exclusion, too, takes a toll in lowered productivity. For the productivity of others enhances my productivity, whereas their dependency drains the communal resources to which I contribute. As the U.S. Congress put the point in its findings prefacing the ADA, "the continuing existence of unfair and unnecessary discrimination and prejudice denies people with disabilities the opportunity to compete on an equal basis . . . and costs the United States billions of dollars in unnecessary expenses resulting from dependency and nonproductivity."[196] Exclusion thus invites squandering public assets.

In sum, although Buchanan understands well *that* disability is relativized to the physical and social environment, he is not equally sensitive to *how* it is relativized. Moreover, he seems to suggest that the dominant cooperative scheme evolved naturally to maximize productivity, and as a by-product those who naturally were most productive became powerful. Both the sign language case and the Windows case, however, suggest that power rather than productivity is the preeminent driver of dominance in the domain of cooperative schemes.

Seen in this light, Buchanan's faith in the scheme that is dominant being the most productive seems to be based on nothing more than a sociobiological application of the medical model's conflation of normal or commonplace practice with biologically warranted practice. The exclusions society imposes on the disabled because of their impairments, and the artificial limits they face, are rarely of a kind designed to advance efficiency. While Buchanan is right that to be disabled is to be disadvantaged by social arrangement, there is no evidence that imposing such disadvantage is the price of having a society that maximizes productivity. It is a price exacted from the disabled for the convenience, not for the productivity, of the nondisabled.

To grasp this last point, we need only consider the testimony of citizens who described to the U.S. Congress how they had been denied normal opportunity on the basis of their disabilities: the children in wheelchairs barred from schools because they were considered "depressing;" the children with Down syndrome ordered out of the zoo because the director

---

196. Sec. 2-a 9.

claimed they would scare the monkeys; the blind businessman refused an account at the neighborhood bank because, the manager wrote, he did not fit the bank's customer image. Only through the influence of enormous bias could anyone imagine that such exclusions, all of which were testified to by congressional witnesses during efforts to pass the ADA, promote productivity.

Suppressing Talent

Cooperative schemes maintained through arrogance, greed, fear, or sloth all may sacrifice talent, and therefore productivity, to continue the powerful in an environment that comforts them. Buchanan argues against such waste. The democratic value of equalizing opportunity operates as a strategic policy for increasing productivity, he says. Equalizing opportunity minimizes waste by preventing sacrifices of talent. Compensatory action is called for where oppressive social arrangements stifle talent, improperly elevating those with less natural ability over those more gifted. The state thus has an interest in protecting people with disabilities, one predicated not on their being weak and incompetent but rather on their having been arbitrarily, incorrectly, or unfairly excluded from contributing their strengths and talents to the community.[197]

In arguing this way, Buchanan advances what is known in jurisprudence as a "mainstream centrist" view, a position justifying state intervention to induce rational conduct on the part of employers. On this account, according to legal theorists Mark Kelman and Gillian Lester, employers are required to treat employees as if they were in a:

> thoroughgoingly rational, impersonal market. Firms [that] follow irrational customs whose impact adversely affects protected groups' members do not treat [them] market-rationally. . . . [A]n unbigoted profit-maximizing employer might refuse to hire those against whom his customers are prejudiced. . . . [T]he unambivalent and unambiguous refusal of courts to allow employers to raise customer preference defenses [means] the courts are simply refusing to allow the employers to act as agents of the customers' economic irrationality. Similarly, reliance on false stereotypes may preclude market-rational treatment.[198]

197. Allen Buchanan, "Equal Opportunity and Genetic Intervention," *Social Philosophy and Policy* 12, no. 2 (Summer 1995): 105–35.

198. Mark Kelman and Gillian Lester, *Jumping the Queue: An Inquiry into the Legal Treatment of Students with Learning Disabilities* (Cambridge, Mass.: Harvard University Press, 1997), 201–2.

It is crucial to understand the implications of the position Kelman and Lester observe is expressed in American case law. Understood broadly, the premise is that justice requires market considerations to be constrained to prevent their being driven by false or irrational theory. In some such matters, the market is self-correcting. So, for example, a restaurant manager who has certain false beliefs about how wealth is distributed within her market—for instance, who overestimates her potential customers' ability to pay—will lose her business if she prices her menu offerings too high.

But one who irrationally underestimates the ability of African American customers to pay, and therefore offers them disadvantageous service to discourage them from occupying her tables, may not be excluding a segment sufficiently large to injure her market. Nevertheless, such practice, fueled by false theories about the competence of a class of people and diffused throughout the culture, may be part of a pattern that imposes sufficient disadvantage upon the group to compromise its members' opportunities for social participation. (The existence of such patterns of exclusionary practice, and their material implications, differentiates denial of access to African Americans and wheelchair users from denial of access to groups whose lives are not systematically limited by social disregard. This is why we find it unfair for a restaurant to deny access to African Americans and wheelchair users, but not unfair if the restaurant denies access to people who work the swing shift by opening only for dinner.)

In respect to the exclusion of minority market segments, the market itself will not correct unfairness. As a juridical corrective to protect minorities whom past oppression has made too small or economically powerless to protect themselves in the market, the courts have been inclined to shift the burden: rather than relying on the market to demonstrate that the inclusion of protected classes is a business necessity, the courts have placed the burden on businesses (and nonprofit enterprises as well) to defend themselves by demonstrating that excluding a protected class is a business necessity. The ADA extends this corrective to practices that limit the opportunities of individuals on the basis of physical, sensory, or cognitive disability.[199]

---

199. I add this discussion in response to Richard Arneson (comment at the American Philosophical Association meeting, 7 May 1998), who appropriately challenges me to explain why I think formal justice, rather than a calculus of social benefits and costs, best permits us to distinguish between the restaurant owner whose early closing hours excludes swing-shift workers or whose carnivores' menu

A question remains about who is sufficiently talented to be productive. Impairment is itself a lack of talent, Buchanan supposes:

> [W]e cannot make a case for allocating special resources to [someone who is blind] or to anyone with a major natural disability on the ground that . . . she is being excluded as a result of prejudice which demeans and devalues her by classifying her as an inferior individual. . . . [S]he lacks the qualifications for various positions not because she is the victim of past injustices, but because she is naturally blind.[200]

Here we return to the question of just how seeing (or hearing or walking or any other major faculty) is valuable. We should recall that the instrumental, not the intrinsic, value realized by the exercise of these faculties is the matter at issue. Because the functioning of these faculties is merely instrumental to the essential objectives of most kinds of employment, it is a mistake to construe their exercise as a job qualification or their absence as a lack of talent.

Such mistakes plague and disable people with physical, sensory, and cognitive impairments. Let me illustrate from my own story. Many years ago, during one of those cataclysmic upheavals of university hierarchies that requires the reassignment of parking, I was informed that under the new scheme my position as an assistant professor did not qualify me to continue to use the only parking lot near my office and classrooms, for it had been reassigned to be an administrators' parking lot. "If you cannot walk from the parking lot at the bottom of the hill to your classroom at

---

excludes vegetarians, and the restaurant owner whose decision not to install a ramp excludes and diminishes the opportunities of people who use wheelchairs. Civil rights legislation typically is embedded in appeals to social history meant to show the social costs of suppressing the talents of a historically ostracized class as well as the personal costs of such oppression. Where market constraints are ineffective against such costly but historically embedded practice, I am arguing, the mechanisms of formal justice, such as shifting the burden of proof in respect to demonstrating whether an exclusionary practice is a business necessity (see *Griggs v. Duke Power Company*, 1971), are preferable to the mechanisms of distributive justice, such as income transfer schemes that allocate extraordinary resources in an effort to mitigate the harm done by exclusionary social policy or practice. One strand of my argument is that because the former approach, but not the latter, is directed at reforming harmful practice, it will be more effective, more reliable, and less costly in the long run.

200. Buchanan, "Equal Opportunity and Genetic Intervention," 128.

the top, you are not qualified to teach," intoned the official who each morning parked in the lot near my classroom, then jogged to the bottom of the hill and back up for exercise. Notice here that qualifying for the job, a matter of being sufficiently competent and talented to achieve the objectives of the classroom, was elided with qualifying to use the parking lot, a matter unrelated to the talent and competence required for performing well in the classroom. Notice also that efficiency is hardly compromised, nor is productivity reduced, by instituting a parking assignment system that facilitates including qualified but mobility-limited individuals in the university workforce.

Walking normally, seeing or hearing as most others do, are not themselves talents. Rather, the ability to execute these performances enables or facilitates talent. It is not the case that some people are more talented hearers than other people are; rather, they have more talent in listening. Similarly, it is perceiving rather than seeing for which people display talent. We understand describing someone as "she is a talented marathoner" or a "talented cakewalker" or a "talented runway walker" or a "talented mall walker," but it is unclear what virtues a generically talented walker would display.

This example calls attention to the important distinction between performing a function and exercising a faculty. Performing certain tasks may very plausibly be considered essential functions of a job, but exercising faculties is merely the instrument of such performances. One exercise may replace another in many contexts, as, for example, one can communicate by signing as well as speaking, read tactilely by feeling Braille with one's fingers or visually by seeing print with one's eyes, or mobilize by wheeling or by walking.

Individuals who utilize uncommon devices to perform a function—note taking in Braille instead of script to archive information, seeing print captions rather than hearing spoken sounds—are no less talented for doing so. Some work sites permit employees with disabilities flexibility in selecting the most effective mode for executing the essential duties of their jobs, whereas other workplaces with identical missions are rigid about how one accomplishes one's work. It was such rigidity, together with a workplace culture in which maintaining managerial power counted for more than fostering employee productivity and appreciating talent, that inflicted the disability discrimination suffered by Pauline Horvath, whose office supervisor, we may recall, made her hide her wheelchair in a closet and insisted that holding a telephone receiver (rather than using a speakerphone or headset) was a talent required for the job.

So far, I have argued that being physically, sensorily, or cognitively impaired should not be equated with the depletion of talent. Indeed, the distinction between being impaired and lacking talent is so well accepted in some areas of practice as to be diagnostic. For instance, individuals who have high IQs (thought to be an indicator of talent) but low performance in reading or other communication or calculation skills are in virtue of that disparity diagnosed as being learning disabled, while others who display equally low-level performance but low IQs as well are not. Thus, what Kelman and Lester call "the 'tragedy' of the disappointing high-IQ student" is attributed in practice to (so-far unidentified) physical differences that render the standard educational inputs ineffective in assisting these talented but disabled individuals to acquire basic skills.[201]

Of course, in a disabling environment, impairments are likely to be instrumentally disadvantageous to the expression of talent wherever the cooperative scheme reduces opportunity by narrowing the permissible modes of executing various functions. In view of their impediments, trying to equalize people with disabilities by providing equitable opportunity for the exercise of talent thus might seem to prolong rather than mitigate their disadvantage. It is Veatch's belief, for example, that "to the extent that we live in a world that distributes its assets on the basis of talent . . . the handicapped are going to lose."[202]

However, Veatch has confused being awarded fair opportunity to use one's talents with being rewarded for being talented. He complains, "It is simply not possible to give [a cognitively impaired individual who needs speech therapy] the educational services he needs to have a real opportunity in life and hold to the idea that educational opportunity should be distributed on the basis of talent."[203] But his complaint is misdirected, I think, by his unclarity as to why the services benefit the individual in question.

In Veatch's example, the cognitively impaired individual can speak understandably, but not normally.[204] If the point of the service is to normal-

---

201. Kelman and Lester, *Jumping the Queue*, 133.
202. Veatch, *Foundation of Justice*, 168.
203. Veatch, *Foundation of Justice*, 178.
204. Veatch, *Foundation of Justice*, 3.

ize him by bringing him into as close compliance as possible with so-called normal patterns of speech, then Veatch is right in thinking that it cannot be defended as education deserved on the basis of talent. But that is beside the point, for in this case it is misleading to portray the service as an educational rather than a health care benefit. That current federal law requires school systems to provide such therapy no more makes this therapy educational than an analogous rule requiring schoolchildren to have measles inoculations makes such disease prevention educational.

Health care facilitates the exercise of talent, but to allocate health care on the basis of the amount of talent a patient demonstrates would be a ludicrous approach to rationing. Indeed, the point of the speech therapy Veatch describes is to facilitate the cognitively impaired individual's expression of the talents he possesses but cannot exercise. For example, speaking distinctly may facilitate his communicating with a supervisor and coworkers or his asking for the products he needs at a store. So the individual in Veatch's example need not lose, and quite likely will gain, if assets are distributed on the basis of their potential to expand opportunities for exercising talent.

More generally, productivity is compromised if we are placed in competition with one another simply to gain opportunity to exercise the talents we have. For the opportunity to apply our talents productively is a prerequisite, not an option, for a fair competitive scheme. It follows that to promote fairness where the outcomes of our exercising our talents will be judged competitively, we must be on guard to ensure against practices framed by theory that equates having a disability with lacking talent.

Equalizing: Repairing the Results of Bias

The last fifty years have seen advanced conditions for persons with serious physical, sensory, or cognitive limitations. And, despite the persistence of their being viewed as deficient and burdensome, they enjoy an unprecedented (for this class) degree of opportunity to participate in society—in work, in education, in public and family life. Throughout American society and culture, there has been a profound transformation in our consciousness of citizens with disabilities. A *New York Times* writer comments on the change: "antidiscrimination laws have had a real impact, allowing disabled people who might once have spent their lives in seclusion to work, take public transportation and just generally be visible."[205] The success of this movement is manifested by the increasing diversity of instrumental options: the availability of ramped curbs and taxis, the appearance of televised captioned subtitles to translate aural into visual communication, or the tightening of Internet standards to ensure that graphical user interfaces do not impede the use of the screen-reading technology used by visually impaired individuals.

These are among the displays of their presence that are beginning to supplant the historical invisibility of persons with disabilities. They emerge in a climate suited to dislodge the traditional practices that have subordinated these individuals to hostile social and built environments. The development of adaptive devices such as those just mentioned, which greatly increase our power to adapt the physical circumstances that bear upon our functioning, reverse the expectation that impaired individuals should conform to the environment. Mandating accessibility—requiring that cities ramp curbs, that television sets contain caption decoders, that software manufacturers attach "ALT" tags to graphics—furthers the idea that where exclusionary circumstance bars the disabled, their isolation must be remedied by an environment made more accommodating to them.

At both the federal and state levels, a large body of recent statutory and case law reflects this analysis of the disability problem. That lawmaking process began with the Architectural Barriers Act of 1968 to mandate access to the built public environment and reached full expression in the 1990 Americans with Disabilities Act. When Sections 503 and 504 were added to the Rehabilitation Act in 1973, the idea of revising exclusionary educational and employment practices instead of altering impaired individuals so as to effect the latters' participation in the former slowly began to take hold in American law.

This idea gained momentum with the 1974 amendment of the Rehabilitation Act's definitions (described earlier in the section entitled "Disability as Difference"). But the provisions of this and other sections of the Rehabilitation Act, including those requiring universities and other recipients of federal funds to make their programs accessible to employees and

---

205. Angier, "Joined for Life," B15. Angier goes on to comment, "[T]he dominant culture appears to be moving in two contradictory directions: more accommodation of disabilities in adults, but less tolerant of imperfections in children."

clients with disabilities by eliminating physical barriers and providing adaptive equipment and aides, continued to be dominated by the medical model of disability. That is because the ultimate purpose of the Rehabilitation Act is to restore impaired people to normal functioning, so it focuses on the individual to be repaired rather than on the environment to be reformed.

Thus, when Sections 503 and 504 were read within the context of the Rehabilitation Act, their requirement that recipients of federal funds provide "reasonable accommodation" to persons with disabilities often was interpreted as mandating a rehabilitation service rather than a far-reaching reform of practice. Where, for instance, the Rehabilitation Act stipulates that people with disabilities be offered accommodations such as sign language interpreters for people who are deaf and catalogues on tape for people who are blind, these were treated as group-differentiated entitlements or social services meant to further a national policy of rehabilitation rather than as an expansion of the options available for acquiring information. In support of this interpretation of Sections 503 and 504 as supplying benefits to the disabled, some federal rehabilitation dollars were passed through to states to remove architectural barriers at public program sites, primarily at universities. Notwithstanding this effort, state officials typically complained that, unlike other parts of the federal rehabilitation program, Sections 503 and 504 carried with them little federal money to defray the costs of implementing them.

Searching for an administrative approach for complying with these new requirements, most program providers, but especially universities, fastened on the model of the rehabilitation agency. They conceived of themselves as offering special services to a marginal and vulnerable group rather than as broadening access to their programs by eliminating artificial and arbitrary barriers to the exercise of talent. Parenthetically, during the 1980s, the growing perception that to be disabled is to be eligible for special services and exemptions correlated with an unpredicted increase in university students identifying themselves as disabled. During the same period, an expansion of the medical and personal services benefits allowed by the federal social security program correlated with a precipitous increase in the Social Security disability rolls.

The Americans with Disabilities Act

Becoming law in 1990, the ADA reiterated the amended Rehabilitation Act's test for identifying who is protected against the hostility of built or arranged environments that exclude them from opportunities they are otherwise competent to pursue. The ADA shares some definitions and substantive provisions with the Rehabilitation Act. But it promotes a very different conception, namely, the view that not special benefits but, instead, access similar to other people's is a basic requirement for acknowledging that the lives of people with disabilities are as worth living as others' lives are. The ADA is propelled by the theory that their social isolation will be diminished, and their social equality furthered, by a different kind of protection from that advised by the medical model of disability—namely, by protecting them against external obstructions of their physical and social access rather than from their internal flaws and failings. The ADA thus marks a significant evolution of the status of citizens with disabilities by advancing them beyond confinement to a class subject(ed) to special treatment and by joining them with other minorities as classes explicitly designated to command equal treatment.

The ADA constitutes an attempt to make the equal protection guaranteed to citizens by the U.S. Constitution's Fourteenth Amendment meaningful to individuals whose physical or mental impairments substantially limit one or more major life activities. Congress found the policy created by the ADA to be required for the public interest because "unlike individuals who have experienced discrimination on the basis of race, color, sex, national origin, religion or age, individuals who have experienced discrimination on the basis of disability have often had no legal recourse to redress such discrimination."[206] First and foremost, the ADA is meant to abate that legal disability from which women and people of color were freed earlier in the century. To meet this challenge, the ADA offers legal recourse against the propensity to view impairments as excusing the inferior treatment of those whose bodily or cognitive functioning is anomalous. In doing so, the ADA disputes assumptions that to be impaired is to be inferior. It shifts the burden of proof to whoever's practices are built on such false and biased theorizing.

The ADA takes a minimalist approach to achieving social equality for the disabled in that it emphasizes formal rather than material equality. That is, the ADA offers recourse to individuals when mistaken or misleading assumptions about disability weight commonplace practices against them. It challenges the unreflective expectation that the conventions of

---

206. P.L. 101–336 Sec. 2–4.

social interaction and organization be keyed to "normal" modes of performance, and the biasing hypothesis that social disadvantage is the natural corollary of impairment. It denies the unreflective expectation that to be exceptionally limited in one's mode of performance inescapably reduces the quality of living, and the biasing hypothesis that diminished well-being is the normal outcome of impairment. It defies the unreflective expectation that the burden of demonstrating one's competence and worth reasonably falls more heavily on people in virtue of disability. Broadly, the ADA furthers formal justice by promoting the refashioning of the biased dialogical structures in which these unfair expectations heretofore have found expression. As I am construing it here, formal justice thus aims at reforming processes central to the achievement of moral connectedness so as to ensure their inclusiveness regardless of disability.

The Congress diagnosed that "the continuing existence of unfair and unnecessary discrimination and prejudice denies people with disabilities the opportunity to compete on an equal basis and to pursue those opportunities for which our free society is justly famous." So the ADA constrains the nondisabled majority from actions that deny the disabled access to the opportunities for social participation the rest of the population enjoys. Thus, it establishes both a ground and a process that liberates the disabled minority from social arrangements that artificially disadvantage the members of this class.

That the ADA emphasizes formal rather than material justice does not mean that its implementation must be abstract. Formal justice not only is compatible with but entails criticism of the morality of community practices that are exclusionary because they are arbitrarily predicated on performances not all community members can execute. To illustrate how formal considerations can have substantial material impact, we may turn to one of the pillars of U.S. antidiscrimination law, *Griggs v. Duke Power Company* (1971), in which the Supreme Court established that, where there is a prima facie (i.e., a formal) case that a practice disparately disadvantages a protected class, the burden shifts to the employer to prove that the practice is not arbitrary—that is, that it is job related and required by business necessity.[207] In the context of disability discrimination law, the emphasis on eliminating exclusionary practices whenever they are arbitrary is a formal consideration that broadens the application of rectificatory jus-

---

207. Colker, *The Law of Disability Discrimination*, 80.

tice by making it less "backward looking." For in the absence of proof that exclusionary practices are not arbitrary, rectification can be authorized even in the absence of identifying the moment and agency when and by which causative wrongdoing took place.

As Kwame Anthony Appiah observes, the ADA recognizes that we can take collective responsibility as a society for harms we did not cause, specifically, for the costs in inappropriate treatment that exclusionary practice visits upon those who are "different."[208] Appiah's point is that the ADA requires reform even of conditions that are inadvertently rather than intentionally discriminatory, and even at a price borne by citizens who did not create the discriminatory conditions. For example, the absence of wheelchair-accessible bathrooms in a public building is discriminatory, according to the ADA, even if no explicit policy of excluding people in wheelchairs guided the omission. To rectify discrimination, opportunities made available to the public within the building must be offered to people in wheelchairs even if doing so constrains opportunities for nonwheelchair users, as may ensue if constructing a wide stall for wheelchairs reduces the number of narrow stalls available to nonwheelchair users. Because the latter's opportunities previously were unfairly enlarged at the expense of the former, this is not unfair.

The ADA also emphasizes formal equality in that it protects all, equally, against disability discrimination. As we have seen, whether or not one actually has "a physical or mental impairment that substantially limits one or more of the major life activities" or is "regarded as having such an impairment," one is protected from being discriminated against on the basis of such an impairment. So it offers redress against suffering the unwarranted attenuation of opportunity incurred when false and biased theorizing about people's physical or cognitive functioning stipulates falsely as to their incompetence. This marks another departure from the medicalized approach, for no "eligibility test"—proof of weakness or incapacity—must be satisfied to qualify for ADA protection.

To understand how else the ADA furthers the formal equality of disabled persons, it is useful to review what behavior is guarded against here and what is not. The ADA does not offer broad protection against unfavorable treatment, regardless of cause, to individuals with substantially limiting impairments. Primarily, the law forbids the exclusion or segrega-

---

208. Appiah and Gutmann, *Color Conscious*, 101.

tion of any individual, or relegation of that individual to lesser services or opportunities, because the individual is or is regarded as impaired. But the law does not speak to the exclusion of impaired individuals for other reasons, such as lack of qualifications. So, for instance, job applicants with disabilities must meet employment position qualifications, as long as these are necessary for performing the essential functions of the job and thus are not arbitrary. Applicants for a poetry editor's job, for instance, might reasonably be required to possess a doctorate in English literature as evidence of being widely and knowledgeably well read, even if it is much more difficult for a blind person than for a sighted one to attain this degree. But applicants cannot be required to have good vision for this job, for it is arbitrary to demand that poems be accessed by looking at texts rather than by hearing them spoken by a human reader or a computer's voice output or by reading them in Braille.

One product of ADA implementation has been to induce employers to clarify what they take to be the essential duties of jobs, in distinction both from peripheral functions and from fashions of performing functions. Thus, employers must hold all employees to the same standard. If, for instance, employees generally are evaluated on the quality of their output, then a prospective or current employer must focus on the known facts about disabled workers' output, not on speculation about their future output or on discomfort.

A *New York Times* letter to the editor about the disability discrimination complaint made by the golfer Casey Martin against the Professional Golf Association (PGA) further illustrates how formal justice is substantive. Complaining about the *Times*'s editorial and sports page support of a federal court decision overriding the PGA tournament prohibition against use of a golf cart, letter writer William J. Wheeler engages in classic "sky is falling" speculation: "invoking the ADA, as Martin has, opens the door for consideration of players with special circumstances that could make a level playing field impossible." Wheeler goes on to imagine that because a mechanical aid—that is, a golf cart—is permitted to accommodate Martin's inability to walk long distances, other mechanical aids also will be permitted—for example, a mechanical device to replace a damaged left forearm or a range finder to accommodate an individual who has lost binocular vision. The familiar specter of disability, cast as incompetence compensated for at the expense of average people, is called up by this writer when he suggests that normal golfers will find themselves competing against bionically amplified contenders.

Wheeler concludes, "I appreciate Casey Martin's dilemma, but the case could set a precedent that would require altering the rules of the game."[209] Precisely so. The ADA facilitates formal intervention into the rules of social games by permitting questions to be raised about the justification of whatever disparately disadvantaging impact they may have. Where, for example, PGA tournament rules bar golfers, however talented, from competing unless they can walk for eighteen holes, the ADA requires evidence that skill or talent in distance walking either is a criterion of excellence in tournament golf or directly affects satisfying such a criterion. That there is no such clarity about the role of walking in golf was demonstrated in the Martin case by the animation with which golfers weighed in on both sides of the debate, some claiming that the eighteen-hole walk is so exhausting as to give an advantage in energy to whoever need not perambulate this distance, but others insisting that whoever does not walk the course disadvantageously loses the "feel" of the ground and fails to remain limber.

As is illustrated by the PGA case, the ADA simply demands of rules or practices which disparately disadvantage some among a group of equally talented individuals that such a discrepancy be justified as being essential to achieving the publicized institutional or recreational objectives. How substantive the reforms ultimately demanded by the ADA will be thus depends on the degree to which prohibitive or exclusionary mandates, mechanisms, or common manners of social transaction turn out to be arbitrary.

The formal justice promoted by the ADA does not address easing the lives of people with physical, sensory, or cognitive impairments so that their difficulties are reduced to the level experienced by people who are not similarly impaired. To illustrate, although public transportation systems must be made accessible, the disabled are owed only that level of mobility enjoyed (or deplored) by public transportation users, not the higher level achieved by private automobile users, despite the fact that many people with disabilities cannot drive and thus do not have mobility equivalent to nondisabled car owners. The comparatively greater inconvenience of using public transportation is visited equally upon disabled and

---

209. William Wheeler, "Golf Cart Gives Disabled Athlete No Advantage," *New York Times*, 23 January 1998: A18.

nondisabled nondrivers. Consequently, this is not an instance of disability incurring a discriminatory lesser level of service.

Related legislation adopted by the U.S. Congress offers added insight into the biased practices that must be arrested if people with physical, sensory, or cognitive impairments are to increase their social participation. For instance, the 1988 Air Carriers Access Act intervenes to relieve travelers with physical or sensory impairments from being ill treated on the basis of their disability. This legislation, fleshed out by Department of Transportation regulations, gives passengers a claim to have certain kinds of adaptive equipment, such as wheelchairs and guide dogs, handled as extensions of their bodies rather than as luggage. So, for instance, guide dogs and (folding) wheelchairs are transported in the same cabin as the passengers for whom they see or roll. Such an arrangement does not privilege passengers with disabilities; it simply affords them protection against loss or damage similar to that afforded the eyes and legs of other passengers.

Among other provisions, the act also constrains airlines from imposing special restraints on the travel of passengers with disabilities in the absence of demonstration that the particular passenger poses a specific hazard.[210] This prohibition protects people with disabilities from the injurious consequences of being stigmatized as burdensomely or dangerously incompetent travelers just because they are disabled. Specifically, air carriers are forbidden to require people with disabilities to bring attendants with them when they travel (except under very special circumstances). This is because, almost a decade earlier, airlines had proposed barring any blind or wheelchair-using passenger who was not accompanied by a personal attendant. Had such a policy been enacted, thousands of persons with disabilities whose employment required them to travel but who neither needed nor could afford attendants would have been put out of work arbitrarily.

---

210. 49 U.S.C. 41705. However, during the decade following adoption of the Air Carriers Access Act, several deaf-blind travelers have had to file suit against airlines that refused to offer them passage unless they were accompanied by an attendant. In April 1997 Georgetown University Law Center's Institute for Public Representation filed suit in federal court on behalf of a deaf-blind student, an experienced air traveler, whom an airline refused to carry unless she was accompanied by an attendant. The case was tried in November 1997, and the plaintiff prevailed, establishing that airlines cannot substitute their own speculations about safety for the unbiased regulations developed by the Department of Transportation to implement the ACAA.

From a public policy point of view, the ADA, as well as the Air Carriers Access Act, some sections of the Rehabilitation Act, and a few other statutes, focus on acting affirmatively to maintain a replete array of alternative or adaptive modes of accessing the usual social options. But the mandate is to respond only to repair social arrangements that marginalize people with disabilities. To satisfy their material needs, they must pursue opportunity with no more advantage than other people enjoy. Does such formal redress, directed at equalizing practices rather than at elevating people, respond sufficiently to the challenge of extending social justice to individuals with physical, sensory, and cognitive impairments?

Equalizing Environments

Applying a distinction Ronald Dworkin draws between two ways of equalizing to an example offered by Martha Minow, Christine Koppel argues that equal treatment is useless to people with disabilities. Koppel writes:

> In a world where ablebodied people are the norm, a person in a wheelchair . . . has her right to equal treatment respected even if nothing is done to accommodate her difference. She is being given the same treatment as everyone else. The right to treatment as an equal, on the other hand, focuses on the differential effects her disability has on her opportunities . . . Her formal equal right of access is without substance.[211]

Unlike Koppel, however, the ADA does not reduce equality of treatment to any treatment that is the same. To do so would be to impoverish how we conceptualize formal equality. The reduction seems plausible to Koppel because she fails to notice that not every level of describing an action is similarly relevant to the justice of the action. Pursuing formal equality requires carefully distinguishing descriptions of how people are treated that reveal the scope of the treatment's instrumentality from other levels of description. To assess its efficacy, the scope of instrumentality permitted by the purportedly equalizing treatment must be known. This is because physical, sensory, and cognitive impairments reduce one's instrumental options. So treating people similarly will not be treating them

---

211. Christine Koppel, *Perspectives on Equality: Constructing a Relational Theory* (Oxford: Rowman & Littlefield, 1998), 168.

equally in cases in which the actions instrumental to pursuing opportunity are so narrowly or rigidly constrained as to exclude people with (certain) impairments.

To illustrate, suppose my dog-sitter places two bowls of dog food, one for my Great Dane and one for my dachshund, on a four-foot-high table. Because the Dane has more options in regard to reach, actions that will be effective in getting the food are available to the Dane but not to the dachshund. So my dog-sitter fails to follow my instruction not to favor one of the dogs, for although she similarly puts out food, she does not equally give each his dinner. That is to say, there is one description of her action—placing the bowls on the table—that is the same for both the dogs, despite their different heights, but another description—giving them their dinners—is not the same for both, as is evident because the Dane has his dinner but the dachshund does not.

Analogously, a program that can be accessed only by climbing stairs does not treat persons in wheelchair and persons who can climb stairs equally precisely because, although the door is similarly open to both groups, entrance is open only to the latter. In the case we have been considering, it is access to the program, not access to the stairs, that must be made the same if formal equality is to be achieved. Furthermore, formal equality requires sameness of opportunity in respect to securing equitably effective instrumentalities. In this regard, securing equitable treatment by enhancing the permissible repertoire of instrumental options emphasizes that formal justice does not depend on people's being the same. Informed as it is by the social model of disability, the ADA levels without homogenizing, as, for example, leveling the entrance to a building so as to make the programs within it accessible does not erase the variations in how guide dog owners, wheelchair users, toddlers, and Olympic sprinters travel through it.

Failure to provide instrumentally effective accommodation illegitimately impinges on the negative freedom of disabled program users and workers. To illustrate, absence of access to public transportation limits impaired people's freedom to be employed, be educated, be refreshed by recreation. The limitation is arbitrary: access to this social necessity is absent only because impaired people happen to be a disregarded minority rather than an influential majority. For were a majority rather than a minority of users disabled, the initial designs of public transportation would have had to accommodate them, or there would have been too few riders.

More generally, the theory that inspires the ADA sets neutralizing the historical inequality of people with disabilities as the benchmark against which to assess whether current practice is just. The ADA is affirmative in that it compensates for errors made in the past by the dominant social group. In this respect, the ADA appeals to a sense of justice similar to that which energizes affirmative action programs for people of color and women. There are, however, important differences. For instance, one argument made for affirmative action programs is that African Americans are owed reparations for having the evils of slavery visited upon them. This thesis draws objections in view of the attenuated link between the ancestral slaves and slaveowners and the nation's current population, both black and white. That is, many who benefit from affirmative action programs, as well as many who feel harmed by them, inevitably will be the progeny of relative newcomers to American society and consequently will be the descendants of neither slaves nor enslavers. So, the objection continues, as so many current members of the creditor and debtor classes bear neither disadvantage nor advantage because of slavery, why should they receive reparations or pay them?

In contrast, past disregard of people with disabilities punishes current as well as earlier members of this class. In virtue of their imagined inferiority, the nation's capital assets, as well as its infrastructure, developed using procedures that excluded and continue to exclude them from the terms that frame, and the processes that further, enjoying a cooperative commercial and civic life. It thus is the strategy of the ADA to remedy the environmental outcomes of disablist oppression by requiring that whoever operates a facility or program must reform arrangements that exclude individuals with disabilities unless doing so would constitute an undue hardship, as measured against the overall financial resources of the facility or program. (To provide for fair distribution of the responsibility to alter exclusionary practices and their products, there is an "undue hardship" exemption to keep the resources that any entity can be required to expend for accessibility in proportion to the entity's total expenditures. But Congress explicitly rejected an amendment that would have capped expenditures for making workplaces accessible to any disabled employee to a specified percentage of her salary. In doing so, Congress took the position that "workers must be paid in accord with gross, not net, output, even when no claim could be made that social output will ultimately increase if they are so entitled."[212])

Historical Counterfactualizing

Recognizing that accessibility would be a commonplace, not a novelty, were the majority, not the minority, of us disabled makes this mandate compelling. Rather than speculating on how the subjective personal responses of unimpaired agents would be transfigured by the onset of physical or mental impairment (i.e., asking nondisabled people what they think they would want if they became impaired), this standard calls for projecting how objective social practice would be transformed were unimpaired functioning so atypical as to be of merely marginal importance for social policy. Sociologist Irving Zola describes experiencing such a transformation when he spent some time in residence at Het Dorp, a Dutch village designed for people with mobility impairments. Zola records the relief he experienced when, for the first time in his life, he found himself in a built environment that welcomed rather than defied bodies like his. Although the majority of residents used wheelchairs, no feature of Het Dorp's adaptive design excluded unimpaired individuals.[213] (This approach to arranging the built environment, now beginning to be taught more widely in U.S. architecture schools, is called universal design.)

Because it projects how living would be different had history been otherwise so that different social practices or arrangements obtain, historical counterfactualizing reflects the consciousness of crucial difference(s). Such historical counterfactualizing facilitates our identifying what features of our artifactual environment have been adopted in the belief that people with physical, sensory, or cognitive impairments have no full claim on social participation. Building stairs rather than ramps, installing Windows rather than DOS, substituting telephones for teletypes all stand out as prohibitive when thought about this way. Historical counterfactualizing thereby invokes our imaginations to help correct the social deprivation that their historical characterization as a weak and incompetent class has visited upon people with disabilities.

---

212. Kelman and Lester, *Jumping the Queue*, 206–7.
213. Irving Zola, *Missing Pieces: A Chronicle of Living with a Disability* (Philadelphia: Temple University Press, 1982), 64, 133.

Historical counterfactualizing helps to assess the formal justice of proposals for equality of treatment by taking into account whether an agent's identity is with a group whose domination, or else whose suppression, has historically shaped our moral associations. It thus brackets the effects of the material influence of power relationships. Furthermore, historical counterfactualizing fosters recognition of how social identities have been formed in the crucible of oppression without miring those same identities in retribution and regret. For counterfactual projection acknowledges difference but frees it of its deleterious meanings. That is because the ADA seeks equal, not exceptionally privileging, treatment to secure protection of its subject class.

Comparing two strategies for addressing the historical exclusion of people with disabilities, one required by the ADA and one untouched by its provisions, further illuminates the contrast between formally equalizing and materially privileging policies. In respect to the first strategy: by requiring bus ramps and lifts (devices different from steps) and teletyping phones (devices different from voice phones), the ADA effects equal access to standard public utilities for taxpayers who happen to be disabled. Adding a lift to a bus or a TTY device to a phone satisfies no individual's special need but, rather, the common needs, shared by disabled and nondisabled alike, for public transportation and communication. Understood in this light, expenditures for retrofitting are seen to be compensatory rather than privileging, for these are responses to the deleterious outcomes of exclusionary past practice rather than to the personal neediness of individuals.

Were a majority rather than a minority of users disabled, the initial designs of public transportation and communication systems would have accommodated them, making unnecessary the extraordinary remodeling expenditures needed to include them later on. Accommodating people with disabilities does not block access for people without disabilities, as the failure to adapt designs does for people with disabilities. Thus, even though accommodations appear to be responsive to individual impairments, making accommodations secures the similar treatment of all people, not any special treatment of special needs.

Compare this strategy, and its rationale, with a second one, not supported by the ADA. Although responsive to the historical exclusion that makes employment available to only a smaller percentage of individuals with disabilities than of any other U.S. minority, the ADA does not mandate the provision of compensatory income for people with disabilities. Is this equitable to a group that historically has been penalized in the workplace? Here counterfactualizing reveals nothing arbitrary or inequitable if society supplies no such care. For there is no reason to think that, were the disabled the majority instead of the minority, they could command compensatory income. Were most people disabled, it would surely be very difficult for the able-bodied minority to care for and sustain so many people with disabilities. Were the nondisabled in the minority, it is less rather than more likely that they could guarantee to provide subsistence for the disabled.

Parenthetically, by assuming that individuals with disabilities can perform the essential functions of many types of jobs, and by declaring that the denial of employment in virtue of disability to otherwise qualified disabled applicants violates their civil rights, the ADA deconstructs the expectation that the disabled do not work. In doing so, the ADA also deconstructs the assignment of people with disabilities as a weak caste or class of incompetents.

Historical counterfactualizing is a formalizing device that universalizes over a minority's differences. It permits us to imagine how the artifactual environment would be shaped were it to be equitably supportive of individuals regardless of whether they are of common kind, very few or singular, whether they are ordinary or anomalous, whether they are normal or impaired. Furthermore, historical counterfactualizing distinguishes between responses to disability that are appropriate regardless of the proportion of impaired to unimpaired individuals—that is, regardless of whether the majority or minority of people consists of unimpaired individuals—and responses that are self-defeating or otherwise unimaginable should the dominant majority become the subordinate minority. It abstracts away and frees our thinking from the conceptual residue of a biased history in which people with impairments have been suppressed. Historical counterfactualizing looks, instead, to a future in which much more will be possible.

Compensatory Justice

Considering, as we have just done, why guaranteeing a disability income neither addresses nor repairs the bias endured by people with disabilities makes clear both how the ADA is compensatory and how it is not so. The

ADA is an instrument of rectificatory justice. As such it removes inequalities resulting from unfairly injurious conduct or practices.

The ADA imposes general duties of rectification, such as the obligation to repair prohibitive programmatic policies and practices and to remodel inaccessible facilities. The positive duties the statute imposes on both commercial and nonprofit entities require them to compensate for their previous disregard of the group of people with physical, sensory, and cognitive impairments. But no further compensatory duty of welfare enhancement is owed to individuals taken singly or singled out for benefit.

The ADA protects individuals from being penalized because their group has been unfairly identified as being incompetent. It thus is incorrect to think of a reasonable accommodation as advantaging the individual for whom it is made. Rather, an accommodation refashions an existing practice or site to eliminate bias against the group of people whom that individual represents. The summative result of making reasonable accommodations will be to remodel disablist behaviors and reform practices shaped by disablist theoretical assumptions.

We may recall here that the U.S. Congress explains the need for the ADA by citing the history of segregation, inequitable treatment, and powerlessness that people with disabilities have endured because they have been stereotyped as incapable of being contributing citizens. For purposes of rectificatory justice, we construct emancipatory collective identities that call out for compensation. Having forebears with a history of being victimized by stereotyping or bias is constitutive of the relevant kind of identity. These predecessors may actually be our ancestors, or they may be virtual or symbolic predecessors as the quarter million individuals with disabilities destroyed by the Nazis are for contemporary American disability activists.

In "The Context of Race," African American legal theorist David B. Wilkins explains further how emancipatory identities are constructed:

[B]lacks cannot forget for one minute that they have a race; a race that links each individual black to the fate of every other black. Whether one takes the casual racism of the cab driver who refuses to pick up a black man on the assumption that he is a criminal, or the sophisticated "statistical discrimination" of employers who judge individual blacks by the mean achievement levels of all blacks, black Americans know that their individual chances for achieving success in America are linked to the advancement of the race as a whole.[214]

---

214. Appiah and Gutmann, *Color Conscious*, 22.

Similarly, people with disabilities cannot forget that they are impaired when they encounter the disablism of the cab driver who refuses to stop for the person in a wheelchair on the assumption that she will need extraordinary assistance or the disablism of the prospective employer who panics about whether he could use a computer if he were blind. Americans with disabilities likewise know that their personal opportunities are linked to advancing the disabled generally. As these examples illustrate, doing so means challenging stereotyping theories that equate disability with being weak or incompetent.

As I argued earlier, we are in no position to know, and hence it is highly speculative to affirm, how little, or for that matter how much, dysfunction would continue to accrue to individuals with disabilities in an environment fully suited to them. Nevertheless, it is fair to consider whether further compensation is due people because of their physical, sensory, or cognitive impairments in the event that reforming the built and social environment does not eliminate the difference between their well-being and that enjoyed by nonimpaired individuals.

Equalizing: Repairing the Results of Difference

The difficult choice facing people with disabilities is not just how to seek their rights but, more fundamentally, which kinds of rights to seek. Claims of people with disabilities to equalized opportunity and to special benefits clash because they leave the public conflicted as to whether to interact with impaired individuals as equals or to focus on their having "special" needs. The discordance of these views about what is involved in extending social justice to people with physical, sensory, and cognitive impairments goes far toward accounting for the cultural ambivalence toward disability highlighted earlier in the discussion.

This conflict in the conceptualization of disability is evident in the difference between current federal mandates that apply to educating people with disabilities. The Individuals with Disabilities Education Act (IDEA), covering public providers of education for grades K through 14, provides that the learning needs of children with disabilities be met, where "needs" are understood to include skills (such as toileting) nondisabled children usually acquire prior to entry into formal schooling, even if providing for such needs means offering special programs or separate settings. On the other hand, the ADA, covering all public and private providers of educational programs, makes no provision for special or personal needs of students with disabilities but requires that reasonable accommodation be made to give them access to whatever education is offered to nondisabled students.

Under the IDEA, sign language interpreters are mandated as a service to those deaf youngsters who cannot otherwise perform adequately in school but are not a right of those whose academic performance is at least average despite their having only the partial access to information that lipreading can achieve. Under the approach to just treatment embedded in the IDEA, these latter need not be compensated because their achievement is "normal" despite their limitations. But under the ADA, sign language interpreters are considered a necessity for all deaf youngsters who can benefit from them, regardless of how well these students perform in the absence of signing. The assumption is that those who perform well without interpreters nevertheless deserve the same opportunity to excel, by having the same full access to information that their hearing peers enjoy.

However, under the IDEA, learning disabled students receive academic coaching if they claim such help as a special need. Under the ADA, regardless of learning disabled students' needs, tutoring is required for them only if there are tutoring programs for all students, in which case learning disabled students conceivably could prevail in claiming that tutoring must be available in a form equitably accessible to them. Because the IDEA does not extend through university level, whereas the ADA covers all educational programs regardless of level, disabled university students who have been accustomed to having their needs met in special programs offered by their schools sometimes lack the self-reliance useful to pursuing equal access to university programs.

Allocating Equality

To model disability rights on civil rights presumes that people with physical, sensory, or cognitive impairments are capable of flourishing without special care just as long as they have meaningful access to social opportunity. Such a model embodies a "centrist" view of the responsibilities of the state, according to Kelman and Lester. That is, the civil rights model is politically liberal but jurisprudentially centrist in that it permits public intervention in private affairs in order to promote people's opportunities to be rewarded commensurate with their talents.[215] However, in that it is intended "to rid the world of the animus, false stereotyping, and perhaps rational statistical discrimination . . . that block members of subordinated groups from receiving 'marginal product' payments," what each person would receive in a perfected impersonal market, modeling disability rights this way is on the whole more mainstream than it is liberal, in Kelman and Lester's terms.[216]

This conception of how to equalize people with disabilities presumes that, if freed from arbitrary barriers, people with disabilities can be competitive. That is, absent a biased cooperative scheme and environment, they will fare as well as the nondisabled in a competitive climate, or, if not as well, at least satisfactorily. But is this realistic? To some it seems a dangerous delusion.

These critics of modeling disability rights on civil rights complain that people with disabilities are too often urged to "overcome" their impairments, and their courage and good character placed in question if they fail. For people who cannot undertake or do not aspire to such a strenuous style of life, equality that is achievable only in virtue of heroic striving appears at best to be vacuous. Equalizing opportunity, it is argued, can do no more than level a field on which only the highest-functioning impaired people can thrive. If left to compete with the nondisabled on a level playing field, they suppose, most seriously impaired people, and particularly those with the most limited physical and/or cognitive capacity, are incapable of advancing.

The civil rights model thus is criticized for favoring people who are capable of functioning competitively as long as the environment supports their alternative or adaptive modes of performing. It is blamed for disregarding people whose impairments make them incapable of competitive functioning even with an accommodating environment. This model is also condemned for promoting individualism—that is, for aiming at personal rather than social good—and for equating social identity with social productivity. That Congress's justification for enacting the ADA references how disabled individuals have been arbitrarily excluded from contributing social roles opens this law to such criticism. "Reaffirming the link between

---

215. Kelman and Lester, *Jumping the Queue*, 206.
216. Kelman and Lester, *Jumping the Queue*, 200.

work and a person's self-worth and . . . value in the community hardly helps," insists British university lecturer R. G. Smith.[217]

Instead, disability studies scholar Paul Abberley has argued, the appropriate understanding of people with disabilities demands "asserting and stressing real differences" at the same time it "combats false and oppressive explanations of the origin and nature" of the "quantitative and qualitative aspects of difference between the lives of disabled and non-disabled people."[218] Abberley urges a system that acknowledges the needs of people with disabilities as being different from "normal" people's.[219] Supposing it to be possible that life with a disability can flourish as expansively as any other life (a prospect not readily admitted by many people), isn't the difference that people with impaired physical, sensory, or cognitive abilities need more support than others to make their lives worth living? And because they are especially vulnerable, do not people with disabilities deserve special entitlements or exemptions—group-differentiated rights that are supposed to compensate for their disadvantageous impairments? Do not their claims for basic support and care take precedence over other people's desires for gratifying or enhancing goods?

For the critics who raise these questions expecting they cannot but be answered affirmatively, equalizing the environment rather than the persons disabled by it is viewed as a retreat from special supportive policies that shelter impaired people. Reforming practice so as to integrate the disabled into the general population is condemned by this line of criticism as being generalized and detached policy making that depersonalizes and is indifferent to them. Rather, the critics insist, equalizing means giving people with disabilities a distributive claim to resources to repair their personal dysfunctioning, and, to the extent repair falters, equalizing means securing for them a level of well-being equivalent to that enjoyed by people without disabilities.

Equalizing Capabilities

Supporters of the view that equalizing must offer more than unrealized opportunity urge that something more than leveling the playing field must

---

217. Private E-mail from university lecturer R. G. Smith, disability-research@-mailbase.ac.uk listserve, 6 January 1998.

218. Paul Abberly, "Disabled People: Normality and Social Work," in *Disability and Dependency*, ed. Len Barton (London: Falmer, 1989): 55–68.

219. Davis, *Enforcing Normalcy*, 64.

be done. Individuals also must be made capable of leaving the starting gate, even if doing so involves an initial unevenness in how goods and services are allocated. For example, allocating resources for such measures as rehabilitative treatment, medication, and orthotic, prosthetic, and other personal assistive devices can improve an impaired person's capabilities so as to raise his level of functioning. Analogously, allocating resources for such measures as housekeeper services, clothing, companionship, and personal income can improve an impaired person's well-being regardless of his level of functioning.

Equalizing capabilities enhances positive freedom by increasing the scope and effectiveness of a person's functionings. Persons with physical, sensory, or cognitive impairments often are, in virtue of their conditions, in deficit for some capabilities (although a wealthy, intelligent, or industrious but impaired person conceivably may be more capable than a poor, dull, or lazy but able-bodied one). Since this is so, impaired people may have greater occasion than others to seek to be restored or rehabilitated through mitigating health care measures.

But do they have a group-specific right to these interventions? And what considerations should decide which measures should be taken, and how much risk to incur, for the possibility of being made more normal? If persons with physical, sensory, and cognitive impairments have a right to restoration because their impairments reduce their capability to function sufficiently well to compete, then whosoever is threatened with an equivalent reduction in capability has an equally strong claim, but to preventative rather than restorative care. This makes health care that secures effective physical, sensory, and cognitive performance a general good but not a special requirement of just treatment for people with disabilities.

For people without disabilities who adopt this view of how importantly the health of citizens weighs for social justice, the existence of incurables will seem to be a failure of justice, the evidence for which can be avoided by eliminating the presence of whoever is disturbingly abnormal. However, for individuals with impairments something troubling attaches to promoting such a broad social affirmation for the provision of health care, or at least to affirming such a broad social interest in maintaining a "normal" population. Justice for people with physical, sensory, or cognitive impairments should not be couched in expectations that they be cured. How can laying claim to the right to be altered so as not to be an impaired individual be central to any person's self-respecting self-identity as an individual with a disability?

The concern is warranted if the rationale for distributing health care resources is to escape the company of the disabled by normalizing them. Historically, social welfare health care schemes like this have been accompanied by efforts to reduce the numbers of high-end consumers. Such schemes invite rationing (such as that proposed in Oregon) to avoid "wasting" costly procedures on already "damaged" individuals, sterilization and prenatal testing to preclude the procreation of more such individuals, and worse. So, for the irreparably impaired, it is difficult to see why the distributive right to procedures for being restored to normal is a more effective route to equality than is the civil right to command respect and inclusion regardless of whether other people think that one is normal.

In sum, promoting the equitable distribution of normal capabilities does not also argue for recognizing the disabled minority's right to social participation. Rather, the distributive model celebrates homogenizing, with the consequence for those whose differences cannot be overcome being isolation and a solitary lifestyle. For both those who are impaired and those not yet so, this approach to equality promotes the right to be free of impairment and, by implication, of the impaired minority. Thus, eliding equalizing with homogenizing authorizes the very motivation that we earlier found to have spawned the current, seriously flawed disability system. That is, the perspective from which equalizing is normalizing is discordant with the analysis of equality on which people with disabilities are owed social inclusion through full recognition of, rather than despite, their impairments.

Distributive Justice

There is all the difference in the world between conceiving of people with disabilities as equal and thereby as deserving only such differentiated treatment as is needed to reform social practice that excludes them and thinking of them as deficient and thereby as deserving of special benefits, entitlements, and exemptions to sustain them in their exclusion from the mainstream of commercial and civic life. Policies that promote the former view controvert the beliefs about people with disabilities that motivate the latter view. Policies informed by the latter view enfeeble the purpose needed to implement the former view.

Because disability discrimination is the misperception that being limited in performing major life activities means being incompetent to produce and contribute, the ADA emphasizes the justice of removing barriers to the display of competence. In contrast, entitlements, benefits, and other compensatory allocations distributed to individuals deemed eligible because they are disabled are aimed at equalizing the well-being of people considered too incompetent to fend for or support themselves.[220] This observation brings us back to the question of whether justice is advanced by distributing personal services of the kinds supposed to equalize disabled people. The thrust of our discussion is to conclude that it does not.

Congruent with the theory that informs the ADA, I have construed our democratic obligation to equalize people with disabilities as meant to secure rectificatory justice. Nozick argues that rectification need not be (re)-distributive: it is a " 'process' principle rather than an 'end-state' principle; it regulates the ongoing transactions of individuals, but does not attempt to adjust the outcome of those transactions so as to bring it into line with some ultimate ideally 'fair' end-state."[221] At the very least, justice is not served by reallocating resources to give beneficiaries advantages over those from whom the resources come. So, to preserve justice, distributive schemes must indemnify the contributors of the resources they redistribute against the elision of compensatory with privileging allocations by ensuring that the scheme's beneficiaries remain inferior. Doing so typically invites the introduction of mechanisms to penalize beneficiaries, often to such an extent that to operate the distributive program is to defeat its purpose.

A further price exacted by distributing special services is the inducing of nonproductive competition among those who wish to become service providers and also among those who want to receive services. An often cited case is the Dutch welfare system that distributed what have been described as "lavish" benefits to people designated as disabled. The Dutch "disease," as it has been named in social policy literature, instances a difficult problem for distributive justice— namely, the tendency of welfare systems to commodify impairment. In a policy paper entitled "A Cautionary

---

220. Anita Silvers, "Disability Rights," in *The Encyclopedia of Applied Ethics*, ed. Ruth Chadwick (San Diego: Academic Press, 1997).

221. John Cottingham, "Rectificatory Justice" in *Encyclopedia of Ethics*, ed. Lawrence Becker and Charlotte Becker (New York: Garland, 1992), 662.

Tale of European Disability Policies: Lessons for the United States," Leo
Aarts, Richard Burkhauser, and Philip DeJong explain:

> Public policy in the Netherlands . . . allowed everybody to be comfortable in
> the face of illness. . . . It was comfortable for the worker who received the
> benefit, comfortable for the employer who no longer had to take responsibil-
> ity for accommodating the worker, comfortable for the worker's union who
> saw this as a way of not only protecting a fellow worker but also perhaps
> opening a new position for an unemployed union member, and even com-
> fortable for the government if it meant the official unemployment rate was
> lower.[222]

To induce such comfort, the Dutch system offered generous nursing and
attendant care for the disabled. According to DeJong, "market employment for workers with disabilities became virtually inaccessible."[223] Repre-
sentatives of business and labor collaborated in managing disability programs so as to shift support of workers regarded as problematic to public
funds. Eventually, so large a number of individuals had been so characterized as to create significant unemployment, disguised as a humane effort
to relieve aging and disabled people from having to labor in order to live.

By 1984, almost one million Dutch people had established themselves
as sufficiently impaired or ill to receive benefits. But only four times that
number constituted the labor force from whom these resources allocated
for benefits payments were drawn.[224] Individuals hoping to command the
income offered to caregivers worked to expand the market of care receivers, the strategy we earlier saw was adopted by institutions for the "feeble-
minded," which transformed their mission from training to custodial care
and thereby created a larger clientele. Individuals striving to acquire the
assistance offered to care receivers collaborated in this effort by trying to
broaden the boundaries of eligibility for benefits. With this and many simi-

---

222. Leo Aarts, Richard Burkhauser, and Philip DeJong, "Policy Studies Paper
No. 6," Syracuse: The Maxwell School of Citizenship and Public Affairs: Syracuse
University (1992): 5.

223. Philip DeJong, "U.S. Disability from a European Perspective," in *Disability: Challenges for Social Insurance, Health Care Financing, & Labor Market Policy*, ed. Virginia Reno, Jerry Mashow, et al. (Washington, D.C.: National Academy
of Social Insurance, 1997), 31.

224. Wolf Wolfensberger, "Human Services Policies: The Rhetoric vs. the Reality" in *Disability and Dependency*, ed. Len Barton (London: Falmer, 1989), 37.

lar examples of self-defeating social welfare programs in view, it is hard to see how defining the disabled as those who have special needs can have merit when the most familiar outcome of such a program is to make serving their needs so profitable for nondisabled people.

The project of guaranteeing every citizen against undeserved poverty, with the twin goals of security and productivity for all, emerged from a wartime proposal drafted by Winston Churchill and Franklin Roosevelt in 1941 to depict how, as the aftermath of a democratic victory, society could be remade afresh to protect against the cataclysmic economic insecurity that had preceded the war.[225] Although this worthy project was assimilated into postwar recovery policy on both sides of the Atlantic, the strategies for pursuing it differed both in assumptions and emphasis. Most Western European cultures assumed a public responsibility to ensure all citizens access to an adequate level of resources, but, by identifying disability with extraordinary neediness, and thereby designating it as justifying exceptional allocations, these programs invited the disabling results described previously.

In contrast, the United States has lodged the responsibility for achieving the projected goals in a dynamic of commercial and public interests. (Re)-distributive benefits programming disrupts this dynamic when it exaggerates the neediness of people with disabilities. By characterizing them as a class of incompetents and commodifying their (imagined) personal deficits, I have argued, distributive programs facilitate their exclusion from commonly proffered social opportunity. With its focus on repairing individuals rather than on reforming biased practice, distributive justice thus cannot do justice to the challenge posed by disability.

Conclusion

Throughout this essay, I have invoked the voices and the history of people with disabilities to urge that their being recognized as social persons in a full and meaningful sense should take priority over other issues more copiously addressed in the philosophical literature that touches on disability. How can they acquire this status if the means for achieving it presumes their spectacular neediness? Well-intentioned and charitable people have

---

225. Aarts, Burkhauser, and DeJong, "U.S. Disability," 32.

an almost visceral protective response upon perceiving neediness. In communities that esteem civility, compassion, and generosity, such a response to perceived weakness is sustained, systematized, conventionalized, and embedded in the culture through a network of supportive practices.

Doubly protective tendencies drive such practices. That is, practitioners of generosity care for the weak and also shield them from being burdened by demands for reimbursement. Integral to these practices is the conviction that needy individuals deserve protection but, in virtue of their neediness, cannot be expected to respond reciprocally.

Thus, to be consigned to the class of the needy is to be resisted rather than recruited for inclusion in productive partnerships. It is to be excused from those collaborative practices in which a participant's welcome depends on how thoroughly other participants can rely on her for protection and sustenance—that is, those practices in which participants relieve each others' neediness. Distributive schemes that cast people with disabilities as supported by others rather than as supporting others thereby diminish their opportunities by denying them the identities they need to initiate mutual or reciprocal relationships.

To enlarge the artificially depressed social opportunities available for people with physical, sensory, and cognitive impairments, we must reconfigure the circumstances that depress their opportunities. To do so, we must reform practice, which is biased against them. As we have seen, the signature of biased practice lies in appeal to false theories positing their incompetence and, thereby, excusing their exclusion. Exclusionary practice lays down a self-enforcing circle: biased practice creates conditions hostile to the manifestation of competence by people whose bodies or intellects differ from the commonplace, while simultaneously adducing the resulting absence of signs of their competence in its own defense. To shatter this cruel circle we must reshape biased practice, eliminating schemes and systems that presume people with disabilities to be categorically weak or dependent.

Several years ago, in separate articles and without reference to each others' work, Ron Amundson, Gregory Kavka, and Susan Wendell, all philosophers with disabilities, remarked with dismay that contemporary philosophy alludes to disability primarily in discussions of whether to kill, or to let die, fetuses, neonates, or elderly individuals with disabling conditions.[226]

---

226. Susan Wendell, "Toward a Feminist Theory of Disability," *Hypatia: A*

Philosophy thus has been inclined to ignore the majority of people who have disabilities. Do their claims to be recognized compel us to revise our philosophical expectations about the levels of physical, sensory, and cognitive performance we take to be crucial for exercising moral responsibility and participating in civic life?

To illustrate, suppose we are committed to a dialogical account of moral activity and the good life. Do we then insist that whoever cannot communicate with others in the normal way cannot flourish? To reform biased expectations, we will have to reconceive dialogical practice so creatively as to engage, on an equal footing, many individuals now excluded because they do not speak, or hear, or cognize as the majority does. It is complexly constructive and imaginative transformative thinking such as this, I have argued, that justice for people with disabilities calls for in a liberal democracy.

Historically, mistaken theories about the intrinsic badness of being impaired have shaped social practice so as to exclude individuals whose differences are interpreted as weaknesses or loss. This being so, philosophical accounts that assume rather than critically assess and constructively reform such flawed views about the competence of people with disabilities subvert justice. Moral intuition inclines us to expend larger than usual resource allocations on people with severe impairments so as, for example, to offer an individual who cannot walk the mobility provided by a wheelchair. Political morality should recognize that the democratic value secured thereby lies not in relieving disabled people's neediness but instead in liberating their talent and thereby eliciting their contributions through full and meaningful citizenship.

It will be argued, against this view, that physical, sensory, and cognitive impairment can be so global as to make implausible the prospect of achieving meaningful social participation for the impaired individual. I grant that this is sometimes true, although for how many impaired individuals it is true is an empirical study that cannot be reliably undertaken in a climate shaped by biased practices. To illustrate this last caution, we should recall that many people we now take to be dysfunctional because they have intellectual disabilities would have found productive roles in the era prior to

Journal of Feminist Philosophy 4, no. 2 (Summer 1996): 104–24; Gregory Kavka "Disability and the Right to Work," *Social Philosophy & Policy* 9, no. 1 (1992); and Amundson, "Disability, Handicap."

institutionalization, but from the time when our current disability system took hold, they have been rendered nonproductive to better suit them to be the means for nondisabled people's productivity.

Nothing I have argued here precludes supporting a distributive scheme to benefit profoundly impaired people. But we should understand that such allocative schemes neither do justice to people with disabilities generally nor equalize them. Instead, they are based on the proposal that there are (a few) individuals for whom no possibility of surviving except in extended dependency exists and who therefore will never be equal. Recognizing this to be the case about such schemes draws to our notice that they collectively defray obligations owed not to the disabled recipients of the benefits but to those who otherwise would be called upon to expend their personal resources disproportionately to support individuals who are in extended dependency.

Programs that assume the extraordinary costs of caring for profoundly impaired people in extended dependency respond directly to those citizens who otherwise would have to shoulder alone the responsibility for this care. Within this context, resource allocation supports (and sometimes offers income to) people who accept the role of what Eva Kittay calls a "dependency worker" (personal attendants and other helpers).[227] Distributing resources for caregiving though the mediation of dependency workers mitigates the inequality of the burdens caregivers otherwise would be called on to assume alone. Such distributive schemes consequently address the caregiver's situation and promote their opportunity to secure their contributing citizenship and their expression of talent, but the schemes do not further the equality of their dependents.

So distributive justice schemes equalize nondisabled rather than disabled people by transforming their personal responsibilities for giving care into collective obligations. Indeed, the history of positive social response to physical, sensory, and cognitive impairment has been focused mainly on developing social service systems meant to avert disadvantage that would otherwise be borne by prospective caregivers rather than to allay disadvantage that accrues to people with disabilities. Mistaking who is treated justly

---

227. Eva Kittay, "Not My Way, Sesha, Your Way, Slowly: Maternal Thinking in the Raising of a Child with Profound Intellectual Disabilities," in *Mothering in the US Today*, ed. Julia Hanisberg and Sara Ruddick (New York: Beacon, 1998). This essay also appears in Eva F. Kittay's *Love's Labor: Essays on Women, Equality, and Dependence*. New York: Routledge, 1998.

for who is served by distributive schemes distracts us from the importance of devising formally just practices. The result, as we have seen, has been the needlessly debilitating proliferation of neediness.

Listening to the voices of people with disabilities in their own words quoted throughout this essay, we cannot help but have observed that, foremost, they desire a public sphere that embraces their presence. For them, equality means taking their places as competent contributors to well-ordered cooperative social and cultural transactions. For them, justice must offer, first, the visibility of full participatory citizenship, not a spotlight that targets them as needing more than others do.

2

Distributive Justice

David Wasserman

Introduction

Our society currently makes several sorts of provisions for people with disabilities, with different, possibly inconsistent rationales. It provides treatment to confer or restore normal functioning, as part of the free medical care available to all indigent and elderly citizens. It makes monthly cash payments to indigent and formerly employed citizens found to be permanently disabled, the former at a flat rate, the latter at a rate based on their previous earnings. It mandates a "free appropriate education" for children with cognitive disabilities in the "least restrictive environment," regardless of cost. And it requires employment, public accommodations, and transit systems to be accessible to people with disabilities; it treats the failure to provide equal opportunity or access as illegal discrimination, unless it is exempted by risk or hardship.

One overarching distinction cuts across this patchwork of legislative entitlements and civil rights. Some provisions are restorative or compensatory: they seek to return the individual to some benchmark of functioning or well-being or to compensate him for the failure to achieve that level. The benchmark varies: the status quo before an injury or disease, some social minimum, or the average in the society. The form of compensation also varies: in some cases, it is medical treatment designed to restore normal functioning; in some cases, rehabilitative training to compensate for normal functioning; in some cases, cash. But in each case, the individual receives goods or services greater than or different from those received by other people, on account of his disability.

147

In contrast, some provisions are proscriptive. They aim to prevent discrimination against people with disabilities, to prohibit others from denying them the same opportunities or services that others receive, from transit to education. The distinction may not be as clear-cut as it first appears: equal opportunity or access for people with disabilities often requires structural changes to accommodate them; the education appropriate to children with cognitive disabilities may differ in significant respects from that appropriate to children with normal cognitive functioning. But although both types of provision aim at equality and mandate similar modifications to achieve it, the compensatory and antidiscrimination rationales differ in one fundamental respect: the latter seeks to eliminate an independently identifiable wrong.

It is sometimes claimed that these two rationales are not only different but inconsistent. In treating people with disabilities as requiring special assistance, the first rationale, it is argued, treats them as defective and thereby justifies or underwrites the very discrimination that the second rationale seeks to eliminate. This argument is often made with respect to provisions designed to "normalize" people with disabilities: to make them function as much as possible like people with the standard complement of sensory, motor, and cognitive functions. But it can also be raised against measures designed to compensate people for failing to achieve normal functioning, rather than to restore such functioning. And it can be raised even more broadly against measures designed to raise people with disabilities to any benchmark of functioning or well-being that they are assumed to fall short of as a result of their impairments.

In this essay, I argue that the claimed inconsistency can be avoided. The compensatory rationale need not demean people with disabilities if it is understood as part a general account of justice in the design of society and the provision of services, rather than as a special allowance for people with impaired functions. But if the compensatory rationale requires a broader account of distributive justice, so does the antidiscrimination rationale. Far from being freestanding, the notion of structural discrimination that informs it can only be understood with reference to the structural arrangements that would be found in a just society.

The recognition that disability involves a mismatch between an individual and her environment suggests that justice cannot be complete if it is distributive in a narrow sense; that because the physical and social organization of society is responsible for much of the disadvantage experienced by people with disabilities, its modification is as much a matter of justice as the distribution of income. For this reason, a just society cannot limit its response to disability to medical treatment and financial subsidy.

But recognizing the social contribution to, or construction of, disability does not simplify the prescription for its redress. Even if we adopt a strong presumption for environmental modification over medical intervention, we must still decide how people with varying abilities are to be fairly accommodated, and we must still adjudicate conflicts among the structural and organizational arrangements that best suit different groups of people. We cannot avoid these issues even if we hold that the core injustice to people with disabilities is their deliberate exclusion, or their lack of power and participation, unless we want to take a purely procedural approach and accept as just whatever accommodations would result from a shift in power or a broadening of participation.

At the same time, justice for people with disabilities cannot be understood as a matter of compensating them for their natural disadvantages. There is no principled basis for distinguishing social from natural sources of inequality or for apportioning disadvantage between natural and social causes. For purposes of justice, the disadvantages associated with disabilities are no different from those arising from fluctuation in the economy, changes in technology, or shifts in the climate. This does not mean that principled limits cannot be set on the extent of redistribution or reconstruction but rather that those limits must be based on a difficult balancing of political values.

Disabilities and the Just Distribution of Resources

In the contemporary philosophical literature, disabilities usually come in to challenge the adequacy of a proposed "currency" of well-being for distributive justice. Thus, consider the scheme of resource equality developed by Ronald Dworkin, in which each member of a society begins with an equal share of its external resources.[1] To simplify matters, assume that the notion of external resources is clear, and ignore the issue of how those resources get produced. Giving everyone equal shares of those resources—

---

1. Ronald Dworkin, "What Is Equality? Part 2: Equality of Resources," *Philosophy and Public Affairs* 10, no. 4 (1981): 283–345, 285ff.

defined in economic terms as bundles of resources divided up so that no one envied anyone else's—would obviously leave some people much better off than others, in some intuitive sense of "better off." Some people, healthy and happy, would be satisfied with their initial share even before they mixed their labor with it to enhance its value. Others would be dissatisfied because their demanding tastes could not be satisfied by their initial allotment or, *ex hypothesi*, by anyone else's. Still others would be unable to keep themselves comfortable, active, or even alive on their initial share. Among this last group would be some people we classify as having serious diseases or disabilities.

Many philosophers would contend that this last group had not been treated fairly under an equal-resource scheme and would reject any notion of equality that was satisfied by that scheme. To rely exclusively on external resources to assess well-being, ignoring their variable impact and utilization, would be to display "commodities fetishism."[2] But how can we take account of the disparate impact of external resources on well-being? Consider two alternatives: (1) we could include "internal resources"—physical and mental endowments—among the resources to which people had an equal claim; (2) we could take the proper subject of distributive justice to be people's welfare—their happiness or well-being. Both of these, however, seem at least as unsatisfactory as an external resource standard.

The equal distribution of internal resources would require either the actual redistribution of those resources to achieve equality or their figurative redistribution in an arrangement that would give everyone an equal share in everyone else's bodies and talents. While the latter, unlike the former, would not require surgical incursions, it would require those with valued abilities to pay dearly for their own leisure time, creating a "slavery of the talented."[3]

A welfare metric would demand enormous sacrifices from some for slight gains to others—not only to those with impairments but to those with extravagant tastes—a "social hijacking" that has led most contemporary philosophers to reject welfare as an appropriate metric of political justice.[4] If a welfare standard demands too much for some, it demands too

---

2. The phrase, taken from Marx, is used by Amartya Sen, *Resources, Values, and Development* (Cambridge: Harvard University Press, 1984).

3. Dworkin, "What Is Equality," 311–12.

4. See, for example, G. A. Cohen, "On the Currency of Egalitarian Justice," *Ethics* 99 (July 1989): 906–44; Norman Daniels, "Equality of What: Welfare, Re-

little for others. It requires no special provision for people whose severe diseases and disabilities are offset by euphoric dispositions or modest expectations, and it would be satisfied by giving cheap drugs or therapy to people with severe diseases and disabilities to improve their dispositions or lower their expectations.

One way of preserving the primacy of welfare in the assessment of well-being while reducing the risk of social hijacking is to require only equality in the *opportunity* for welfare and to treat disabilities as limiting that opportunity. Thus, Richard Arneson argues that equality of the appropriate sort obtains when each member of political community "face[s] an array of options that is equivalent to every other person's in terms of the prospects for preference-satisfaction it offers"[5]—when each member of the community has an equal opportunity for welfare, understood as preference satisfaction. An obvious problem in applying this standard of equal opportunity for welfare to disabilities is that people with impairments, particularly congenital ones, may form preferences so closely tailored to their conditions that their opportunity for welfare is extremely high. To avoid the problem of "small mercies"—the easy fulfillment of depressed expectations[6]—it seems necessary to refer to some set of hypothetical or standard preferences, and that recourse may undermine the understanding of welfare as subjective preference satisfaction. But though welfare may have serious drawbacks as the underlying metric of well-being, the attempt to understand disability in terms of limited opportunity has a much broader appeal.

Liberal philosophers have been understandably anxious to avoid the trilemma of commodities fetishism, the slavery of the talented, and social hijacking. If people with impaired functions are seen as lacking some prerequisite for the adequate utilization of a wide range of goods, for a wide range of ends, then perhaps measures to restore or compensate them for what they lack can alleviate their disadvantages without imposing onerous burdens on others or violating neutrality among different ends. This way

---

sources, or Capabilities?" *Philosophy and Phenomenological Research* 50 (Fall 1990) suppl.

5. Richard J. Arneson, "Equality and Equal Opportunity for Welfare," *Philosophical Studies* 56 (1989): 85.

6. David Crocker, "Functioning and Capability: The Foundations of Sen's and Nussbaum's Development Ethic, Part 1," *Political Theory* 20, no. 4 (1992): 601–2.

of looking at impairments has shaped several very different attempts by recent political philosophers to take account of disabilities.

Some have preserved a resource metric but made special provision for those whose physical or mental endowment limits their capacity to utilize or benefit from external resources. Two types of provisions have been proposed: medical and therapeutic services designed to increase the capacity of people with greater needs to benefit from external resources, and increases in the external resources allotted to those people, to compensate for their greater difficulties in using those resources. Other philosophers, however, including Amartya Sen, have argued that the disadvantage of people with disabilities must be taken account of through a different measure of well-being, more sensitive than a resource metric to individual differences in function. In my essay, I begin with resource-based approaches, reserving Sen's capabilities approach for a later section, in which I consider whether liberal theories of justice and disability can meet some of the more trenchant objections raised by their critics.

Disability in a Rawlsian Framework

Given the apparent centrality of normal sensory and motor functioning to the pursuit of a wide range of human ends, and the difficulties in treating those functions as resources subject to distribution, several writers have suggested that they should be seen in terms of equal opportunity, which in the Rawlsian framework has priority over the distribution of (other) primary social goods.[7] Two proposals that embody this general approach are Norman Daniels's account of "normal species functioning" as necessary for fair equality of opportunity and Thomas Pogge's proposal for roughly equal "health protection."

Fair Equality of Opportunity

Norman Daniels argues for the priority of health care, including corrective measures for impairments, as a means of achieving fair equality of

---

7. The parentheses around *other* reflect the fact that Rawls includes opportunities in his list of primary social goods, goods that people are presumed to want whatever else they want. Their distribution is governed by the difference principle, permitting inequalities only when they benefit the least advantaged people. But Rawls also holds that fair equality of opportunity is categorically more important than the distribution of primary goods in conformity to that principle (Rawls, *A Theory of Justice* [Cambridge: Harvard University Press, 1971]: 299–303).

opportunity. A society cannot hope to eliminate all natural differences among people that may affect their well-being, but health care needs have priority because of "their unequal distribution and great strategic importance."[8] Daniels understands the goal of health care to be the restoration or maintenance of normal functioning; he argues that "we have special claims on others only when our functioning falls short of the normal range."[9] Deficits in skills and talents do not give rise to such special claims, whatever disadvantages they confer, if they involve no departure from normal functioning.

Daniels takes his notion of functioning within the normal range from the biological account of health and disease proposed by Christopher Boorse. For Boorse, (physiological) functions are to be understood as contributions to the individual organism's survival and fitness—the function of the heart is to pump blood, not, say, to make thumping sounds.[10] Normal functioning is defined relative to the species; it occurs when "each internal part [performs] all of its statistically typically functions with at least statistically typical efficiency." Abnormal functioning "occurs when some function's efficiency falls more than a certain distance below the population mean."[11]

Although Daniels does not define "skills and talents," he apparently intends them to be understood in an ordinary sense, in which they bear a highly variable relationship to normal functioning. Certain skills and talents are defined in terms of anatomical form and physiological function: skill in running or jumping requires certain kinds of leg movements, so that someone without legs cannot be skilled in running or jumping (unless he is equipped with artificial limbs), however proficiently he can move around or up by other means.[12] Other skills and talents, perhaps the vast

---

8. Norman Daniels, "Justice and Health Care," in *Health Care Ethics: An Introduction*, ed. Donald Van DeVeer and Tom Regan (Philadelphia: Temple University Press, 1987), 311–13.

9. Daniels, "Equality of What?" 283.

10. Christopher Boorse, "Health as a Theoretical Concept," *Philosophy of Science* 44, no. 4 (1977): 556.

11. Boorse, "Health as a Theoretical Concept," 558–59.

12. Is this also true of playing the violin or piano? One can certainly display virtuosity on the piano with only one hand, but perhaps not without hands (natural or artificial). Someone who could play tunes with his feet might display a kind of virtuosity, but unless he could play with a finesse that seems anatomically impossible, we would hesitate to call him a talented pianist. And matters are even more

majority, have a more contingent relationship to specific physiological functions: they are defined in such a way that they can be performed with various combinations of functions, though some combinations may be more conventional, and in some environments, more efficient. Clearly, the impact of abnormal functioning on skill and talent will vary with both the specific abnormality and the social delineation of skills and talents: some abnormalities may affect few if any talents in most societies; some may have a comprehensive impact. But why should abnormal functioning in general give us "special claims on others"?

Daniels first rejects the suggestion that abnormal or impaired functions have only contingent urgency, because they tend to reduce happiness. Rather, impairments of normal species functioning are of special concern because they "reduce the range of opportunity open to the individual in which he may construct his 'plan of life' or conception of the good life"[13] and thereby deny people with impairments fair equality of opportunity. While deficits in talent and skill obviously affect the opportunity range as well, they do not deny fair equality of opportunity, since equality only requires that opportunity "be equal for persons of similar skills and talents."[14] By definition, then, impairments deny equality of opportunity while deficits in talents and skill do not.

There is no formal reason that opportunity should not be assessed relative to functioning rather than skills and talents: we could *define* equality of opportunity to require that opportunities be equal for persons with similar levels of physiological (or mental) functioning. Daniels's inclusion of skills and talents, but not levels of functioning, as part of the opportunity baseline needs to be justified; otherwise, it begs the question of why the normalization of functioning should be required for fair equality of opportunity when the equalization of skills and talents is not.

Intuitively, it is not obvious that those with impairments are denied fair equality of opportunity by the failure to restore them to normal functioning any more than are those with mediocre talents by the failure to improve their level of performance. Daniels observes that "[l]ife plans for which we are otherwise suited are rendered unreasonable by impairments

uncertain with cognitive skills, in which the meaning of normal functioning, and the relationship of function to talent, are much less clear.
13. Daniels, "Equality of What?" 280.
14. Daniels, "Equality of What?" 281.

of normal functioning."[15] But life plans for which we are otherwise suited are also rendered unreasonable by deficits in talent. Consider the legions of would-be musicians and actors with the temperament and commitment for artistic careers, whose life plans are shattered simply because they lack the talent to make it in a highly competitive market.

The lack of any categorical difference between the opportunities available to the impaired and untalented is even more striking when we consider the whole array of functions, skills, and talents a person has. A single impairment denies fair equality of opportunity, in Daniels's sense, while a full set of talents barely within the normal does not. Daniels's fair equality of opportunity thus has little to do with the actual range of opportunity that people enjoy. Even without medical intervention, a genius with a sensory or motor impairment may have a far greater range of opportunity than an able-bodied mediocrity.

If there is intuitive appeal in Daniels's claim that fair equality of opportunity is denied by impairments in functioning but not by deficits in talent, it may arise from his implicit contrast of *acquired* impairments with *congenital* deficits. Daniels mentions only "deformities and disabilities that result from trauma" in discussing impairments of normal biological functioning, "as when, say, a ballerina is paralyzed or a mechanic loses a hand."[16] An acquired impairment denies opportunities that were actually available to a person; those opportunities are especially salient, and their denial especially wrenching. The failure to develop or maintain talents will typically have a less visible, if no less substantial, effect on a person's opportunity range. But this difference should not matter to Daniels, since he wishes to abstract from "the perspective of an individual who has a particular plan of life and has developed certain skills accordingly."[17] If we eliminate the confounding sense of loss, we can more clearly see the arbitrariness of treating fair equality of opportunity as relative to talent but not to functioning.

---

15. Daniels, "Justice and Health Care," 301.

16. Daniels, "Justice and Health Care," 301, 302.

17. Daniels, "Equality of What?" 282. It may be that Daniels, like Dworkin, assumes that people's ambitions are inextricably bound up with their talents but not their functions or abilities, so that deficits in talent cannot cause the kind of frustration often produced by impaired functions. But, as I argue against Dworkin, this assumption is unsupported and implausible, once we distinguish acquired from congenital deficits.

In explaining the priority he accords to the restoration of normal functioning, Daniels draws an analogy between the opportunities lost to disease and impairment and the opportunities lost to "racism and sexism."[18] In the latter case, however, the opportunities are lost as the result of an independent injustice—the racially or sexually discriminatory allocation of resources. The limitation of opportunity due to disease and impairment may involve a "natural injustice," but if so, that injustice is also found in the unequal distribution of skills and talents. There is a narrower analogy to racism and sexism, discussed later, which claims a similar discrimination against people with disabilities in the physical design and social organization of society. But that analogy, as we will see, favors the reconstruction of society, not the restoration of normal functioning; it treats the alleviation of disability as primarily a problem of social engineering, not health care.

A final argument for including talent but not functioning in the opportunity baseline is suggested by Daniels's observation that in Rawls's scheme, "unequal chances for success resulting from unequal talents may be compensated for in other ways, by the constraints on inequality imposed by the Difference Principle."[19] But there is no reason to suppose that the unequal chances for success resulting from impairments of normal species functioning would *not* be compensated, since those with severe disabilities and diseases would be at least as likely as those with deficient skills and talents to be among the worst off in primary goods, the Rawlsian currency of comparative advantage. Admittedly, the compensation afforded to people with disabilities by the Difference Principle may be inadequate or inappropriate. But Daniels offers no reason to think that the compensation would be more adequate or appropriate for the untalented than the impaired.

Daniels recognizes that the priority he accords to normal functioning will sometimes yield results that appear morally arbitrary. For example, in the case of two extremely short children, one with hormone deficiency, the other with short parents, only the first will be entitled to human growth hormone, even though both will be limited in the same ways by their short stature.[20] Daniels defends his notion of fair equality of opportunity by ar-

---

18. Daniels, "Equality of What?" 281, n. 23.
19. Daniels, "Equality of What?" 281.
20. Norman Daniels, "The Distribution of Scarce Medical Resources," in *The Human Genome Project and the Future of Health Care*, ed. Thomas Murray, Mark

guing that, despite the occasional anomalies it may yield, it is faithful to the standard conception of equal opportunity in our society, which is relativized to skill and talent. Many critics, however, would contend that that conception is confused or unstable.[21]

Daniels also argues that his distinction between abnormal functioning and lack of talent captures and helps maintain the strong social consensus on the importance of health care; he worries that eliminating or blurring the distinction, by adopting a more expansive standard for compensation, would undermine that consensus.[22] But his own approach poses a similar threat, because of the rigid priority that the Rawlsian framework accords to the fair equality of opportunity that disease and impairment deny. As several critics have observed, Daniels would appear to prohibit a society from devoting *any* resources to reducing wealth or income disparities, however great, until it had done everything possible to restore normal functioning to those who lacked it. Indeed, much of the current public dissatisfaction with health care spending arises from the perception, however accurate, that technology-intensive measures to restore functioning are given priority over other, more important social goals.[23]

The political consequences of the dichotomy Daniels imposes can also be seen in the current controversy over the proliferation of diagnosed

---

Rothstein, and Robert Murray (Bloomington: Indiana University Press, 1996), 191–93.

21. See, for example, Christopher Jencks, "Whom Must We Treat Equally for Educational Opportunity to Be Equal?" *Ethics* 98 (1988): 519–20.

22. Daniels, "The Distribution of Scarce Medical Resources," 191–93.

23. Moreover, there is a more cynical explanation for the consensus Daniels invokes about the importance of treating disease and disability. Mark Kelman and Gillian Lester argue that "it is surely the case that conservative support for programs that benefit the disabled, rather than to other needy constituencies, has been high over the last two decades; federal legislative support for the disabled intensified during an era of pronounced welfare state entrenchment." They suggest that people, particularly children, with disabilities are now regarded as the quintessentially "deserving" poor; "the unfortunate, utterly blameless blind man contrasting with the undeserving, parasitic, never-married 'welfare mother.' " *Jumping the Queue: An Inquiry into the Legal Treatment of Students with Learning Disabilities.* [Cambridge: Harvard University Press, 1997]: 201–2. Daniels, as a good Rawlsian, would no doubt deplore the retrenchment of welfare programs and the denigration of the majority of recipients. My only point is that he should be a little more wary of the consensus he marshals for the importance of treating disease and disability.

learning disabilities, driven less, critics claim, by changes in the incidence of such impairments than by the advantages that accrue from their diagnosis under the Individuals with Disabilities Education Act (IDEA): special services and the waiver or relaxation of academic requirements. A student who has little talent for math gets lower grades; a student with "dyscalculia" gets tutoring, extra time for exams, or a waiver of math proficiency requirements. While educational conservatives rail at the privileged treatment received by those diagnosed with learning disabilities, the real problem is the priority accorded to children with diagnosed disabilities over those with limited talent. Much of the accommodation students receive as a result of a diagnosis of disability should not require one; perhaps more flexible exam times and course requirements should be more broadly available; perhaps our school systems should oriented less toward performing a screening function for employers and more toward providing an "appropriate education" for *all* children, not just disabled ones. Daniels's notion of fair equality of opportunity may demand too much for too few, obscuring the broader problems of social justice in what has increasingly become a "winner take all" society.

Equal Health Protection

Thomas Pogge argues that the priority Daniels accords to the restoration of normal functioning is based on a misinterpretation of the Rawlsian imperative to nullify the accidents of natural endowment. According to Pogge, Rawls rejects a stronger interpretation of that imperative, which would require a society to *compensate for* natural inequalities by providing greater opportunities and resources for those with poorer natural endowments. Instead, Rawls adopts a weaker interpretation, which merely requires a society to *mitigate* natural inequalities by ensuring that the scheme of social cooperation does not compound or aggravate them.[24]

---

24. Thomas W. Pogge, *Realizing Rawls* (Ithaca: Cornell University Press, 1989), 177. This distinction, between full and semiconsequentialist conceptions of justice, bears some resemblance to the distinction Christopher Jencks draws between strong and weak humane justice ("Whom Must We Treat Equally"; Kelman and Lester, "Jumping the Queue," 121–24): strong humane justice requires the state to compensate individuals for both genetic and environmental disadvantages; weak humane justice, only for environmental ones. But what is required to mitigate natural inequalities may be more or less than what is required to compensate for environmental disadvantages.

For Pogge, the use of primary social goods to assess comparative advantage reflects that limited commitment. Because political justice is "concerned with citizens' *social* positions or *shares*, not their overall *situations* or *standards of living*," it is appropriate for Rawls to "leave aside differences among persons that affect how useful a given bundle of social goods will be to each"; it reflects a political morality limited not in vision, as Sen claims, but in scope.[25]

In applying this limited imperative to health care, Pogge rejects Daniels's claim that health care needs are an exception; that a just society would attempt to equalize health before distributing primary social goods.[26] It would be impossible to restrict compensation for natural differences to this one domain: we would also have to compensate bad looks through the distribution of clothing, and low intelligence through the distribution of educational services. Such across-the-board compensation would require the comprehensive appraisal of well-being that Rawls rejects, as well as a bankrupting level of expenditure. But even if it remained an exception, the priority accorded to the restoration of health would impose oppressive burdens in the face of expensive and barely tractable disorders.

At the same time, however, Pogge recognizes the "great strategic importance" of medical care, since "its distribution crucially affects a person's access to all forms of the human good."[27] He requires a means of distributing such care according to variable need that would not commit a society to the stronger form of compensation that Daniels embraces.

Consistent with his commitment to the weaker form of nullification—to prevent social arraignments from amplifying natural inequalities—Pogge proposes a scheme that would reduce the dependence of health on wealth by imposing constraints on the distribution of "health protection:" resources for maintaining or restoring health.[28] Pogge develops this proposal for equal medical opportunity by analogy to his proposal for equal educational opportunity. The latter requires universal "access to a roughly equivalent education, with equivalence defined in terms of cost."[29] Equal medical opportunity would not require equal health, any more than equal

25. Pogge, *Realizing Rawls*, 44–47.
26. Pogge, *Realizing Rawls*, 183–84.
27. Pogge, *Realizing Rawls*, 182.
28. Pogge, *Realizing Rawls*, 185–86.
29. Pogge, *Realizing Rawls*, 175.

educational opportunity requires equal educational achievement. It would, however, ensure that medical care was not distributed only as a means to achieve greater productivity or more primary social goods for the worst-off. Everyone would be entitled to roughly equal resources for health protection even if that lowered the position of the worst-off in terms of (other) primary social goods. The lexical priority accorded these measures indirectly reflects the centrality of health and normal functioning to well-being, by recognizing the adverse effect that large disparities in health care would have on the self-respect of the worst-off citizens.[30]

Applied to disabilities, Pogge's proposal would require that poor people have access to most of the corrective and assistive measures available to people of average means. The only relevant comparison, though, would be between poor and middle-class people with disabilities; the disparity in advantage between people of any class with and without disabilities would not be relevant to political justice. Pogge apparently relies on the self-interest of the middle-class to guarantee a decent minimum of treatment and accommodation: if middle-class people with disabilities were able to get wheelchairs and hand signers, so would poor people with disabilities.

At the same time, Pogge qualifies this assurance by allowing the political process to determine which conditions get covered. He contends that the alternative of guaranteeing access to all kind of medical care would involve "the dubious view that an institutional scheme . . . should operate in a remedial way, should distribute benefits and burdens so as to balance out things among its participants for the sake of the overall fairness of the universe."[31] The right to treatment for specific conditions would smack of the broader compensation that Rawls rejects. Pogge concedes that under his more modest proposal, conditions for which most people were not at risk might get short shrift. But "if more is required for those who, through no fault of their own, are genetically handicapped, then why should not more be required also on behalf of those who, through no fault of their own, have run out of health protection?"[32]

Pogge's assurance that such gaps in coverage would be unlikely overlooks the status of people with disabilities as a vulnerable, underrepresented minority, whose needs could be ignored even in a society that

30. Pogge, *Realizing Rawls*, 182.
31. Pogge, *Realizing Rawls*, 189.
32. Pogge, *Realizing Rawls*, 189.

would not tolerate significant disparities in health care among economic classes. We could imagine a rationing plan broader than Oregon's, applicable to the middle class as well as the poor, that gave very low priority to the mitigation of congenital and early-onset disabilities (which Oregon's did not), compared with prevention and emergency interventions.[33] Such a plan might well satisfy Pogge's criteria for equal medical opportunity, without providing any form of therapy or treatment, or any assistive device or accommodation, except perhaps for the late-onset impairments and traumatic accidents to which a majority of the population felt vulnerable.

This suggests a basic disanalogy between educational and medical resources, as Pogge defines them. He presents education as a single service or resource, whether conferred on gifted or retarded students, but he presents medical services and resources as indefinitely divisible. Since he regards education as a single resource, he can assume that the less intelligent, whether poor or middle-class, will be assured significant educational benefits: because middle-class people of high intelligence will buy significant educational resources for themselves, slow learners in the lower and middle classes will be entitled to the same generic educational opportunities. In contrast, because health protection can be divided into distinct categories, the self-interest of middle-class people without disabilities may offer little relevant health protection to middle-class or poor people with disabilities.

Perhaps education could also be divided into categories that would allow the more intelligent to educate themselves without making comparable provision for the less intelligent under an equal opportunity standard: all children would have the "opportunity" to learn abstract algebra, but only gifted children could take advantage of that opportunity; no children would have the "opportunity" for remedial reading and arithmetic, but only slow learners would be disadvantaged by that lack of opportunity. That refinement would preserve the analogy between equal educational and medical opportunity but deprive the former of its moral appeal.

Pogge does leave an opening for a more expansive social response to disease and disability. Consistent with his view that a cooperative scheme

---

33. For an account of Oregon's health prioritization plan, see Dan W. Brock, "Justice and the ADA: Does Prioritizing and Rationing Health Care Discriminate against the Disabled?" *Social Philosophy and Policy* 12, no. 2 (Summer 1995): 159–85.

must not exacerbate natural inequalities, he insists that if a medical condition is socially produced, then justice requires "full health protection," lest people be left with a significant net burden as a result of their participation in a cooperative scheme. He regards diseases caused by pollution, highway accidents caused by other drivers, and injuries from crime as socially produced. He also recognizes that it will be difficult to distinguish natural and socially produced medical conditions, because of such complexities as genetic susceptibility to environmental disease.[34]

But there is a deeper source of uncertainty: our health and disease susceptibility are pervasively affected by living in a modern society, so that almost any affliction, except perhaps a few brought on by single-gene mutations, will have both natural and social causes: a car crash caused by a heart attack has a natural cause, as Pogge asserts, but it also has obvious, if less proximate social causes, such as the stress and diet that contributed to the attack. Much the same could be said for death by AIDS, influenza, or TB, natural diseases that owe their epidemic character to various features of urban or cosmopolitan societies.[35] Given the difficulties of teasing apart natural and social causes or of apportioning causal responsibility, it might be tempting to adopt a state-of-nature baseline and require "full health protection" only for those with worse health than they would have enjoyed outside a scheme of social cooperation. But this baseline is hopelessly speculative, and even if it were not, it would yield anomalous results: it would, for example, appear to make life expectancy in a state of nature the cutoff point for full health protection; beyond that point, any medical intervention would be a net gain.

The line between natural and socially produced disadvantage is even harder to draw for disabilities, since they involve, by definition, an interaction between a person's "natural endowment" and her environment. The social environment is involved at two levels: first, in helping to deter-

---

34. Pogge, *Realizing Rawls*, 109–93.

35. Pogge may intend his distinction between natural and socially produced disease to conform to the distinction between what an institutional scheme brings about and what it merely lets happen (*Realizing Rawls*, 44–47). But the latter distinction seems narrower than the former. While an accident caused by another driver is, according to Pogge, socially produced, it does not seem to be brought about by the institutional scheme. If Pogge were to adopt such a broad understanding of what an institutional scheme brings about, he would also have to include most maladies associated with urban and cosmopolitan living.

mine, through rearing and education, the traits a person will acquire; second, in determining how useful those traits will be to the pursuit of various goals. Thus, the development of particular intellectual skills depends to a large if debatable extent on the individual's family and educational environments; the utility of those skills depends on the division of labor and the prevailing technology. Thus, to take a familiar example, the development of reading ability is shaped by the early social environment, while the utility of that ability depends on the society's level of literacy.

To anticipate the discussion in the "Disability and Discrimination" section, the problem is not that we cannot make useful generalizations about whether specific biological characteristics are advantageous or disadvantageous across the range of possible social environments; it is that we lack any natural baseline with which to compare the effects of various cooperative schemes. If we consider the situation of a cognitively impaired child or adult, we may be able to claim that he began life with below-average intellectual potential, but we have no basis for apportioning his overall disadvantage between natural and social causes. We cannot view the benefits conferred by primary social goods as "superimposed" on his natural goods and ills, to use Pogge's words,[36] since we cannot separate out the pervasive effects of the prevailing scheme of social cooperation on his traits and prospects to determine what his natural goods and ills would be. The difficulty of distinguishing natural and socially produced disadvantage makes it hard for Pogge to draw the line between limited and full health protection.

Comparing the Two Rawlsian Approaches

Pogge's standard of equal health protection makes only modest and highly contingent provision for disease and disability, while Daniels's fair equality of opportunity gives rise to distributive demands as oppressive as the ones he hopes to avoid. These complementary extremes in part reflect the rigidity of the Rawlsian framework, which gives lexical priority to opportunity over other primary social goods. If equality of opportunity takes absolute precedence over raising the position of the worst-off in terms of those other goods, equal opportunity must be a very modest goal if it is not going to be an oppressive one. Pogge settles for a very minimal notion

---

36. Pogge, *Realizing Rawls*, 46.

of health protection to keep the priority of opportunities from becoming oppressive, while Daniels requires a potentially bankrupting priority for health care.

Despite these differences in their approaches, both Pogge and Daniels are attempting to find a principled basis for mitigating severe disparities in well-being while avoiding a commitment to the full equalization of well-being. The lexical priority that both accord to health care rests on two assumptions: (1) that if a resource or function has broad utility—if it is useful or critical for a wide variety of ends—its equalization has priority over the equalization of other resources or functions; (2) that health and normal functioning are useful or critical for a wide range of ends. The first assumption lies behind the claim that the equalization of opportunity has priority over the equalization of other goods; the second lies behind the claim that health and health protection are valuable because of the opportunities they preserve. Neither assumption is as valid as it may first appear. As to the first, James Griffin has argued that giving priority to more general needs may reflect a conflation of versatility and urgency: the fact that a good or function is useful for almost everyone's life plan does not give it priority in any particular conflict among goods or values.[37] Individuals and societies often trade off the satisfaction of more "basic" interests like nourishment and safety to satisfy less universal ones, like knowledge and beauty—individuals go hungry in the pursuit of esoteric research; societies increase injury and death by building scenic parkways instead of highways with broad shoulders and high barriers. Admittedly, the broad utility of a resource or function may make its acquisition or possession a useful indicator of well-being for a government unable to ascertain individual life plans or for an individual denied that knowledge by a veil of ignorance.[38] But even granting this, it is questionable whether the number of opportunities

37. James Griffin, *Well-Being: Its Meaning, Measurement, and Moral Importance* (Oxford: Oxford University Press, 1986), 41–53.

38. It is worth noting that Rawls does not appear to base the priority he accords to fair equality of opportunity on any such inference from versatility to urgency. Rather, his notion of fair opportunity is based on a concern for the openness of economic and political institutions to all qualified individuals. His concern for versatility across the range of reasonable conceptions of the goods is reflected in inclusion of opportunities in his initial list of primary social goods and his rationale for the list—that they are goods that people would tend to want more of, whatever their ends (*A Theory of Justice*, 299–303).

one has, above some minimum, or the size of one's opportunity range contributes much to well-being individually or serves as a useful social indicator. I will return to this issue in "Back to Distributive Justice," when I consider the effort to capture quality of life in terms of capabilities.

The second assumption, that health and normal functioning are necessary for a wide range of ends, glosses over an important distinction between disease and impairment as threats to well-being. Although impairments of functioning often results from disease, they generally do not involve chronic or acute pain, progressive debilitation or loss of function, or an imminent threat to life, in contrast to many diseases. (As Ron Amundson notes in carefully distinguishing disease and disability, a person can, in common parlance, be impaired and perfectly healthy.) But though the failure to treat disease and impairment separately undoubtedly contributes to a distorted picture of the impact of impairment on the opportunity to pursue most reasonable ends, it is not the only source. A similar distortion is found in the scheme for hypothetical disability insurance proposed by Ronald Dworkin, a scheme that assimilates impairments not to disease but to deficits in talent.

Hypothetical Disability Insurance

Dworkin proposes to treat disabilities as resource deficits that can be insured against in a hypothetical market.[39] In contrast to Pogge, who allots the same amount of resources for health protection to each individual regardless of their health, Dworkin's insurance payoff would vary with the severity of the condition, to reflect the amount of insurance a person could be expected to have purchased against it.[40] It thereby offers a far more flexible and generous alternative than Pogge's to the wholesale redistribution of internal resources.

Dworkin's account also improves on Daniels's in one important respect. It treats the difference between disabilities and talent deficits as "one of degree,"[41] and it proposes the same kind of hypothetical insurance scheme to compensate for both. Dworkin appears to recognize (as Jerome Bicken-

---

39. Dworkin, "What Is Equality?" 296ff.
40. Dworkin, "What Is Equality?" 297–98.
41. Dworkin, "What Is Equality?" 314.

bach notes[42]) that the disadvantages associated with impairments as well as talent deficits arise from an interaction between biological endowment and social environment. But he insists that it is possible to generalize about the impact of impairments on life plans in a way one cannot generalize about the impact of talent deficits, since "the connection between talents and ambitions is much closer than that between ambitions and handicaps."[43] He assumes that standard impairments like blindness and limb paralysis have an adverse effect on a sufficiently broad range of life plans that people will insure against them in ignorance of their own plans.

Dworkin's recourse to hypothetical choice allows him to rely on social consensus to decide not only what conditions to compensate but how much to compensate them. People insure against their absence because, in ignorance of their actual life plans, they believe that they are likely to want them for almost any life plans they choose. Dworkin thus takes account of the versatility of typical functions without endowing them with objectively greater urgency or priority.

His scheme is worth examining in some detail, because despite, or because of, these significant virtues, it so clearly illustrates two of the most significant pitfalls in liberal theories of distributive justice as applied to disabilities: first, in appraising the impact of impairments on life plans and well-being, the hypothetical choice situation invites the conflation of absence and loss; second, in focusing on individual distributive shares, it has difficulty underwriting the structural and organizational modifications that most effectively alleviate the limitations associated with many impairments. While Dworkin's hypothetical insurance market permits disabilities to be accommodated more flexibly than either Pogge's or Daniels's proposals, it cannot account for the types of accommodation to which people with disabilities seem most clearly entitled.

Dworkin treats disabilities as "features of body or mind or personality that provide . . . impediments to [a successful life]."[44] These "impediments" complicate Dworkin's proposal for equality of resources: a hypothetical division of the community's resources that would leave no one envying anyone else's share. If disabilities are not treated as resource defi-

---

42. Jerome Bickenbach, *Physical Disability and Social Policy* (Toronto: University of Toronto Press, 1993).

43. Dworkin, "What Is Equality?" 316.

44. Dworkin, "What Is Equality?" 303.

cits, people with disabilities will receive no provisions beyond their materially equal shares, which seems inconsistent with the underlying imperative of equal concern and respect. But if abilities are resources, they cannot be "resources for the theory of equality in exactly the same sense that material resources are," since "they cannot be manipulated or transferred, even so far as technology might permit."[45] Productive abilities—skills and talents—are not subject to equal distribution, as they cannot be transferred from person to person but only "bought out" by those to whom they are assigned by nature; those with an abundance will effectively be indentured to those with a dearth, since they will have to buy out the expensive shares that others own in their abilities.[46]

Since we can neither ignore disabilities nor treat abilities as assignable resources, what options are available to a resource egalitarian? Dworkin rejects the suggestion that the community's resources first be used to raise everyone to a minimum level of functioning, with the remainder distributed equally—a proposal that sounds in rough outline like Daniels's. Such an adjustment would require "a benchmark of normal human abilities" to guide it, a benchmark that Dworkin is more skeptical than Daniels of finding.[47] Even if such a benchmark could be found, achieving it would exhaust the society's resources in the face of intractable disabilities or, more likely, lead to political compromise that would leave only stinting provisions for disability—the specter haunting Pogge's proposal.

Dworkin proposes that compensation for deficient abilities be based on the average level of insurance against deficiencies that people ignorant of their powers would buy in a hypothetical market. This assessment is made on the admittedly counterfactual assumption that "everyone had . . . the same risk of developing physical or mental handicaps in the future . . . but that the total number of handicaps remained what it is." The buyers in this hypothetical market are not ideal, rational decision makers, but people just like us; Dworkin suggests that actual insurance markets might provide a rough approximation. This proposal for determining compensation does not rely on a benchmark of normal powers, because it lets the hypothetical insurance market determine which conditions get compensated.[48]

---

45. Dworkin, "What Is Equality?" 301.
46. Dworkin, "What Is Equality?" 311–12.
47. Dworkin, "What Is Equality?" 300.
48. Dworkin, "What Is Equality?" 297. This is essentially the same procedure Dworkin uses to set compensation for insufficiently remunerative talents, in which

Dworkin recognizes that significant variability in people's willingness to insure would be fatal to a hypothetical insurance market. If the amount of insurance that a person would buy varies too widely with her life plans, a hypothetical insurance market would not be possible, since we could arrive at a standard amount of insurance only through the crudest sort of averaging. But he argues that "we do not need . . . to make counterfactual judgments that are so personalized as to embarrass us,"[49] since there is a consensus about the disvalue of significant disabilities: "It would makes sense to suppose that . . . most people would make roughly the same assessment of the value of insurance against general handicaps, such as blindness or the loss of limb, that affect a wide spectrum of different sorts of lives."[50]

With this assumption, Dworkin attempts to maintains value neutrality in somewhat the same manner as Rawls does. In effect, he recognizes a group of primary abilities that people want whatever else they want. Dworkin identifies such abilities not by sociological and psychological generalization, as Rawls does for primary goods, nor through biological theory, but through social consensus.

The prudential judgment of the auction bidders provides a value-neutral basis for compensating disabilities. They do not insure against blindness because they regard sight as inherently good, but because they regard themselves as likely to have life plans that require sight. If they thought their plans were unlikely to require sight, they would insure less against blindness. Such prudential judgments can plausibly claim neutrality.[51] This

---

the disadvantages insured against clearly arise from the vagaries of the marketplace rather than any general deficit in biological endowment ("Equality of Resources," 314–23).

49. Dworkin, "What Is Equality?" 298.

50. Dworkin, "What Is Equality?" 299.

51. For this reason, it seems mistaken to argue that in awarding compensation to "general handicaps" such as blindness, Dworkin has violated value neutrality. Larry Alexander and Maimon Schwarzchild complain that "blindness is a handicap only for those who value sight or goals requiring sight, and it is conceivable that someone with particular religious beliefs might even value blindness as, say, a sign of divine grace." They find "no *neutral* basis" for insuring against expensive handicaps but not expensive tastes ("Liberalism, Neutrality, and Equality of Welfare vs. Equality of Resources," *Philosophy and Public Affairs* 16 (1987): 85–110, 101). But the preferences of people in the hypothetical auction are intended to provide just such a neutral basis.

is, after all, one of the virtues of hypothetical choice: that it derives distributional principles from constrained prudence.

But there are several acute difficulties in basing the accommodation of disabilities on the insurance that would be purchased against them in a hypothetical auction. In part, they arise from Dworkin's conception of distributive justice as a matter of dividing up society's resources into individual bundles. In part, they reflect the particular difficulty of using hypothetical ignorance to ascertain the requirements of justice for people with atypical sensory and motor functions.

First, Dworkin's auction cannot account for the distinctive moral features of disability claims: their general limitation to remedial or compensatory devices—to "in-kind" payments—and their application beyond individual assistance to accommodation in the design of physical structures and social institutions. Both these features are difficult to explain in terms of the individual entitlements generated by a hypothetical auction.

If we were insuring against disability in the stipulated state of ignorance and only against our own disability, it is hard to see why we would not insist on cash rather than in-kind payment. We might prefer the cash to any assistive or compensatory devices, and if we did not, we could always apply the money to the purchase of those devices. Dworkin recognizes that hypothetical bidders would insure more heavily against disabilities if there were better remedial technology, but his auction would not restrict the payoff to such remedial measures.[52] It might be that we would prefer that *all* payoffs be in kind, since the existence of such a large reserve of encumbered funds would greatly enhance research and development in this area. But since each person is only purchasing insurance for herself, this raises an obvious problem of collective action.

The poor fit between the recognized claims of people with disabilities and the payoff of a hypothetical insurance policy reflects, to some extent, the limitations of any approach that conceives distributive justice as a matter of dividing society's resources into individual shares. For Dworkin, as

---

It must be conceded, however, that Dworkin offers a more dogmatic reason for denying insurance against expensive tastes: that tastes, unlike abilities, cannot be viewed as resources at all, since they are too closely identified with the person who has them. There may be less tendentious reasons for not insuring against expensive tastes, having to do with the difficulty of identifying the conditions that would trigger compensation.

52. Dworkin, "What Is Equality?" 299.

for other liberal political philosophers, the problem of accommodating disabilities is "one of determining how far the ownership of material resources should be affected by the differences that exist in physical and mental powers, and our theory should speak in this vocabulary."[53] While Dworkin is arguing in this passage against the proposal to treat physical and mental powers as transferable resources, his framing of the problem, which limits the solution to changes in the individual ownership of material resources, ignores modifications in the structure and organization of society to permit access and participation by people with disabilities. Such modifications are hard to derive from a hypothetical assignment of the community's resources to individuals. Even if we assume that the disabled could pool their allowances to obtain structural improvements, that oblique derivation of the right to public access would fail to capture the direct entitlement we recognize.

There is also a problem with the idea that the hypothetical "willingness to insure" against disabilities can provide a basis for fair compensation. Research on decision making and risk suggests that the willingness to pay for reductions in the probability *or* magnitude of harm is a problematic basis for valuing actual harm, because of systematic errors and biases in the evaluation of risk. For example, it may be that most people discount the small risk of having a disability, and are willing to purchase very little insurance. Because we regard attitudes toward risk as part of a person's character (as Dworkin would insist), we feel that people are bound by the decisions under uncertainty they actually make. But it is quite a different thing to base compensation for a disability on the insurance that people *would have* bought against it.

This problem may be eliminated if we substitute rational decision makers for ordinary mortals in the hypothetical choice setting.[54] But there is a

---

53. Dworkin, "What Is Equality?" 301.

54. Gregory Kavka argues that rational decision makers would establish strong legal protections for people with disabilities if they were supplied with adequate information about the incidence and impact of disabilities in contemporary society, the resources available for ameliorating disabilities and raising the level of well-being of people with disabilities, and the pervasive consequences of disabilities, especially for self-esteem. But important as this information is, it is radically incomplete, because it does not include any intimation of the experience of disabilities ("Disability and the Right to Work," *Social Philosophy & Policy* 9, no. 1 (1992): 262–90).

broader problem in using hypothetical choice to yield binding agreement that remains even if we assume that the decision makers are fully rational. We cannot stipulate away their knowledge about disabilities as readily as, say, their knowledge about economic status. Since most of those invited to imagine themselves taking part in a hypothetical auction do not have serious disabilities, they will have difficulty assessing the prospects of people with disabilities. The very centrality of walking and seeing to the lives of people with typical sensory and motor functions may make paralysis and blindness less conceivable than other adversities, such as insult or hunger.

Ironically, the danger may be that the "abled" will greatly exaggerate the misery of living with disabilities. This danger is suggested by the controversy over the Oregon health prioritization plan, for which able-bodied people appear to have rated the value of continued life with disabilities much lower than people with disabilities.[55] There is also the complementary risk that hypothetical decision makers will place excessive weight on correcting or restoring functions because they do not appreciate the possibilities for flourishing with impaired functions. While some of the problems with a Dworkinian veil, such as risk biases, can be eliminated by stipulating that the hypothetical decision makers are rational, this one cannot be. We can expect the decision makers to be rational but not Tiresian: they cannot compare the perspectives of people who have been born with, or long acquired, different sets of sensory and motor functions.

The problems with hypothetical choice are exacerbated by the kind of choice elicited, about whether and how much to insure. Actual insurance is bought against *loss*—either the actual loss of an existing object or function, like a house or a limb, or the loss of an expected outcome, like a crop. But for those insuring against the *absence* of functions, this approach is quite misleading.

People born without the standard complement of sensory or motor functions will not experience the loss of functions they have already acquired or expected to acquire (although they may experience disadvantage or envy), nor will they experience the disruption of their life plans by loss—their life plans will be formed around the functions that they do possess. As I suggest later, a person's atypical physical or mental functions may form part of their "context of choice"—the basis on which they assess possible life plans. Dworkin has no basis for assuming that a person's ambi-

---

55. See Brock, "Justice and the ADA."

tions are inextricably bound up with his talents but not his functions; the connection between functions and life plans is much closer than Dworkin acknowledges.

Moreover, Dworkin does not even suggest an argument that the life plans available to people with congenital or early-onset impairments will provide a lower quality of life than the plans available to people with a standard complement of functions. People with the standard complement of functions will, however, inevitably regard the quality of life without them as far lower. The invitation to insure against hypothetical loss makes it even more difficult than it would otherwise be to divorce one's own plans and attachments from an appraisal of the value of standard sensory and motor functions.[56] The intuitive plausibility of the generalizations required by Dworkin's insurance scheme depend, no less than the plausibility of Daniels's assumptions concerning opportunity and disability, on this conflation of absence and loss.

Disability and Discrimination

The liberal philosophers who have addressed disability have come up with proposals that bear a depressing similarity to the status quo. Daniels gives us unrestricted allowances for corrective surgery and therapy, making available in theory the unlimited state-funded medical assistance already available in theory to the permanently disabled. Pogge would allow only those corrective measures that a flat allotment for health protection could buy and that the political process would select for coverage, a rationing scheme that resembles the controversial Oregon plan writ large. Dworkin's elaborate scheme of hypothetical insurance yields the most inadequate provision of all, an income supplement for people with disabilities that they would receive, unlike Supplemental Security Income (SSI) and Social Security Disability Insurance (SSDI), regardless of their actual income or capacity to earn a living.

These approaches differ radically in their prescriptions, but they share a

---

56. Dworkin himself speculates that in the absence of corrective technology, an insurance payoff to a person born blind would "simply swell a bank account they could not, in any case, use with much satisfaction" ("Equality of Resources," 299).

common framing of the problem of impairments for distributive justice. They all treat impairments as deficiencies in the individual's capacity to convert external resources into well-being or to press external resources into the service of their chosen ends. Like expensive tastes or vaulting ambitions, impairments result in frustration and unhappiness, but because unlike most tastes and ambitions, they are involuntary, a just society must somehow compensate for the shortfall in well-being that they produce. Daniels and Pogge respond to this shortfall by making a threshold allotment of resources to fix the deficiency—an unlimited allotment for Daniels, a very limited and contingent one for Pogge. Dworkin, on the other hand, offers compensation rather than adjustment. Although he recognizes an element of social contingency in the hardships of people with disabilities, he shares the assumption that their core problem is a lack of generally valuable internal resources.

Several philosophers have challenged this assumption and the narrowly distributive response associated with it. They argue that framing the problem as one of appropriate compensation for a deficit in internal resources conceals the primary injustice: the construction or maintenance of a handicapping environment. People with disabilities have difficulty utilizing external resources to serve their own ends in large part because the physical structure and social organization of society make it difficult for them to do so. Theories that frame the issue of fair treatment for people with disabilities in terms of society's obligation to compensate for natural inequalities ignore the extent to which the inequalities associated with natural differences are social. If people with disabilities fail to flourish even with an equal share of society's external resources, it may be because those resources are already divided up or structured in ways that limit their utilization to people with normal functions. Much or most of the disadvantage suffered by people with disabilities is, in Anita Silvers's phrase, "the stubborn artifact of inequitable social arrangements."[57] Ascribing that disadvantage to a deficit in internal resources "naturalizes" the injustice and makes its rectification a matter of special assistance, a response that obscures the source of injustice and reinforces the impression of internal inadequacy.[58]

---

57. Anita Silvers, " 'Defective' Agents: Equality, Difference and the Tyranny of the Normal," *Journal of Social Philosophy*, 25th Anniversary Special Issue (1994): 168.

58. See, for example, Silvers, " 'Defective' Agents," 162–63.

Those who see disability primarily as a problem of discrimination rather than distributive justice begin with the broadly accepted analysis of disability as an interaction between a person's physical or mental functioning and her environment.[59] As Ron Amundson points out in a representative passage:

> A person with a disability [impairment] is handicapped only with respect to a particular environment and a particular goal . . . Blind people are handicapped with respect to access to information because so much information in the present social environment is stored only in visually accessible form. Wheelchair users are handicapped with respect to travel because so little public transportation is accessible to wheelchairs.[60]

Proponents of an antidiscrimination approach do not, however, merely insist on the environmental origin of much of the disadvantage associated with disability or on environmental reconstruction as the presumptive social response to disability. They also see such modification as having greater moral urgency than other claims for more equitable construction or distribution. They agree with Daniels that the elimination of the disadvantages associated with impairments must take priority over the alleviation of mere distributive injustice—they merely disagree on the reasons for that priority and on how those disadvantages should be alleviated.

---

59. The interactive character of disability is obscured by a common equivocation between biological or statistical and normative senses of "impairment," an equivocation that leaves the false impression of a classification that is both scientifically grounded and normatively significant. If "impairment" is defined biologically or statistically, its undesirability appears to be an entirely contingent matter. For example, one standard biological account defines impairments as departures from species-typical functioning and regards such functions as presumptively valuable because of their contribution to reproductive fitness. But the fact that a function is species-typical reflects the vagaries of evolution, and the environmental conditions that made the function typical may no longer prevail. Moreover, departures from species-typical functioning may be desirable for an individual even if they reduce his reproductive fitness. At best, departures from species typicality are relevant to social policy only as weak evidence of disadvantage. There is no reason to suppose that any other biological account of impairment would make its relationship to well-being less contingent. On the other hand, if "impairment" is defined normatively, as an undesirable variation, its use begs the question of why such variation is undesirable.

60. Ron Amundson, "Disability, Handicap, and the Environment," *Journal of Social Philosophy* 23, no.1 (1992): 110.

But the recognition that the disadvantages associated with disability are mediated by the social environment does not, by itself, give claims for reconstruction greater urgency than (other) claims for the redistribution of resources, let alone exempt the former from trade-offs with other reforms. The attribution of their disadvantage to the social environment gives people with impairments the same kind of grievance as people with obsolete skills, differing only in degree. We need an additional reason, not supplied by the environmental analysis of disability, for treating the grievance of people with disabilities as differing in kind.

The additional claim is that the disadvantages associated with impairments have their source in pervasive attitudes of contempt and disrespect. Unlike people with obsolete skills, but like people of color, people with disabilities are not regarded as moral equals by the larger society, and the disadvantages they face reflect their devaluation. Because those disadvantages arise from contempt and disrespect, they bear a moral taint lacking in distributive injustices arising from greed, insularity, or oversight.[61] For this reason, even when the disadvantages associated with disability do not result from purposeful exclusion, their elimination has greater moral urgency than the elimination of distributive injustices that arise from the vagaries of the market or the political process. Compensating for the adverse effects of prejudice and contempt must take priority over other forms of redistribution.

Even if we accept the proposition that the alleviation of disadvantages has greater moral urgency when they arise from disrespect than from some more innocent source, it is necessary to defend the claim that the disadvantages associated with impairment do have such a tainted source. Otherwise, the claim of greater urgency will merely look like special pleading. As Kelman and Lester observe, in criticizing the priority accorded to children with learning disabilities in underfunded public education systems, "it will always be tempting to 'jump the queue' by claiming that one's distributive interests take priority over the interests of another group: claim hopping on the ideological backs of instances of genuine victimiza-

---

61. I develop this analysis of the core evil of discrimination more fully in Wasserman, "Discrimination, Concept Of," *Encyclopedia of Applied Ethics*, vol.1 (San Diego: Academic, 1998): 805–13. A similar analysis of the moral underpinnings of equal protection analysis is found in Andrew Koppleman, *Antidiscrimination Law and Social Equality* (New Haven: Yale University Press, 1996).

tion."[62] The question is whether the disadvantages associated with disability are attributable to "genuine victimization" and thus have a moral taint that appropriately jumps them up the queue.

That claim gains plausibility from the recognition that an impairment is not merely a functional variation but a stigma, the marker of a despised and oppressed group. In his classic work on the subject, Erving Goffman introduced the notion of "spoiled identity" to describe the categorization and treatment of people who depart from the norm in certain ways:

> While the stranger is present before us, evidence can arise of his possessing an attribute that makes him different from others . . . and of a less desirable kind. . . . He is thus reduced in our minds from a whole and usual person to a tainted and discounted one. . . . By definition, of course, we believe the person with a stigma is not quite human. On this assumption, we exercise varieties of discrimination, through which we effectively, if often unthinkingly, reduce his life chances.[63]

Among the most important and pervasive ways that we have "effectively, if unthinkingly, reduced the life chances" of people with disabilities is in the design of the physical structures and social organization of society to accommodate only those who fall within an extremely narrow range of physical and mental variation. The formal neutrality of such a design masks a structural bias against people with disabilities.

This understanding of people with disabilities as a minority group, and of disability as a product of discriminatory social arrangements, informs the Americans with Disabilities Act (ADA) of 1990. The congressional findings prefacing the ADA hold that people with disabilities are "a discrete and insular minority," "subject to a history of purposeful unequal treatment." The ADA seeks to eliminate that inequality by prohibiting discrimination; strikingly, it defines discrimination against people with disabilities to encompass the failure to provide equal access and opportunity to benefit (e.g., to make reasonable modifications in the workplace; to remove architectural and communication barriers in public facilities and accommodations). While the ADA might appear to smuggle in a substantive standard of equal treatment under its antidiscrimination rubric, it can

---

62. Kelman and Lester, *Jumping the Queue*, 226.

63. Erving Goffman, *Stigma: Notes on the Maintenance of Spoiled Identity* (Englewood Cliffs: Prentice Hall, 1963), 5.

instead be seen as informed by the view that discrimination against certain groups is characteristically expressed by standards and practices that are neutral on their face but grossly unequal in their impact. As such, the ADA's treatment of discrimination presents an interesting hybrid of claims concerning recognition and redistribution:[64] the disregard and devaluation of people with impairments are expressed by the neglect of their needs in physical design and social organization, and the inequities in design and organization are particularly objectionable just because they are expressions of disrespect.

The ADA's treatment of people with disabilities as a minority group, and its treatment of unequal access and opportunity as forms of discrimination, are rejected by some scholars, who find the analogy to race and gender inapt. Jerome Bickenbach argues that

> it is a fundamental mistake to characterize disability as the identifier of a minority group, and the process of disablement, with the denial of equality it entails, as discrimination. Quite the contrary, physical and mental difference is a universal human condition and people whose lives are, or will be, affected by impairments and disabilities are not a minority, nor are they discrete and insular. . . . Not only are the social responses to different forms of mental and physical difference vastly different, there is almost no commonality of experience, or feelings of solidarity, between people with diverse disabilities.[65]

Bickenbach is surely right that people with disabilities are not a discrete and insular group in the same sense that many racial and ethnic minorities are and that we cannot see their treatment simply in terms of the kind of intentional discrimination that those racial and ethnic groups have experienced. But behind the variety of social responses Bickenbach observes may lie a pervasive stigmatization that endows otherwise different people with deep, if unwelcome, commonalities. It is characteristic of a stigma to "spoil" identity by suppressing vast differences in the experience of people with different impairments and of different people with the same impairments. Moreover, the pervasiveness of disability is hardly proof against invidious discrimination; the contempt often displayed toward children

---

64. Nancy Fraser, "From Redistribution to Recognition: Dilemmas of Justice in a 'Post-Socialist' Age," *New Left Review* 212 (1995): 73.

65. Jerome Bickenbach, "Equality, Rights, and the Disablement Process," paper presented at the American Philosophical Association, Central Division Meetings, Chicago: April 1996, 3.6.

and elderly people suggests that we are quite capable of devaluing our own past or future selves. Finally, the concept of discrimination has been enlarged by a generation of scholars and activists to cover the kinds of disregard to which people with disabilities are typically subject. This enlarged concept may not be able to do the work required of it, but I think its potential is worth exploring.

The notion of structural discrimination embodied in the ADA was shaped by the feminist critique of earlier civil rights law, with its narrow focus on the direct and indirect effects of intentional discrimination. Feminists argued that the design of physical structures and social practices for just one group—able-bodied males—constitutes a significant form of discrimination against the rest.[66] Women and people with disabilities must choose between a formal equality that ignores their distinct needs and special treatment that reaffirms the dominant norm and merely accommodates their "abnormality." Thus, feminists reject the choice between employment policies that make no accommodation for pregnancy and those that treat it as a "special need" of women or, worse, as a disease.

Similarly, feminists argue that the structures and practices of our society embody a norm of healthy functioning, just as they embody a norm of male functioning. As Susan Wendell argues, "Life and work have been structured as though no one of any importance in the public world . . . has to breast feed a baby or look after a sick child. . . . Much of the world is structured as though everyone is physically strong . . . as though everyone can walk, hear and see well."[67] Once we reject the dominant norm, we will reject the preferential satisfaction of the latter as discriminatory.

This position was anticipated a generation ago by Jacobus tenBroek, who argued that the right of the disabled "to live in the world" required comprehensive changes in our physical and social order: not just in the design of buildings and public spaces but in the duties of care owed by

---

66. More broadly, feminists argue that discrimination against disabled people can be better understood by analogy to sex discrimination. While gender may be a significant biological category, its significance has been destructively exaggerated. Like the disabled, women suffer from false beliefs about the magnitude and relevance of their physical differences. Like the disabled, women are excluded by standards, which, while facially neutral, are needlessly exclusionary in their effect, such as the height and weight standards for fire and police departments.

67. Susan Wendell, "Toward a Feminist Theory of Disability," *Hypatia* 4, no. 2 (1989): 111.

able-bodied pedestrians, drivers, common carriers, and property owners to disabled people traveling in public places.[68] The refusal to make these changes denied the disabled their right to live in the world as much as the exclusion of blacks and women from public facilities.[69]

The analogy has been strengthened by a recognition that the equal treatment of women may require different, more expensive facilities. In some jurisdictions, women's rest rooms in public buildings must contain more stalls, to accommodate the anatomical differences that lead to slower queues for women than men. This requirement reflects a belief that non-discriminatory treatment may require more than formal equality. If different, more expensive, structures are needed to fairly accommodate women, different, more expensive structures may also be required to fairly accommodate people with disabilities.

But the elimination of structural discrimination involves a more extensive commitment for disabled people than for women. As one judge commented about the ADA's predecessor statute:

> What must be done to provide handicapped persons with the same right to utilize mass-transportation facilities as other persons? Does each bus have to have special capacity? Must each seat on each bus be removable? Must the bus routes be changed to provide stops at all hospitals, therapy centers, and nursing homes? Is it required that buses be able to accommodate bedridden persons?[70]

While the ADA mandates equal access to public transit, its specific requirements for access leave most disabled people with a far greater burden of mobility than most other people. Such disparities are permitted under the ADA if further equalization would not be "readily achievable" or would

---

68. Jacobus tenBroek, "The Right to Live in the World: The Disabled in the Law of Torts," *California Law Review* 54 (1966): 841–919.

69. The structural discrimination faced by women was highlighted when the six women elected to the Senate in 1992 discovered that congressional offices only had men's rest rooms. One commentator argued that the lack of disabled-accessible restrooms was equally objectionable: "If it's discriminatory for women to have to go farther, then it's discriminatory for disabled people to be forced to do the same thing" (*New York Newsday*, 14 November 1992, col.1, 16).

70. Quoted in Judith Welch Wagner, "The Antidiscrimination Model Reconsidered: Ensuring Equal Opportunity without Respect to Handicap under Section 504 of the Rehabilitation Act of 1973," *Cornell Law Review* 69: 404.

pose either an "undue burden" or "a direct threat to the health and safety of others." Perhaps the ADA should provide a less generous exemption, as some disability advocates have urged.[71] But it is not easy to see how any structural improvements could fully eliminate all such inequalities,[72] and the marginal cost of further improvements is likely to increase as inequality is reduced.

Even tenBroek concedes that "the policy of integration has its limitations: it cannot be pushed beyond the physical capacity of the disabled."[73] But the limitations are not physical so much as technological and economic. The "physical capacity of the disabled" depends on available technology, which in turn depends on the resources invested in research and implementation. For example, opening doors is "beyond the physical capacity" of many disabled people, but that limitation can be overcome by electric door openers. Securing the right of people with disabilities to "live in the world" involves an indefinite commitment of resources.[74]

---

71. Jonathan C. Drimmer, "Cripples, Overcomers, and Civil Rights: Tracing the Evolution of Federal Legislation and Social Policy for People with Disabilities," *UCLA Law Review* 40 (1993): 1405.

72. We might come close to structural equality in an entirely human-made environment, such as a space station, in which button pushing was the only basic action required for most activities. In such a world, most people with motor and sensory impairments could do almost everything that able-bodied people could, *except* see, hear, and walk. We might have reservations about creating such a world, however, since its technology would bring about a radical cleavage between practical action and the exercise of our sense organs and musculoskeletal system.

73. tenBroek, "The Right to Live in the World," 914.

74. Similarly, tenBroek notes that negligence law has long imposed duties of care on blind pedestrians that are far more demanding than those imposed on the sighted. For example, most jurisdictions hold a blind pedestrian contributorily negligent for falling into a hole in a public sidewalk, if the mishap could have been prevented by the proper use of a cane. Thus, a blind man will be not be able to recover if he falls into a hole that is surrounded by a thin fence, adequate to give tactile warning, but too weak to stop someone from falling in. TenBroek faults the courts for treating such pitfalls as inevitable, and placing the burden on the blind to avoid them ("The Right to Live in the World," 881). But unless tenBroek insists that the actual burden of precaution on disabled people, however great their disability, cannot exceed the burden imposed on able-bodied people, a balance must be struck between the burden of extra precaution imposed on the disabled and the burden of accommodation imposed on the community. While courts may often have struck the wrong balance, there is no simple formula to give the right one.

This is not a problem for the ADA itself; its standards of "reasonable accommodation" and "undue burden" will be fleshed out and refined on a case-by-case basis. But it is a problem for the antidiscrimination analysis that underlies the ADA. How can the reconstruction of the physical and social environment be regarded as a matter of civil rights, if it is subject to the exemptions and qualifications found in the ADA? Imagine a civil rights law that permitted the owners of public facilities to exclude blacks or women when their admission posed an "undue burden." If the bounds of reasonable accommodation are a matter of uncertainty, dispute, and negotiation, how can the mere failure to make such accommodation be taken to express a denial of the moral equality of people with disabilities? While the utter lack of accommodation that prevailed before the Vocational Rehabilitation Act of 1974 clearly bore the taint of contempt and disregard, it is hardly fair to impute such taint to arrangements and practices that reflect reasonable disagreement about what reasonable accommodation requires—rubber margins on all subway platforms, fees for "disabled" parking spaces to remove the incentives for misuse by able-bodied drivers, exemptions for retrofitting of certain historic buildings, or the widening and paving of trails in natural and wilderness areas.

If this indeterminacy complicates the application of an antidiscrimination analysis, it also poses a significant practical challenge. It is one thing to agree that physical structures and social practices have been designed for those who fall within a very narrow range of physical and mental variation; it is quite another matter to decide how we should redesign those structures and practices to end discrimination against people who fall outside the range, let alone to compensate them for past discrimination. What norm should we adopt? Those who seek a general principle are likely to regard case-by-case determination under the ADA as excessively ad hoc and context-specific. As Amundson asks, "is there any principled way of guaranteeing access rights to disabled people (or to certain classes of them) without risking bankruptcy from social hijacking?"[75] A requirement that structures and practices be designed to strictly equalize burdens or benefits (e.g., the time to get by public transit from point A to point B) for all people in every conceivable mental or physical condition is obviously problematic and has not, to my knowledge, ever been proposed by a disability advocate. And any standard based on the structures and practices

---

75. Amundson, "Disability, Handicap, and the Environment," 116.

that would obtain if we did not neglect and devalue people with disabilities would require that we suspend attitudes that we have every reason to regard as entrenched and pervasive.

Two proposals for qualifying or refining the antidiscrimination approach have been made by philosophers who subscribe to an environmental conception of disability. One would distinguish the failure to remove natural barriers from the imposition of artificial ones, treating only the latter as a civil rights violation; the other would test present social arrangements against those that would prevail in a society where people with disabilities were not a relatively powerless minority. Both offer a basis for treating certain handicapping features of the social environment as discriminatory, requiring modification without recourse to the cumbersome and often distorting apparatus of a comprehensive theory of justice.

Distinguishing Natural from Artificial Handicapping Features

Ron Amundson suggests that the specter of social hijacking has been greatly exaggerated. Concerns about hypothetical issues like the cost of accommodating a blind person who wants to be an airline pilot are, from a civil rights perspective, "the equivalent of 'would you want one to marry your sister' or 'will we be forced to use coed restrooms.' Most significant accommodations, such as curb ramps and tactile signage, are small, one-time expenses that often benefit even non-disabled people."[76] Yet Amundson recognizes that this will not always be the case:

> Other modifications (e.g., wheelchair accessible public transportation, or employer-funded readers for blind employees) may end up being very expensive. . . . The wide range of kinds and degrees of disability make the civil rights approach to access troubling. Is there any principled way of guaranteeing access to disabled people (or to certain classes of them) without risking bankruptcy by social hijacking? That is, does the environmental concept of handicap lead to the conclusion that civil rights requires the remediation of all consequences of disadvantage?[77]

Amundson suggests that this conclusion can be avoided by making a distinction between natural and constructed limitations: "It may be possible

---

76. Amundson, "Disability, Handicap, and the Environment," 116.
77. Amundson, "Disability, Handicap, and the Environment," 116.

to tease apart those features of the handicapping environment which are socially constructed from those which are independent of human choice. Humans construct stairways, but they do not construct the laws of gravity."[78] Amundson argues that while socially constructed barriers constitute civil rights violations, the remediation of "fully and genuinely 'natural' " barriers may fall within the purview of distributive justice. In effect, he proposes to draw the same line as Pogge, although his prescriptions for both sides of the line are quite different. But it is no easier for Amundson than Pogge to distinguish natural from socially constructed barriers.

While we can identify the natural features of a handicapping environment, their handicapping effect will almost always be mediated by human choice. Thus, although stairs are built by people, their handicapping effect is (largely) due to the force of gravity. And while gravity is "fully and genuinely natural," it may function as an artificial barrier, as it would, for example, if a town held its public meetings on a hilltop that wheelchair users could not reach. It would seem perverse to claim that the exclusion of wheelchair users from social and political participation by gravity would be subject to any less stringent standards for remediation than their exclusion by stairways (e.g., if the town held its public meetings on the second floor of a building lacking ramps or elevators).

More broadly, in a world where humans have the technological capacity to alter most features of the environment, few barriers are "independent of human choice," and the distinction between artificial and natural barriers is difficult to maintain.[79] Amundson might refine his distinction along the same lines as Pogge, by distinguishing barriers that humans create from those that they merely allow. But the distinction between doing and allowing is even more elusive for disability than disease, because, as Amundson insists, a disability is not an internal condition but rather an interaction between a person's functions and her environment. It may be reasonable to claim that a society merely allows a person to remain or

---

78. Amundson, "Disability, Handicap, and the Environment," 116.

79. As Phillip Cole argues: "[I]t is a combination of natural handicap and social practice which deprives the disabled person of the capacity to attain certain goals— and even if the natural handicap *is* unalterable, or irretrievable, the social practice *may well not be*. But we do not even have to concede this much, for the Natural/ Social distinction falls completely when we recognize that there is nothing *necessarily* unalterable or irretrievable about any natural handicap" ("Social Liberty and the Physically Disabled," *Journal of Applied Philosophy* 4, no.1 [1987]: 38).

become blind if it declines to finance a novel and expensive medical intervention to preserve or restore sight. But it is not so obvious that it merely allows the associated loss of mobility, access, or participation, since that loss is also caused by the social decision to use visual rather then tactile signage and instruction. Moreover, much of the access and participation that disabilities limit is inherently social: a community engages in activities that are more or less accessible to people with various impairments. The community could almost always structure its activities so that they were more accessible, and it seems unsatisfactory, if not disingenuous, to claim that if the community fails to do so, it merely allows people with impairments to be excluded.

We might look to the marginal impact of a social decision and direct our inquiry to the access that people with disabilities enjoyed at an earlier time. To decide whether the absence of lifts on buses constituted a civil rights violation rather than a possible distributive injustice, we would have to assess the mobility enjoyed by people with motor impairments before the creation of the transit system or, more narrowly, the introduction of bus service, to see whether its net effect was disabling.

We can certainly assess the disabling effect of some technological changes by comparison with the status quo ante. Thus, Allen Buchanan has argued that a society effectively chooses who will be disabled in any setting where it can exercise political control over the development and applications of new technologies that affect the complexity and accessibility of the "dominant cooperative scheme."[80] By examining the marginal impact of such choices (which are not confined to the technological frontier), we can see how innovations that do not directly affect people with particular disabilities can be indirectly handicapping, by causing social practice to change in a way that excludes them. This was certainly the case for the telephone, which caused much business and social communication to shift to a medium to which deaf people had no access, and it threatens to become the case for icon-based computer software, which appears considerably harder for blind people to access than the DOS software it has replaced. While such post/ante comparisons have considerable normative force, they yield only constraints, not prescriptions: they treat the level of

---

80. Allen Buchanan, "Choosing Who Will Be Disabled: Genetic Intervention and the Morality of Inclusion," *Social Philosophy and Policy* 13, no. 2 (Summer 1996): 40–45.

access and participation previously enjoyed by people with disabilities as a moral floor, which future technologies must maintain, but they do not prescribe increases in access and participation, even increases that technology has made feasible and inexpensive. They appear to leave theories of distributive justice with the lion's share of the work. Moreover, the floor that they impose depends on the kindnesses of past generations: the telephone or iconic software would not have had a disabling effect in a society where deaf or blind people were already excluded from most social and business communication. Even if we raised the standard by requiring that the *relative* mobility of people with motor impairments not be decreased—compared with the mobility of other people—we could not condemn as a civil rights violation any feature that did not make a comparatively bad situation worse.

It is doubtful that Amundson, any more than Pogge, could find a more general and morally appropriate benchmark by looking to the condition of people with disabilities in a state of nature. Our actual prehistory is unknowable and of limited relevance, since it might have been rife with cruelty and oppression. And there are an indefinite number of hypothetical states in which people might exist without a government or an organized civil society. In some, people with particular impairments would fare quite well, relative to the rest of the population; in some, they would fare very badly. Thus, for example, we could compare "states of nature" with the two forms of equal ownership envisioned by G. A. Cohen.[81] In a primitive agrarian society in which all land was jointly owned, such that its appropriation or utilization required universal consent, the veto power enjoyed by people with impairments might assure them a relatively comfortable existence. In contrast, in a primitive agrarian society in which land was divisible into equal shares, people with severe physical impairments might starve while their neighbors flourished. Far from prescribing what accommodations are fair or just, the state of nature we adopt as a baseline for comparison already embodies those judgments.

The Majority-Disability Standard

Anita Silvers proposes a test for the moral adequacy of accommodation that avoids the pitfalls of the natural/artificial distinction as well as the

---

81. G. A. Cohen, "Self-Ownership, World Ownership, and Equality: Part II," *Social Philosophy and Policy* 3, no. 2 (Spring 1986): 89–90.

distorting effects of hypothetical choice on the appraisal of disability. In contrast to Amundson, who seeks to limit the scope of distributive justice, Silvers wants to replace it altogether, with a strict standard of equal opportunity. Her test can be seen as offering a more general or determinate answer to the question of what counts as "reasonable accommodation":

> Suppose that most persons used wheelchairs. Would we continue to build staircases rather than ramps? Suppose most were deaf? Closed-captioning would be open captioning and would have been the standard for television manufacturing long before July 1, 1993. By hypothesizing what society would do were persons with disabilities dominant rather than suppressed, it becomes evident that systematic exclusion of the disabled is a consequence not of their natural inferiority but of their minority social status. They are inferior not because they are too defective, but because they are too few. As I describe it here, this counterfactualizing technique tests the nature of practices to reveal whether they arise out of an incipiently inequitable distribution of power or population. . . . [O]ne simply considers what would be the rule in a kingdom in which one's unimpaired functioning had become so atypical as to be marginalized by social arrangements.[82]

I will call Silvers's test a demographic one, although there is some ambiguity in its formulation, since people with disabilities might well be suppressed even if they were a numerical majority, such as women in many countries or, until recently, South African blacks. But even if we assume that political power would accompany majority status, the scope of the counterfactual is unclear. Is the kingdom in which "unimpaired functioning" has become atypical one in which a single impairment predominates, or several? Is it surrounded by kingdoms with similar demographics, or are the able-bodied preponderant outside its borders?

Silvers's questions about the accommodations we could expect in a society in which wheelchair users or deaf people predominated are intended to be rhetorical, but the plausibility of her answers may depend on the extent to which she holds other things constant. While it may be reasonable to assume that such societies would differ from our own mainly in the degree of accommodation they afforded people with common impairments, it is also possible that their trajectory of development would have been different enough to make the answers to Silvers's questions far more speculative. H. G. Wells envisioned a country of the blind that was far less

---

82. Silvers, " 'Defective' Agents," 168–69.

sophisticated technologically than his own but well adapted to the sensory functions of its citizens.[83] One wonders how such a country would have been imagined by a contemporary blind writer, particularly a congenitally blind one. Indeed, although Silvers hopes to "reconfigure the operation of moral imagination to rely on social rather than psychological extrapolations," I suspect that the social extrapolations of able-bodied people would be subject to many of the same distortions as their psychological ones.

Thus, the uncertain counterfactual scope of Silver's test, and the speculation it requires, make its application far less determinate than she supposes. But there is a deeper problem with its use as a standard for accommodation. First, in the case of people with some impairments, such as severe cognitive disability, multiple sensory impairments, or total limb paralysis, we might plausibly assume that a society in which they predominated would make far worse provisions for them than they enjoy in at least some existing societies. It is difficult to imagine how people with such impairments could enjoy political power commensurate with their numbers or, if they did, how they could make better arrangements for themselves than they have at present. Perhaps this is just a failure of imagination on my part, or perhaps cognitive disability is a special case, but the point remains: it is possible that Silvers's demographic test would require only very limited provision for people with certain impairments, worse than they now enjoy in some societies. I do not think this prospect argues for more limited accommodations.

If the counterfactual test does not set a maximum, which we are not obliged to exceed, it also does not set a minimum, which we must not fall below. For even if we assumed that a society dominated by people with a given impairment would accommodate them far better than we do now, we cannot conclude that justice requires that level of accommodation in our own society, in which they are in a small minority.

This point becomes apparent in considering the fair treatment of a group of people whom even the politically incorrect among us would describe as differently abled rather than impaired. Thus, imagine the difficulties of accommodating six-inch Lilliputians or sixty-foot Brobdingnagians, people whose physical dimensions differed greatly from our own but

---

83. H. G. Wells, *The Country of the Blind and Other Stories* (Freeport: Books for Libraries Press, 1971).

who have the same proportions and the same size-proportionate abilities and functions, health prospects, and life expectancies as "normal" six-footers. In their own kingdoms, Lilliputians and Brobdingnagians would live much as we do in ours; their lives would be much like our own, writ small or large. Because we regard their endowments as normal in this sense, we would not see them as impaired, however great the practical disadvantages they encountered in diverging so greatly from our population norms. We would hesitate to prescribe growth or shrinkage hormones to "correct" their problem, in part because we would be reluctant to have them relinquish the distinctive sensibilities and perspectives of life at their different scales. Yet the costs of accommodating them would likely be far greater than the costs of accommodating people with many "index" impairments.

It is likely that Lilliputians or Brobdingnagians would be able to design their own societies to comfortably accommodate people of their respective statures.[84] Comparing their prospects in their own societies with their prospects in ours, we might regard their present disadvantages as socially constructed, an artifact of their minority status. But the fact that they would enjoy vastly better accommodation in a society in which they predominated would hardly require us to offer them similar accommodation, regardless of cost. We would not feel compelled to make enormous sacrifices in our own quality of living to provide slight gains in access and opportunity to people whose physical dimensions diverged so greatly from our own.[85]

Nevertheless, although we might reject the "social hijacking" of resources by the effort to achieve equal access for Lilliputians and Brobdingnagians, we would also recognize an obligation to go beyond formal

---

84. I state this tentatively because scale might actually affect flourishing on our planet in a variety of ways. For example, while our fauna would offer very meager sustenance to Brobdingnagians, they would prey on Lilliputians. But we can assume that there are compensating advantages for each race.

85. It might be claimed that Lilliputians and Brobdingnagians would not be members of our species, since, among other reasons, we would hardly be able to breed with them. But even if they were not *Homo sapiens*, they would still be persons, and our grounds for denying them full equality could not be that we lacked the same moral and political obligation to them that we had to members of our own species. If they were the same size as us, we could hardly deny them equal accommodation on the grounds that they could not coreproduce; to do so would be the crassest form of "speciesism."

equality, to make some alterations or modification in our structures and practices to accommodate them. The extent of the modifications we felt obliged to make would depend on the distribution of sizes in the population as well as on the available technology. Virtual interaction, for example, might drastically reduce the importance of size for social participation and the ease of accommodating people of vastly different sizes. But it would not eliminate the trade-offs we faced in physical construction, from ceiling height to toilet-seat circumference, trade-offs that would be more acute the greater the variation in size. Our projection of the arrangements that differently sized people would make for themselves in a society in which they predominated might affect the balance we struck, but it would hardly be dispositive. Thus, even if Silvers's demographic test yielded determinate answers, it would not yield morally compelling ones.

Back to Distributive Justice

The uncertainty about the accommodation owed the "differently sized" suggests that the impairment classification itself has limited relevance to the issue of just accommodation. Even if we disfavor medical intervention for people we regard as differently abled rather than impaired, we may still be conflicted or uncertain about the accommodation they are owed. Thus, proponents of Deaf culture argue that congenital deafness is not an impairment and should not be routinely subject to medical "correction."[86] But it is one thing to question the imperative for corrective measures like cochlear implants, quite another to determine the extent to which a just society must contribute to the flourishing of Deaf culture.

The question is not how, or whether, a just society should compensate people for their natural misfortune or deficiency—as I have argued, it is difficult to even make a coherent distinction between natural and socially produced disadvantage—but rather of how it accommodates the range of variations in sensory, motor, and cognitive functioning among its members. This is not a special problem of disability policy but a general problem of justice. The conditions classified as impairments are merely some of the more significant, and conspicuous, variations that a just society must accommodate.

---

86. See, for example, Harlan Lane, *The Mask of Benevolence: Disabling the Deaf Community* (New York: Knopf, 1992).

The question of fair accommodation is not a problem of distributive justice in a narrow sense, because it is not concerned solely with the allocation of specific goods and services. But no contemporary theory of justice, even those using primary goods as a metric of comparative advantage, is solely concerned with who gets what—Rawls, after all, gives equality of liberty absolute priority over the distribution of resources.[87] And if such theories of justice are *re*distributive, it is not because they require some people to compensate others for their natural or accidental disadvantages but because the current pattern of entitlements in almost any society will almost certainly be found wanting.

While liberal theories of justice are not concerned only with who gets what, they *are* distributive in the sense that they assess the fairness of the physical and social organization of a society in terms of its impact on its individual members. And that assessment requires some metric of comparative advantage. The challenge is to take account of variations in function without treating them as inherently disadvantageous. While wide variations in health and functioning suggest the need for a more comprehensive measure of well-being, the plurality of ways in which people with varying sensory and functions can flourish, and the difficulties in making comparisons among them, may favor a *less* comprehensive measure of well-being for political justice.

Even if we can find an adequate measure of comparative advantage, we must still decide how much disparity in advantage justice can tolerate. These two issues are not independent, because the more comprehensive the measure of well-being we adopt, the more demanding the task of equalization may be.

Enlarging the List of Primary Goods

To preserve neutrality among varying conceptions of the good, Rawls adopts a metric of comparative advantage that takes little account of varying physical and mental functions. He proposes to measure well-being for purposes of political justice in terms of "primary social goods": income, wealth, and other goods that people want more of, whatever else they want. These goods are neutral in the sense that they have broad utility for

---

87. Rawls, *A Theory of Justice*, 60–61.

a wide variety of ends.[88] Yet, as we have seen, the use of primary social goods as a metric for well-being appears to ignore disparities in well-being that arise from differences in physical and mental functioning.

Rawls himself (at least in his later writings) regards his list of primary social goods as incomplete and negotiable. He suggests that it might be expanded to include other goods, such as leisure and the absence of pain.[89] Several political philosophers who share or sympathize with Rawls's commitment to neutrality among varying conceptions of the good have proposed other ways of understanding or modifying the list of primary good to better accommodate background differences among people that mediate the impact and value of they external resources they receive.

In attempting to justify special protections for vulnerable cultures, for example, Will Kymlicka has argued that the importance of cultural mem-

---

88. Rawls, *A Theory of Justice*, 62. Any approach that gives priority to a set of primary goods can be charged with nonneutrality among competing conceptions of the good, since that set of goods will be more conducive to the fulfillment of some conceptions than others. I think such criticism reflects an unduly stringent sense of neutrality. The neutrality that political liberals seek does not require equal impact. A policy of religious toleration, for example, would not violate neutrality just because it caused some religions to flourish and others to decline. So long as the policy of toleration was not designed to advance some religions at the expense of others or justified by religious doctrine, disparate impact would not violate neutrality.

Similarly, an index of primary goods based on a survey of, or generalization about, the range of life plans in a society could plausibly claim neutrality among those plans, even though it would always be more closely correlated with the fulfillment of some plans than others. Thus, Rawls's index of primary social goods does not violate neutrality among life plans even if it correlates much more closely with one life plan—"commodities fetishism"—than with any other.

The examples chosen by critics also seem to ignore the fact that different life plans vary in the extent to which they depend on the state for their fulfillment. A life of material or sensory deprivation, for example, may be fully compatible with public largess, as long as the goods dispensed are easily relinquished. Those who believe that "the last shall be first" or that "a rich man can enter heaven as easily as a camel can pass through the eye of a needle" may view resources as an encumbrance, but they do not require the state to rid them of that encumbrance. Even those who regard abundance, relinquished or not, as a sign of damnation have no cause for complaint about a munificent state, which would merely be the bearer of bad tidings.

89. John Rawls, "Priority of the Rights and Ideas of the Good," in *Political Liberalism* (New York: Columbia University Press, 1996), 178–87.

bership for individual well-being can be understood in a Rawlsian framework by treating such membership as a primary good: "it is a good in its
capacity of providing meaningful options for us, and aiding our ability to
judge for ourselves the value of our life plans."[90] Kymlicka treats cultural
membership as similar to Rawls's "social bases of self-respect," in being a
precondition for the appreciation of other goods. For this reason, he argues that the loss of culture is not compensable with monetary benefits.
Interestingly, he contrasts that loss with "natural handicap or natural di-
saster," for which monetary benefits are

> fair compensation for disadvantages . . . , since they compensate for unde-
> served limitations of the capacity to achieve one's ends through one set of
> means by extending one's capacity through another set of means. But cultural
> membership is not a means used in the pursuit of one's ends. It is rather the
> context within which we choose our ends, and come to see their value, and
> this is a precondition of self-respect, of the sense that one's ends are worth
> pursuing. And it affects our very sense of personal identity and capacity.
> When we take cultural identity seriously, we'll understand that asking some-
> one to trade off her cultural identity for some amount of money is like expect-
> ing someone to trade off her self-respect for some amount of money. Having
> money for the pursuit of one's ends is of little help if the price involves giving
> up the context within which such ends are worth pursuing.[91]

We can accept Kymlicka's insight about culture but reject his contrast
with disability. As I have already argued in considering Dworkin's hypothetical insurance scheme, monetary compensation is also of dubious value
for many "natural handicaps." In part, this is because it is highly unlikely
that individual compensation would ever be adequate for obtaining the
structural and organizational modifications necessary for meaningful economic, social, and political participation. But it is also because growing up
with an atypical set of sensory or motor functions may itself provide a
"context of choice," affecting the individual's evaluation of the desirability
as well as the feasibility of various life plans.

The similarity to ethnic and linguistic cultures is closest in the case of
Deafness, which its proponents claim to be a language-based culture as
complete and encompassing as any other.[92] Whether or not one accepts

---

90. Will Kymlicka, *Liberalism, Community, and Culture* (Oxford: Clarendon,
1991), 166.
91. Kymlicka, *Liberalism, Community, and Culture*, 192–93.
92. See, for instance, Lane, *The Mask of Benevolence.*

this claim in its entirely, it seems clear that monetary payments to Deaf individuals would be poor recompense for the loss of their language or of the economic support and social structures needed to maintain its viability. And although people with other impairments may not have developed cultures as distinct and encompassing as the Deaf, their sensibilities, social practices, and self-understanding may also provide a context of choice in Kymlicka's sense. The threat to those choice contexts may militate against the correction of atypical functions as it does against the assimilation of minority cultures.[93] That threat may also militate against programs of accommodation designed to integrate people with that function into the larger society. For these reasons, many Deaf activists favor separate schools for Deaf children, as incubators of a distinct culture, and reject the mainstreaming policy that has been the centerpiece of disability education for the past thirty years.[94]

If a just society is constrained to respect existing cultures based on atypical functions, it may also be required to promote the formation of inchoate cultures. (If this seems presumptuous or condescending, it is worth recalling that sign languages for the deaf were developed by hearing as well as Deaf people.) On a more modest level, a just society may enhance the contexts of choice and social bases of self-respect of citizens with atypical functions by promoting opportunities for fellowship and community among people with similar functions. (Sometimes, as in the case of cognitive disability, a society may face a difficult choice between promoting the fellowship of a very limited subculture or marginal participation in the much richer culture of the larger society.)

---

93. In a similar vein, Shelley Tremain argues that the social bases of self-respect can serve as a constraint on corrective measures. She rejects the demand, pressed by Bonnie Tucker and others, that people with atypical sensory or motor functions either avail themselves of corrective technology when it becomes available or forfeit any claim to more expensive accommodation (Bonnie Poitras Tucker, "The ADA and Deaf Culture: Contrasting Precepts, Conflicting Results," *Annals of the American Academy of Political and Social Sciences* 551 [January 1997]: 24–36). While the availability of corrective technology may make Deafness a choice, "some choices are more urgent than others precisely because they are intimately interwoven with the self-respect of those who make them"—for example, "the choice to uphold Deafness in an audist culture." To establish equality in the conditions for self-respect, a society must provide support for such choices (Tremain, "Statement on Impairment" presented at Roundtable on Challenges to the Impairment Classification, Joint Bioethics Meetings, Baltimore, Maryland, 6 November 1997).

94. See Lane, *The Mask of Benevolence.*

But the recognition of cultural membership as a primary good does not resolve the question of how much a just society must devote to maintaining or nurturing "expensive" cultures built around atypical functions. Some cultures (and not only those based on atypical functions) require more economic resources and social support than others to develop or survive, and some individuals (and not only those with atypical functions) require more resources and support to take part in minority or mainstream culture. Of course, some of the expense in maintaining a minority culture may arise from a long history of discrimination, and the resources needed to redress those effects may be claimed under the more stringent standard of corrective justice. But even if we cannot apply the distinction with any certainty, it seems clear that other expenses arise from accidents of demography, and still others from the character of the culture.

As important as the maintenance of the social bases of self-respect may be, then, it is not always dispositive. Some minority cultures may become impossible to nurture or preserve, or they may be sustainable only by the sacrifice of other urgent projects.[95] Perhaps the specter of social hijacking by "extravagant cultures" is no less exaggerated than the specter of social hijacking by intractable impairments. But my point is not to urge austerity—it is merely to insist that claims based on the self-respect of people with atypical functions do not enjoy categorical priority; they compete with each other, as well as with other social projects, for limited resources.

The recognition of such trade-offs is a strength, not a weakness, of the expansion of primary goods. It is surely more appropriate, as well as less demeaning, to see the disadvantages faced people with impairments as arising from a shortage of such important resources as the social bases of self-respect rather than from a comprehensive deficit in the capacity to utilize resources. And it is surely more appropriate, and less demeaning, to see their disadvantages as competing with those of abled-bodied people for alleviation, rather than as receiving absolute priority because of their magnitude or urgency.

---

95. Moreover, although justice may require at least a limited state commitment to preserving vulnerable and expensive cultures, that claim has virtually no political currency in the late twentieth-century United States. There is much stronger, albeit eroding support, for the claim that the state has an obligation to help people who are disadvantaged through no fault of their own, which provides a far more secure, if far less appealing, foundation for the resources needed for access and participation.

But the sheer diversity of the items in the enlarged list of primary goods make it very difficult to assess the trade-offs: how do we weigh income and wealth against self-respect or cultural support? I may be offered a job that raises my income and status but attenuates my cultural membership; we may have to choose between programs that improve the material resources of a group but encourage assimilation and programs that preserve both their cultural integrity and their privation. In confronting such trade-offs, we may be tempted to look beyond a comparison of primary goods to a more comprehensive metric of well-being.

Disability and Capability

Several philosophers have argued that the claims of people with disabilities are better addressed with a metric of well-being more sensitive to individual differences in function than primary goods, one that shifts the focus from the resources people have to what those resources enable them to do. They argue that it is a serious mistake to measure well-being in terms of those resources, or in terms of the subjective experiences or preferences of their recipients. As Sen contends in a well-known passage:

> If it is argued that resources should be reduced to remove or substantially reduce the handicap of the cripple despite there being no marginal utility argument (because it is so expensive), despite there being no total utility argument (because he is so content), and despite there being no primary goods deprivation (because he has all the goods that others have), then the case must rest on something else.[96]

Jerome Bickenbach provides a concise summary of what Sen thinks that "something else" is:

> What is required, Sen argues, is equality of capability. To formulate this account of equality more precisely, Sen defines "functionings" as the things and activities that people have a realistic choice between. A functioning is not merely a physical and mental capability (or absence of impairment), it is also the set of all other preconditions to achievement (that is, absence of disability) that infringe on positive freedom. A "capability," then, is a set of functionings over which a person has a choice, so that the set of a person's capabil-

---

96. Amartya Sen, "Equality of What?" in *Tanner Lectures on Human Values I*, ed. S. McMurrin (Salt Lake City: University of Utah Press, 1980), 218.

ities constitutes her actual freedom over alternative lives that he or she can
lead.[97]

The notions of functioning and capability appear well suited to capture
the disadvantages associated with disabilities and to prescribe an appropriate social response. For example, a person with a mobility impairment
has the same claim as everyone else to be able to move about from place
to place. That claim is not satisfied by making him rich or happy but only
by ensuring him the appropriate means of locomotion. And that, in turn,
does not require the restoration of normal functioning; it may be achieved
far more effectively and appropriately by improved building access, curb
cuts, ramps, and a wheelchair than by surgery. Thus, the capabilities approach can acknowledge the distributive claims arising from impaired mobility without treating it as an internal deficit or a health care problem.

Despite these significant virtues, the capabilities approach runs into difficulties when it tries to assume less schematic form. In generating a list of
valuable functionings, it is pulled toward an exhaustive enumeration of
human goods; in explaining the importance of capabilities, it is drawn
toward a more abstract emphasis on positive freedom as a good in itself.
But the former tends toward a rigid and dogmatic account of human
flourishing, while the second tends toward an "opportunities fetishism."
Both tendencies exaggerate the value of standard sensory and motor functions, and thereby lend support to the presumption for corrective measures.

Thus, Martha Nussbaum regards certain sensory and motor functional
capabilities as essential components of a "thick, vague conception" of the
human good.[98] She maintains that "being able to move from place to
place" and "being able to use the five senses" are essential to human
flourishing.[99] The problem lies in justifying or grounding Nussbaum's
claim about the indispensable contribution of standard sensory and motor
functions to well-being.[100]

---

97. Jerome Bickenbach, *Physical Disability and Social Policy* (Toronto: University of Toronto Press: 1993), 266.

98. Martha Nussbaum, "Aristotelian Social Democracy" in *Liberalism and
the Human Good*, ed. R. B. Douglass, G. Mara, and H. Richardson (New York:
Routledge: 1990).

99. Nussbaum, "Aristotelian Social Democracy," 219, 225.

100. If we look for reasons that standard sensory and motor functions should

I doubt Nussbaum would deny that *some* individuals flourish without particular senses or with very restricted mobility. Between the most successful lives of blind, deaf, or paralyzed people and the most successful lives of "able-bodied" people, there is the same sort of incommensurability that there is among the latter. The flourishing of people with sensory and motor impairments can be characterized in terms of other valuable functionings (e.g., affiliation, play, imagination, and practical reason), but few of these functionings, or the capabilities for them, appear to be individually necessary for flourishing.[101] As Jerome Segal has argued, many people flourish with less than a full set of the functional capabilities that Nussbaum regards as essential: some live rich lives without sex or the opportunity for sex, cut off from the natural world, or with little or no capacity for play and mirth; we may not envy their lives, but we can acknowledge their quality.[102] It is doubtful that any formula could specify the minimum combinations of functionings or capabilities necessary for flourishing, especially since functionings and capabilities can be described at different levels of generality or abstraction. It might be claimed that it was intrinsically harder for people with limited sensory or motor functions to achieve almost *any* minimum combination (e.g., to form friendships, have

---

be regarded as integral to human flourishing, one obvious consideration is their aesthetic value—their beauty, richness, and complexity. But we do not accord high priority to the correction of color-blindness, tone deafness, and impairments of smell or taste, despite the great aesthetic loss they entail. Nor do we feel deficient in lacking atypical sensory functions in which we might find equally great aesthetic value. While we may regret that we lack a sixth sense or, less fancifully, the acoustic range or olfactory sensitivity of a normal dog, we do not feel ourselves impaired in lacking them, and we might well decline to undergo surgery to acquire them. Certainly, the lack of typical sensations is more salient and more likely to be a source of envy. But that provides only a psychological explanation for the priority of correction over enhancement—in the case of enhanced functions, we do not know, or sufficiently appreciate, what we are missing. That saving ignorance would be lost if enhancement procedures became routinely available, and we learned from those who underwent them about the array of sensation and experience we were missing.

101. For sensory and motor functions themselves, the line between functionings and capabilities has little significance; for example, it is only in extreme and peculiar circumstances that one would be *able* to see without seeing.

102. Jerome M. Segal, "Living at a High Economic Standard: A Functioning Analysis," in *Ethics of Consumption: The Good Life, Justice, and Global Stewardship* (Lanham, Md.: Rowman & Littlefield, 1998), 347–48.

198 *David Wasserman*

fun, or engage in practical reason). But that case has not been made, and Nussbaum does not even attempt to make it.

It might be argued, however, that *fewer* minimally adequate combinations were available on the average to people with sensory and motor impairments than to able-bodied people, so that the "capability sets" of the former were smaller. Moreover, it would be plausible to deny that this difference was socially constructed—people with more or better sensory or motor function have, in general, more ways of doing things in almost all environments. But the question is why having a bigger capability set should matter: why should the number of ways of flourishing available to a person make any difference to the appraisal of his well-being?

Several factors are associated with the size of one's capability set that do seem relevant to the appraisal of well-being. Clearly, it is objectionable to lose options as a consequence of some independently identifiable injustice, such as prejudicial exclusion. I would feel aggrieved at being denied the opportunity for military or medical training because of my race, regardless of whether I had any interest in military or medical service. But if a smaller range of options does not result from such an injustice, what is the grievance?

We might also value a larger capability set to increase the likelihood of finding a satisfactory life plan—it is more likely that one will find one's favorite dish on a long than a short menu (of the same type). But we do not confront possible life plans the way we confront items on a menu—with fully formed preferences. Our preferences among ways of living are formed in the light of our capacities and limitations; a person born blind is unlikely to chafe at the constraint of being unable to pursue a career in which the sense of sight is central, as long as there are other respected, remunerative careers that satisfy his taste for challenge and adventure.[103] Sen and Nussbaum are anxious to withhold approval of the severely circumscribed capability sets available to people, particularly women, in many less developed countries, and they are right to reject subjective satisfaction as a criterion for acceptability. But while it is true that people have a remarkable capacity to adapt to stifling and oppressive circumstances, it is also true that people can flourish with comparatively limited options.

---

103. A person who loses his sight after forming his life plans may, of course, be devastated, but having a life plan thwarted is, as I have stressed in criticizing Daniels, far worse than having it unavailable from the start.

Another reason that a larger capability set might appear more valuable is in giving the individual a fuller choice and thus more of what Scanlon calls the value of choice—the value that comes from having an outcome arise from one's own decision.[104] Both Sen and Nussbaum insist that certain activities are only valuable, or more valuable, for being chosen.[105] As options narrow to the vanishing point, choice may become default. But above some elusive minimum, the value of choice may be as greater or greater in choosing among fewer options. To value more ways of flourishing when fewer will do is to indulge in a kind of opportunities fetishism. We may envy privileged and talented people their apparently boundless options, but the size of their capability sets has only a tenuous connection with their flourishing.

These misgivings about the application of the capabilities approach to disabilities mirror a broader uncertainty about how the insights of Sen and Nussbaum about the multiple aspects of human flourishing can be refined into a usable metric of comparative well-being. While a reliance on external resources is surely insufficient to capture the disadvantages associated with disability, it certainly provides a useful starting point. The most salient social fact about people with disabilities is their poverty and unemployment. One does not need to deny that people can flourish in poverty and without regular employment to regard the poverty and unemployment figures for people with disabilities as a useful index for political purposes of their comparative disadvantage. Perhaps justice requires that our society make available more ways of living well without wealth or full employment, but it also requires some reduction in poverty and unemployment.

Segal has suggested that the resources of a capabilities approach are best employed, for purposes of political justice, not in attempting to assess "the good life or human well-being in all its richness" but in focusing more narrowly on an adequate measure of economic well-being, a standard of

---

104. Thomas Scanlon, "The Significance of Choice" in *Tanner Lectures on Human Values VIII*, ed. S. McMurrin (Salt Lake City: University of Utah Press, 1988), 177–85.

105. See David Crocker, "Functioning and Capability: The Foundations of Sen's and Nussbaum's Development Ethic, Part 2," in *Women, Culture, and Development*, ed. Martha Nussbaum and Jonathan Glover (New York: Oxford University Press/Clarendon, 1995), 182–86.

living.[106] He proposes a fairly complex measure, which takes account of such aspects of economic well-being as clothing, housing, food, transportation, health, education, work, security, and leisure. Such a measure would be "relatively stable across alternative visions of the good life,"[107] and it would clearly be an improvement over such standard measures as income and expenditure in assessing the economic well-being of people with disabilities. Living well economically would not be necessary for every variety of human flourishing, but it would be a central component or aspect of man if not most life plans. For that reason, it might be appropriate to treat large disparities in that living standard associated with impairment, as well as with race and gender, as a presumptive injustice.

A theory of justice that adopts a capabilities metric will require more than this, however, to guide the accommodation of people with atypical physical and mental functions. A society in which people with atypical functions enjoyed roughly the same standard of living as the general population, in terms of food, clothing, housing, work, security, and leisure, would clearly be more just than our own society. But that society could still be faulted if its impaired citizens, despite their comfort, security, and leisure, had little opportunity for friendship, adventure, or cultural enrichment. It is unclear, though, how we could assess their comparative disadvantage without recourse to a more comprehensive account of human flourishing. And it is unclear how such an account could avoid consigning people with impairments to very low levels of well-being simply by virtue of their lack of valuable functionings or their smaller capability sets.

The Complexity of Distributive Justice: Equality, Utility, Priority

Even if we have an adequate metric of well-being, we must still decide how much disparity in advantage justice can tolerate. It is doubtful that any plausible scheme of social cooperation would yield complete equality on any metric of well-being that was not based entirely on material resources. It is therefore likely that we will have to choose between schemes that have higher average (or total) well-being and schemes that have smaller disparities in well-being.

Few political theorists, even those who describe themselves as egalitar-

106. Segal, "Living at a High Economic Standard," 354.
107. Segal, "Living at a High Economic Standard," 359.

ian, would consider only the disparities in, and not the absolute levels of, well-being or would consider it just to reduce everyone to the lowest level of well-being in the society. This might be taken as evidence that most egalitarians are really pluralists, that they give weight to other values besides equality, such as total or average well-being. It might be argued that a commitment to what Dworkin calls "equal concern and respect" underlies egalitarianism and that such a commitment entails a concern for well-being as well as equality. For to treat people with equal concern, we must have concern for them, and such concern would seem to require us to give some weight to their absolute levels of well-being. But it may also be, as Parfit suggests, that much of what passes for egalitarianism is really "prioritism"—a commitment to according absolute or weighted priority to the worst-off, regardless of the effect on the overall distribution.[108] Unlike egalitarianism, "prioritism" would not favor reductions in the well-being of the better-off that did not redound to the benefit of the worst-off.

Any theory of justice that either is committed to equal concern rather than formal equality, or that acknowledges the sometimes competing claims of beneficence must weigh average well-being against disparities in well-being—a conundrum associated with, but not limited to, utilitarianism. While people with impairments have been unfairly typecast to illustrate this conundrum, as individuals with the worst and the least tractable disadvantages, a less distorted understanding of impairment hardly eliminates the problem. Thus, consider the father's dilemma presented by Thomas Nagel:

> Suppose I have two children, one of which is quite normal and happy, the other of which suffers from a painful handicap. . . . Suppose I must decide between moving to an expensive city where the second child can receive special medical treatment and schooling, but where the family's standard of living will be lower and the neighborhood will be unpleasant and dangerous for the first child—or else moving to a pleasant semi-rural neighborhood where the first child . . . can have a free and agreeable life. . . . [Suppose] the gain to the first child of moving to the suburb is substantially greater than the gain to the second child of moving to the city. . . . [T]he . . . benefits will not make [the second child] happy but only less miserable. For the first child, on the other hand, the choice is between a happy life and a disagreeable one.[109]

---

108. Derek Parfit, "Equality and Priority," *Ratio* 10 (n.s.), no. 3 (December 1997): 213.

109. Thomas Nagel, "Equality," in *Mortal Questions* (Cambridge: Cambridge University Press, 1979), 123–24.

This dilemma does not evaporate with a more realistic understanding of disability. Even if most familiar impairments would not present the father with such a stark choice, there are surely some conditions, such as painful, degenerative neuromuscular disorders, for which Nagel's framing of the alternatives would be plausible. Moving to the city would clearly be the egalitarian decision, as well as the prioritarian one. If the difference in benefit to the two children were only slight, it would clearly be the fairer decision. But if we recognize other values besides formal equality or do not give absolute priority to the interests of the worse-off child, we would find it unfair to the first child to reduce him to the same level of misery as the second for very slight gains in the second child's well-being.

A second general problem of justice that confronts the accommodation of people with impairments is the moral significance of numbers. A group appears to have a stronger claim, to more extensive accommodation, the larger its size. It makes no difference whether the claim for accommodation involves variations in bodily dimensions, in language, or in physical and mental functions. The number of people in a community who speak Spanish, or Chinese, as a first language is frequently adduced in support of, or opposition to, demands for bilingual education or signage. Similarly, the ADA is prefaced by a congressional finding that forty-three million Americans have one or more disabilities and that the proportion will increase as our population ages. (For this reason, the reduction in the number of people with various impairments by selective abortion may disadvantage people with those impairments. Although, as Buchanan notes, a reduction in numbers may free up more funds for corrective measures, it also reduces the "moral capital" for accommodation.)

But the moral significance of numbers, assumed in policy debate, raises vexing problem for political philosophers who reject the summation or averaging of well-being across individuals to determine the overall goodness of a state of affairs (or who reject the assumption that a basic structure or society is to be appraised morally by its overall goodness).[110] If the

---

110. Contractarian theories sometimes accord significance to numbers indirectly, by regarding justice as determined or constituted by the rules or basic structure that self-interested people would adopt in ignorance of their actual circumstances. The underlying commitment to equality is expressed procedurally, through the universal ignorance in which the cooperative scheme is chosen. For some of these contractarian theories, the number of people at a given level of well-being is significant in this context because it determines the likelihood of finding

number of people with similar claims affects the weight of their claims, it cannot be because their individual claims are any stronger or weaker.[111]

It might be argued that the relevance of numbers to social choices has been misconstrued. The number of people with a given characteristic or condition is relevant not because the claims or more people are cumulatively stronger or because they suffer a larger net deprivation from the failure to meet them. Rather, the numbers are relevant because once there are enough individuals with a linguistic or functional variation, they become a cognizable social group, and the failure to accommodate such a group is demeaning to its members in a way that the failure to meet their individual claims is not. But this claim would seem implausible unless the individuals were so closely identified with their group that the slight to the group would be more damaging to their self-respect than the mere failure to meet their individual claims. This level of identification will not always be found for individuals in a linguistic or functional minority. Moreover, this claim would regard numbers beyond the threshold for group recognition as irrelevant, which would conflict with strong, widespread intuitions about their continuing relevance.

Another account of the relevance of numbers would rely not on group identity but on the social fact that larger numbers are *perceived* as having greater claims. In light of this social fact, the failure to provide people with a given condition . . . a level of accommodation commensurate with their numbers would betray or express a societal devaluation of their individual claims. The fact that the numbers usually count, even in the absence of a clear moral justification for their counting, makes the selective disregard of numbers an affront. This argument has greater force as a critique of current social practice, however, than as a prescription for future practice. If the numbers should not count, they should count for no one, and it might be more just to disregard them consistently.

---

oneself at that level of well-being and thereby affects the expected outcome of a cooperative scheme. Other contractarian theories, notably that of Rawls, reject the recourse to expected outcome, in part because they think that the extremely high stakes make such calculations inappropriate.

111. Thus, Nagel insists that the claim of his second child would not be weakened if he had *two* healthy children with conflicting interests: "Suppose a third child is added to the situation, another happy, healthy, one, and I am faced with the same choice in the allocation of indivisible goods. The greater urgency of benefiting the second child remains" ("Equality," 124).

These fundamental issues of justice are writ large in the allocation of educational resources for cognitively disabled children. The Individuals with Disabilities Education Act (IDEA) mandates a "free appropriate education" for all children, regardless of ability. Its mandate has been variously construed to require merely "some educational benefit" for severely disabled children, to require that disabled children receive benefits fully "commensurate" with those received by normal children, or to require that they receive the "maximum possible" benefit. Special education can be very expensive, and many financially strained school systems claim that providing more than minimal benefit to severely disabled children requires drastic cutbacks in other programs, such as honors classes for gifted students.

One type of case arising under the IDEA concerns cognitively normal or "gifted" children with a sensory or motor impairment. Amy Rowley, the plaintiff in the leading case of this type, was an above-average student with a hearing impairment who sued the school system because it refused to provide her with a classroom interpreter. The U.S. Supreme Court took her academic and social progress as evidence that she had received an appropriate education with the less extensive accommodation the school offered—a hearing aid and training in lip-reading.[112] *Rowley* can be seen in the ADA's quite different terms as raising the question of whether an interpreter is reasonable accommodation for an "otherwise-qualified" student. In cases such as *Rowley*, it is easy to see the failure to accommodate, reasonable or not, as denying the student an opportunity to develop her cognitive potential. A different sort of dilemma arises for cases in which the student's impairment is itself cognitive.

Unlike Rowley, who required only a change in the medium of classroom communication to excel academically, children with severe cognitive impairments may require intensive tutoring to achieve far more modest academic goals. Whether such tutoring was an alternative or a supplement to regular classroom instruction, it would be difficult to treat it merely as an accommodation for a different learning style, such as the interpreter demanded by Rowley. But the case for tutoring seems no less compelling than the case for an interpreter. Some cognitive functions, such as memory and practical reason, arguably have the general importance mistakenly as-

---

112. *Board of Education of the Hendrick Hudson Central School District v. Rowley* 458 U.S. 176 (Superior Court 1982).

cribed to particular sensory and motor functions. For that reason, the case for correcting cognitive impairments is perhaps stronger than it is for any sensory or motor impairment. Moreover, the distinction between correction and accommodation is blurred in an educational context, since all children are thought to need schooling to "correct" their ignorance and intellectual immaturity; changing them is the point of the whole enterprise. It is hard to deny that more intensive, customized education for cognitively impaired children would be an unequivocal good, if it could be provided without increasing their isolation and stigmatization. But such education may be extremely expensive.

There are, of course, several familiar ways of denying or mitigating the school system's dilemma. We may claim that conflicts arise only because of an unjustly meager allocation for public schooling. We can deny that psychometric measures of intelligence adequately capture cognitive potential. We can also insist that our society should drastically reduce the disparities in social and economic outcomes for people of varying cognitive skill.

But conflicts will inevitably occur on the margins of any educational budget, however large, and there is no reason to believe that large disparities and severe deficits in cognitive skill will disappear with more appropriate ways of measuring it. And while it would be far better if our society provided more dignified ways of living and forms of work for people with limited cognitive functioning, and gave them greater control over their lives, it seems hard to deny that severe cognitive impairments limit the prospects for flourishing in a way that few motor and sensory impairments do.

The issues of distributive justice raised by the IDEA are the subject of an entire book by Robert Veatch, who focuses on the hypothetical case of Eddie Conrad, a mentally retarded ten-year-old boy with visual and hearing impairments and a speech impairment that can be alleviated, but not eliminated, by regular therapy.[113] Hiring the additional speech teacher needed to provide this therapy would force the school system to eliminate physical education at an elementary school level. Veatch concludes that justice is best understood as equality of outcome, objectively assessed, and that as such, it requires the speech therapy for Conrad, even at the expense of the physical education program.[114]

---

113. Robert Veatch, *The Foundation of Justice: Why the Retarded and the Rest of Us Have Claims to Equality* (Oxford: Oxford University Press, 1986).

114. Veatch, *The Foundation of Justice*, 164.

But what if Conrad would benefit significantly not only from regular speech therapy but from intensive daily tutoring, and the expense of those tutors would require significant cutbacks in basic education for other students? Even with the cuts, and despite the tutoring, the objective educational outcomes of most other students would probably still be far higher than Conrad's, so they would still be objectively better off. More broadly, Veatch would be committed to a budget that left the most "gifted" children at the same level of educational development, or general well-being, as the most severely impaired child (far more impaired than Eddie Conrad), as long as additional educational resources to the most severely impaired conferred some marginal benefit.

Many people who regard themselves as broadly egalitarian would find such an allocation grossly unfair. Their objection would not necessarily be based on the number of normal and gifted children adversely affected. Nor would it necessarily reflect the conviction that society had only a limited duty to correct the results of "the natural lottery." The disadvantages associated with cognitive impairment cannot be attributed to the natural lottery alone; many of them arise from the increasing premium on literacy in modern societies. Moreover, few people would feel that the claim of an impaired child to additional educational resources would be significantly stronger if his particular impairment did not occur in preindustrial societies and was attributable in a general way to the physical environment of a modern society.

On the other extreme of broadly egalitarian positions, Pogge's equality of educational opportunity, which I discussed earlier, would merely require the same monetary allotment for each student, regardless of cognitive ability.[115] That proposal would be open to many of the same objections as Pogge's scheme for equal health protection, since it would leave cognitively impaired children with no claim to greater educational resources, no matter how well they would do with them or how poorly they would do without them. Many people who find Veatch's standard too demanding would find Pogge's too stinting.

A middle road is suggested by William Galston, who proposes a standard of commensurate benefit:

> In spite of profound differences among individuals, the full development of each individual—however great or limited his or her natural capacities—is

---

115. Pogge, *Realizing Rawls*, 173–80.

equal in moral weight to that of every other. . . . [A] policy that neglects the educable retarded so that they do not learn how to care for themselves and must be institutionalized is, considered in itself, as bad as one that deprives extraordinary gifts of their chance to flower.[116]

But technology makes "natural capacity" and "full development" terribly elastic notions, which raises serious problems for any standard that requires a comparison of actual and potential development.

In the end, we may be able to do no better than to strike an ad hoc balance between equality and utility or between the urgency of benefits to the least well-off and the magnitude of benefits to the better-off. Rawls warns that such recourse to intuition limits the possibilities for meaningful deliberation:

> The assignment of weight is an essential and not a minor part of a conception of justice. If we cannot explain how these weights are to be determined by reasonable ethical criteria, the means of rational discussion have come to an end. An intuitionist conception of justice is, one might say, but half a conception.[117]

However, the prospects for a more principled and determinate assignment of weights do not appear very good, and we may decide that half a conception is better than none.

---

116. William Galston, *Liberal Purposes: Goods, Virtues, and Diversity in the Liberal State* (New York: Cambridge University Press, 1991), 192–93.
117. Rawls, *A Theory of Justice*, 41.

3

A Feminist Standpoint

Mary B. Mahowald

Introduction

Several years ago, I wrote an article entitled "On Treatment of Myopia," in which I argue for the incorporation of a feminist standpoint into the process of ethical decision making and the development of public policy on issues related to health care.[1] As "feminist," a feminist standpoint may articulate any of the various versions of feminism.[2] While these represent different, sometimes conflicting philosophical orientations, the different versions of feminism arise from a common recognition of gender injustice and aim to reduce or eliminate that injustice. As "standpoint," a feminist standpoint articulates a particular perspective that is not "dominant." In general, the dominant perspective of white, middle-class, able, heterosexual males who predominate in positions of social power defines the rules and practices that are applied to everyone in their society.[3] In contrast, a

---

1. Mary B. Mahowald, "On Treatment of Myopia: Feminism, Standpoint Theory, and Bioethics," in *Feminism and Bioethics: Beyond Reproduction*, ed. Susan Wolf (New York: Oxford University Press, 1995), 95–115. To critics who would prefer language not associated with visual impairment, I apologize for not being able to find a better metaphor than myopia to express my thoughts.

2. Alison Jaggar and Paula Struhl, *Feminist Frameworks* (New York: McGraw-Hill, 1978); Rosemarie Tong, *Feminist Thought* (Boulder, Colo.: Westview, 1989).

3. As an exemplar of the dominant standpoint, which to the dominant individual is universally applicable, see Thomas Nagel, *Equality and Partiality* (New York: Oxford University Press, 1991). Nagel distinguishes between a personal and im-

feminist standpoint is the perspective of those who have little or no part in determining those rules and practices because they mainly occupy a nondominant position in society. It thus provides a corrective lens for the inevitably limited perspective (i.e., the myopia) of the dominant group.

Admittedly, all of us are myopic, even those in nondominant groups, in that we only experience or see the world from where we stand in it. From there we cannot see very far, nor can we see from all angles. Moreover, because our singular perspectives limit our vision, we inevitably miss or mistake the trees for the forest. A feminist standpoint imputes privileged status to nondominant perspectives not because those perspectives are more valid or more accurate (although sometimes they are) than the dominant perspective but because nondominant perspectives are typically missing from the perspective that dominates society at large.[4] Living in that

---

personal standpoint, arguing that the latter is indispensable to ethics (10–20). In contrast, a feminist standpoint argues that an impersonal standpoint is neither feasible nor desirable because knowledge is inevitably "situated." As Donna Haraway puts it, an impersonal standpoint suggests the "god trick of seeing everything from nowhere." Her account of the "embodied nature of all vision" is particularly pertinent to a discussion of disabilities. A feminist standpoint, for Haraway, is based on "a doctrine of embodied objectivity," which involves "partial, locatable, critical knowledges sustaining the possibility of webs of connections called solidarity in politics and shared conversations in epistemology." See Donna Haraway, "Situated Knowledges: The Science Question in Feminism and the Privilege of Partial Perspective," *Feminist Studies* 14 (1988): 581–84.

4. In addition to Haraway, authors to whom I am indebted for my understanding of a feminist standpoint include Nancy C. M. Hartsock, "The Feminist Standpoint: Developing the Ground for a Specifically Feminist Historical Materialism," in *Feminism and Methodology: Social Science Issues*, ed. Sandra Harding (Bloomington: Indiana University Press, 1987), 136–62; Dorothy E. Smith, "Women's Perspective as a Radical Critique of Sociology," in *Feminism and Methodology*, 85–96; "Rethinking Standpoint Epistemology: 'What Is Strong Objectivity'?" in *Feminist Epistemologies*, ed. Linda Alcoff and Elizabeth Potter (New York: Routledge, 1993), 49–82; Marianne Janack, "Standpoint Epistemology without the 'Standpoint'? An Examination of Epistemic Privilege and Epistemic Authority," *Hypatia* 12, no. 2 (Spring 1997): 125–39; Sara Ruddick, *Maternal Thinking: Toward a Politics of Peace* (New York: Ballantine, 1989), 127–39; Nel Noddings, "Ethics from the Standpoint of Women," in *Theoretical Perspectives on Sexual Difference*, ed. Deborah L. Rhode (New Haven: Yale University Press, 1990), 160–73; Catharine A. MacKinnon, "Feminism, Marxism, Method, and the State," in *Feminism and Methodology*, 136–56; Terry Winant, "The Feminist Standpoint: A Matter of Language," *Hypatia* 2 (Winter 1987): 1123–48; Alison M. Jaggar, *Feminist Poli-*

society, nondominant groups and individuals cannot help but be aware of the dominant group's perspective, while the dominant group may be totally unaware of the nondominant groups' and individuals' perspectives unless it grants privileged status to them. In other words, dominant people need nondominant people more than the latter need the former to reduce the limitations of their perspective.

Because women belong to multiple nondominant groups, advocacy for gender justice implies advocacy for women not only as women but as members of other nondominant groups also. A version of feminism that fails to express such advocacy by opposing discrimination against any non-dominant group ignores or denies its own essential goal. A feminist stand-point thus demands advocacy for persons with disabilities.

Feminists have not always recognized that advocacy for people with disabilities is logically and practically required by their commitment to gender justice. This is unfortunate not only because so many women are disabled and those who are currently able will eventually become disabled but also because they share the same battle against stereotypes of dependence, passivity, and inferiority.[5] Men who are disabled are thus dominant vis-à-vis women who are disabled. As Adrienne Asch and Michelle Fine put it, "concerns with 'emasculation' may promote efforts directed toward those at the locus of the *masculinity-dependence* contradiction, not toward those at the redundant intersection of *femininity* and *dependence*."[6]

As is true of men with disabilities, many individuals are dominant in some respects while nondominant in others. While nondominant by gender, for example, I am dominant by class, sexual orientation, ability status, and racial identity. These dominances suggest the need to acknowledge at the start of this essay the limitations that they inevitably entail. Although I have attempted to reduce my nearsightedness by learning from those

---

tics and Human Nature (Totowa, N.J.: Rowman & Allanheld, 1983), 369–71, 377–89.

5. These stereotypes are also more likely to be attributed to women because of their longer life span. Persons with disabilities in the United States number from thirty-five million to forty-three million, depending on how disability is defined; one-third of these are over sixty-five years of age, with women comprising the bulk of that population. See Joseph P. Shapiro, *No Pity* (New York: Times Books, 1993), 6.

6. Adrienne Asch and Michelle Fine, "Introduction: Beyond Pedestals," in *Women with Disabilities*, ed. Michelle Fine and Adrienne Asch (Philadelphia: Temple University Press, 1988), 3.

whose views emerge from nondominant experiences that I lack, I undoubtedly fall short of the understanding that emerges from reflection on
one's own experience of disability. All that I write here, then, should be
interpreted within the context of my own inevitable myopia.

Myopia extends to other areas of my life as well. For example, I am a
life-long citizen of the United States, who has only visited other parts of
the world on occasion. Except for three years when I lived and taught
junior high school in a poor Latino neighborhood of New York City, I
have spent most of my adult life in a middle-class environment. Trained as
a philosopher, I lack the academic skills of the social scientist, the basic
scientist, or the clinician. Nonetheless, through interactions with clinicians
in a medical school/hospital complex for many years, I have often been
involved in specific cases, some of which are cited in this essay.

Throughout most of my adult life, I have been a feminist.[7] This is a
nondominant standpoint in its own right. Although my feminism was
sparked more by the observation of gender stereotyping and discrimination in the lives of others than in my own, I have had my share of pertinent
experiences in that regard.[8] Theoretically, however, my feminism is part
and parcel of a commitment to an egalitarian ideal whose underpinnings
are socialist and religious.[9] In accordance with that ideal, the concepts of,
and relation between, equality and differences are crucial to the standpoint
I bring to this essay. In what follows, therefore, I examine these concepts
in relation to each other, applying that account to disabilities, which are
different but not equal, and to people with disabilities, who are different
but equal. Gender is the difference I emphasize because it relates to two
issues I explore more fully: (1) the possible conflict between feminism as
advocacy for women and advocacy for the disabled, as exemplified in the

---

7. The first publication in which I identified myself as such was entitled "Feminism, Socialism, and Christianity," *Cross Currents* 25 (1975): 33–50.

8. Some of these experiences are recounted in Mary B. Mahowald, "A Feminist
in the Medical Academy: An Idealistic Pragmatist Account," in *Women in Medical
Education*, ed. Delese Wear (New York: State University of New York Press, 1996),
47–58.

9. In the article cited in n. 7, I wrote that I considered myself socialist and
Christian as well as feminist, distinguishing between individualistic and "communalistic" interpretations of those terms. As will be clear from what follows, my
commitment is to a communalistic interpretation of feminism. This should not
be equated with communitarianism, which, in my judgment, may be inimical to
feminism.

issue of prenatal testing and termination of pregnancy for disabling conditions, and (2) the role of caregivers, most of whom are women, in caring for those who are disabled.

In the theoretical part of the essay, my main goal is to explicate how discrimination (injustice) does not necessarily or justifiably follow from differences. In the empirical or descriptive part, my main goal is to illustrate the range of differences that are morally relevant to an analysis of disabilities based on a feminist standpoint. My approach is characterized as *a* feminist standpoint rather than *the* feminist standpoint. It thus represents a particular version of feminism, with which other feminists may disagree.

Differences and Equality

Although differences are often associated with inequality, this is not a causal or necessary relationship. Both terms may refer to quantitative relationships, as when the term *difference* is used for the remainder in subtraction, which can be but usually is not equal to the minuend or the subtrahend. More often, "difference" simply identifies changes or contrasts that have nothing to do with equality or inequality. I am different from my sister, for example, because I have a different nose structure, eye color, and life plan; none of these differentiating factors render us, or the elements being compared, unequal or different in value. The term *equal* means that different elements on both sides of an equation have the same value. Different things may therefore be equal, but that does not make them the same. In the abstract world of math, equality signifies sameness if the elements on both sides of the equation are identical, as in $X = X$ or $2 + 3 = 2 + 3$. In the real world, however, two things are never exactly the same. Even things that are descriptively identical, such as identical twins or all of the matches in a matchbox, are not the same because each individual twin or match occupies a different place in the world or in the matchbox.

In math or algebra, when different entities are declared equal, the equation may look like $2 + 3 = 4 + 1$ or $X = Y$. If we were to change the variables in the algebraic equation, we could illustrate the equality between women and men by using the letters that indicate their different chromosomal arrangements; thus, $XX = XY$.[10] We could also illustrate the equality between people of the same sex who have different chromosomal arrangements, as in $XO = XX$, or in people of either sex who have diverse chromosomal arrangements, so that $XX = XY = XO = XXY = XYY$.[11] Because some of these chromosomal arrangements may connote a disability, the last equation is intended to illustrate equality between people who are disabled and those who are not and also among those who have different disabilities.

A feminist standpoint is primarily concerned with gender equality or gender justice. Admittedly, equality is not necessarily equivalent to justice; some people distinguish between equity and equality, relating the former to justice but not the latter.[12] On the account of equality described earlier, however, gender equality *may* be construed as gender justice. This usage accords with a popular tendency to use the terms interchangeably, for example, in discussions of racial justice or racial equality. Racial equality and gender equality signify different but overlapping goals for those who oppose discrimination based on race or sex. Comparable terms, such as *ability justice* or *ability equality* (or *disability justice* or *disability equality*) are needed to identify the overlapping goal of overcoming discrimination against the disabled. As already suggested, a feminist standpoint is opposed not only to sexism but also to racism, classism, heterosexism, and ableism.

A feminist standpoint is also opposed to inequalities that occur within

---

10. I introduced the analogy between human chromosomal diversity and algebraic equations in "Gender Justice in Genetics," *Women's Health Issues* 7, no. 4 (July/August 1997): 230–33.

11. XO, XXY, and XYY represent chromosomal abnormalities, but whether they also connote disabilities depends on how disability is defined. XO refers to Turner's syndrome, a condition of females that involves infertility and shortness of stature; in some texts the O is dropped because it simply refers to the absence of a chromosome. XXY refers to Klinefelter's syndrome, a condition that involves infertility. XYY is associated with increased stature and severe acne; although greater aggressivity has also been alleged in XYY males, this finding is not supported by the evidence to date. See R. J. M. Gardner and G. R. Sutherland, *Chromosome Abnormalities and Genetic Counseling* (New York: Oxford University Press, 1989), 195, 196.

12. For a fuller elaboration of the meaning of equality that underlies my perspective, see my *Women and Children in Health Care: An Unequal Majority* (New York: Oxford University Press, 1993), especially chap. 1, "An Egalitarian Overview," 2–23.

any of the groups designated previously. These occur in part because individuals simultaneously belong to different groups and, in addition, because they sometimes defy the generalizations with which their group memberships are associated. As Henry Louis Gates, Jr., puts it, "there isn't one way to be white or black, gay or straight, Hispanic or Asian, liberal or conservative, male or female, Jewish or Christian."[13] Neither is there only one way to be able or disabled. If inequalities are to be minimized, the inevitability of differences within distinct ethnic and cultural groups demands the avoidance of a tendency to equate group designations with definitions of particular human beings. Gates calls this tendency "the omnipotence of the label" and says it "can be as dangerous as any of the ideologies it annexes."[14] A feminist standpoint reduces this tendency by insisting on attention to individual as well as group differences.[15]

Identifying and assessing differences from a justice or equality perspective suggests a strategy by which the two principal approaches to contemporary bioethics may be incorporated. These approaches are the principle-based method proposed by Tom Beauchamp and James Childress in *Principles of Bioethics*[16] and the case-based method proposed by Albert Jonsen and Stephen Toulmin in *The Abuse of Casuistry*.[17] Beauchamp and Childress elaborate four principles that they consider applicable to specific ethical dilemmas: respect for autonomy, beneficence, nonmaleficence, and justice. They consider these principles derivable from what they call a "common morality."[18] Jonsen and Toulmin advocate a method called casuistry, which, in their judgment, has been misinterpreted and unfairly

---

13. Henry Louis Gates, Jr., "Ethics and Ethnicity," *Bulletin of the American Academy of Arts and Sciences* 51, no. 1 (September/October 1997): 45.

14. Gates, "Ethics and Ethnicity," 46.

15. I argue for an extension of a feminist standpoint beyond nondominant groups to nondominant individuals in "On Treatment of Myopia," in *Feminism and Bioethics*, 101–3.

16. Tom L. Beauchamp and James F. Childress, *Principles of Biomedical Ethics* (New York: Oxford University Press, 1994).

17. Albert R. Jonsen and Stephen Toulmin, *The Abuse of Casuistry* (Berkeley: University of California Press, 1988). Other principle-based and case-based approaches, as well as approaches that combine principle-based and case-based reasoning, are outlined in Mary B. Mahowald, "So Many Ways to Think: An Overview of Approaches to Ethical Issues in Geriatrics," *Clinics in Geriatric Medicine* 10, no. 3 (August 1994): 403–18.

18. Beauchamp and Childress, *Principles of Biomedical Ethics*, 37.

derided since medieval times. For Jonsen and Toulmin, casuistry involves comparison of the specific circumstances of a new case with those of para-digmatic cases, applying the maxims followed in the best-fitting paradigm to the new case, with the certainty of the resolution dependent on the fit of the new case with the old.

Some ethicists collapse the principles of beneficence and nonmaleficence into one, arguing that the obligation to avoid harm and do good are part of a continuum, nonmaleficence representing the more demanding end of the spectrum and beneficence representing the less demanding end. Beauchamp himself has elsewhere identified the conflict between auton-omy and beneficence as the major conflict of bioethics.[19] In that context, justice may be construed as a mediating principle for resolving conflicts that inevitably arise not only between respect for autonomy and benefi-cence/nonmaleficence but also in determining whose autonomy should be respected when the preferences of different individuals are at odds, and whose benefits or burdens weigh more heavily when they are unequally distributed among those affected. Taking justice as the mediating principle elevates it to a position of preeminence over the other two (or three). A feminist standpoint reflects this view in its call for justice toward all of those who are unequally affected by what is done or not done.[20]

Casuistry's attention to the particular circumstances of cases may be de-scribed as attention to differences. Only to the extent that the impact of specific differences is understood can justice be maximized or injustice minimized in any particular case. Just as for Jonsen and Toulmin, each case is different, but there are generalities that allow valid and useful compari-sons, so with our understanding of gender differences and ability differ-ences.[21] The differences involve conflicting preferences, burdens and bene-fits that may make it impossible to give priority to either respect for autonomy or beneficence or nonmaleficence for a particular individual or

---

19. Laurence McCullough and Tom L. Beauchamp, *Medical Ethics: The Moral Responsibilities of Physicians* (Engelwood Cliffs: Prentice Hall, 1984), 13–51.

20. A libertarian feminist might disagree with this interpretation. However, I subsequently argue that a libertarian version of feminism fails to advocate for the interests of all women.

21. Jonsen and Toulmin would employ "maxims" used in precedent-setting cases to address new cases. Although the maxims are more specific than the princi-ples of Beauchamp and Childress, they still represent a level of generality or else they would not be helpful in addressing new cases.

group. Justice is the mediating principle by which the circumstantial differences are to be interpreted in an effort to balance, or at least reduce, the
inequalities that occur. Before this principle can be applied, however, the
specific differences that characterize a particular case or issue need to be
delineated. The remainder of this essay is mainly devoted to that delineation. While I identify some of the inequities or inequalities associated with
these differences, my remarks in that regard are suggestive and illustrative;
in no way do they constitute a complete account of morally relevant differences between groups and individuals, whether men or women, able or
disabled.

Differences among Disabilities

Just as the "culture of women" spreads across different ethnic and cultural
groups, so too does the "culture of persons with disabilities." And just as
some women do not identify with a "feminist culture" whose goal is gender equality, some people who are deaf do not identify with the "culture
of persons with disabilities."[22] The Deaf culture in fact sees itself not as a
group of people who are disabled by hearing loss but rather as a culture
whose language is sign language.[23] Moreover, individuals who do identify
with the culture of persons with disabilities experience significantly different disabilities. These differences may be better appreciated by examining
the following overlapping distinctions: the cause or etiology of the disability, its time of onset, its expected duration, the severity of its impact on
the individual and society, the type of impairment associated with it, and
its recognizability or unrecognizability to others. Because each of these is
relevant to a feminist standpoint, I will consider them all, albeit briefly.

---

22. Many women with disabilities view feminists as having virtually ignored
them and their interests. See, for example, Anita Silvers, "How Can Women with
Disabilities Countenance Feminist Bioethics?" in *Embodying Bioethics: Feminist
Advances*, ed. Laura Purdy and Anne Donchin (Lanham, Md.: Rowman & Littlefield, 1998).
23. Jamie Israel, Margaret Cunningham, Helen Thumann, and Kathleen
Shaver Arnos, "Deaf Culture," in *Cultural and Ethnic Diversity: A Guide for
Genetics Professionals*, ed. Nancy L. Fisher (Baltimore, Md.: Johns Hopkins University Press, 1996), 224. According to Shapiro, an increasing number of those
with disabilities "proclaim that it is okay, even good to be disabled" (*No Pity*, 4).

Cause or Etiology

Some disabilities are caused by nature, some by other persons, and some by oneself.[24] Disabilities caused by nature are generally involuntary.[25] Genetic disabilities, for example, are involuntary, although some may consider them "chosen" by parents who decide to have children while aware of specific genetic risks or positive prenatal diagnosis.[26] It is the child, however, who is chosen rather than the disability. Moreover, the affected fetus or child surely does not choose the disability. Other natural causes of disability include calamitous events such as hurricanes, earthquakes, and the like, which may inflict disabling conditions on those affected. The common denominator for disabilities caused by nature is that no person is to blame for them so long as the impact of the calamitous event was not escapable by the affected individuals or avoidable through the interventions of others.

Disabilities caused by the behavior of others or oneself may be accidental or deliberate. Consider, for example, the increasing number of persons who are disabled through deliberate violence (e.g., the victims of land mines or gang shootings). Those who placed the land mines or engaged in the shooting acted deliberately; those disabled as a result did not.[27] Infectious agents may also cause disabilities. Although the HIV virus has been deliberately transmitted to another, it is usually transmitted indeliberately. One may unintentionally or accidentally transmit an infection to which one is resistant and nonsymptomatic to an individual who is susceptible to the disease and its associated disability. Unintentional exposure to

---

24. According to Shapiro, fewer than 15 percent of people with disabilities in the United States were born with their disabilities. See *No Pity*, 7.

25. The term *nature* is of course problematic because it may be used more broadly to encompass the (natural) autonomy of human beings. I use it here in the narrower sense that distinguishes between human nature and the realm of nature in which and by which human beings live, but with which they do not identify themselves.

26. Laura Purdy assumes parental autonomy in such decisions when she argues, controversially, that parents have a moral responsibility to avoid the conception or birth of children with disabilities. See her *Reproducing Persons* (New York: Cornell University Press, 1996).

27. A relevant caveat involves the possibility that some individuals on either side of the issue may have acted in a counterintuitive capacity (i.e., that those who planted the land mines did so involuntarily and those who were disabled by them had anticipated and chosen the resultant disabilities).

infectious bacteria or viruses, such as those that cause polio or meningitis, illustrates a genuinely accidental cause of disability. So does hereditary transmission of genetic disease by carriers who are unaware of their carrier status. A less clear but appropriate example of a deliberate cause of disability is drunk driving. Because drinking is a deliberate behavior, referring to a disability as caused by a "drunk driving accident" is rather misleading if the "accident" is attributed to the drunk driver. It is an accident, however, for the nondrunk victim.

Perhaps the least recognized cause of disabilities is the myopia of the currently able[28] dominant group that structures society for "its own kind." This group organizes the world to facilitate its own interests on the basis of its usual requirements for optimal functioning, mainly ignoring the requirements for similar functioning on the part of those who have other requirements for optimal functioning. So, for example, those who are currently able design public facilities with curbs and stairs that deny access to wheelchair users who might otherwise use the facilities not only for their own benefit but for that of the larger society as well. To the extent that society is built, solely or mainly, to serve the interests of those who are not (yet) disabled, it fails to serve the interests of those who are disabled. From a feminist standpoint as from other egalitarian perspectives, the inequality that results is morally unacceptable.

Time of Onset

Some persons are disabled throughout their lives; others become disabled as children or adults. For people who are born with disabilities or acquire them early in life, education is often inferior or interrupted, and they are more likely to be stigmatized and abused in childhood. The lack of opportunity to establish solid work histories before becoming disabled typically impairs their ability to find or sustain meaningful employment.

Those who incur disabilities later in life may fare worse in other ways than those who incur them earlier. For example, a person born deaf, particularly one raised in a Deaf culture, where soundless communication

---

28. I prefer this term to *temporarily able* because whether a current ability is temporary is not ascertainable in advance, at least not in all cases. It is true, however, that most able people are only temporarily able because they become disabled at some point in their lives, especially in old age.

abounds, may not experience deafness as a burden but simply as an ordinary way of being for the linguistic minority to which he or she belongs.[29] In contrast, someone who once heard and then lost hearing would probably experience deafness as a disability.

A similar point may be made for family or friends of individuals with disabilities. Even though we are all always susceptible to disability, relating to someone who has always had, so far as we know, a particular disability requires no adjustment to the transition from ability to disability, or disability to ability, in our relationships to that person. In contrast, a disability that interrupts or alters someone's way of being or interacting challenges others as well as the affected person to adjust to the change.

Most of us become disabled in old age, and since the majority of the aged are women, the majority of disabled persons are women.[30] Stereotypical expectations thus present a triple hurdle for women, those who are currently able as well as those who are disabled. Ageism, sexism, and ableism may all conspire to limit the options of women who could and would remain productive as they get older.

Although time of onset usually refers to the time at which symptoms of a particular disorder appear, it may have a different meaning in the context of genetic testing. Even before a disabling condition is physiologically expressed, an individual may be socially disabled by psychological trauma, social stigmatization, and loss of insurance or employment triggered by the positive result of a genetic test. Uncertainty about the time of onset of symptoms compounds the psychological burden when the disorder is as predictable as Huntington's chorea;[31] in most situations, however, the ge-

29. Presumably, this is why Nancy Fisher includes Deaf culture in her book on *Cultural and Ethnic Diversity*, which does not focus on disabilities. Compare Israel et al., "Deaf Culture," 220–39.

30. According to Stephen G. Post, women comprise over 90 percent of the nursing home population, and "their likelihood of suffering serious dementia is much higher than for men simply because of their life span." See Stephen G. Post, "Women and Elderly Parents: Moral Controversy in an Aging Society," *Hypatia* 5, no. 1 (Spring 1990): 84.

31. Huntington's chorea is a devastating, progressive, neurological disorder, whose usual onset of symptoms occurs in adulthood, in the midst of or after one's reproductive years have been completed. Because it is autosomal dominant, it occurs in 50 percent of the offspring of those who are affected. A genetic test is now available to identify those who carry the mutation for the disease that will eventually be expressed, provided they live long enough.

netic test simply identifies susceptibility to the disorder, leaving the person unsure whether she will ever become symptomatic.[32] Except for the psychological trauma that may be unavoidable, the disabling impact of positive testing for susceptibility to genetic disorders is socially induced.

Expected Duration

Some disabilities, such as epilepsy and other seizure conditions, are episodic; others, such as cystic fibrosis, muscular dystrophy, and some forms of vision and hearing loss, are progressive. Some conditions, such as loss of a limb, are static and permanent; others, such as cancer and paralysis, can occasionally go away.

Permanent disabilities (or those thought to be permanent) are generally considered more burdensome than those that are (thought to be) temporary. But the certainty that the former entail, whether correctly assessed as such or not, may facilitate adjustment to the impairment. In this age of advancing medical technologies, fewer and fewer conditions are viewed as permanently disabling. Neurological and genetic disorders that were previously incurable are now being treated with some success.[33] The result is that many persons with disabilities for which there is still no cure or relief in sight harbor hope that medical science will discover effective treatment during their lifetime. Potential parents whose fetuses have disabling conditions sometimes continue their pregnancies with the expectation that a cure will be found during the child's lifetime. Persons who test positive for late onset disorders may live in expectation that by the time they reach the usual age of onset, a cure will be available.

Despite the advances of modern medicine, it is impossible to know whether some disabilities are transient or permanent. Repetitive stress injury, for example, may arise from overuse of a particular set of muscles, such as the hands of a typist or musician. This condition can be so severe that it causes constant pain and inability to use one's hands even for ordi-

---

32. Breast cancer is an example of a disease for which genetic susceptibility testing is now available. Although a positive test forecasts an 85 percent lifetime risk of becoming symptomatic, this prediction varies with the mutation identified and the age of the person tested.

33. For example, the use of fetal neural tissue for treatment of Parkinson's disease. See Lois M. Nora and Mary B. Mahowald, "Neural Fetal Tissue Transplants: Old and New Issues," *Zygon* 31, no. 4 (1996): 615–33.

nary life functions, yet physicians do not know whether the condition is permanent or temporary.[34] Consequently, people affected with these disorders live in a state of limbo.

Degree of Impact on the Individual and Society

Disabilities may be minor or major in their impact, often because of social adaptation or lack thereof. For example, extreme nearsightedness would be a major disability without corrective lenses; deafness could be experienced as a minor disability if most people knew and used sign language. The severity of the disability is also dependent on the degree of impairment that a particular expression of the condition entails. Cerebral palsy, for example, may be mild enough that an affected individual can walk unaided or so severe that he or she is unable to ambulate at all. Some people with this condition are gifted intellectually but unable to speak intelligibly; others can speak clearly but have only average intelligence. Because intelligence is often gauged, inappropriately, by articulateness, people with cerebral palsy who are intellectually able are sometimes treated as disabled cognitively as well as physically.[35]

The example of cerebral palsy illustrates another point about disability—namely, the difficulty of determining what degree of impairment or divergence from the "norm" should count as a disability for legal or social purposes. Consider, for instance, a sixteen-year-old named Joe who has an awkward gait due to irreparable anoxic damage at birth. He carries a diagnosis of mild spastic diplegia or cerebral palsy. Joe is intelligent, sociable, and musically talented. Through much of his childhood he has been embarrassed by his body and teased by his peers because of his "funny walk." Although he loves sports and yearns to participate, he cannot play team sports. In comparison with his peers and in light of his diagnosis, Joe *may* be described as disabled. However, in comparison with peers who have no diagnosable disability but are less intelligent, less sociable, and tone deaf, Joe is currently able or even advantaged.

---

34. This particular disorder illustrates a new social cause of disability. In many cases, it has been induced by long-term, repetitive use of computers in situations in which neither users nor their tutors are aware of the disability risks involved unless they observe specific health precautions.

35. For example, a sixty-five-year-old patient at one of our teaching hospitals had never had regular schooling because he was assumed retarded. His only disabilities were physical.

The severity of some conditions depends mainly on the goals of the affected individual—for example, hand injury to a pianist or a surgeon compared with the same injury to a professional runner. Admittedly, people's goals may be modified by the experience of disability. For example, a severely impaired university student was totally dependent on mechanical support and personal assistance for ordinary life functions. Intellectually and creatively, however, he was superior to nearly all of his peers, composing poetry that dazzled his professors. His professional goal, which he had already achieved, to some extent, was to be a writer. Had he not been so physically disabled, he might have chosen a different goal.

Societal costs of providing equitable treatment and equal opportunities and access to public facilities depend on the nature of the disability, the willingness and ability of the dominant group to address the needs and interests of people with disabilities, and the socioeconomic status of individuals who are disabled. For some, even those with profound disabilities, there are no financial costs to others because their medical care and other needs are totally covered by insurance. For those who are uninsured or underinsured, however, there may be devastating financial costs to them and their families.[36] Some people with disabilities are able to provide for their own needs through their own income, and some need little or no financial assistance because the burden of their disabilities cannot thereby be reduced.

The impact of disabilities on society is positive in its potential for broadening social awareness of the range of human capacities and their tenuousness throughout the course of a lifetime. Depending on their different talents, the majority of persons with disabilities contribute a great deal to society empirically as well as morally. In virtually every walk of life, they can and do excel, despite the discriminatory attitudes that often make the same degree of success more easily achievable by others. Recognition of these achievements contributes to the defeat of stereotypical prejudices in general and serves as an incentive to those who are currently able.

Type of Impairment

Disabilities may involve appearance, mobility, ability to perform other physical functions, cognitive ability, psychological capacity, energy level,

---

36. Because of the phenomenon that Diana Pearce refers to as the "feminiza-

ability to communicate, sensory function, life span, or ability to function without pain.[37] Each of these types of disabilities provides a very different kind of experience for the affected person. Some, such as those involving appearance, are only disabling because of societal expectations or prejudices. Many, especially those involving mobility, might not be disabilities at all except for lack of the enabling societal structures that have been designed for those who are currently able.

Cultural differences also play a significant role in determining whether or to what degree a specific individual is disabled. For example, in a community in which physical labor is the mainstay, mobility and physical stamina are more important values than intellectual strengths; the reverse would be true in a community that especially values the life of the mind. In some cases, gender differences defined by a culture may actually inflict disabilities, as in the ancient practice of foot binding of women in China.[38] Anorexia, a psychologically disabling, life-threatening disorder that mainly affects women, is a modern example of a culturally influenced disability.[39]

Fortunately or unfortunately, the culture of modern medicine routinely attributes greater importance to health of mind than health of body. The following case illustrates this point:

A little boy named Chris suffered a prolonged umbilical cord prolapse at birth. The event left him completely immobilized from the head down. He

---

tion of poverty," these costs affect women and their children more than men. See Diana Pearce, "The Feminization of Poverty: Women, Work and Welfare," *Urban and Social Change Review* 11 (February 1978): 28–36. See also Ruth Sidel, *Women and Children Last* (New York: Penguin Viking, 1986), 133–56.

37. This is not intended to be a comprehensive list. It simply illustrates the huge array of different impairments that individuals experience. Shapiro observes that "there are hundreds of different disabilities," but I suspect that is an underestimate (*No Pity*, 4). Scholars who maintain a sharp distinction between disease and disability might disagree with this assessment.

38. Another, more controversial example is female circumcision or genital mutilation, which in many cases makes sexual intercourse painful thereafter.

39. The cult of thinness is the cultural factor that encourages adolescent girls to starve themselves in anorexia nervosa. Although the tendency to develop this and other eating disorders is undoubtedly influenced by other factors also, gender socialization is a significant factor that deserves therapeutic social intervention. See Mary B. Mahowald, "To Be or Not to Be a Woman: Anorexia Nervosa, Normative Gender Roles, and Feminism," *Journal of Medicine and Philosophy* 17 (1992): 233–51.

was also blind, and possibly deaf. At three months of age Chris remained prone in a hospital crib, depending on medical technology for all vital functions, including respiration and nutrition. There was no realistic expectation that he would ever be weanable from his dependence for survival on extensive medical technology. In the past, his caregivers, in accordance with parental wishes, had removed life support from infants whose basic bodily systems were functional but had suffered severe brain hemorrhages predictive of massive and irreparable cognitive damage. With Chris, the situation was the reverse, leaving his caregivers much more ambivalent than they were in the other cases about whether to continue his treatment. "He has a good brain," one said. "How can we let him go?"

From a feminist standpoint, the same criteria that would justify treatment or nontreatment are applicable to Chris as to the other infants: the principles of beneficence and nonmaleficence, which are equivalent to the infant's own interests. Moreover, the same criteria apply to adults, with the caveat that respect for the person's autonomy is also relevant, sometimes overriding beneficence or nonmaleficence.[40] Rather than automatically assume that caregivers ought to treat an infant without severe brain damage who is otherwise severely impaired more aggressively than an infant with the opposite situation, the priority of the child's interests demands a more individualized calculation. Among the significant factors to be considered in this case was the fact that Chris might suffer more because of his physical disabilities than someone who had little or no cognitive capacity to recognize them. This suggests a stronger basis for letting Chris go than for letting the other infants go. On the other side, however, because Chris had never known any other way of being, he could not experience the loss of abilities he once enjoyed as would someone whose disabilities occurred later in life.[41] Moreover, Chris's cognitive development would be slowed but not eliminated because of his sensory impairment.

---

40. Respect for the patient's autonomy is more compelling than respect for a proxy's autonomy because the patient is directly affected by the decision, whereas the proxy is not. In deciding for their infants, parents, as proxies, are expected to act in their infants' interests. Where this is not so or where it is contestable, the best interests of the infant may be determined by the courts, overriding the parents' decision.

41. The case of Joseph Saikewicz was decided on grounds such as those described here but in a different context. Saikewicz was a sixty-eight-year-old, with a mental age of less than three years. He had no known family members. Chemotherapy for his acute myeloblastic monocytic leukemia would involve extensive

A feminist standpoint does not foreclose the possibility of terminating life support for a person with physical disabilities any more than it does for someone with mental disability, providing the same criteria are followed for either of them as for someone who has as yet no disability. Beneficence, nonmaleficence, and respect for autonomy sometimes justify letting go, but they never justify it if the principles are not equally applied to everyone.

Recognizability or Apparentness to Others

Some disabilities, such as chronic fatigue immune dysfunction syndrome, are unrecognizable to others, and many are only apparent in circumstances in which a specific function is expected and cannot be performed.[42] Disabilities of appearance, such as those that neurofibromatosis sometimes involves, may be associated with physiological dysfunction but especially with a socially disabling impact on the affected person. To some extent, disabilities can arise from the mere perception of them by others. Obesity and stuttering, for example, may not themselves be disabling but evoke discriminatory practices if they are perceived as such. The history of discrimination against persons who are nonsymptomatic carriers of sickle-cell disease should count as a warning in this regard.[43] Similarly, disability

---

suffering and possibly serious side effects to provide a 30 to 50 percent chance of remission for two to thirteen months. Without chemotherapy, he would die within weeks or perhaps a few months. Acknowledging that "most reasonable persons with this disease choose treatment," the court decided that Saikewicz, nonetheless, would not have chosen treatment. While I agree that the harms suffered by aggressive therapy would be greater than those suffered by someone who knew the purpose of the treatment, it seems illogical for the court to base its decision on what a person who never had the ability to choose would have chosen. Beauchamp and Childress, *Principles of Biomedical Ethics*, 171, 215.

42. For a philosophically rich feminist account of disabilities, stemming from the experience of someone with myalgic encephalomyelitis or chronic fatigue immune dysfunction syndrome, see Susan Wendell, *The Rejected Body: Feminist Philosophical Reflections on Disability* (New York: Routledge, 1996).

43. In the 1970s, people who were carriers for sickle-cell disease were discriminated against by being excluded from jobs as well as education, despite the fact that their carrier status in no way implied that they had, or would ever have, symptoms of the disease. See, for example, David Suzuki and Peter Knudtson, *Genethics: The Clash between the New Genetics and Human Values* (Cambridge, Mass.: Harvard University Press, 1989), 162–63.

evoked by the perception of disability may arise from the fact that an individual tests positive for susceptibility to a late onset condition for which he or she has as yet no symptoms. As the human genome project unfolds and genetic tests for multifactorial and late onset conditions proliferate, the last category is bound to expand.

Nonrecognizability is both a curse and a blessing.[44] It is a curse because it often makes others distrustful of the reality. The reality must be disclosed to others if they are to believe it and react appropriately. Nonrecognizability is a blessing because it reduces the likelihood of stigmatization or condescension by others. Between recognizability and nonrecognizability there are degrees of both that may stretch credibility or incline toward stigmatization on the part of others. Even for someone with an unrecognized but severe disability, self-doubt may arise as to whether she is actually disabled because self-concepts emerge and are sustained in a social context. The more recognizable the disability, the less likely this is to occur because its reality will be manifest to, and therefore believed by, others.[45]

A Feminist Standpoint Regarding Different Disabilities

Different socialization and cultural values influence not only the attitudes and practices of those who are currently able toward those who are disabled but also the attitudes and practices of persons with specific disabilities toward others with different disabilities. It may be difficult, for example, for those who are mobility impaired but intellectually superior to tender equal respect to those who are cognitively or emotionally impaired but physically able.[46] As someone who has lived in a university community

---

44. Barbara Hillyer describes this phenomenon as one in which disabled persons "pass" for people who are currently able; she compares it with the experience of lesbians who pass as heterosexuals. *Feminism and Disability* (Norman: University of Oklahoma Press, 1993), 136–62. By constraining self-disclosure, passing may also exert a toll on the person with disabilities (150).

45. Although there is truth to the adage that "seeing is believing," we may also believe on the basis of what we know or hear or smell or feel. Even so, our senses can deceive us, and our supposed knowledge can fail us as well.

46. "Cognitive disability" may encompass mental retardation or mental illness. The latter may be the subject of even greater prejudice than the former.

for many years, I have not only observed but been guilty of a certain disdain, prejudice, or lack of equal respect toward those who are cognitively impaired. Ironically, it seems to me a sign of disrespect for colleagues who are intellectually able but physically disabled to deny that they have the same proclivity, although perhaps to a lesser degree.

A feminist standpoint looks toward an equitable balance of both advantages and disadvantages, burdens and benefits, among all of those affected by decisions and policies. In that context, consider a case involving a severely disabled young man, who was mainstreaming at a midwestern university in the 1970s.

> Tom Brown was twenty years old and lived about twenty miles from the university. Born ten weeks prematurely, he experienced oxygen deprivation during parturition. Although he could not walk, hold a pencil, or turn his head, he could speak very slowly and softly. Because he was unable to articulate his words clearly, it was extremely difficult to understand him unless one spent considerable time learning how to interpret his speech. Understanding him was also facilitated by kneeling in front of him when listening so that one could see the words he was mouthing. In contrast, he could understand others easily.

Tom's mother drove him to the university twice each week for classes and stayed to help him with personal needs. Most of his exams were taken orally, and his mother typed papers that he dictated to her.[47] Although his grades were excellent, Tom did not participate in discussions in large classes, which disappointed him. His professors were willing to answer his typed questions in class or meet him in private to discuss the course, but they were unwilling to take the time required to understand his oral questions during class time.

A gathering of health professionals discussing Tom's case considered the issue of whether the university had an obligation to ensure that Tom's oral questions were heard during class time, just as the questions of at least some of the currently able students' questions were heard and answered during that time. I asked the following question of this group: Do you think that Tom and his mother have considered responsibilities to the other students in their plans for his mainstreaming at the university? The

---

47. That Tom's mother was his principal caregiver is not unusual. While all of us have both fathers and mothers, mothers are by far the principal caregivers of young people who are disabled.

immediate and obviously irritated answer of one person to my question was, "No, never, fortunately. No disabled person should ever consider such things."

That answer, I believe, is paternalistically disrespectful of both Tom and his mother. Both are clearly moral agents, who as such should consider the impact of their decisions on other persons. Respect for them involves an expectation that they consider such matters. To deny or fail to acknowledge their moral responsibility in this and other regards is to impugn their moral agency.

Possibly my respondent thought that I was opposed to Tom's mainstreaming or that Tom would not be mainstreaming if he considered the burden it might entail for others. In fact, I had quite a different sentiment—namely, that Tom's mainstreaming was a boon rather than a burden not only for other students but also for faculty and staff, whose nearsightedness might thereby be reduced. In other words, university personnel would or should have considered Tom's presence an educational advantage for others on campus. While I did not know for sure whether Tom and his mother had weighed the impact of their plans on others, I believed that they had, and that that was in fact a compelling reason for mainstreaming.

If Tom had been intellectually rather than physically impaired, he no doubt would not have been mainstreaming at the university, and he would have had a very different experience as a disabled person. In general, it is easier for academics who are currently able to be open to those with physical disabilities than those with cognitive disabilities. In contrast, it may be difficult not only for academics who are currently able but also for those who are physically disabled to be genuinely open to persons who are cognitively disabled. Although I have attended a number of public panels and conferences involving persons with physical disabilities, some devoted specifically to consideration of disability issues, I have never attended one in which people with mental disabilities participated. Yet persons with cognitive disabilities are a major group in society, and those who are currently able or have other disabilities generally represent a dominant perspective in their regard.[48]

---

48. In the United States, for example, it is estimated that 1 percent of the population is mentally retarded and 22.9 percent of fifteen to fifty-four-year-olds have mental disorders. See *Diagnostic and Statistical Manual of Mental Disorders*, 4th ed. (DSM-IV) (Washington, D.C.: American Psychiatric Association, 1994)

Reduction in the inevitable nearsightedness of those who are cognitively able regarding those who are cognitively disabled requires recognition of our myopia and desire to reduce it. It also requires that those who are cognitively disabled be involved in the process to the extent that they are capable of such involvement. Presumably, the profoundly retarded cannot be involved because their cognitive deficit is too great, but many who are mildly or moderately retarded are capable of indicating their own needs and interests more accurately than others might indicate them. Those who cannot speak for themselves deserve advocates in their behalf. The charge of such advocates is to indicate what they believe the person they speak for would want and where that is impossible to discern what they believe is in the person's best interests.[49] All of these measures are supported by a feminist standpoint, as one that imputes privileged standing to the non-dominant perspectives of those most affected by specific policies or decisions.

Potential Conflicts between Feminism and Advocacy for Persons with Disabilities

Gender justice underlies all versions of feminism, and feminism generally involves advocacy for those with disabilities. However, there is one issue on which some versions of feminism may be at odds with that advocacy. This is the issue of prenatal testing and elective abortion of fetuses found to have particular disabilities.[50] Although some feminists object to medical

---

44, and Beatrice A. Rouse, ed. *Substance Abuse and Mental Health Statistics Sourcebook* (Washington, D.C.: U.S. Government Printing Office, 1995), 33.

49. In other words, advocates are expected to be substitute decision makers for incompetent patients, making the same decisions they believe the person who cannot speak would make in her own behalf or, where that is impossible, the decision that is in the person's best interests. These expectations represent casuistic maxims that are derivable in particular circumstances from the principles of respect for autonomy, beneficence, and nonmaleficence.

50. Sources on this topic include authors with disabilities as well as those who are currently able. See, for example, Deborah Kaplan, "Prenatal Screening and Diagnosis: The Impact on Persons with Disabilities," in *Women and Prenatal Testing: Facing the Challenges of Genetic Technology*, ed. Karen H. Rothenberg and Elizabeth J. Thomson (Columbus: Ohio State University Press, 1994), 49–61; Marsha Saxton, "Disability Rights and Selective Abortion," in *Abortion Wars: A*

technologies that usurp women's control over their bodies, many women embrace the technologies that provide them with means of controlling otherwise uncontrollable aspects of their lives. Prenatal testing is one of these technologies, abortion is another, and the two are intertwined. Ordinarily, abortion is the only means through which a woman whose prenatal test is positive for a specific condition can avoid giving birth to a child with that condition.[51]

The desire to avoid having children with disabilities is apparently the main motivation for prenatal testing. This is clear from the fact that most medical referrals for prenatal testing are based on maternal age, which is associated with an increased incidence of chromosomal abnormalities, especially Down syndrome. Although congenital anomalies, particularly cardiac defects, occur more often in infants with Down syndrome than in other infants, the only anomaly that the syndrome always entails is mental retardation. Consequently, the predominant rationale that underlies prenatal testing and termination of affected fetuses is avoidance of the birth of a child who is mentally retarded. Some women choose to continue their pregnancies after a positive diagnosis of a fetal anomaly, but most women do not.

Does feminist advocacy for the right to terminate pregnancy because of fetal anomaly imply disregard for persons with disabilities? Related to that question are others: Does advocacy for persons with disabilities imply the right to terminate an unaffected fetus so as to ensure (as far as possible) the birth of an infant with a specific condition, such as achondroplasia or deafness? Does advocacy for either group imply support for the right to become pregnant or to continue a pregnancy despite inability to care for an infant without public or professional assistance? Does it also imply the right to medical assistance to become pregnant? Answers to these ques-

---

Half Century of Struggle, 1950–2000, ed. Rick Solinger (Berkeley: University of California Press, 1998, 374–93); Adrienne Asch, "Reproductive Technology and Disability," in *Reproductive Laws for the 1990s*, ed. Sherill Cohen and Nadine Taub (New York: Humana, 1988), 69–124; and Allen Buchanan, "Choosing Who Will Be Disabled: Genetic Intervention and the Morality of Inclusion," *Social Philosophy and Policy* 13 (1996): 18–46.

51. Because most results of prenatal testing are negative, some genetic counselors believe that it actually decreases the incidence of abortions. If they could not be tested, women at risk for fetal anomalies might terminate their pregnancies to avoid the possibility of having an affected child.

tions depend on the version of feminism that is operable and on different construals of "reproductive rights." Questions involving the right to terminate a pregnancy also involve the moral status that is imputed or denied to the fetus.

Different Versions of Feminism

Basically, different versions of feminism stem from different conceptions of justice.[52] Among other possibilities, the conceptions may be libertarian, liberal, or egalitarian. In feminist versions of these theories, a necessary emphasis is placed on justice toward women, as generally representing the disadvantaged side of the relationship between the sexes. Libertarian and liberal feminists affirm that justice entails equal liberty for women and men as the primary value to be promoted. Justice mainly entails the promotion of liberty for individual women by refraining from interference with their choices. Libertarian feminism does not require social measures to reduce material inequality; in fact, it opposes such measures because they allegedly compromise the liberty of those who are materially advantaged (e.g., through graduated income tax).

A libertarian framework thus supports the right of disabled women to make choices but opposes governmental requirements of means to implement their choices. In contrast, liberal feminism *may* support such requirements, and egalitarian versions of feminism *insist* on them. Whether liberal feminism supports governmental requirements that reduce the disadvantages of the disabled depends on the extent to which it accepts the decreased autonomy this may entail for those who are currently able (i.e., the dominant group). Like liberalism in general, liberal feminism encompasses a variety of positions within a range of liberal feminist positions. For example, some liberal feminists oppose restrictions on surrogate gestation,

---

52. On different versions of feminism, see authors cited in n. 2. I have developed a simpler rendition in "Gender Justice and Genetics," in *The Social Power of Ideas*, ed. Yeager Hudson and Creighton Peden (Lewiston, N.Y.: Mellen, 1995), 225–52; some of the material in this section appears in that article. One version of feminism may be at odds with the concept of justice, namely, "cultural feminism," as described by Tong. "Cultural feminism" refers to the care-based ethic that is particularly found in women. In the section on caregivers I deal with this view and feminist concerns about it.

while others support them.[53] Because both libertarian and egalitarian versions of feminism are clearer than liberal feminism in their implications regarding advocacy for the disabled, these illustrate the stark contrast between certain versions of feminism and their compatibility with advocacy for people with disabilities. To the extent that liberal feminism emphasizes equality, it is consistent with egalitarian feminism; to the extent that it emphasizes individual liberty, liberal feminism is consistent with libertarian feminism.

Egalitarian feminists (such as I) give priority to women's material equality with men as a condition for their individual liberty.[54] Because women belong to different races, classes, and sexual orientations and have different abilities and disabilities, the material equality to be promoted must take account of those differences as well. As I have already suggested, therefore, gender justice demands racial justice, socioeconomic justice, sexual justice, and ability justice. For egalitarian feminists, the individual liberty of some women and men may be curtailed if the expression of that liberty increases or sustains material advantages of them over others.[55]

Advocacy for persons with disabilities, like advocacy for any other nondominant group, may mean support for their choices, their welfare, or both. Their advocacy is thus based on the principles of respect for autonomy, beneficence, and nonmaleficence, which, they argue, should be equally applied to the currently able and the disabled. The goal of providing equal opportunities to both groups entails advocacy of measures that enable the disabled as much as possible. The Americans with Disabilities Act (ADA) of 1990 accords with this aim. To the extent that the legislation applies to women as well as men, it exemplifies liberal or egalitarian feminism.

---

53. See, for example, Lori B. Andrews, "Feminism Revisited: Fallacies and Policies in the Surrogacy Debate," *Logos* 9 (1988): 81–96, Christine Overall, *Ethics and Reproduction: A Feminist Analysis* (Boston: Allen & Unwin, 1987), 11–136, and Mary B. Mahowald, *Women and Children in Health Care*, 104–10.

54. By material equality I mean a situation in which differences associated with inequalities are reduced as much as possible.

55. Amartya K. Sen's account of egalitarianism would not be so restrictive. According to Sen, "virtually all the approaches to the ethics of social arrangements" are egalitarian in some respect. Even "pure libertarians," he says, "demand equality with respect to an entire class of rights and liberties." See *Inequality Reexamined* (Cambridge, Mass.: Harvard University Press, 1992), ix. Obviously, the concept of liberty associated with this interpretation is not material equality.

Feminists with disabilities are as likely as those who are currently able to support a pregnant woman's right to abortion. Many, however, are particularly concerned about the societal implications of abortions based on fetal disability. In general, they worry that such decisions strengthen "the widely-held belief that life with a disability is not worth living," sending "a message to children and adults with disabilities, especially people who have genetic or prenatal disabilities, that 'We do not want any more like you.' "[56] Because of the priority it imputes to individual choice, a libertarian version of feminism is more likely than other versions to tolerate this view if not endorse it; in doing so it betrays the interests of many women, including those who are currently able. Accordingly, Jenny Morris observes that "[i]t is not in the interests of either women or disabled people to rely on liberal individualism for the furtherance of our rights."[57]

All versions of feminism involve advocacy for women, but whether "women" include female fetuses, as potential women, is unclear. Since no fetus is autonomous, there can be no advocacy for fetal "choice." Accordingly, in a libertarian version of feminism, fetuses themselves are not a relevant consideration, regardless of whether they are male or female. They may nonetheless be relevant to persons who are moral agents.[58] Although an argument may be made in support of the potential woman's choice regarding tests and interventions during her fetal development, such an argument would be highly speculative and hardly convincing. However, a liberal version of feminism might include, and an egalitarian version would definitely include, the welfare of the fetus as a morally relevant consideration in decisions about prenatal tests and interventions. Not only the possibility of damage to the potential child but the possibility of fetal pain would be relevant to decisions about procedures. These factors are relevant to liberal and egalitarian feminists because respect for autonomy does not always trump beneficence and nonmaleficence. Justice is the principle needed to determine whether respect for different choices, burdens, and benefits are equitably distributed among those affected.

---

56. Wendell, *The Rejected Body*, 153, 154.

57. Jenny Morris, *Pride against Prejudice: Transforming Attitudes to Disability* (Philadelphia: New Society, 1991), 81.

58. H. Tristram Engelhardt exemplifies this view in his account of persons, including parents, as moral agents. See *The Foundations of Bioethics* (New York: Oxford University Press, 1996).

Reproductive Rights and the Moral Status of the Fetus

The right to become pregnant, to continue or end a pregnancy, or to obtain medical assistance with regard to any of these goals is generally considered under the aegis of "reproductive rights," which most if not all feminists support. Although the right to raise a child is often viewed as a reproductive right, the parenting on which newborns and children rely is both legally and morally separable from the right to reproduce. The separability derives from the fact that children, unlike embryos or fetuses, have clearly established rights based on their own interests. Moreover, the extent to which reproductive rights are supported vis-à-vis other rights or others' rights varies with the different versions of feminism. A libertarian feminism supports a woman's right to choose among reproductive options for any reason but would not coerce others to assist her medically or economically in implementing her choices. In contrast, an egalitarian version of feminism would maintain that the moral exercise of reproductive rights calls for consideration of their impact on others, including potential children. To what extent, if any, that consideration should be legally mandated is debatable even within the context of an egalitarian feminism.

Whether support for pregnant women's choices is compatible with advocacy for persons with disabilities depends also on one's view of the moral status or standing of the fetus.[59] If the fetus has no moral status, then the two issues are separable, and there is neither logical nor ethical connection between support for persons with disabilities and denial of support for disabled fetuses. There may be an emotional or social link, which may have ethical implications. In general, however, if the fetus has no moral status or standing, women's decisions about pregnancy have nothing to do with their decisions about newborns with disabilities; their choices may justifiably be overridden with regard to their children, but not with regard to their fetuses. Asch and Fine support this point of view.[60] Birth defines the moment at which an individual with a disability has rights and responsibilities equivalent to persons who are currently able.

---

59. L. W. Sumner distinguishes between moral status and moral standing, but his distinction is not helpful here. See his *Abortion and Moral Theory* (Princeton, N.J.: Princeton University Press, 1981), 26. Either term is applicable to a being to whom moral agents have moral responsibilities, regardless of whether the being has reciprocal responsibilities.

60. Adrienne Asch and Michelle Fine, "Shared Dreams: A Left Perspective on Disability Rights and Reproductive Rights," in *Women with Disabilities*, 297–305.

A contrasting view is based on the assumption that the fetus has a moral status equivalent to that of a born individual. A woman's decision to terminate a pregnancy because the fetus has a disability may then be regarded as morally equivalent to terminating a person who is born with a disability.[61] In a sense, every fetus may be considered disabled because, at least until viability, it is totally dependent on another (i.e., the pregnant woman) to sustain its life. Whether the fetus is disabled or not, however, if its moral status is equivalent to that of a newborn, terminating it is tantamount to homicide. Support for the woman's choice is therefore incompatible with support for those who are disabled, some of whom are women. Since fetuses cannot choose, this position implies support for those who can choose over those who are unable to choose.

A number of views about the moral status of the fetus are gradualist; that is, they impute some moral status to the fetus as it develops but not full moral status until it is born. These views include those who impute moral status to the implanted embryo but not the zygote and those who deny that early embryos have moral status but posit some point during gestation, such as the onset of brain activity or viability, at which moral status is present.[62] Whether these gradualist views allow compatibility between the pregnant woman's right to choose and advocacy for the disabled depends on the weight attributed to one or the other at the point when some moral status is imputed to the fetus. If the fetus achieves full or nearly full moral status in late gestation, nonmaleficence toward it may outweigh the autonomy of the pregnant woman at that point. If the fetus has minimal moral standing until it is viable, the woman's autonomy may trump nonmaleficence toward it.

The Compatibility Question

A libertarian version of feminism (i.e., one that emphasizes the individual woman's choice as paramount) fully supports the decisions of autono-

---

61. The analogy between the two limps badly, however, because the fetus is still within the body of the woman whereas a newborn is not. This point is morally significant even when a fetus at term is developmentally more mature than a premature infant.

62. For example, L. W. Sumner, "A Third Way," and Baruch Brody, "Against an Absolute Right to Abortion," both in *The Problem of Abortion,* 3d edit., ed. Susan Dwyer and Joel Feinberg (Belmont, Calif.: Wadsworth, 1997), 88–117.

mous women, whether currently able or disabled, to initiate, terminate, or continue pregnancies for any reason. In cases involving prenatal diagnosis and termination of pregnancies because of fetal anomaly, this view is incompatible with advocacy for persons with disabilities unless (1) the fetus has no moral status or (2) obligations that follow from its moral status are not as compelling as the woman's choice. To the extent that some women lack autonomy (e.g., because of retardation or mental illness), libertarian feminism ignores their interests if those interests are not pursued by autonomous individuals, such as family members.

An egalitarian version of feminism (i.e., one that places greater emphasis on equality, broadly construed) implies that other values besides women's autonomy are morally relevant to decisions about initiation, continuation, or termination of a pregnancy. With regard to prenatal diagnosis and termination of affected fetuses, this view is consistent with the pregnant woman's right to choose and with the rights of the disabled if the fetus has no moral status. But if the fetus has moral status or standing, egalitarian feminism can only be consistent with advocacy for women's choice and for the disabled if (1) the moral status of a fetus is deemed less compelling than the pregnant woman's autonomy or (2) the decision is not based on the ability or disability of the fetus. Concerning the latter factor, the decision may be based on the inability of the caregiver or of society to provide adequate care for the potential child. As already mentioned, to an egalitarian feminist, choice is not an absolute value. From an egalitarian feminist perspective, therefore, pregnant women, whether they are currently able or disabled, are morally obliged to consider the welfare of the potential child in their decisions about initiating, continuing, or terminating pregnancy. This does not imply that they should be legally obligated or coerced to do so.

What I have said thus far is as applicable to fetuses without disabilities as it is to those with disabilities. The applicability to both suggests a criterion to be followed if advocacy for women's choice and advocacy for persons with disabilities are to be reconciled: *in itself, the fact of the disability is irrelevant to the choice.* Admittedly, there are cases both during and beyond gestation in which suffering, whatever its cause, may be unrelievably so overwhelming that letting the suffering individual die seems like a merciful or humane thing to do.[63] The criterion in that case, however, is not

---

63. For example, when an infant has a profoundly devastating, incurable, pro-

the disability itself but the suffering of the individual with the disability. Moreover, the crucial caveat in situations of overwhelming suffering is that it be unrelievable by others. As many authors attest, much of the suffering associated with disabilities is socially induced and relievable.[64] For autonomous persons with disabilities, another crucial variable is respect for autonomy; this consideration is relevant to pregnant women but not to fetuses.

My suggested criterion for reconciling feminism with advocacy for people with disabilities is also applicable to the issue of assisted suicide, which presents another possibility for discrimination against persons with disabilities. As one disabilities activist framed her concern, "They (i.e., supporters of the legalization of assisted suicide) just want to get rid of us."[65] From an egalitarian feminist standpoint, however, if assisted suicide is a legal right for those who are currently able, it should be equally a right of those who are disabled. For both groups, measures must be taken to ensure that the decision is made autonomously. Circumstances that compromise autonomy such as treatable depression and social causes of disability must be adequately addressed before an individual's decision is regarded as genuinely autonomous.

An egalitarian version of feminism is more coherent in its own right and more compatible with advocacy for the disabled than a libertarian version. It is more coherent because individual choice is not an absolute moral right; other rights and others' rights may be more compelling. Egalitarian feminism is compatible with advocacy for the disabled because it embraces all of the disabled, including those who are not autonomous. Persons with disabilities, like persons who are currently able, are not always autonomous or equally autonomous any more than they are equally intelligent, talented, or attractive. The goal of an egalitarian feminism is to treat different individuals fairly in the face of these differences, both changeable and unchangeable. This returns us to the notion of gender justice as essentially

---

gressive condition such as Tay-Sachs disease or Lesch-Nyhan disease or when someone is dying of an incurable, painful cancer.

64. For instance, Wendell, *The Rejected Body*, 35–56, Asch and Fine, "Introduction," in *Women with Disabilities*, 5–6, Silvers, this volume and elsewhere.

65. This statement was made by a person with disabilities who attended a workshop funded by the Ethical, Legal, and Social Issues Program of the National Center for Human Genome Research in Zanesville, Ohio, 16–19 May 1996. The principal investigator for the workshop on Women and Genetics in Contemporary Society was Helen Bequaert Holmes.

tied to justice toward individuals with disabilities. An obligation to treat everyone justly assumes that no one's autonomy is absolute, whether women or men, able or disabled, young or old, whatever their class, color, ethnicity, or sexual orientation. In addition, treating everyone justly requires the persistent attempt by all reasonable means to reduce whatever disadvantages individuals or groups experience vis-à-vis one another. An egalitarian feminist standpoint demands this.

Asch and Fine illustrate the compatibility between feminism and advocacy for people with disabilities while identifying a concrete measure by which an egalitarian feminist standpoint may be promoted: the provision of much better information to potential parents of children with disabilities than is typically provided by genetic counselors and physicians. They contend that "given proper information about how disabled children and adults live, many women might not choose to abort."[66] As already suggested, however, their support for a woman's right to terminate her pregnancy depends on a denial that fetal interests ever outweigh a pregnant woman's interests. According to Asch and Fine, "we must recognize the crucial 'line' separating the fetus—residing in the body of her mother—and the infant, viable outside the womb."[67] Once the infant is born, their position shifts drastically. While staunchly defending the right of disabled infants to be treated over the objection of their parents, they argue just as forcefully for the right of every woman to abort a disabled fetus so long as she has adequate information about its actual life potential.

Caregivers of People with Disabilities

Both formally and informally, women are by far the predominant caregivers of the young, the aged, and those with disabling conditions, regardless of their age.[68] Formally, women concentrate in direct care roles that are less prestigious and less remunerated than the roles occupied by those in positions of power over them, who are mainly white, relatively affluent,

---

66. Asch and Fine, "Shared Dreams," 302. Shapiro maintains that less than 50 percent of women told that a fetus has a serious genetic defect choose abortion (*No Pity*, 278).
67. Asch and Fine, "Shared Dreams," 302.
68. Post, "Women and Elderly Parents," 83–5.

currently able men.[69] Informally, potential mothers do all of the care of their children before their birth and most of the care afterward. As daughters, spouses, and sisters, they also do most of the care of their kindred who are sick or disabled. Here too, their care often draws little notice and is seldom remunerated.

While I acknowledged at the start that I lack the experience of a person with a disability, I do not lack the experience of an informal caregiver of the disabled. That experience has brought home to me quite vividly that caregiving experiences are as diverse as the experience of different disabilities. The differences have to do with the type and extent of caregiving required; the relationship between the caregiver and the person with disability; the age, health, and stamina of the caregiver; the attitudes of others toward the caregiver; the burdens and benefits of caregiving both for the caregiver and for the person with disability. Before elaborating on these, however, the meaning of care, and women's relation to caregiving needs to be further examined.

Feminism and a Care Ethic

Although the practice of care is as old as humankind, the concept of care has rarely been articulated by philosophers, let alone examined.[70] Recently, however, the terms *care* and *caring* have been explicitly discussed in the literature of moral psychology and ethics. In that context, a care-based model of moral reasoning is applicable to all interpersonal relationships, not only those that occur within the health care system or between people with disabilities and their personal attendants but also among persons who are currently able. This model should not be confused with the meaning of

69. In 1994, women comprised 19.5 percent of the physicians in the United States. Four-fifths or 85.6 percent were in patient care, concentrating in internal medicine, pediatrics, family practice, psychiatry, obstetrics and gynecology, and anesthesia. See Lillian Randolph, Bradley Seidman, and Thomas Pasko, *Physician Characteristics and Distribution in the U.S.* (Chicago: American Medical Association, 1996), 44.

70. Warren Reich has tracked the history of the concept of care in the *Encyclopedia of Bioethics* (New York: Macmillan, 1995). To do so, however, he has interpreted various other terms, such as *sympathy* in Schopenhauer, as synonymous with its meaning. Needless to say, those who chose those other terms might disagree with his interpretation.

care that, as Shapiro observes, "the disability rights movement consciously steers clear of . . . [because it] suggests that a disabled person is a sick and passive recipient of an attendant's help."[71] Care in that sense is totally unacceptable to an egalitarian feminist. I disagree, however, that a caregiver, whether a personal attendant or someone who provides assistance in other ways to a person with disabilities, should be regarded merely as "an item of social liberation—just like a lightweight wheelchair or a bus lift," which, according to Shapiro, is how disability rights activists characterize personal attendants. From a feminist standpoint, personal attendants, whether called caregivers or not, are persons equal to persons with disabilities, even as those with disabilities are equal to those who are currently able.

Many caregivers are not simply equal to those with disabilities; they are disabled themselves. This double status of being a caregiver and being disabled applies more prevalently to women than to men in their reproductive years as well as later in life. When women with disabilities become parents, they are as likely as currently able women to be the principal caregivers of their children. And due not only to the influence of gender roles but also to women's longer life span, a woman is more likely to be the principal caregiver of her partner, even though both may be disabled.

The meaning of care elaborated by moral psychologist Carol Gilligan is based on her study of the decision making of women facing an unwanted pregnancy. Her data, as reported and interpreted in her book *In a Different Voice*, provided a major impetus for critiquing mainstream philosophers' emphasis on justice, impartiality, and individual rights as the appropriate basis for ethical decision making.[72] While Gilligan's mentor, Lawrence Kohlberg, had developed a strategy for assessing moral development that fit nicely with traditional philosophical ethics, Gilligan found the tradition wanting.[73] It failed, she maintained, to match the reasoning of most women and some men, for whom the preservation of particular relationships figured tellingly in their decisions. Gilligan called the tradi-

---

71. Shapiro, *No Pity*, 254. As a person who is currently able, Shapiro imputes this view to others.
72. Carol Gilligan, *In a Different Voice: Psychological Theory and Women's Development* (Cambridge, Mass.: Harvard University Press, 1982).
73. Lawrence Kohlberg, *The Philosophy of Moral Development* (San Francisco: Harper & Row, 1981).

tional ethic an ethic of justice, contrasting it with an ethic of care.[74] Both types of moral reasoning, she maintained, are present in most individuals, but care predominates in women and justice in men.

Nel Noddings also developed an ethic of care or caring, based on her observation of maternal behavior as exhibiting a natural drive to attend to the needs of the newborn. She proposes that "ethical care" should be based on this model.[75] Unlike Gilligan, however, Noddings eschews an ethic of justice, arguing that a feminine or maternal ethic of care justifiably excludes concerns about equality because it focuses on particular others whose interests one wishes to advance. While she apparently considers her view feminist, those of us who identify feminism with advocacy for gender equality do not agree.

Some feminists have argued for an essential relationship between care and justice. Joan Tronto, for example, argues that justice and care are not only compatible but essentially related.[76] For Tronto, care is in fact a way of promoting social equality. Her definition of care goes well beyond that of Noddings: "*a species activity that includes everything that we do to maintain, continue, and repair our 'world' so that we can live in it as well as possible.*"[77] Obviously, this definition is congenial to an egalitarian version of feminism.

The concepts that Gilligan, Noddings, and Tronto construe as care and caring are not necessarily equivalent to the activities of caregiving that occur within the health care system. Their views capture a subjective element in the activity of caregiving that is sometimes lost in the motivations and experience of caregivers and those for whom they care. This is particularly evident in the tendency to equate treatment with care.[78] Nonetheless, care and caring are surely related to caregiving, and women remain the

---

74. Carol Gilligan, "Moral Orientation and Moral Development," in *Women and Moral Theory*, ed. Eva F. Kittay and Diana T. Meyers (Totowa, N.J.: Rowman & Allanheld, 1987), 19–33.

75. Nel Noddings, *Caring: A Feminine Approach to Ethics and Moral Education* (Berkeley: University of California Press, 1984). Note that Noddings uses the word *feminine* rather than *feminist* to describe her approach.

76. Joan C. Tronto, *Moral Boundaries: A Political Argument for an Ethic of Care* (New York: Routledge, 1993).

77. Tronto, *Moral Boundaries*, 103. This definition was formulated with Berenice Fisher.

78. See Mahowald, *Women and Children in Health Care*, 268, concerning the distinction between the two.

principal caregivers within society, whether or not they embody that subjective element.[79] According to one survey, women in the United States typically spend about seventeen years caring for children and about eighteen years after that caring for adult relatives (other than their spouses) who are ill or disabled.[80]

Differences in Caregiving

It may be impossible to determine whether women's predominance in caregiving roles arises from natural or culturally induced tendencies. Indeed, the assumption that the two influences are distinctive or separable is challengeable in its own right.[81] It is possible, however, to identify some of the areas of impact on women's lives of assuming these roles. From a feminist standpoint, these areas need to be identified and assessed so as to reduce, as much as possible, whatever inequities are associated with them. They involve, but are not limited to, the following factors, each of which will be examined, albeit briefly: the type and extent of caregiving; the relationship between the caregiver and the person with the disability; the age, health, and stamina of the caregiver, whether male or female; societal attitudes toward caregivers; and the burdens and benefits of caregiving for caregivers and for persons with disabilities.

Type and Extent of Caregiving

Caregiving is needed not only by some people with disabilities but also by others, especially children. Caring for a child who is disabled, however, may be much more demanding than care of one who is not. All of the differences regarding disabilities that were mentioned earlier have their

---

79. According to Shapiro, "three-quarters of caregiving is provided by unpaid relatives, 70 percent of whom are women" (*No Pity*, 252).

80. "Crisis of Elder Care," *Ms* (October 1989): 73, cited in Wendell, *The Rejected Body*, 140.

81. Hillyer, for example, argues that the "nature-culture dichotomy," which is "empirically false," has been used "to confine women to the private domestic sphere in contrast to men, whose ability to 'reason' supposedly fits them for the political world." This dichotomy, according to Hillyer, is still at work in shaping "not only our public policy, academic disciplines and the organization of family life, but even—especially—our language" (*Feminism and Disability*, 164–5).

counterpart in the caregiving experience. Some persons with disabilities, for example, require personal assistants around the clock; others require assistance on a regular but not persistent basis; others require caregiving only occasionally, just as those who are currently able require it. Others still do not require personal caregiving at all but require social accommodations or equipment to allow them to function normally within the environment designed for those who are currently able.

Some forms of caregiving entail little more than attendance and attention to potential emergencies for intervention. Other forms require constant scrutiny and responsiveness to someone's needs. The responsibilities of caregivers may extend to individuals in institutions, in sheltered workshops, or at home. Caregiving sometimes demands physical strength such as the ability to lift an adult or a wheelchair; technical skills such as the ability to use and monitor medical devices or equipment; nursing skills; or therapeutic, psychological, and educational skills. More mundanely but no less demandingly, caregiving may simply require ordinary life skills performed in another's behalf or the maintenance of personal contact that is indispensable to anyone's survival or flourishing.

The tasks of caregiving may be as basic, and possibly as distasteful, as cleaning someone after a bowel movement, as mundane as doing laundry and tying shoelaces, or as apparently superficial as trimming someone's nails or putting on her lipstick. Needless to say, when a person needs a caregiver to assist in the fulfillment of personal or professional tasks, as in reading for the blind or signing for the deaf, the preparation and experience of the caregiver is quite different than it is for the caregiver who provides for more basic needs.

Relationship between the Caregiver and the Person with Disability

The relationship between caregivers and persons with disabilities may be familial, friendly, professional, or a combination of these. Sometimes a relationship may develop from one into the other, as when a family member becomes a nurse, a physical therapist becomes a friend, or a person with disabilities marries a caregiver. Relationships, however, are much more complicated than these terms express. For example, familial relationships may be genetically close but psychologically distant or even hostile. Friendships may be intense or casual, constant or sporadic, and a relationship between caregiver and cared-for that starts with friendship may become unfriendly. Professional relationships may be warm or cool, chosen or coerced, with varying degrees between each of these opposing pairs. Familial relationships are always mutual, friendship may be one-sided, and the professional-client relationship is always one-sided. When one person is in need of the services of the other, and not vice versa, the relationship is inevitably one-sided.[82]

Familial relationships are particularly complex, sometimes introducing feelings of obligation or resentment on the part of the familial caregiver. Depending on the degree and type of impairment, the person with the disability often recognizes this sentiment. In other situations, the family caregiver may relish the opportunity to show love for the other through caregiving, and this too may be recognized by the person cared for. Professional caregivers may also act out of a sense of obligation that will be communicated to their client, performing their caregiving duties as a job rather than a choice. But both friends and professionals may have a transient relationship to the person cared for, while family members remain family members even if the relationship becomes strained or resentful.

Mothers who care for those with disabilities may be subjected to criticism from a variety of sources, including professional caregivers, people with disabilities, and feminists. Hillyer describes this phenomenon as one of mother blaming.[83] Apparently ignoring the responsibilities of fathers, professional caregivers are prone to blame mothers for not providing children with disabilities with an exorbitant amount of attention and care, at times expecting an impossible expenditure of energy, ability, and resources. In contrast, and ironically, persons with disabilities and advocates for them sometimes blame mothers for being overprotective of children with disabilities, impeding their full expression of autonomy. The same mother may be the target of criticism from both sides.

Feminist mother blaming arises from the view that mothering in general, and mothering of those with disabilities in particular, involves perpetuation of feminine stereotypes of subservience. According to Hillyer:

> The remarkable tenacity of this idea among feminists who in other contexts know perfectly well that men and patriarchal institutions have a great deal to

---

82. Admittedly, some caregivers seem to need to care more than the cared-for needs care.

83. Hillyer, *Feminism and Disability*, 86–107. As the mother of a daughter with multiple, severe disabilities, Hillyer apparently experienced mother blaming herself.

do with human options is probably a result of the fact that all of us have been daughters and only some of us mothers.[84]

Feminists as well as persons with disabilities and professional caregivers who indulge in this kind of mother blaming have apparently ignored their own myopia regarding the experience of mothers of people with disabilities.

Age, Health, and Stamina of the Caregiver

The majority of formal and informal caregivers of disabled children are young and middle-aged women. The majority of health professionals who care for disabled persons are also young and middle-aged women. As persons with disabilities get older, however, their informal caregivers also tend to be older. Because of the longer life span of women in comparison with men, along with the fact that they typically marry older men, elderly women are often the principal caregivers of their aging, disabled husbands. Moreover, an increasing number of grandmothers are the sole caregivers of their grandchildren, both able and disabled. Many of these elderly caregivers have their own health problems as well as the reduced stamina associated with the normal aging process. Because of the cost of caregiving, not only psychologically but financially,[85] many caregivers are constantly "on call" or work the "night shift" after working outside of the home each day. Because disabled husbands are typically heavier than their caregiver-wives, some of the ordinary caregiving requirements of care may not only deplete their energy but threaten their own health.

Next to wives, adult daughters and daughters-in-law tend to be the principal caregivers of disabled parents, as well as the principal caregivers of their children or other disabled relatives. Moreover, as medical advances have extended the life span of the disabled at all ages, the duration of their lives through which women fulfill their caregiving roles toward others continues to increase. One example of this multigenerational caregiving is a sixty-five-year-old woman with major caregiving responsibility for her eighty-five-year-old mother, her seventy-year-old husband, and her adult

---

84. Hillyer, *Feminism and Disability*, 92.

85. For an overview of the psychological and economic costs of caregiving for the disabled, see Mary B. Mahowald, Dana Levinson, Christine Cassel, et al., "The New Genetics and Women," *Milbank Quarterly* 74, no. 2 (1996), 268–70.

child, all living in the same home and all disabled. Most geriatricians are familiar with such cases.

Social Attitudes toward Caregivers

Unfortunately, societal attitudes toward the majority of caregivers, whether they work in institutional or home settings, tend to be positive in rhetoric but not in practice.[86] The discrepancy between rhetoric and practice may be measured by the gap between the income and power of a few versus the majority. The minority of caregivers who are already in prestigious positions are physicians. Most are still men, with the increasing number of female physicians concentrating at the lower levels of power.[87] Physicians work in hospitals or offices where they provide care acutely or episodically rather than constantly and are well rewarded economically. In contrast, hospital nurses, who are still mainly women, provide continuous care by shifts, are often less respected, and are usually less remunerated.[88] Within the health care system as a whole, women predominate as caregivers at the levels of least prestige and income. Blacks and Hispanics, regardless of their gender, represent an even greater proportion of those who are least remunerated.[89] To an egalitarian feminist, the racism suggested by this disproportionality is as regrettable as the sexism it suggests.

---

86. On occasions when I have observed personal attendants of people with severe disabilities (e.g., involving ventilator dependence) in the workplace, I have been troubled by what struck me as disrespectful treatment of the attendant, totally ignoring his presence, as if the assistance rendered was coming from a piece of equipment or a machine rather than a person. I did not observe this from the person with the disability but from those interacting with him. Similar lack of acknowledgment of those who assist people in more powerful positions often occurs in the workplace—unfortunately and unjustifiably from a feminist standpoint.

87. In 1994, women represented almost one-third (32.6 percent) of all residents in training. Surgical residents were still predominantly male (80.3 percent) but pediatric residents were predominantly female (62.4 percent). See Appendix II—Graduate Medical Education. Table 1: Resident Physicians on Duty in ACGME-Accredited and in Combined Specialty Graduate Medical Education (GME) Programs in 1996, *Journal of the American Medical Association* 278, no. 9 (3 September 1997), 775–76.

88. Some experienced nurses in administrative roles have higher salaries than medical residents.

89. In the United States, women comprise only 21.5 percent of physicians and dentists but 86.2 percent of registered nurses, pharmacists, dietitians, therapists,

As already noted, women predominate as caregivers in their homes and others' homes, and here the gap between rhetoric and practice is widest. The work that women typically do in the home is unremunerated and expected rather than respected; when men do similar work, they are often respected because it is not expected. When a member of the household becomes disabled, the person who does the work in the home is expected to extend her responsibilities to the new required tasks. Only occasionally are the extra demands of caregiving even recognized as extra. When a caregiver leaves a job outside the home to care for a relative with a disability, she loses not only prestige and income but the social supports of the workplace.[90] In time, the self-concepts of caregivers in such circumstances are more likely than not to be depleted by these societal attitudes and practice.

Attitudes of the disabled toward their caregivers may be positive or negative as well. While there is always a certain dependence of the cared-for on the caregiver, the caregiver may be dependent on the cared for both emotionally and financially. In some instances, the dependence is mutual, as individuals are both caregivers and cared-for vis-à-vis one another. In many instances, persons with disabilities are better educated and more affluent than their caregivers. Because they are as human as their caregivers, persons with disabilities are also capable of conveying disrespect for the role of caregiver. Generational differences may exacerbate this disrespectfulness, with children expecting sacrificial care from their mothers, and elderly parents expecting it from their daughters.

Burdens and Benefits of Caregiving for Caregivers
and for Persons with Disabilities

As any mother might say, caregiving has its rewards as well as its burdens, even if the rewards are neither income nor prestige. People who care

---

and physician assistants. Blacks and Hispanics comprise only 3.7 percent and 4.4 percent, respectively, of physicians and dentists. *Statistical Abstract of the United States 1995* (Washington, D.C.: U.S. Government Printing Office, 1995), 411.

90. Naomi Breslau, "Care of Disabled Children and Women's Time Use," *Medical Care* 216 (1983): 620–29; Naomi Breslau, David Salkever, and Kathleen S. Staruch, "Women's Labor Force Activity and Responsibilities for Disabled Dependents, *Journal of Health and Social Behavior* 23 (1982): 169.

for persons with disabilities might say the same. I assume that people with disabilities would say the same also. If Noddings is right that mothers have a natural drive to care for their totally dependent infants, it may also be true that women in general have a natural drive to care for others who are dependent, including people with disabilities.[91] And if fulfillment of that natural drive entails satisfaction for mothers, women may be more likely than men to find satisfaction in caring for those who are disabled.

It may also be the case that Noddings's notion of ethical care, as distinct from natural care, is the drive that motivates women to be caregivers. Through the impact of gender socialization in which maternal nurturance is equated with self-sacrifice, women tend to internalize the notion that they *ought* to be the main caregivers of their children, the aged, the sick and the disabled. There again, fulfillment of the ought may entail satisfaction for them, although not without cost.

Costs of caregiving include payment for therapies, medications, nursing care, hospitalizations, and medical equipment, as well as stress, time loss, and chronic fatigue.[92] The physical and psychological toll for the primary caregiver includes ill health, guilt, and anger.[93] Symptoms of mothers who are primary caregivers are strongly influenced by three factors: their perception of how severely disabled their child is, the actual severity of their child's disability, and their relationship with the child's father. Not surprisingly, positive relationships between the child's parents may be correlated with milder symptoms, while the severity of the disability, whether actual or perceived, is correlated with more problematic symptoms. Women who are primary caregivers are more likely to experience depression than their male counterparts, but this is true of women in general.[94] Unfortunately, studies of the psychological impact of caregiving on those who care for

---

91. Noddings, *Caring*.

92. C. Eiser, "Psychological Effects of Chronic Disease," *Journal of Clinical Psychology and Psychiatry* 31, no. 1 (1990): 85–98; Susan Hillier Parks and Marc Pilisuk, "Caregiver Burden: Gender and the Psychological Costs of Caregiving," *American Journal of Orthopsychiatry* 61 (1991): 501–9.

93. Parks and Pilisuk, "Caregiver Burden," 501–9.

94. Eiser, "Psychological Effects," 85–98. On the incidence of depression in women, see R. C. Kessler et al., "Lifetime and 12-Month Prevalence of DSM-III-R Psychiatric Disorders from the National Comorbidity Survey," *Archives of General Psychiatry* 51 (1994): 8–19.

the disabled seldom address gender differences, referring only to "parental" or "family" impact. In gathering their data, however, the researchers
typically interview mothers rather than fathers.[95]

Men as well as women may of course find satisfaction in caring for their
infants and caring for others, whether or not the satisfaction derives from
fulfillment of a natural or ethical drive. If so, how sad that so few men, in
comparison with women, fulfill those drives. Beyond the possibility that
men do not naturally have as great a drive toward (unremunerated, non-
prestigious) caregiving as women, another explanation for the gender imbalance in caregiving is that the financial cost for men is likely to be
greater. This is because their income from work outside the home is typically higher than that of their wives or their female counterparts in the
workplace, and that advantage would of course be lost if they were to
spend their days caring for a relative at home.[96] Nonetheless, women are
sometimes required to give up their only earned income to provide care,
and the poverty that many experience in old age is often triggered by that
loss.

For caregivers who have no other or better source of income, an obvious
benefit of caregiving is that it provides some income, no matter how meager. To persons with disabilities, the fact that basic caregiving is not well
paid is an ambivalent benefit because they would probably like to see their
caregivers paid better, but they may not have the means to pay them better
or the power to see that others do so. From a feminist standpoint, the
inequity that caregiving responsibility usually involves for the caregiver,
whether male or female, can and should be rectified by practical changes
in laws and social policies. As already suggested, however, the rhetoric that
often favors such rectification is seldom matched by practice.

Conclusion

The foregoing sketch of differences in disabilities and in caregiving responsibilities is by no means an adequate account of the real differences and

95. For example, A. Kathleen Barlew, Robert Evans, and Carlton Oler, "The
Impact of a Child with Sickle Cell Disease on Family Dynamics," *Annals of the
New York Academy of Sciences* 565 (1989): 162.
96. On the average, women in the United States earn seventy-one cents for
every dollar earned by men. The earning discrepancy between men and women

real inequities experienced by people with disabilities and their caregivers. Nor could it be, as written by one who has but limited experience of either situation. The different versions of feminism and of views about the moral status of the fetus are not fully developed either, although these may be less inadequate because they are theoretical rather than empirical accounts.

While acknowledging my own myopia, both theoretical and practical, I believe this account is less nearsighted than it might have been because it has been influenced a great deal by those who have had different experiences and theoretical constructs than I have had.[97] Even without those remedial lenses, it constitutes the perspective of a particular currently able woman with a particular feminist standpoint that has some legitimacy in its own right. I leave it to others, especially my coauthors, to provide stronger corrective lenses.

---

applies to blacks, Hispanics, and whites but is greatest between white men and white women. See Charity Anne Dorgan, ed., *Statistical Handbook of Working America* (Detroit: Gale Research, 1995), 567.

97. Among others, Judy Panko Reis, Adrienne Asch, Marsha Saxton, and Anita Silvers have been helpful in this regard. I particularly want to thank Susan Wendell for generously reviewing an earlier version of this manuscript and providing constructive criticisms and suggestions.

4

Response

Silvers on Wasserman and Mahowald

Silvers on Wasserman

David Wasserman tackles the job of delineating how fairness in allocating resources to people with disabilities can be achieved. His treatment of the question is thorough, thoughtful, and tuned to the complexities that must be weighed whenever we are faced with claims about allocating more to some kinds of people than to others. Wasserman, if anyone, could allay my concerns about the price that is extracted for distributively privileging people because of their disabilities. But it will come as no surprise, especially to him, that he has not yet succeeded in doing so. To admit this is not to suggest that a chasm of political disagreement separates our views. For the division between us is limned not by a dispute about whose interests—people hampered by disabilities or people free of them—are more important to serve but by a profound difference in how we frame the moral rationale for social responsiveness to the "problem" of disability. For me, justice for people with disabilities is predominantly compensatory, and the question is whether formal or distributive reasons more appropriately ground the requisite reparation. This is not an open question for Wasserman, for whom compensation seems to be nothing other than distributive. For me, then, the philosophical problem disability initially poses for a theory of justice has to do with identifying whether formal or distributive considerations constitute the primary ground for compensation, whereas Wasserman apparently does not think that there need be such an argument about how to ground a just compensatory response to disability.

Formal justice, I argue, stipulates that to differ from the majority—that is, to be in the minority—is not itself sufficient to justify the imposition of social disadvantage, nor does their benefiting the majority excuse public policies that cause minorities to be worse off. I argue that justice for people with disabilities is most consistently and compellingly motivated by recognizing disabling circumstances to be mainly the outcome of thoughtless and oppressive social choices. These deserve redress because they artificially, needlessly, and systematically disadvantage a discrete minority of citizens, a violation of the fundamental formal commitment to equality of treatment. Thus, formal justice supports the compensatory reform of those civic and commercial practices that impose artificial disadvantages on individuals who are in the minority in virtue of their physical, sensory, or cognitive impairments.

Distributive motivations for compensation are more obscure to me. Distributive justice imagines that individuals can be compensated for their natural disadvantages. But it is not at all clear why we should be required to compensate for disadvantages that are not the result of one group's having enjoyed privilege to the detriment of another. Nor is it evident how we are to rank competing claims for restoration from nature's harms.

Wasserman's account does not take the moral force of our duty to re-fashion unfair privileging practices sufficiently seriously. Because for him only distributive justice is compensatory, his position is pervaded by perplexity about how to decide among competing claims for compensation. Very many people suffer from natural disadvantage, which manifests itself in very many different ways. Given the wide range and frequent incidence of disadvantage that is not traceable to social choice, and the potential magnitude of calls to compensate for it, the beneficence from which we are moved to offset natural disadvantage can generate no more than very imperfect duties. While I appreciate the love of humanity that prompts exercises in compensatory distributive justice, it seems to me to be too sporadic to be of broad and dependable use in equalizing the social participation of people with disabilities. Wasserman thus circumscribes compensatory policy too narrowly by casting it in distributive terms.

I have argued that the difficulty in determining which individuals deserve extraordinary allocations commonly corrupts compensatory systems. To determine to whom to distribute special benefits and what these benefits should be, policies granting compensatory entitlements typically reify individuals with certain disabilities into prototypes of all disability, and the circumstances that will benefit these individuals arbitrarily become programmatic missions that cannot help but be exclusionary. So Wasserman's position is also to be distinguished from mine by his acceptance, and my rejection, of compensatory processes that are initiated by determining who is disabled. The preferable approach, I urge, initially identifies disabling social practices and then is guided in refashioning them by the particular experiences and concrete modes of achieving successful functioning of those whom they disable.

Wasserman furthermore distinguishes between (1) compensatory responses, those aimed at returning individuals with disabilities to the commonplace level of functioning or subvening those individuals' well-being in case restorative procedures fail, and (2) proscriptive responses, those aimed at prohibiting the discriminatory obstruction of those same individuals' access to opportunity. I, in contrast, take the distinction that Wasserman tries to draw to differentiate two kinds of compensatory responses: (1) compensating individuals on the basis of their deficits, a class of policies roughly coextensive with Wasserman's compensatory category, and (2) compensating groups for the residual damage of past social wrongs, a class of policies roughly coextensive with Wasserman's proscriptive category. My understanding of the ADA differs from Wasserman's because I take this law to exemplify my second policy category and therefore to be mainly an instrument of formal rather than distributive justice.

Several reasons prompt my interpretation. The first draws on the language of the "findings" Congress positioned to serve as a preface to the prescriptive sections of the ADA. Here Congress identifies people with disabilities as a discrete and insular class subject to the continuing existence of unfair and unnecessary discrimination and prejudice that denies them "the opportunity to compete on an equal basis and to pursue those opportunities for which our free society is justifiably famous." The second reason is that the ADA and its implementing regulations do more than proscribe disability discrimination. The ADA is more affirmative and proactive than the proscriptions Wasserman takes to comprise his second category; it is prescriptive in that it requires the refashioning of practice to accommodate to people's disabilities.

While Wasserman questions whether the ADA can improve individuals with physical, sensory, or cognitive impairments so that they are elevated to the functional level of nonimpaired individuals, I do not take the direction of this law to be the improvement of individuals, although many individuals have found their personal situations bettered because of it. I interpret the ADA as being, primarily, a vehicle of formal justice in that it prescribes reforms in discriminatory practices, especially practices that suppose people with disabilities need not participate in civic and commercial transactions or partake of public goods. The ADA thus is designed to secure equal social participation and benefit by reforming practices that privilege those who do not have physical, sensory, or cognitive impairments over those who do. It is in this sense that the ADA compensates that group of individuals barred from public and commercial buildings by stairs—namely, by reforming the manner in which the opportunity to enter is offered, even if rectifying the wrong done by building designs that bar them is costly.

Doorways must be widened and ramps installed regardless of whether a wheelchair-using individual has yet come forward with the wish to enter. This is because access is owed first of all to the class of wheelchair users and only derivatively to individual wheelchair users. Of course, how compensation migrates from a wronged class to its individual members is a significant issue for any scheme that is intended to secure compensatory justice. Compensation is meant to be leveling, not privileging, so it must be clear that individuals who benefit from compensation have themselves been wronged and are not simply enjoying advantage because some fellow members of their class have been wronged.

In this regard, my hesitation about adopting Wasserman's proposal to compensate for disabilities by equalizing people's capabilities is that it blurs the distinction between individual- and group-targeted compensation. Regrettably, to do so is to perpetuate the unclarity about whether justice calls for revising disadvantaged persons so that they measure higher on a metric of properties needed for human flourishing or, first and foremost, for revising practices so that they expand their scope in facilitating human flourishing.

In this volume, as in his previous writing on this law,[1] Wasserman is concerned that, regardless of its mandating achievable access to transit, the ADA "leaves most disabled people with a far greater burden of mobility than most other people." However, as I argued earlier, citizens with

---

1. David Wasserman, "Disability, Discrimination, and Fairness," *Report from the Institute for Philosophy & Public Policy* 13, no. 1/2 (Winter/Spring 1993): 7–12.

disabilities are owed only that convenience of mobility enjoyed (or deplored) by public transportation users, not the greater degree of convenience achieved by private automobile users, despite the fact that many people with disabilities are prevented from driving because of their impairments. The comparatively greater inconvenience of using public transportation is visited equally upon disabled and nondisabled nondrivers. For to further compensate those whose residual transportation burden is due to their impairments, but not those for whom poverty, lack of language skills, or other deficient circumstances impose a similar degree of burden, is to privilege disability over other disadvantages without justification.

Wheelchair ramps and voice output computers clearly equalize, and just as clearly do not privilege, those who would have no access without them. Nor do they disadvantage those who previously enjoyed privileged access, as all users, disabled or not, can preserve access when these devices are available to facilitate opportunity. Were all computers to speak their texts as well as show them, people who are blind would gain equal access, while the access for people who are deaf would not diminish. Were all elevated built spaces ramped rather than staired, athletes would not be kept out because mobility-limited people were let in.

Granted, retrofitting buildings and machines to provide access is not costless. But we have the strongest reason to shoulder their costs—namely, that of rectifying past wrongs that could have been avoided, often with relative ease. This is remediation that would not be needed but for the oppressively negligent past. Nor can it be denied that those from whom reparative resources are drawn—namely, the nondisabled general public— have heretofore gained personal benefit from having precisely that access to facilities and programs the disabled also desired but were denied.

Parenthetically, Wasserman's analysis echoes the complaints of those individuals within the disability community who believe that the ADA has failed because people with disabilities still have less access to public programs and to the workplace than other people do. For instance, that no steep rise in the employment of people with disabilities followed the signing into law of the ADA has caused some commentators to call for a return to the entitlement approach and to propose that employers be assigned quotas for hiring disabled people.[2] Before adopting quota-driven entitle-

---

2. Jane West, *Federal Implementation of the Americans with Disabilities Act 1991–94* (New York: Millbank Memorial Fund, 1994), 18. Marjorie Baldwin,

ments that many are sure to perceive as privileging, we would do well to consider why people with disabilities are not hired. In addition to the so-called work disincentives—namely, the imprudence of jeopardizing their federal support and medical services for jobs that promise less security—the discrimination they have previously suffered persists in hampering them. For, of course, those who have not previously held jobs and have no employment experience are at a disadvantage in finding new work.

It could take a generation to overcome this result of past discrimination. But not only should the future population of a wronged class enjoy the benefits that flow from formal justice; the current population should do so as well. A faster and fairer remedy would have us examine our practices of assessing candidates for employment and reweight the importance of past work experience in the light of recognizing that its absence may be the artifact of oppression. Despite complaints that the ADA has failed because a considerable amount of noncompliance with it remains, the ultimate success or failure of the ADA will depend not on whether the handrails or electric outlets of various facilities match the implementation regulations but on whether people with physical, sensory, and cognitive impairments now begin to figure prominently and influentially in the population for whom such facilities are designed.

Against my claim that the ADA is a policy directed at group rather than individual compensation, it might be objected that its provision for reasonable accommodation is famously individualized. It is well known that compliance with this law involves assessment on a case-by-case basis rather than the application of first or fundamental principles. What should be realized, however, is that an accommodation is a makeshift remedy required to adapt to a discriminatory practice that cannot easily be reformed. For example, conveying information through speech rather than pictures is a convention that excludes people who are deaf. Reforming the practice to make it nondiscriminatory requires all conversationalists to add signing to their speech, a formidable demand on hearing individuals that is partially and temporarily relieved by the use of sign language interpreters.

"Can the ADA Achieve Its Employment Goals?" *The Annals of the American Academy of Political and Social Science, The Annals of the American Academy of Political and Social Science* (Special Issue on the Americans with Disabilities Act: Social Contract or Special Privilege?) 549 (January 1997): 37–52; Richard Scotch and Kay Schriner, "Disability as Human Variation: Implications for Policy," in Johnson, *The Annals*, 148–59.

Once we see that both categories of response—both the distributive and the proscriptive, as Wasserman has them—are compensatory, we can begin to understand why policies furthering the first are confusing as well as misguided. They are confusing because they are confused with the second kind of policy. I do not claim that these two policy categories are inconsistent with each other. But I do make the practical point that these rationales become conflated in such a way that they undermine each other. For what is appropriate for redressing a wrong may be excessive for mitigating a disadvantage.

For instance, it is a commonplace that whoever has been wronged should be made whole by the wrongdoer. So formal justice requires that, wherever feasible, public resources be expended to reform exclusionary public practice so as to extend access to people with disabilities. On the other hand, aside from this formal rationale becoming obscured by a different, distributive one, it is hard to see what obligates us to elevate all those in physical, sensory, or cognitive deficit—that is, to make them whole or normal. It is even harder to determine just who is obligated to forego earned resources to do so.

This leads to my next point of difference with Wasserman. While I agree with his criticisms of Daniels and find them more elegant and eloquent than my own along the same line,[3] I think he undercuts his own position by admitting that those with "severe disabilities and diseases would be at least as likely as those with deficient skills and talents to be among the worst off in primary goods." This supposition illustrates how easy it is to slip into stereotyping the disabled as being needy when one is considering distributing goods. To the contrary, many people with disabilities, even "severe ones," are well endowed with goods. Disability can occur at any stage of an individual's career, so some individuals with disabilities have accumulated goods, or acquired the skills to earn them, prior to becoming disabled. Moreover, many people flourish in productivity despite their disablement.

This observation leads to yet another concern about distributive compensation—namely, the fairness of exacting resources from some people

---

3. Anita Silvers, "A Fatal Attraction to Normalizing: Treating Disabilities as Deviations from 'Species-Typical' Functioning," in *Enhancing Human Capacities: Conceptual Complexities and Ethical Implications*, ed. Eric Parens (Washington D.C.: Georgetown University Press, forthcoming).

with disabilities to reimburse other people with disabilities because of the latter's disabilities. Need-based compensatory schemes do not take into account how disability discrimination equally oppresses rich and poor alike. The individual who plans to buy caviar in the grocery store but cannot gain access is no better off than the individual who equally cannot gain access to buy tuna fish. So it is unclear why the former individual must compensate the latter for her disability, for neither is it in his direct interest to do so, nor has he enjoyed any privilege for which paying compensation is the penalty. On the other hand, it is crystal clear why it is in the interest of both well-off and indigent individuals with disabilities alike to contribute to the reform of discriminatory practices.

Schemes that take disability to be a problem for distributive rather than formal justice to solve, Wasserman's included, usually reduce the difference disability makes in lives to states of neediness in regard to one or another desirable condition. For such an approach, to be disabled and to be flourishing is virtually an oxymoron. Furthermore, although disability affects well-off and indigent individuals similarly, most distributive entitlement schemes differentiate between them on the basis of means tests or other eligibility criteria. If both the employed mobility-impaired individual and the unemployed one need to use wheelchairs, assessing the former to pay for the latter's mobility may prevent the employed person from purchasing her own wheelchair. It is, moreover, not unusual for public benefits programs to set a higher reimbursement level for equipment and assistance for their clients than the market otherwise would settle on. Thus, a system that compensates people who are both indigent and disabled may have a market impact that constricts the functionality of nonindigent people with disabilities.

In regard to my position, Wasserman labors under a misunderstanding that results from his failure to see how substantive formal justice can be. My counterfactualizing proposal is meant to test the oppressiveness of practices—that is, as an imaginative exercise to reveal whether a practice excludes people with disabilities merely because they are in the minority among people. By no means should counterfactualizing be taken as an instrument for setting specifications for distributive policy.

Nevertheless, Wasserman takes counterfactualizing to be a test of the adequacy of accommodations. But it is a lapse of imagination on his part that leads him to think me interested in what accommodations would be made in a society in which the disabled are the dominant group. To the contrary, I argue, in such a society, individuals would only rarely seek to have their disabilities accommodated, for practices would already suit the fashions in which they function. There would be no need for a special practice of making accommodations if our common practice was itself inherently accommodating. So the way Wasserman puts this argument appears to prolong the notion that the social inclusion of people with disabilities must be an extraordinary, and burdensome, achievement rather than a conventional expectation.

One factor affecting whether we eventually will think of inclusion as ordinary or special is how imaginative and how thorough we are about refashioning our practices. For instance, an inherently accommodating society would neither reduce nor enlarge its size-related expectations to include both Lilliputian and Brobdingnagians (to continue with Wasserman's example). Instead, practices would be reshaped to facilitate the interpersonal transactions of a much more physically diverse population than we now provide for. As an example, we would want to replace our habit of charging into empty spaces as we ambulate with a more caretaking process of moving forward. For just as "normal" human walking practice now places the frail elderly, children, and people walking on canes and crutches in jeopardy of being knocked over, Brobdingnagians who did not reform their carefree walking practices would harm "normal"-sized humans, whose aggressive walking habits would in turn harm Lilliputians.

Parenthetically, it is hard to understand why Wasserman concludes that disruptions of our practices required to extend inclusion to previously marginalized groups of people are a form of social hijacking. Surely we would not similarly characterize the changes complained of by certain older males forced to work side by side and equally with women as social hijacking. Some males still experience working on an equal basis with women as so disruptive one imagines they might be less agitated by laboring next to male Lilliputians and Brobdingnagians than by being teamed with ordinary-sized females. We laugh at them. Wasserman objects that diversity like that introduced by Lilliputians and Brobdingnagians might call for trade-offs unheard of in a more homogeneous population. I agree that acknowledging human diversity makes our interpersonal transactions more complex. But I take this to be a compelling fact of our current social situation, one that an adequate theory of justice should highlight, not obscure.

Silvers on Mahowald

I have learned much from Mary Mahowald's clear, comprehensive, and discerning analysis of disability from a feminist standpoint. Its richness offers much to stimulate thought, too much to address thoroughly in a short space. Consequently, I will take up just two of the important points she makes. Both have to do with how people with disabilities relate to nondisabled people.

From a feminist perspective, connectedness between people should be foregrounded. Mahowald is on target to ask whether disability changes the character of our affiliations. To connect with other members of a just community, one must not only avail one's self of justice fostered by others but be just oneself. I thoroughly concur with Mahowald's contention that one is not exempted from moral responsibility by being disabled and that any practice to the contrary is both paternalistic and patronizing. But to acknowledge people with disabilities as being fully accountable agents raises the question of what principles govern their execution of this role.

Let us recall the case of Tom, who wishes to participate in the discussion part of a lecture/discussion class but whose difficulty in speaking will require that he be allocated more than the usual share of class time (time is arguably a depletable resource). Mahowald rightly rejects the proposal that his disability exempts Tom from considering how his participation, while bettering him, might disadvantage his classmates. To the contrary, she proposes, he must weigh the benefits his participation would secure against the disadvantage it might impose on other students.

In doing so, Mahowald thinks, he and others should perceive that his participation would on balance be "a boon rather than a burden not only for other students but also for faculty and staff, whose nearsightedness might thereby be reduced. . . . [U]niversity personnel . . . should have considered Tom's presence an educational advantage for others on campus." So, while Tom's entering into classroom discussion compromises other students' usual opportunities, it creates a different opportunity for them. But this is to consider Tom to be a means for others' improvement, not to consider him as an equally important end. Being afforded the opportunity to speak, a prospect other students take for granted, should not impose any additional burden of justification on him. In general, students do not speak in class in the conviction that their participation advances the common good, nor should there be any special burden placed on people with disabilities to do so. I discuss the unfairness implicit in the expectation that people with disabilities bear the burden of proving the value of their presence in the remarks introducing my section on "(Why) Is Disability Bad?"

To achieve equitable and inclusive participation that is not unfairly burdensome either to people with disabilities or to people who are not disabled calls for imagination rather than justification. We need to reform practice to make it more functional for people with and without disabilities alike. Faced with the case Mahowald describes, it is more productive, I think, to consider what the purpose of classroom questions may be—is it to make the questioner visible to the professor and class, to elucidate the question, to elaborate on the points presented for the benefit of the professor and class, or is some other advantage obtained by classroom participation?

In what ways can each of these objectives be achieved equitably for all students alike? It will turn out that there are many mechanisms, more inclusive than asking questions in class and also better adapted to achieving the presumed objectives of public dialogue, that can be substituted. As more and more students with disabilities appear in our classes with expectations of equal access, we must exercise more imagination in how we communicate, interact, assess, and perform other standard pedagogical functions. In doing so, we must recognize that our familiar activities and approaches are the product of a history of privileging people without impairments to the detriment of people who are impaired, so it is unrealistic to expect the latter to fit in without changing the lives of people in the former group.

This being so, we would do well to acknowledge that change has a cost to whoever is well supported by current exclusionary practice. At a minimum, the price exacted will be the effort needed to alter a system one will gain no personal benefit from changing. This is the commitment democratic morality extracts from the currently privileged for their commitment to equality.

From a democratic point of view, people with disabilities owe neither gratitude nor compensation to nondisabled persons who reform a system in which they themselves are privileged, making it more broadly and inclusively beneficial and less privileging. There thus is no reason for people with disabilities to indemnify the nondisabled majority for any costs incurred in extending justice. Nor should there be a call for demonstrating that their presence serves the common good; rather, what need be shown is only that justice is offended by their arbitrary forced absence. Nevertheless, people with disabilities do owe appreciation and admiration, as does everyone alike, to those nondisabled individuals who pursue justice consistently.

Having addressed the interconnectedness of the moral responsibility of people with and without disabilities, I want to comment on Mahowald's characterization of the interconnectedness of caregivers and care receivers. Mahowald observes, "There is always a one-sidedness regarding one aspect of the relationship: the fact that one person is in need of the services of the other, and not vice versa." So care receivers are made vulnerable by their dependence. On the other hand, as she also notices, the connection makes caregivers needy as well. Caregivers need appreciation and remuneration but too often realize mostly criticism and inadequate pay or other deprivation of goods in return for the services they render.

Insofar as the issue between people with disabilities and those who care for them is reciprocity, Mahowald is right in emphasizing that both must find the connection rewarding. However, caregivers often find themselves linked to people with disabilities by bonds other than those shaped by receiving, and reciprocating for, services. For instance, caregivers and care receivers may find themselves equally limited by hostile environments that magnify how much physical, sensory, and cognitive impairments reduce functionality. Such hostility makes people with impairments less able to care for themselves; concomitantly, in hostile environments caregivers find themselves with less respite from giving care.

Another tie, much debated within the disability community but little noticed beyond it, is incurred by caregivers and service providers who identify with disability. Prominent among these are parents of children with disabilities. Unlike the fortifying experience of mothers who identify enjoyably with the nondisabled children who flourish under their care, identifying with an individual with a disability is itself disabling. As one parent of a child with a disability writes:

> Especially when the child is young, . . . society confers . . . stigma upon whole families of the disabled. . . . It is one's affiliation/acceptance of a differently embodied other that situates the friend or family member as "disabled," too. In other words, there is an identity-politics issue for parents. Not to mention

that wherever my son could not go (because of wheelchair inaccessibility), I could not go. And when he was captive in a "special school," I, too, forfeited a "status" image—because all my friends were parents of kids in "regular" schools. Then there is the identity one absorbs as a . . . frequent visitor to hospitals, etc. Believe me, this works on one's identity.[4]

We agreed earlier that individuals with disabilities should consider how their social participation might affect, by way of limiting, other people's, but that they bear no special obligation to justify their presence. Nevertheless, it must be of concern to parents with disabilities that their nondisabled children are subject to the social rejection evoked by their parents' differences. To illustrate the problem, Paul Preston reports in *Mother Father Deaf: Living between Sound and Silence* that hearing children of deaf parents envy deaf siblings who can remain unaware of how their families are the subject of loud ridicule.[5] That hearing children of deaf parents must share the penalties society imposes on people for being deaf both afflicts the parents and embitters these children. Furthermore, children with disabilities typically cannot help but feel a need to justify their existence when they are made aware of their families' suffering because their own limited access to social goods also visits constraints on their parents and siblings.

Not everyone agrees that it is proper to characterize those intimately associated with people with disabilities as disabled themselves. Vic Finkelstein, one of the founders of disability studies, comments that parents who identify with their child's disability are only transiently disadvantaged by disability:

> But how can you then say that you are "disabled and handicapped" by life circumstances "which is a result of disability"? . . . Surely, . . . you are most emphatically NOT "disabled and handicapped" as a result of disability, but by the absence of support systems when these are required. . . . On the other hand your children would still have faced choices concerned with identity.[6]

But, I believe, an ambiguity of identity plagues caregivers and complicates how care receivers relate to them. For to become identified with a

---

4. E-mail correspondence from Donna Avery.

5. Paul Preston, *Mother Father Deaf: Living between Sound and Silence* (Cambridge, Mass.: Harvard University Press, 1994).

6. E-mail correspondence from Vic Finkelstein, 6 December 1996.

class for whom opportunity is compromised and constricted because its members are viewed as needing special care, but to do so without one's self either requiring or receiving the benefit of care, confounds relationships. There is a sense, then, in which association with the disabled exposes those nondisabled individuals who choose such relationships or are thrust into them to social jeopardy. This is itself a factor that exacerbates the isolation of people with disabilities. Already attenuated, the opportunity people with disabilities have for connectedness is further threatened because people without disabilities avoid relating to them in view of the liability these incur and, as important, because people with disabilities choose not to impose the liability of disability discrimination on loved ones who otherwise could remain oblivious to it.

This brings us back to the question of what special responsibilities accrue to individuals because they have a disability. Framing this question within the social model of disability illuminates it, I think, for the issue there becomes a matter of the extent to which one may justifiably expose one's nondisabled intimates, persons not otherwise threatened by disability discrimination, to the damaging effects of marginalization and oppression. To understand the interconnectedness of people with and without disabilities in this light suggests the complexity with which such relationships are nuanced in an environment made artificially hostile to some of them.

We who espouse democratic morality should not need to be convinced that injustice injures interconnectedness, for any relationship between people society privileges and people it disadvantages cannot help but be deformed. So, much as I admire the evenhandedness of feminist standpoint theory with its concern to give all standpoints standing, I do not see how standpoints can be equitably influential if they are expressed in practices that support some kinds of people but ignore others. And much as I applaud the concreteness of feminist descriptions of interdependence, I remain suspicious of centering practices, such as some of the familiar modes of caregiving, that have emerged within and are shaped by environments hostile to people with disabilities. Just as gender justice cures the corrupted connectedness between women and men by reforming practices that perpetuate inequities between men and women, a theory of justice of equivalent transformative force is called for to fashion practices that permit people with and without physical, sensory, and cognitive impairments to flourish together.

Wasserman on Silvers and Mahowald

Wasserman on Silvers

In her skillful interweaving of philosophy and social history, Anita Silvers makes a powerful case that the way we think about human functional variation has profound and often harmful consequences. I am persuaded by her narrative that the accommodation of human difference suffered a grave setback with the emergence of "the normal" in the nineteenth century as a dominant statistical, explanatory, and regulative concept. I disagree, however, about how we can best liberate our thinking and policy making about disability from that historical legacy.

Silvers draws three main conclusions from her analysis and historical review. First, she rejects medical correction as a legitimate, or at least as a primary, goal of disability policy: "Justice for people with physical, sensory, or cognitive impairments should not be couched in [the] demand that they be cured." Second, justice for people with impairments should not be understood in distributive terms, since that inevitably treats those people as deficient, "as needing more than others do." Third, justice of people with impairments requires only formal equality, understood to include the removal of barriers to full social participation and the elimination or redress of the effects of past exclusion.

I largely agree with the first thesis, and I devoted much of my own chapter to arguing that it did not have the close relationship with the second thesis that Silvers assumes; that distributive justice is not committed to, and has the resources to reject, medical normalization as the modal response to impairment. I will not repeat those arguments here. Rather, I wish to focus on Silvers's third thesis, that justice for people with impairments can be satisfied by formal equality.

Silvers's commitment to formal equality appears to have two sources: first, her conviction, already mentioned, that any more comprehensive approach will relegate people with impairments to positions of dependence and inferiority; second, her assumption that distributive justice is a matter of "decid[ing] whose assets to transform into common assets and whose to supply from common assets." This assumption strikes me as profoundly misleading; it reflects Robert Nozick's view that people's entitlements to their assets are relatively clear[7] and that the redistribution of assets that

---

7. Robert Nozick, *Anarchy, State, and Utopia* (Cambridge, Mass.: Harvard University Press, 1974), 149–53.

have not been acquired by force or fraud will almost always be a matter of robbing Peter to compensate Paul. As G. A. Cohen has argued, the threshold problem of distributive justice is in deciding how the world's assets are owned, in assessing Peter's moral title to the resources he holds and Paul needs.[8] I will not attempt to address this larger issue here; I merely want to point out that Silvers's understanding of distributive justice appears to reflect a hostility toward the whole enterprise. What I will argue is that Silvers's own claims about the entitlements of people with disabilities *require* a theory of distributive justice, that they go well beyond formal equality, even as Silvers understands it.

In her effort to keep equality formal rather than distributive, Silvers makes a sharp distinction between external barriers and internal deficits: removing the former is a requisite of formal equality, while alleviating the latter is a matter of distributive justice; the former provides equal treatment for people with disabilities, the latter subjects them to a homogenizing equalization. Yet in developing her approach to equal treatment for people with disabilities, Silvers articulates two more specific principles that, I will argue, undermine that distinction and demand a more substantive equality. One requires equal access to the means of satisfying common needs or interests; the other, equal opportunity to display talents. Silvers's own application of these principles suggests the arbitrariness of the line between external barriers and internal deficits and the limitations of her underlying notion of formal equality. Her own examples suggest that justice does not always require the removal of external impediments and that it may sometimes require the alleviation of internal deficits. The specific principles of equal treatment that Silvers adopts, and the intuitions she elicits in their support, require a comprehensive and broadly distributive theory of justice.

To illustrate her principle of equal access, Silvers argues that her two dogs would not have received equal treatment in the relevant sense if her dog-sitter set their dinner bowls on a four-foot-high table, accessible to her Great Dane but not her dachshund. While both dogs would have had their bowls set out for them, the former would have gotten his dinner, while the latter would not have. The table height is an external barrier for

---

8. G. A. Cohen, "Self-Ownership, World-Ownership, and Equality," in *Justice and Equality Here and Now*, ed. Frank Lucash (Ithaca: Cornell University Press, 1983).

the dachshund, and equal treatment requires the placement of his bowl at an accessible height. It is a small step from this example to bus lifts and TTY devices, which make transportation and communication accessible to disabled individuals, satisfying needs they share with nondisabled people.

To return to the two dogs, however, Silvers would presumably be equally unhappy with her dog-sitter if she gave her Great Dane the same small amount of food as she gave her dachshund. Although both dogs would get a bowl of food, the dachshund would get a full meal, while the Great Dane would not. There is no external barrier for the Great Dane, however; there is simply not enough food. (On the other hand, it seems odd to describe the Great Dane as having an internal deficit in this respect.) It strikes me as morally arbitrary to accuse the dog-sitter of denying equal treatment to the dachshund when she sets his bowl too high but not to the Great Dane when she gives him too small a portion.

Silvers herself insists that in identifying the "treatment" that must be equalized, we should employ "descriptions of actions as directly instrumental to individuals' interests." If equal treatment is understood in terms of the actions instrumental to individuals' interests, we will be concerned with feeding the dogs, not simply placing food in front of them. If the dog-sitter fails to treat the two dogs equally when she sets the dachshund's food at Great Dane height, she also fails to treat them equally when she gives the Great Dane a dachshund-size portion.

More broadly, if we are concerned about access to the means of satisfying an individual's interests, it is hard to see how the equalization of access can be limited to the removal of external barriers. Cohen, for example, argues for equality of access to "advantage," a broad, eclectic category that includes virtually everything that makes people's lives go better.[9] Understood in this expansive sense, access may be equalized by removing external barriers, by providing varying amounts or types of resources, or by correcting internal deficits.

Silvers may well favor a much narrower notion of access than Cohen's, one that reflects the distinction between external barriers and internal

---

9. G. A. Cohen, "On the Currency of Egalitarian Justice," *Ethics* 99 (July 1989): 906–4. Cohen takes "advantage" to include both welfare and resources: "[R]esource deficiencies and welfare deficiencies are distinct types of disadvantage, and . . . each of them covers pretty distinct subtypes: poverty and physical weakness are very different kinds of resource limitation, and despondency and failure to achieve aims are very different kinds of illfare" (920–21).

deficits. But if so, she needs to specify what it is that people must have equal access to. She must also reconcile her narrower notion of access with her understanding of equal treatment in terms of individual interests. And if the narrower notion she favors would not give her hungry Great Dane the same basis for complaint as her hungry dachshund, she must explain why this is not a morally arbitrary result.

In one area, Silvers does seem prepared to override the distinction between external barriers and internal deficits. She allows that a school system might be required, as a matter of equal treatment, to provide speech therapy for a cognitively impaired child, as long as that therapy "served to facilitate the . . . expression of talents he does possess—perhaps permitting him to communicate with a supervisor and coworkers or ask for the products he needs at a store." Silvers thus appears to accept speech therapy as a means of enlarging the opportunity to express preexisting talents, even if it has "internal" improvement as a goal and normalization as a side effect. For unlike Amy Rowley's interpreter, Eddie Conrad's therapist is trying to modify an internal deficit, even if her goal is serviceable communication rather than normal speech.

But Silvers's approval of internal modifications is highly circumscribed: if she is willing to accept speech therapy to facilitate the expression of preexisting talents, she is wary of speech therapy aimed at creating or developing talents. She would apparently not require schools to offer therapy to prepare students for jobs in which normal speech was a required talent (e.g., work as a receptionist or an announcer). In that case, the failure to provide therapy would not hinder the expression of a talent the student already had but merely fail to develop one he lacked. Why, though, should compensatory measures be permitted only to facilitate the expression of existing talents rather than to cultivate or enhance talent? Particularly in the context of primary education, it seems highly artificial as well as morally arbitrary to limit intervention to measures that facilitate "the cognitively impaired individual's expression of talents he does possess."

Schools are in the business of nurturing or developing talents in those who cannot be said to possess them except in the most inchoate form. It is certainly true that background differences make it far easier for some children to acquire talents than others and that we may use "talent" interchangeably with "potential" in referring to those differences. But few children, however talented in this sense, come into school with the talents necessary for an adult job or for responsible citizenship; it is the school's job to develop a wide range of general talents, a task that may require considerably more educational resources for some children than others. Silvers's goal of facilitating the expression of talents the child already possesses sounds more appropriate to an employment agency than a primary school.

But even if we limit ourselves to preexisting talents, formal equality will not ensure "the opportunity to apply our talents productively," which Silvers regards as a "prerequisite . . . for a fair cooperative scheme." Formal equality does not require that jobs or tasks be structured so that they provide opportunities, let alone equal opportunities, for people to express their talents; it merely requires the consistent application of job or task requirements. In Silvers's words, "employers must hold all employees to the same standard."

This requirement of consistency certainly imposes some constraints: it is violated when an employer inflates the requirements for a job to exclude a person whose employment poses some small inconvenience. Thus, Silvers is clearly right to object to having her parking space removed by a university administrator on the grounds that "if you cannot walk . . . to your classroom, you are not qualified to teach." While there is a wide range of views about what constitutes teaching competence in philosophy, ambulatory capacity has never been thought to be a part of it (except, perhaps, for the Peripatetics); a job description for a philosopher that included both classroom teaching and walking would look obviously gerrymandered.

But if some composite requirements are clearly pretextual, some are clearly bona fide, such as running, swimming, and bicycling in a triathlon. (Others, such as walking the length of a golf course in tournament play, may be contested or uncertain.) As long as the requirements for a particular job or task are consistently defined and applied, formal equality imposes no limits on their composition—a triathlon is no more or less fair than a marathon.

Clearly, the opportunity to apply one's talents productively requires more than consistency in the application of job or task requirements. A society that offered only composite tasks like triathlons would not offend formal equality, but it would slight the interests of people with a narrow or nonstandard array of talents. To ensure an adequate opportunity for those people to display their talents, it is not enough for individual employers to "clarify what they take to be essential duties for jobs." It is also necessary that the society as a whole divide up its jobs and tasks in such a way that their requirements can be met by people with widely varying arrays of talents.

How can Silvers assume that formal equality will ensure adequate opportunity for people with disabilities, when it imposes no constraints on the way jobs and tasks are structured? Her faith in the adequacy of formal equality appears to rest in part on her conviction that impairments do not entail a lack of talent, so that the way jobs or tasks are structured should not affect the opportunities available to people with disabilities. She distinguishes the operation of a faculty, which is (by definition) impaired, from the performance of a task, which need not be. Since impairments are, per Ron Amundson, defined at the level of basic or personal actions, they have no necessary implications for non-basic actions or performances.[10] While blind people cannot see, and most people read by seeing visual characters, this does not mean blind people cannot read; they read by touching Braille characters. There will usually be alternative means to perform a task available to people who cannot, because of an impairment, perform it the standard way.

I think this is an important point, which sharpens the central distinction between impairment and disability. But I think Silvers makes too much of it. First, it may rest on a questionable hierarchy of actions, although I will leave it to others to pursue that concern. But second, there are tasks that, as a practical matter, a person can only accomplish by performing a basic action (or one of a small set of such actions) precluded by a particular impairment. The familiar example of driving a car comes to mind: it is simply not feasible for a blind person to drive a standard automobile by herself in heavy traffic, although she might well have skills that, in some technologically more advanced world, would permit her to drive high-speed vehicles as well as anyone with sight. And even if it is not practically impossible for a person with a particular impairment to perform a particular task, it may be much harder, or much more expensive. There is no reason to assume that alternative means will always be as easy or cheap (even in a society in which most people were impaired in the same way) or that we could define the relevant task at a level of generality at which difficulty and cost could be equalized (and how would be know what the right level of generality was?).

10. Ron Amundson, "Disability, Handicap, and the Environment," *Journal of Social Philosophy* 23, no. 1 (1992): 107.

In circumstances in which an individual can only perform some task X in a nonstandard way, which is very difficult or expensive, we could describe him either as having a talent for task X, but lacking certain ancillary conditions for its performance, or as lacking a talent for X, even though he had a talent for the constituent task Y. Thus, we could say that the blind person with superb reflexes, coordination, and sense of direction has the talent for driving but that the cost of permitting her to express that talent (e.g., with an advanced sonar system or a navigator) is prohibitive, or we could say she lacks the specific talents for driving, even though she has superb reflexes, and so forth. Under either description, a cab company would be justified in refusing to hire her—either because the cost of accommodating her would be prohibitive or because she was not qualified. In either case, a just society would ensure that she had a meaningful opportunity to display her formidable talents elsewhere. I do not think the distinction between the two ways of describing her case makes a moral difference, and I think that the fact that it makes so much of a difference for Silvers suggests an infirmity in her account.

Silvers is not alone, however, in placing so much emphasis on the distinction between an employee's lack of talent or qualification and the costs of accommodating her. As Mark Kelman notes, the law of employment discrimination makes a critical distinction between an employee's "output capacity" and "value-added capacity": An employer need not bear the costs of lower employee output, since output is a matter of job qualification; it must bear, up to the elastic limits of "business necessity," the costs of physical accommodation, flexible scheduling, and higher premiums for health care and liability insurance. Kelman argues that this distinction lacks normative force, since an employee does not deserve, or bear responsibility for, her productive or output capacity any more than for the incidental costs her employment imposes. He speculates that the distinction may be preserved by a recalcitrant belief that productive capacity is really deserved or that the employee is somehow more responsible or deserving with respect to "active" output than "passive" input costs.[11] In drawing a sharp line between the core requirements of a job and the incidental costs of

---

11. Mark Kelman, "Concepts of Discrimination in General Ability Job Testing," *Harvard Law Review* 104, no. 6 (April, 1991): 1202–4. For a similar analysis with respect to genetic testing, see Alan Strudler, "The Social Construction of Genetic Abnormality: Ethical Implications for Managerial Decisions in the Workplace," *Journal of Business Ethics* 13 (1994): 839–48.

employment, the law is making a concession to public attitudes it might do better to challenge.

Ironically, in insisting on the irrelevance of impairment to job qualification, Silvers appears as committed as Daniels to a rigid distinction between impairment and deficient talent. Daniels requires the distinction to identify the conditions whose correction receives lexical priority—millions for the rectification of impairments before a cent is spent on the enhancement of limited talents. Silvers requires the distinction to determine when formal equality is jeopardized—never when a difference in outcome is based on a difference in talent, almost always when it is based on a difference in faculties or functions. I do not think the distinction can bear the weight that either Daniels or Silvers places on it.

This does not mean, of course, that we should regard people as untalented or incompetent by virtue of their impairments. To the contrary, it means that we must do more than formal equality requires to structure jobs and tasks so as to give people, impaired or not, a fair or adequate opportunity to display talent and competence. This requires a flexibility in job descriptions and a diversity in job offerings that we can more appropriately demand of the cooperative scheme as a whole than of individual jobs or employers. More broadly, we need to recognize that talent, merit, and competence are no less social constructed than (dis)ability and that opening existing careers to talents is but a small part of treating people as equals.

Rather than concede that treating people as equals will often require the alleviation of internal deficits, Silvers seems prepared to deny that people for whom such intervention is necessary *can* be treated as equals. Thus, while Silvers does not ignore the claims of the most profoundly impaired people, she insists that distributive schemes to benefit them fall outside the scope of justice. "Instead, they are based on the fact that some individuals among us will be in extended dependency and therefore will never be equal." What is most troubling in this claim is the implication that extended dependency, at least if it is unavoidable, makes a person less than equal. Silvers cannot mean that permanently dependent people lack the moral equality on which justice rests. Some human beings of course, lack any self-awareness or capacity for agency, and their presence raises difficult issues about the boundaries and moral significance of personhood. But—and Silvers would surely agree—most profoundly impaired individuals have whatever is required for moral equality, even if they will live in extended dependency; they possess, in Jeff McMahan's words, "certain properties and capacities that give their possessor an inherent worth that demands respect."[12] For contractarians like Rawls, that is enough to place them within the scope of justice. Their dependency may be undesirable if it undermines their self-respect or prevents their flourishing, but it does not place them below the threshold for justice. The social and economic arrangements for people in extended or permanent dependency are as much a matter of justice as the social and economic arrangements for any of the rest of us.

The fact that Silvers denies this suggests that she takes the view that justice is a matter of reciprocity or mutual benefit. If justice is seen in terms of fair exchange or a fair division of the product of social cooperation, then, as Derek Parfit notes, those who cannot produce will be left out altogether, their very survival a matter of charity rather than justice.[13] That implication alone, I think, gives us a compelling reason to reject the notion of justice as reciprocity or mutual benefit.

We can recognize the importance of providing people with the opportunity to develop and express their talents without making reciprocity or mutual benefit the essence of justice. The kind of dependency that people with profound impairments typically experience is profoundly unjust because it undermines their self-respect and limits their flourishing. Thus, for example, the widespread employment of people with disabilities during World War II exposes as unnecessary, and invidious, their high level of unemployment before and after. At the same time, there are, as Silvers recognizes, people with impairments so severe that their full employment is not technologically or economically feasible. But although their permanent dependency may not be unjust, it does not place them outside the scope of justice.

It is also critical to recognize that people can flourish without being economically productive, that the worth of a person's work is not determined by its market value. Modern governments directly subsidize a wide range of vocations and indirectly subsidize an even wider range. While such subsidies are often given in the belief, or on the pretext, that they are correcting market failures, there is a growing recognition that they are

12. Jeff McMahan, "Cognitive Disability, Misfortune, and Justice," *Philosophy and Public Affairs* 25, no. 1 (Winter 1996): 30.

13. Derek Parfit, "Equality and Priority," *Ratio* 10 *(n.s.)*, no. 3 (December 1997): 209.

better justified in terms of the worth or dignity of the activities that they support. Government intervention permits rural workers to engage in traditional livelihoods, it permits artists and scholars to pursue esoteric projects, and it allows severely retarded adults to work in sheltered settings. If farmers, watermen, poets, and literary critics are not demeaned by their dependency, people with profound impairments need not be. It is not the subsidy itself that demeans them; it is the disrespect and contempt with which it is given and administered.

People with disabilities would be less likely to be demeaned and marginalized if nondisabled people saw them as competent and productive, but they would also be less likely to be demeaned and marginalized if nondisabled people saw themselves as pervasively dependent on the provisions made for them by the government and the broader social order. And the latter may be a more realistic objective. As Silvers points out, disabled experience is largely opaque to the nondisabled; the able-bodied may be in a better position to recognize their own dependence than to appreciate the competence and productivity of people with significant impairments. Advocates for the disabled should join feminist scholars in promoting recognition of our interdependence and in rejecting the harshly individualistic ethos that associates dignity and respect with self-sufficiency.

At the same time, the short history of the modern welfare state does give some credibility to Silvers's concerns about the demeaning effects of entitlement regimes. Even in societies that acknowledge universal dependence, some types of people will inevitably be regarded as more dependent than others; perhaps the insidious distinction between "us" and "them" will always reassert itself despite the concerted efforts of policy makers to suppress it. But to make a general case against entitlement regimes, Silvers would have to show that people with impairments fared *worse*, in terms of political and economic participation, social acceptance, and self-esteem, in societies that treated welfare as a general dispensation than in societies that treated it as a last resort. And even if she could show that entitlement regimes were damaging to people with impairments, she would only have shown that the attempt to implement liberal theories of distributive justice tended to produce results that those theories would condemn. It would surely be a disturbing fact if the most appealing theories of justice were self-defeating in this sense. But it would not show their conception of human equality to be fundamentally mistaken.

Wasserman on Mahowald

In her discussion of differences among disabilities, Mahowald suggests that what is true of race is equally true of impairment: that the variability *among* people with disabilities is much greater than that *between* people with disabilities and able-bodied people. This observation lends support to my claim that impairments should be seen as merely some among the many variations in function and capacity that a just society accommodates. But the fact that people with disabilities, like people of color, are treated as a single class despite these differences, and share powerful experiences of stigmatization and exclusion, also supports Silvers's emphasis on discrimination and disrespect as central problems of disability. I will discuss the points of overlap between Mahowald's account and my own, then turn to the one area of significant disagreement: the relevance of selective abortion to people with disabilities.

I ended my own chapter skeptical that we could dispense with moral intuitions in resolving fundamental issues of justice but hopeful that we could make moral progress with an account that relied on such intuitions. Mahowald's sensitive discussion of the varieties of disability rewards my optimism; it suggests that justice, like God, is in the details. But it also highlights the need for a general conception of justice to adjudicate the conflicts and trade-offs among different needs and interests. And this, I think, places it at odds with feminist ethics that reject the importance of moral theory.

Thus, for example, consider the hardships faced by caregivers for people with disabilities, a group that Mahowald sees as neglected in much of the debate on disability policy. A recent article in the *Washington Post* announced the likely passage of a Maryland legislative initiative "to relieve parents of some of the burdens involved in caring for grown children who are disabled or mentally retarded." According to the *Post*, the prospect of such relief comes "thanks to an unusual lobbying effort, a bulging state budget surplus, and the election-year willingness to spend the money."[14] (The article also illustrates Mahowald's contention that women are the predominant caregivers. In the two featured families, both with two parents, the mother does most or all of the caregiving for a severely disabled adult child.)

---

14. Robert E. Pierre, "For Parents of Disabled, Promise of a Respite in Maryland," *Washington Post*, 10 February 1998, 1.

As a Maryland resident, I was appalled that in a state whose tax revenues support an arts and a humanities council—the latter a sometime contributor to our institute—funding for severely disabled residents depends on a large budget surplus and a concerted election-year lobbying effort. I believe that the state's spending priorities are, in this respect, deeply unjust. I suspect that Mahowald would agree. But while the invitation to adopt the standpoint of the overburdened caregivers is a useful heuristic for dramatizing their plight and generating support for its alleviation, I think we need a more general basis for reordering the legislators' priorities. That need is more acute when we consider the array of other urgent projects that the legislators have also slighted, such as the housing, health care, and education of indigent children. A serial exposure to the perspectives of nondominant groups may be essential to the application of any adequately concrete theory of justice. But, by itself, such exposure does more to shame us than to guide us.

It is in this respect that the metaphor of myopia is misleading. Our exposure to unfamiliar and neglected standpoints may reveal the limitations in our own vision, but it does not provide us with a benchmark for correct or adequate vision. The view from almost any standpoint will look flawed or distorted from others' perspective. It is this recognition that motivates the search for a neutral standpoint and the recourse to hypothetical ignorance about one's own position. Critics of contractarian approaches, Silvers among them, have argued that we tend to regard the neutral standpoint as a thinly disguised version of our own and that we smuggle in much of our own standpoint behind the veil of ignorance. But it is unclear how we can do better simply by exposing ourselves to an array of actual standpoints. While sustained dialogue and careful listening may increase mutual access, the perspectives of people with significantly different backgrounds and life experiences are likely to remain, as Silvers fears, mutually opaque. Despite its limitations, however, Mahowald's emphasis on the particular and concrete serves as a valuable corrective to overconfident abstraction, and it contributes to a vital dialectic between generality and specificity in the appraisal of justice.

The one area in which I find Mahowald's analysis mistaken, rather than (perhaps unavoidably) incomplete, is in the framing of the debate between a woman's right to choose an abortion for any reason and the interests of people with disabilities. Mahowald thinks that the moral status of the fetus is central to the debate; I do not. She claims that egalitarian feminism is reconcilable with advocacy for women's choice if the fetus has little or no moral status. But just as support for a woman's right to choose may be consistent with a belief that the fetus has the moral status of a person—that is, if we regard abortion as a failure to aid, as self-protection, or as a woman's exercise of control over her own body—support for restrictions on a woman's right to choose in the interest of people with disabilities may be consistent with a belief that the fetus has little or no moral status.

Advocates for the disabled see three kinds of harm in prenatal testing and selective abortion apart from the death of the aborted fetus: first, the adverse effects of reducing the number of people with a given impairment; second, the adverse effects of the exclusionary attitudes underlying the practice of prenatal testing; third, the expressive significance of that practice. All of these fears are credible; none involves an assumption that the fetus has significant moral status.

Some critics fear that widespread testing will lead to the disappearance of people with certain disabilities, a loss they treat as somewhat akin to the extinction of a species.[15] But this concern may be scientifically implausible, since most disabilities are acquired, and even for those that are largely or entirely genetic, testing will never be universal or completely accurate. But even if testing merely causes a significant reduction in the number of people with certain disabilities (a more realistic prospect), the loss of numbers may itself have an adverse effect on people with those disabilities.

Some bioethicists dismiss this concern, arguing that the fewer the people with a given disability, the more per capita will be spent on research, treatment, and services for their benefit.[16] This is doubtful, however, since larger numbers generate as well as consume more resources. However justifiably, the claims of greater numbers are accorded greater moral weight, and (partly as a result) they tend to have greater political weight. Numbers also matter in providing the intangible benefits of community and culture—the fewer the people with a given impairment, the more socially isolated they may be.

---

15. Marsha Saxton, "Disability Rights and Selective Abortion," in *Abortion Wars: A Half Century of Struggle, 1950–2000*, ed. R. Solinger (Berkeley: University of California Press, 1998).

16. Allen Buchanan, "Choosing Who Will Be Disabled: Genetic Intervention and the Morality of Inclusion," *Social Philosophy and Policy* 13, no. 2 (1996): 40–41.

The second concern is that prenatal testing may harm existing people with disabilities by reinforcing negative social attitudes toward them. A policy encouraging prenatal testing in a society committed to treating all people as equals postnatally might be likened to an immigration policy that makes it difficult for people to enter a country but gives them full citizenship if they do. The analogy suggests the importance of the reason behind the exclusionary policy: Does the society have limited resources, which it is committed to sharing on a first-come, first-served basis? Does it fear that the immigrants will consume a disproportionate share of those resources? Or are the immigrants regarded as undesirable for other reasons? To the extent that exclusion is based on the last of these concerns, its effects may be difficult to contain at the border, as the actual history of U.S. immigration policy suggests. Whatever reasons lie behind the decisions of parents who use prenatal testing or of the institutions that sponsor it—an issue I consider later—it is clear that policies to prevent the birth of, and reproduction by, people with disabilities have long been animated by aversion and contempt toward those people and that the strength and persistence of those attitudes is relevant to the appraisal of the social impact of prenatal testing.

Prenatal testing may also exacerbate prejudice against people with detectable impairments, by encouraging a view of those conditions as preventable misfortunes rather than as an unavoidable aspect of human variation. (And if testing reduces tolerance for people with impairments, it will certainly reduce tolerance for parents who choose to bring such people into the world. As testing becomes routine, the failure to test, or to act on positive results, is likely to be seen, however unjustifiably, as a form of parental neglect or abuse and as a basis for denying such parents medical and economic assistance.) As Lisa Blumberg argues, "a society which engages in a relentless if futile struggle to separate the 'normal' from the 'abnormal' prenatally . . . will end up making outsiders of much of its citizenry."[17]

But even if, as Jonathan Glover suggests, it were possible to prevent such a "spillover" to actual people with disabilities,[18] the question would remain whether the exclusionary policy was consistent with their full citi-

---

17. Lisa Blumberg, "The Politics of Prenatal Testing and Selective Abortion," *Sexuality and Disability* 12, no. 2 (1994): 150.
18. Jonathan Glover, "Future People, Disability, and Screening," in *Justice between Age Groups and Generations*, ed. P. Laslett and J. S. Fishkin (New Haven: Yale University Press, 1992).

zenship. Even if existing people with disabilities suffered no loss of civil rights, social status, or self-esteem from such a policy, it might still be seen as denying them full equality by expressing, in emphatic terms, the belief that their lives are not worth living or have lesser value. This is a fundamentally nonutilitarian objection to actions and policies that deny the moral equality of all people, not to the psychological harm caused by the perceived denial. It is not a concern about the offense intended by those who use or sponsor prenatal testing, but about the offense inherent in the beliefs that underlie the use or sponsorship of such tests. The notion of moral equality is notoriously vague, however, and a variety of beliefs may underlie a given action or policy. Writers in this area have made several distinctions in an effort to clarify the expressive significance of prenatal testing and selective abortion: between devaluation of the impairment and devaluation of the impaired person; between concern *for* the impaired child and concern *about* the child's effect on others; and between the decision of individual parents to test and abort and the social sponsorship of testing.

Allen Buchanan invokes the first distinction, arguing that prenatal testing may express a benign desire to spare people the burden of impairments; it devalues only the impairment, not the impaired person.[19] One does not have to be an essentialist about impairment and personal identity to question this distinction. It seems particularly difficult to maintain in the case of congenital and early-onset impairments, which the individual may not regard as an affliction but as an integral part of her way of living and self-conception, even if she recognizes that she could have existed without it.

It might be thought that prenatal testing conveys no disrespect if it is undertaken out of concern for the people who will be impaired, and not for the society at large. Prospective parents may feel that a child with the disability would have a life so painful and frustrating that it would not be worth living. But for the great majority of people with disabilities, who regard their lives as well worth living, the contrary assumption may well seem disrespectful, in its exaggeration of their burdens and its disregard of their own testimony. Ironically, a decision to abort based on the less extreme belief that the life of an impaired child will be *less* rewarding than the lives of most unimpaired children may convey greater disrespect, since

---

19. Buchanan, "Choosing Who," 30–31.

that decision is clearly not being made for the sake of the impaired child—she would presumably prefer to have a life well worth living than not to exist at all. Rather, that decision reflects the view that happier or more fulfilled lives have greater weight or higher priority.

The decision to test and abort may be less likely to reflect any adverse judgment about the quality or value of life with impairments if it is based on concern for others besides the affected fetus. Parents may simply feel overwhelmed by the prospect of raising an impaired child in a society that fails to welcome such children, or by the prospect of having their expectations about parenting pervasively defeated.[20] Admittedly, there may be an implicit devaluation of people with disabilities in parents' assessment of the economic, social, and psychological burdens they would face in raising a disabled child. But this assessment may also be informed by a belief that they would love an impaired child as much as any other and that the unconditional love they would feel would cause them great pain. Some of the difficulties they anticipate would arise precisely because they could not treat the impaired child with lesser concern, and their apprehension may affirm rather than deny the moral equality of the child. We are far more likely to find an implicit belief in the undesirability or lesser value of lives with disabilities in the public sponsorship of prenatal testing than in parents' willingness to use those tests.

The considerable social investment in prenatal testing is designed to permit women to prevent the birth of children with certain conditions, and that investment clearly suggests that society regards those conditions as undesirable. After all, it does not sponsor costly research and development for tests that would reveal such neutral traits as skin color, even if some parents might be tempted to seek such information in deciding whether to continue a pregnancy, and it strongly disapproves of using existing tests for the purpose of sex selection. The resistance to testing for sex selection offers a striking contrast to the acceptance or encouragement of testing for disability.[21] Moreover, the expressive significance of the sponsorship of prenatal testing by the state must be assessed in light of its responsibility for the economic and social conditions that contribute so

---

20. M. Saxton, "Disability Rights and Selective Abortion"; A. Asch, "Reproductive Technology and Disability," in *Reproductive Laws for the 1990s*, ed. S. Cohen and N. Taub (New York: Humana, 1988).

21. Dorothy Wertz and John Fletcher, eds., *Ethics and Human Genetics: A Cross-Cultural Perspective* (Berlin: Springer, Inc., 1989).

greatly to the difficulties of raising, or being, a child with a disability.[22] In allocating resources to enable parents to prevent the birth of children with disabilities, while failing to support facilities and services that would allow such children (and their parents) to flourish, society devalues the lives of people with disabilities less ambiguously than do the parents who avail themselves of prenatal testing.

The harm and offense that may arise from prenatal testing and selective abortion can be avoided less obtrusively by limiting testing than by restricting abortion. But restrictions on testing also impair a woman's autonomy, since they deny her information she might well find relevant to her reproductive choices. So in the end, I do think there is a tension between respect for women's autonomy and respect for people with impairments, a tension that arises regardless of one's position on the moral status of the fetus. I do not see how either right or interest can be said to trump the other in the circumstances where they conflict. The most appropriate ways of alleviating the tension may involve modest restrictions on the availability and content of prenatal testing—for example, discouraging tests for impairments not associated with life-threatening disease; requiring more balanced information about the challenge of raising a child with an impairment, including the opportunity for contact with parents who have done so successfully. And, of course, I strongly support social and medical provisions for children with impairments that would make the challenge of raising them less onerous. I do not know whether Mahowald would endorse all of these proposals, but I suspect that even our narrow disagreement on this issue is more a matter of theory than practice.

Mahowald on Silvers and Wasserman

As I had hoped, the essays by Anita Silvers and David Wasserman have served to reduce my nearsightedness. I thank them for that. In particular I am indebted to Silvers for her astute analysis of the meaning and models of disability and to Wasserman for his incisive critique of different interpretations of distributive justice. From both coauthors, I learned a great deal about the Americans with Disabilities Act (ADA), expanded and clarified my understanding of variables applicable to disabilities and persons with

---

22. Asch, "Reproductive Technology and Disability."

disabilities, and gleaned insights that would only have been available to me from their different standpoints. However, the more I know, the more I know how little I know. This prompts me to raise two questions that I was not knowledgeable enough to ask before reading their essays.

The first question is why my coauthors apparently do not consider themselves feminists. In early drafts of the book's contents, my essay was entitled "Feminist Justice." I asked that this be changed because it suggests (1) that the other authors' conceptions of justice are not feminist, (2) that there is but one feminist conception of justice, and (3) that my conception is different from theirs. That the second point is false should be clear from my essay; the last point is true, but contingently so (i.e., as dependent on the particular conceptions of justice that they developed). The first point, I believe, is refuted by the authors' own essays. While Silvers and Wasserman provide different accounts of justice, both accounts are not only consistent with, but demand, gender justice. Each thus exemplifies a different version of feminism.

Silvers critiques the notion of care that has troubled many feminists. She also affirms the theme of interdependence, albeit not uncritically, that many feminists emphasize.[23] Her observation that women with disabilities are especially devalued constitutes implicit acknowledgment of the need for a feminist standpoint even within disabilities discourse. Wasserman incorporates a feminist critique into his own critique of structural discrimination. The ADA, he says, was shaped by feminists who challenged earlier civil rights law. According to Wasserman, that law, designed by able-bodied males, forced women and people with disabilities to choose between "a formal equality that ignores their distinct needs and special treatment that reaffirms the dominant norm and merely accommodates their 'abnormality.' "

It is not surprising that these authors do not identify themselves as feminists. Many philosophers have been loathe to do so, treating feminism, for the most part if at all, as tangential to "mainstream philosophy." Yet "mainstream philosophy" embraces such a variety of theoretical orientations, and ethics and political philosophy exemplify so many different theories and address so many different topics, that it is difficult to see why mainstream philosophers would not routinely acknowledge at least some versions of feminism within the proper domain of our discipline.

---

23. See, for example, Joan Tronto, *Moral Boundaries: A Political Argument for an Ethic of Care* (New York: Routledge, 1993), especially 162–64.

Silvers may be loathe to identify with feminism because of past or present neglect of, and sometimes downright hostility toward, people with disabilities on the part of some "feminists." But that neglect mainly shows the lack of a thoroughgoing or consistent feminism on the part of those individuals, who are needlessly myopic; those hostile to people with disabilities can hardly be called feminists because, as I argued in my essay, any version of feminism that excludes support for people with disabilities betrays itself. The only feminism worth identifying with for people with disabilities is one that not only includes them but grants them a privileged status.

Wasserman may be loathe to identify with feminism because he is male. Unfortunately, the word *feminism* is a "put-off" or disincentive to some people, women as well as men, because it suggests to them an exclusive alignment with women. Yet the core element of different versions of feminism, "gender justice," surely applies to members of both sexes. In defense of the term, I would suggest that *feminism* is preferable to *humanism* or *masculinism* because gender injustice is mainly practiced toward women. To feminists themselves, however, whether the term is used or not, anyone who is consistently committed to elimination of gender injustice is a feminist.

My second question is prompted by the distinction between formal and distributive justice that the format of the book assumes: why are these considered as separate or even separable principles? The traditional Aristotelian articulation of the formal principle of justice (i.e., "equals are to be treated equally, and unequals unequally") is clearly compatible with different material principles of justice, even though these may not be compatible with one another.[24] As Amartya Sen has suggested, the key to linking formal justice to a specific version of material justice is the answer to the question, What equality?[25] Silvers's answer to this question, with which I agree, seems to be an affirmation of the equality between people who are disabled and those who are currently able. On Sen's interpretation, with which I also agree, her conception of "people with disabilities as equal

---

24. See Aristotle, *Nichomachean Ethics* V, 3–5. Many authors cite this principle before delineating various material principles of justice; for example, see Tom L. Beauchamp and James F. Childress, *Principles of Biomedical Ethics* (New York: Oxford University Press, 1994), 328.
25. Amartya Sen, *Inequality Reexamined* (Cambridge, Mass.: Harvard University Press, 1995), 3.

and thereby deserving only such differentiated treatment as is needed to reform social practice which excludes them" amounts to a material principle that is compatible with Aristotle's formal principle.

Silvers maintains that "there is all the difference in the world" between her interpretation of formal justice and the view of distributive justice that she apparently imputes to Wasserman: one in which people with disabilities are judged "deficient and thereby as deserving of special benefits, entitlements, and exemptions to sustain them in their exclusion from the mainstream of commercial and civic life." I doubt that Wasserman would agree with this interpretation of his view because he seems to see formal and distributive justice as complementary. However, I do not understand why Silvers thinks that a policy that provides "special benefits"[26] to people considered "deficient and therefore deserving" of them would "enfeeble the purpose needed to implement" the view that people with disabilities are equal to those who are not disabled, and therefore deserving only of such "differentiated treatment as is needed to reform social practice that excludes them." Silvers herself acknowledges that some individuals are so globally impaired that their social participation is "implausible." For this group, her proposal to change social practices so as to include them would not work, and she seems open to "special benefits" for them. Her overall position thus combines elements she had described as at odds with each other.

Interestingly, Wasserman and Silvers have opposite interpretations of the rationale that underlies the ADA. Silvers sees it as embodying formal rather than material justice, while Wasserman sees it as critiquing a forced choice between the two. Silvers alleges that the distributive model of justice "celebrates homogenizing," which leads to isolation and a solitary lifestyle for those whose differences cannot be overcome. Although I agree with her account of the "tyranny of the normal," developed elsewhere,[27]

---

26. The benefits that Silvers describes as "special" are, in my judgment, no more special than the benefits that anyone receives from others, so long as they are based on the unique needs of the individuals who receive them. What Silvers considers "special," I consider "equitable," as equitable as the "differentiated treatment" she proposes as the reforms required to ensure that people with disabilities are not excluded from social practices. If I were to subscribe to Silvers's interpretations of the terms, I would also support "special" and "differentiated" treatment of those who are currently able.

27. Anita Silvers, " 'Defective' Agents: Equality, Difference, and the Tyranny

I do not believe that Wasserman's view calls for such homogenization. In defending either Wasserman or myself on this point, however, the crucial concept is that of equality. Different concepts and applications of the term lead to different theoretical analyses but not necessarily to different practices. Despite their theoretical disagreement, consideration of particular questions in the context of particular cases might well draw agreement between my coauthors.[28]

If equality between individuals means that they have the same value despite their differences, as I argued in my essay, then that value is not distorted through their being provided with different or even unequal services or, as Silvers would put it, "instrumental means" by which to pursue their interests. While Silvers believes that some persons with profound, global disabilities can never become equal to others, I aver that there is no need for this because they are already equal. They do not have the same needs or interests, but they have the same value. This point is applicable as well to those who are currently able, those who are disabled but not profoundly so, and those who are advantaged well beyond the "normal" range of functioning or capability: all are human beings who have equal value as such.[29] The meaning of equality by which one imputes the same value to *different* individuals entails recognition of the differences within those individuals. Treating different individuals equally may be understood as requiring different responses to each difference. As a moral principle, then, respect for equality demands distributive as well as formal justice.

---

of the Normal," *Journal of Social Philosophy*, 25th Anniversary Special Issue (1994): 154–75.

28. According to Albert Jonsen and Stephen Toulmin, this is what happened to participants in the President's Commission for the Study of Ethical Problems in Medicine and Biomedical and Behavioral Research, which addressed a number of bioethical issues from different theoretical perspectives in the early 1980s. Their experience on the commission prompted them to attempt a revival of casuistry, as descriptive of the process. For a full elaboration of the history and method of casuistry, see Albert R. Jonsen and Stephen Toulmin, *The Abuse of Casuistry* (Berkeley: University of California Press, 1988).

29. This does not imply that human beings are equal to one another in all respects. But if each individual were superior to others in some respect, everyone would be inferior to others in some respect. Once we introduce the evaluative language of superiority and inferiority, which I choose to avoid, we run the risk of interpreting differences as necessarily entailing inequality among individuals, which I deny.

Apparently, Silvers does not agree with this conception of equality. She seems, to me at least, to understate the differences among individuals, whether disabled or not, arguing for a conception of equality based exclusively on the need to change social structures so that people with disabilities have the same opportunities as those who are currently able. While she would permit a distributive scheme to benefit "profoundly impaired people" whose situation cannot be improved by social changes, she insists that "we should understand that such schemes neither do justice to people with disabilities nor equalize them." Describing those who are profoundly impaired as unequal to those who are less impaired or currently able belies the same assumptions of inferiority or defectiveness with regard to them that Silvers wants to avoid for everyone who is disabled. To an egalitarian feminist such as I, this as an inequitable attribution of equality.

From a feminist standpoint, Silvers's proposal of historical counterfactualizing presents a compelling strategy for incorporating nondominant standpoints into the development of policies by a dominant group that is incapable of actually obtaining the input of nondominant groups or individuals.[30] Hypothesizing what social arrangements would be desirable if most people were disabled rather than able would surely facilitate more equitable arrangements than we have now, even with the ADA. For example, historical counterfactualizing would both clarify and transform interpretations of the "reasonable accommodation" standard that the ADA requires of employers and business owners. If society launched a broad historical counterfactualizing campaign with regard to other nondominant groups (women, minorities, the poor, etc.), many "reasonable" standards would probably be modified to reflect views that the previously dominant class considered "unreasonable."

Despite the strong appeal of Silvers's proposal, Wasserman's reservations about it give me pause. He worries, for example, about the possibility that counterfactualizing from the standpoint of people who are severely cognitively impaired might lead to worse rather than better social arrangements for everyone. But I doubt that Silvers would view her strategy as

---

30. Being incapable of obtaining input from nondominant groups means that all avenues of obtaining it have been exhausted, which rarely occurs. Such a situation may arise with regard to nondominant individuals who are profoundly, globally impaired, but advocates or family members charged with representing the standpoint of nondominant individuals may be accorded privileged status in their behalf.

either exclusive or adequate to determination of fair social arrangements. It simply provides *a* means of recognizing and reducing the limitations of the dominant standpoint.

Wasserman's criticism alerts me to the need to acknowledge the limitations of nondominant standpoints. It should be noted, however, that the privileged status imputed to nondominant standpoints is not based on infallibility or adequacy, which they lack. Rather, it is based on the necessity or indispensability of nondominant standpoints to overcome the inevitable limitations of the dominant standpoint. A feminist standpoint would add a caveat to its support of Silvers's proposal: the standpoints of those most affected by policies developed by a specific group, whether dominant, nondominant, or both, should be privileged on that basis alone. Lest it be thought that this allows for determination based on numbers, "most affected" is not a simple quantitative measure; it also refers to the extent and kind of impact. Giving special weight to those most affected might justify the imposition of small inconveniences on many to ensure the ability to perform ordinary life functions for a few.

Wasserman's argument for a link between natural and social causes of inequality has also given me pause, mainly because I have argued elsewhere for the importance of establishing this distinction.[31] While I find his argument credible, however, I do not believe it necessary because neither natural nor social causes justify a failure of social will to overcome or reduce the associated inequality or injustice. Even if disabilities are not changeable because they are naturally rather than socially induced, the principle of equality, as I understand it, still calls for rectification rather than special assistance.

Because many human traits or abilities are manifest along a continuum of more or less rather than as discrete and separable qualities or lack thereof, Wasserman's discussion of the relationship between deficiencies and talents is persuasive. In contrast, many clinicians and health care Rawlsians construe "normal" and "abnormal" as discrete conditions. Typically, "normal" encompasses an average range and beyond, while "abnormal" is consigned to what lies below the average range and therefore needs or merits assistance to reach what appears to be the beginning point of "nor-

---

31. See, for example, Mary B. Mahowald, "Genetic Technologies and Their Implications for Women," *University of Chicago Law School Roundtable* 3, no. 2 (1996): 439–63.

mal species functioning."³² Wasserman is right, however, that ignoring the disparities that exist between those who are deficient but within the normal range and those who are talented within that range (and *a fortiori* between the former and those who excel beyond the normal range) undercuts an adequately just distributive scheme. If the health care Rawlsians were to succeed in bringing all of those below the "norm" within the range of normal species functioning, the disparity between them and those at the higher level of the norm or beyond would remain, and with it the associated disadvantages.

A more radically egalitarian point may be made to buttress Wasserman's critique: most if not all of our talents and the successes associated with their exercise are fortuitous rather than earned. Distribution of natural and social advantages is not provably determined by individual effort. Rather, an honest answer to the question "What have you got that you have not been given?" is "Nothing that I know of." While meritarians would surely have a different answer, convincing evidence for their view is hard, if not impossible, to come by. Some talents are undoubtedly developed through effort, but the amount of effort available to the individual is strongly influenced, and possibly determined, by genes, luck, physical and psychological stamina, and environmental nurturance or lack thereof.

While I consider my coauthors feminists, their standpoints are different from mine because they do not focus on gender justice as I do. I regard this focus as remedial, even within the context of ability justice, which is itself remedial. Both Silvers and Wasserman exemplify liberal conceptions of justice, with Silvers leaning more toward the libertarian side and Wasserman more toward the egalitarian side.³³ The feminist standpoint that I bring to the discussion is more egalitarian than Wasserman's and more critical of a Rawlsian account. Like most feminists, I resist a conception of individual autonomy that ignores the context, which often compromises that autonomy.³⁴ Until and unless the compromising influences are re-

---

32. See, for example, Norman Daniels, *Just Health Care* (Cambridge: Cambridge University Press, 1985).

33. I use the term *egalitarian* in a narrower, and more usual, sense than the meaning that Sen attaches to it. By his account, even libertarians are egalitarian because they subscribe to equal distribution of individual liberty. Compare Sen, *Inequality Reexamined*, 3.

34. Susan Sherwin develops this point with regard to "reproductive freedom," an issue that carries particular significance for women with disabilities. According

moved, equal liberty for individuals is not possible. These influences in-clude all of the social biases and empirical obstacles placed in the path of people who belong to nondominant groups; they also include covert obstacles such as internalized biases, psychological pressures, and reduced expectations on the part of the nondominant persons themselves. Material equality, defined as the removal of both internal and external obstacles to autonomy, is thus a prerequisite to equal liberty.

In comparison with other theories, Amartya Sen's view of equality as equal capability comes closest to my perspective as an egalitarian feminist. His answer to the question "What equality?" takes into account not only individual autonomy and equal opportunity but the capacity of individuals and groups to achieve the goals they define for themselves. "Capability," he says, "reflects a person's ability to choose between alternative lives, and its valuation need not presuppose unanimity regarding some one specific set of objectives."[35] In other words, capability is determined from the standpoint of the individual agent or group. Using that concept, we may define ability equality or ability justice as a situation in which differences in ability do not result in greater advantage of one group over the other. Because ability differences inevitably influence the capabilities of men and women, ability justice requires identification of the differences, determina-tion of whether they entail inequality, and efforts to eliminate or amelio-rate the inequalities that occur.

For both changeable and unchangeable differences in ability, their mere occurrence is ethically neutral. This is as true for differences associated with disability as for those associated with ability beyond the normal range. Nonetheless, the disparities in capability that are introduced through these differences carry unavoidable ethical import for individuals and for society. If we agree with Sen that justice demands equalization of capabilities (to whatever extent possible), changeable differences that re-duce the capability of those who are disabled need to be modified so that they no longer do so. The unequal capability that results from unchange-able differences also needs to be reduced (as much as possible) through

---

to Sherwin, "[f]eminism helps us understand that reproductive freedom involves being free from the economic, racist, and sexist oppression that prevents choices in other aspects of life. This freedom cannot be captured by focusing on single choices, in isolation from other factors" (*No Longer Patient: Feminist Ethics and Health Care* [Philadelphia: Temple University Press, 1992], 134).

35. Sen, *Inequality Reexamined*, 83, deleting parentheticals.

social measures whose costs are justifiably defrayed through contributions from the advantaged members of society.

Admittedly, this view entails an egalitarian ideal that is not fully realizable, particularly in so individualistic a culture as ours. The ideal can, however, be better approximated, or more fully realized, than even the ADA supports. To someone who describes herself as an idealistic pragmatist[36] as well as an egalitarian feminist, I find maximal approximation not only morally acceptable but demanded.

---

36. Mary B. Mahowald, "A Feminist in the Medical Academy: An Idealistic Pragmatist Account" in *Women in Medical Education*, ed. Delese Wear (New York: State University of New York Press, 1996), 47–58; compare Mary Briody Mahowald, *An Idealistic Pragmatism* (The Hague: Nijhoff, 1972).

Afterword: Disability, Strategic Action, and Reciprocity

Lawrence C. Becker

The essays in this volume focus on philosophical problems that are extremely difficult. As we have seen, there are problems of definition that threaten to dissolve the distinction between the able and the disabled, problems of moral imagination in identifying and understanding each others' needs, problems about Kantian concerns for human dignity and utilitarian concerns for aggregate welfare, problems about fairness in the allocation of benefits and burdens, problems about the meaning of equality in this context, and problems about the appropriate moral response to the natural evils that befall us all to varying degrees. Equally able philosophers disagree about all of these matters, and it is of course appropriate for them to focus on the most challenging philosophical issues and the most persistent disagreements about them. How else will we make progress on these matters?

Yet there is something in this discussion that does not quite square with my own experience in living with a significant physical disability since my early teens. My experience has been that when my own "disability issues" are framed either in terms of love or in terms of justice, *in the long run* things do not go very well for anyone concerned. Moreover, I have reason to believe that my experience in this regard is not merely idiosyncratic. On the contrary, there is a general philosophical explanation for it in the theory of strategic action coupled with a consideration of norms of reciproc-

293

ity. (No doubt there is also a particular psychohistorical explanation for my experience as well—one that makes a more entertaining story.)

The philosophical explanation interests me because it situates the discouraging difficulties explored in this volume in a larger, less discouraging context. In short, I will argue that we can resolve many conflicts about disability and distributive justice by treating them as coordination problems. And I am hopeful that if we pursue disability issues in this larger context, we will be able both to see their most difficult aspects more clearly and to make some surprising progress in resolving them.

Hardin on the Limitations of Reason

In an important book,[1] Russell Hardin argues that careful attention to our limitations as rational agents is crucial for moral theory. In particular, he emphasizes three limitations that all human agents need to face squarely: the extent of our ignorance about the consequences of our actions, the intractable difficulties of our value theories, and the fact that we can accomplish very little without the active and sustained cooperation of other human agents. Hardin's aim is to use reflection on these limitations to construct a justification for utilitarian moral theory, but his point of departure is a perfectly general one of the first importance. Here I want to focus on the third of the limitations he mentions—the one that gives rise to the strategic dimension of human action.

It is now commonplace in discussions of disability for writers to point out that all human beings have extended periods of dependency during the normal life-cycle—in infancy and early childhood, in periods of illness or injury, in senescence—and in general have great vulnerability, not only in matters of their physical and psychological health as well as life itself but also in their attachments to all sorts of external goods, ranging from the most mundane matters of physical comfort to the most exalted rewards of intimate relationships. At our best, the argument goes, we are only temporarily "abled," and we should reflect on this fact carefully before we decide how to treat the permanently disabled.

Hardin's point is a stronger one: No one is even temporarily able to

---

1. Russell Hardin, *Morality within the Limits of Reason* (Chicago: University of Chicago Press, 1988).

accomplish very much at all by her own actions, independent of the responses of others. No matter how others respond—whether they oppose her, ignore her, help her, or simply stand out of the way—she will need to adapt her conduct accordingly in order to succeed. That does not mean that she will always have to fight the opposition, curry favor, or accept help. (After all, sometimes a soft answer actually does turn away wrath; sometimes a low profile is a good thing; sometimes accepting help is more trouble than it is worth.) It does, however, mean that she will have to consider what to do in the light of the responses she is likely to get from various courses of action she might take. That is to say, if she wishes to act effectively, she will have to act strategically, and not simply as if the problem were simply to decide what is right in some abstract sense, and then to do it, regardless of what others might do. I simply add to this the observation that there is no direct correlation between the *extent* to which one must act strategically and the extent to which one is disabled—though there is sometimes a correlation between the extent of a disability and the range of strategic responses available to an agent.

Now consider three general sorts of strategic situations that we face. Borrowing Hardin's terms we may identify them as situations of pure conflict, pure coordination, or mixtures of conflict and coordination.[2]

We have a pure conflict situation whenever a net gain by one person necessarily involves a net loss by another. Zero-sum (constant-sum) games are examples of this. And in general, whenever we compete for shares of a fixed sum of resources, my gain is necessarily your loss, *ceteris paribus.*

We have a pure coordination situation whenever it is possible (if we simply coordinate our conduct) for everyone to gain. Rules of the road are good examples. It typically does not matter what the rules are (e.g., whether we are to drive on the left or the right); it only matters that we coordinate on the same set of determinate rules. Social norms and conventions often solve pure coordination problems without the intervention of law—as with various arrangements for standing in the registration line in a hotel.

We have a mixture of conflict and coordination if we have a situation in which some options open to us pose problems of pure conflict while other options are pure coordination problems. Think of prisoner's dilemmas: Each target of the investigation is offered immunity in exchange for testi-

---

2. Hardin, *Morality within the Limits of Reason,* 35–53.

mony that leads to the conviction of his accomplice, but only if the accomplice does not accept a similar deal first. Here there are two possibilities that are pure conflict—namely, those in which one prisoner confesses while the other does not. The payoff structure that defines a prisoner's dilemma is one in which each prisoner's top preference is for getting immunity (the jackpot), even though that means the sucker's payoff for his silent accomplice; his second-best option is coordinating with his partner on joint silence; his third-best option is coordinating on joint confession; and his worst option is is the one in which he gets the sucker's payoff because he stays silent while his partner confesses.

Note that if the two opportunities for pure conflict are removed, the prisoners have a pure coordination problem that is easily solved: they both prefer mutual silence to mutual confession. That is why, in the context of our criminal law, we often see elaborate efforts by police and prosecutors to keep all four options open and equally elaborate efforts by at least one of the "prisoners" to remove the pure conflict options. It is of the first importance to notice also, however, that in many other sorts of situations that have this same strategic structure—ranging from mundane business transactions to the control of nuclear weapons—we may *all* have a strong interest in defining social structures that eliminate the pure conflict options.

Now it is fairly obvious that pure coordination problems are, from the standpoint of moral theory, much less difficult than the other strategic problems we face. In pure coordination problems we can all be better off if and only if we coordinate our behavior. Further, if we coordinate, no one gets harmed, or even forced to take a second best option, and aggregate welfare is improved. Sadists, bullies, and the envious aside, then, we do not in general face motivational problems in these situations. Rather, the problems we face are merely those of communication and organization. (Hardin has an instructive example of this in the way Sweden went about changing from left-hand to right-hand driving.[3])

Moreover, it is also clear that mixtures of conflict and coordination problems (such as prisoner's dilemmas) are often more manageable than those of pure conflict. In the former, we at least have the possibility of arranging a second-best outcome for everyone, and better yet, if we can somehow arrange effectively to block serious consideration or implemen-

---

3. Hardin, *Morality within the Limits of Reason*, 51–52.

tation of the pure conflict elements of such mixed situations (e.g., by making them unthinkable or undoable), we have effectively moved these problems into the realm of pure coordination. The Mutual Assured Destruction strategy of nuclear deterrence attempted to do this by making first strike unthinkable; verification treaties attempted to do this by making first strike undoable.

Problems of pure conflict remain, however, and they present us with serious theoretical difficulties as well as grim practical choices. In such situations some people are going to be the losers, and absent motives of beneficence or justice on their part—motives strong enough to make them genuinely willing to yield—getting a stable result will be difficult. Moreover, from the standpoint of moral theory, we presumably do not want to recommend that people be genuinely willing to yield unless their yielding is justifiable. Yet how often is it the case, even in theory, that in matters of distributive justice we can identify precisely who *should* be the loser? Perhaps we can do this in clear cases of intentional wrongdoing by competent adults who are responsible for their characters. But in most cases Yossarian's problem[4] remains as poignant for us as it was for him: he could see why the war had to be fought, and why, if it were fought, people had to die. What he could not see was how it followed from that that he, Yossarian, had to die.[5]

---

4. Joseph Heller, *Catch-22* (New York: Simon & Schuster, 1961), 102.

5. Yossarian famously takes everything personally. It is perfectly clear to him, for example, that German antiaircraft gunners are trying to kill him, and he is not persuaded at all by the argument that they are not shooting at him personally but rather shooting at "everyone." (See Heller, *Catch-22*, 16–17.) But here is the passage relevant to what I call Yossarian's problem. Yossarian says (102):

> "I don't want to be in the war anymore."
> "Would you like to see our country lose?" Major Major asked.
> "We won't lose. We've got more men, more money and more material. There are ten million men in uniform who could replace me. Some people are getting killed and a lot more are making money and having fun. Let somebody else get killed."
> "But suppose everybody on our side felt that way."
> "Then I'd certainly be a damned fool to feel any other way. Wouldn't I?"

This refrain is repeated at the end of the book when, after Yossarian has flown seventy bombing missions, he is considering desertion. (435–36.) It is hard to resist pointing out that Heller's book was published in the same year (1961) as the first edition of Marcus Singer's *Generalization in Ethics*.

Disability, Strategic Action, and Reciprocity

The general point should be obvious: we must all act strategically, but we are well advised to arrange to do so, as much as possible, in situations where we face only problems of pure coordination. I want to suggest that in the context of disability issues, though we must of course consider carefully what to do in cases of pure conflict, we should also examine very carefully the options we have for moving such issues into the realm of coordination problems.

In general, discussing disability issues in terms of equality is not helpful in this regard—whether it is equality of access, opportunity, life prospects, or capacities that we have in mind. Proposals to make people equal in some respect invite us to think in terms of conflict. We want to know whether we are going to have to "take" resources from some in order to "bring others up" to a predefined level, and if so how we can justify this sort of redistribution. We want to know whether we can draw a principled line that will justify such redistribution in the case of some disadvantages (e.g., those arising from bad luck in one's choice of viruses) and not for others (such as those arising from bad luck in one's choice of parents). And we will want to know whether the social costs of pursuing equality for the disabled can be contained or whether they are likely to be ratcheted up by a perpetually expanding definition of disability or an increasingly high standard of equality. All such thoughts distract us from considering the possibilities for dissolving such conflicts by transforming them into coordination problems.

Thinking about reciprocity, however, is helpful here. An effective norm of reciprocity resolves problems of pure conflict by seeing to it that people who are burdened by one aspect of a social relationship, policy, or transaction are benefited in return by another aspect of it. And when reciprocity is "full" or complete, meaning that the eventual return to the one who has been burdened is proportional to that person's sacrifice, then there is no net loss to anyone. The strategic problem of arranging for full reciprocity is a problem of pure coordination, at least as long as envy, greed, and various forms of malice are kept out of the picture. These coordination problems are far from simple ones, but full reciprocity takes many forms other than a direct tit-for-tat exchange.[6] In a setting characterized by gen-

---

6. Lawrence C. Becker, *Reciprocity* (Boston: Routledge, 1986), chap. 3.

eralized reciprocity, for example, both benefactor and recipient can be confident that "what goes around, comes around" and that any recipient will eventually be someone else's benefactor just as surely as any benefactor will eventually be the recipient of someone else's beneficence.

Full Reciprocity and Coordination

Now suppose, as a first approximation to appropriate conduct in these matters, that we consider a social environment (like our own) that is characterized by a robust, complex norm of reciprocity for social interactions—a norm that defines at least a minimal level of justice in social arrangements. Let us leave aside, for the moment, the fact that some people (at least in some circumstances) are not motivated to reciprocate. And let us assume that the people who are motivated to reciprocate also recognize and are often satisfied by reciprocal arrangements that are very indirect, institutionalized, and delayed—as they are, for example, with various forms of insurance. Then let us consider the ways in which some people, against their wishes and choices, may both need an unusual amount of help from others and be unable to reciprocate for it—or at least to reciprocate fully for it.

Surely the appropriate strategic response to this is, as far possible, to make full reciprocity possible for such people. It makes little difference what the cause of their inability is—whether it is polio or poverty, for example. If we can arrange things so that they can and do reciprocate, it is hard to see what objection there could be to that from the standpoint of the initial benefactors, since they will be repaid. And it is equally hard to see what objection there could be from the standpoint of the reciprocally minded disabled themselves, since this strategic response to their disability offers a very powerful and socially benign ratchet mechanism—one which they will control—for their getting all the help for which reciprocal returns will eventually emerge, however indirectly. (As long as each increment proposed by the disabled will be fully reciprocated, it would be stupid for the able to confine rehabilitation or assistance to some arbitrary minimum. This is so not only because the increased benefits will cancel the increased burdens but because there is often a sort of "surplus value" created by increasing the level of functioning for a disabled person. Yet since the benefits of reciprocation are lost when the recipient refuses the proffer of increased help, recipients retain control of this ratchet effect.)

A caution here: I am not proposing that we think along the lines of imposing a direct, tit-for-tat duty of reciprocation on the disabled— something like a loan for a college education, to be repaid directly to the lender by the very person initially benefited. Rather, I am simply proposing that in dealing with disability issues we should first look for new physical and social arrangements that eliminate anyone's serious, persistent inability to engage in fully reciprocal social interactions, however indirect those interactions might be. And I am suggesting that in this context we need not be concerned with refining the definition of disability—or even with singling out a special class of disabled people for special treatment. *Any* persistent inability to reciprocate poses the same sort of strategic problems—which we should, if possible, solve by restoring the ability to reciprocate. Among reciprocally minded people (surely the vast majority in our society), such coordination on reciprocity will pay for itself in the long run and immediately turn disability issues from problems of pure conflict to problems of pure coordination.

Indeed, for that reason I am suggesting that as a first approximation we may as well consider the inability to reciprocate, when it is more than merely transient, to be the very definition of the sort of disability that unambiguously calls for social assistance. Thus, for example, parents, children, or spouses who are persistently exhausted and socially isolated by the burdens of caring for profoundly disabled relatives are effectively disabled in this sense, and their situation warrants appropriate social assistance as much as does an inability imposed by paraplegia or Alzheimer's disease. But the nature and scale of the requisite assistance for all such disabilities, in this first approximation, is to be defined in terms of what can in fact be fully reciprocated, since that is the least problematic issue.

It is worthwhile to reflect on how many issues even this first approximation settles. Having level or ramped access to public buildings, for example, is useful for service technicians, furniture movers, delivery people, and parents pushing baby strollers as well as for wheelchair users, and the reciprocal social benefits begin to accrue immediately, not only from the increased participation of mobility-impaired people but from others' increased efficiency. The standard placement of signage introduced by accommodating the blind and visually impaired has similar immediate benefits for others. And, in general, problems of access to public transportation, accommodations, educational opportunities, medical care, rehabilitative services, and employment opportunities—for those who can and will fully reciprocate for them—can be fully addressed by a strategic concern for achieving full reciprocity.

Partial Reciprocity, Litigant's Dilemmas, and Settlements

The next step is to consider disability cases that present us with a mixture of conflict and coordination problems—ones in which the conflict element cannot be removed because no new physical or social arrangements can be found in which full reciprocity can be restored, even among reciprocally minded people. Some people with profound cognitive disabilities appear to present us with this situation, as do some people with especially severe physical handicaps. In such cases it may be that significant social assistance can dramatically improve the situation for the disabled person but will inevitably impose a net cost on those who provide it.

Let us imagine that this is so in some cases and that the best option for the disabled person (and the worst for others) is to get an enforceable right to maximally effective social assistance, even though it imposes a net cost on others. Conversely, the best option for the others (and the worst for the disabled) is to get an enforceable right to refuse to provide any assistance at all to the disabled beyond what can be reciprocated. These are the pure conflict options. However, the second-best outcome for both parties is a settlement—just below the ignition point for conflict—in which some suboptimal but acceptable level of social assistance is provided to the disabled at a net cost acceptable to the providers, but is reciprocated as far as possible. The third-best option for both parties is a standoff in which neither assistance nor reciprocation occurs. These are coordination points. Schematically, we have these four options:

1. Claim rights to assistance; duties to provide it
2. Mutually suboptimal settlement
3. Standoff
4. No claim rights to assistance; no duties to provide it

And we are imagining that the preference order for these options is 1, 2, 3, 4 for the disabled, 4, 2, 3, 1 for everyone else.

This is, of course, the structure of the payoffs in a prisoner's dilemma, but the strategic situation is rather different from that described by the standard prisoner's dilemma story. In a prisoner's dilemma, when both parties go for their best options, they both confess and get what they agree is the third-best option. Here, in what we may call the "litigant's dilemma," when both parties go for their best options (let us say through a lawsuit) it is not clear what will happen. One party or the other may win outright, or both may get some sort of suboptimal settlement, or it may even be that a standoff results (e.g., if the case is mooted by the courts). In any case, the difficulty is that legal claims for options 1 and 4 must be adjudicated, and moral claims for them go through an even messier process before they become enforceable norms. These decision processes are typically quite unpredictable. Litigation (or moral suasion) is costly for both parties no matter what happens, and if both parties have plausible cases to the extent that it is simply not clear in advance which party has the stronger argument, the outcome is quite uncertain. Even if both parties press the conflict very hard—that is, press for their best options—there is often even no discernible change in the probabilities of the possible outcomes. This is the heart of the litigant's dilemma.

In such situations it is often in the strategic interests of both parties to settle. For one thing, a settlement is within their (joint) control. Opting for conflict is opting for loss of control, and that is not usually desirable. And if one is going to keep control by opting for coordination rather than conflict, then the choice is settlement vs. standoff, and it is hard to see why one would choose the standoff. (Accepting a standoff as a tactical move in a protracted conflict does not count as opting for coordination.) Moreover, coordination is the maximin option in these situations—the only way for each party to immunize herself against her least favored outcome. (By contrast, in a prisoner's dilemma it is conflict—confession—that is the maximin strategy for both.) And again, between the two coordination options, settlement is surely preferable to standoff. Finally, the sort of stability and mutual goodwill achieved by a genuine settlement is a genuine prize. Winners face new strategic problems with losers, and vice versa. In some cases, these new problems are as difficult as the old ones.

For all these reasons, in a reasonably just and beneficent social order of people who are, for the most part, willing to reciprocate, it seems reasonable to suggest that when we find ourselves in a litigant's dilemma with respect to disability issues, we should settle rather than opt for pure conflict—if we have the chance. And it seems to me that such a suggestion is supported by reflection on the multitude of disturbing lawsuits, threatened lawsuits, and administrative and arbitration proceedings concerning students with cognitive disabilities in public schools.

Residues

That leaves cases of pure conflict—cases in which people either cannot or will not reciprocate (or accept either full or partial reciprocity) or in which they either cannot or will not settle for second best in order to avoid conflict. It is here that the classic problems of beneficence and distributive justice find their most severe tests.

I have little to add here, in a mere afterword, to the discussion of those difficult issues. My suggestion is simply that we should take the opportunity, afforded to us by the strategic value of norms of reciprocity, to minimize the range and intensity of such pure conflict in matters concerning human disabilities. It would be a great benefit to us all if we could arrange in this way to make the most difficult and discouraging problems of disability and distributive justice purely academic.

Bibliography

Aarts, Leo, Richard Burkhauser, and Philip DeJong. "Introduction and Over-view." In *Curing the Dutch Disease: An International Perspective on Disability Policy Reform.* Aldershot, U.K.: Avebury, 1996.
———. "Policy Studies Paper No. 6." *Syracuse: The Maxwell School of Citizenship and Public Affairs,* Syracuse, N.Y.: Syracuse University, 1992.
Abberly, Paul. "Disabled People: Normality and Social Work." In *Disability and Dependency,* ed. Len Barton. London: Falmer, 1989.
Albrecht, Gary. *The Disability Business: Rehabilitation in America.* London: Sage, 1992.
———. *The Sociology of Physical Disability and Rehabilitation.* Pittsburgh: University of Pittsburgh Press, 1976.
Alcoff, Linda, and Elizabeth Potter, eds. *Feminist Epistemologies.* New York: Routledge, 1993.
Alexander, Larry, and Maimon Schwarzchild. "Liberalism, Neutrality, and Equality of Welfare vs. Equality of Resources." *Philosophy and Public Affairs,* 16 (1987): 85–110.
Allen, Karen Moses, and Janice Mitchell Phillips. *Women's Health across the Life-span: A Comprehensive Perspective.* Philadelphia: Lippincott, 1997.
Amundson, Ron. "Disability, Handicap, and the Environment." *Journal of Social Philosophy* 23, no. 1 (1992): 114–18.
Andrews, Lori B. "Feminism Revisited: Fallacies and Policies in the Surrogacy Debate." *Logos* 9 (1988): 81–96.
Angier, Natalie. "Joined for Life, and Living to the Full." *New York Times* (23 December 1997), B11, B15.
Appiah, Kwame Anthony, and Amy Gutmann. *Color Conscious: The Political Morality of Race.* Princeton, N.J.: Princeton University Press, 1996.
Arneson, Richard J. "Equality and Equal Opportunity for Welfare." *Philosophical Studies* 56 (1989): 77–93.
———. "Liberalism, Distributive Subjectivism, and Equal Opportunity for Welfare." *Philosophy and Public Affairs:* 158–94.

Asch, Adrienne. "Reproductive Technology and Disability." In *Reproductive Laws for the 1990s*, ed. Sherill Cohen and Nadine Taub. New York: Humana, 1988.
Asch, Adrienne, and Michelle Fine. "Introduction: Beyond Pedestals." In *Women and Disabilities*, ed. Adrienne Asch and Michelle Fine. Philadelphia: Temple University Press, 1988.
———. "Shared Dreams: A Left Perspective on Disability Rights and Reproductive Rights." In *Women and Disabilities*, ed. Adrienne Asch and Michelle Fine. Philadelphia: Temple University Press, 1988.
Asch, Adrienne, and Gail Geller. "Feminism, Bioethics and Genetics." In *Feminism & Bioethics: Beyond Reproduction*. Oxford: Oxford University Press, 1996.
Baier, Annette. "The Need for More Than Justice." In *Science, Morality, and Feminist Theory*, ed. Marsha Hanen and Kai Neilson. Calgary: University of Calgary Press, 1987.
Barlew, A. Kathleen, Robert Evans, and Carlton Oler. "The Impact of a Child with Sickle Cell Disease on Family Dynamics." *Annals of the New York Academy of Sciences* 565 (1989).
Barnartt, Sharon. "Disability Culture or Disability Consciousness?" *Journal of Disability Policy Studies* 7, no. 2 (1996): 2–19.
Barnes, Colin, and Geoff Mercer, eds. *Exploring the Divide: Illness and Disability*. Leeds, U.K.: Disability Press, 1996.
Barron, Karin. "The Bumpy Road to Womanhood." *Disability & Society* 12, no. 2 (Spring 1997): 223–39.
Barton, Len, ed. *Disability and Dependency*. London: Falmer, 1989.
———, ed. *Disability & Society: Emerging Issues and Insights*. London: Longman, 1996.
Battin, Margaret, Rosamond Rhodes, and Anita Silvers, eds. *Physician-Assisted Suicide: Extending the Debate*. New York: Routledge, 1998.
Baynton, Douglas. *Forbidden Signs: American Culture and the Campaign against Sign Language*. Chicago: University of Chicago Press, 1996.
Beauchamp, Tom L., and James F. Childress. *Principles of Biomedical Ethics*. New York: Oxford University Press, 1994.
Becker, Lawrence C. *Reciprocity*. London: Routledge, 1986.
Becker, Lawrence C., and Charlotte Becker, eds. *Encyclopedia of Ethics*. New York: Garland, 1992.
Begun, Nasa. "Doubly Disabled." *Community Care Inside* 24 (September 1992): iii–iv.
———. . . . *Something to Be Proud Of . . . : The Lives of Asian Disabled People and Careers in Waltham Forest*. London: Waltham Forest Race Relations Unit, 1992.
Berkowitz, Edward, and Richard Burkhauser. "A United States Perspective on Disability Programs." In *Curing the Dutch Disease: An International Perspective on Disability Policy Reform*, ed. Leo Aarts, Richard Burkhauser and Philip DeJong. Aldershot, U.K.: Avebury, 1996.
Berube, Michael. *Life as We Know It: A Father, a Family, and an Exceptional Child*. New York: Pantheon, 1996.

Bickenbach, Jerome. "Equality, Rights, and the Disablement Process." Paper presented at the *American Philosophical Association, Central Division Meetings*, Chicago: April 1996.

———. *Physical Disability and Social Policy*. Toronto: University of Toronto Press, 1993.

Blum, Lawrence. "Moral Perception and Particularity." *Ethics* (July 1991): 701–25.

Blumberg, Lisa. "The Politics of Prenatal Testing and Selective Abortion." *Sexuality and Disability* 12, no. 2 (1994): 135–53.

Boddington, Paula, and Tessa Podpadec. "Who Are the Mentally Handicapped?" *Journal of Applied Philosophy* 8, no. 2 (1991): 177–90.

Boorse, Christopher. "Health as a Theoretical Concept." *Philosophy of Science* 44, no. 4 (1977): 542–73.

Bordo, Susan. *Unbearable Weight: Feminism, Western Culture, and the Body*. Berkeley: University of California Press, 1993.

Bosk, Charles L. *All God's Mistakes: Genetic Counseling in a Pediatric Hospital*. Chicago: University of Chicago Press, 1992.

Boss, Judith A. *The Birth Lottery: Prenatal Diagnosis and Selective Abortion*. Chicago: Loyola University Press, 1993.

Breslau, Naomi. "Care of Disabled Children and Women's Time Use." *Medical Care* 216 (1983): 620–29.

Breslau, Naomi, David Salkever, and Kathleen S. Staruch. "Women's Labor Force Activity and Responsibilities for Disabled Dependents." *Journal of Health and Social Behavior* 23 (1982).

Brock, Dan W. *Life and Death*. Cambridge: Cambridge University Press, 1993.

———. "The Human Genome Project and Human Identity." In *Genes and Human Self-Knowledge: Historical and Philosophical Reflections on Modern Genetics*, ed. Robert Weir, Susan Lawrence, and Evan Fales. Ames: University of Iowa Press, 1994.

———. "Justice and the ADA: Does Prioritizing and Rationing Health Care Discriminate against the Disabled?" *Social Philosophy and Policy* 12, no. 2 (Summer 1995): 159–85.

Brody, Baruch. "Against an Absolute Right to Abortion." In *The Problem of Abortion*, ed. Susan Dwyer and Joel Feinberg. Belmont, Calif.: Wadsworth, 1997.

Buchanan, Allen. "Choosing Who Will Be Disabled: Genetic Intervention and the Morality of Inclusion." *Social Philosophy and Policy* 13, no. 2 (Summer 1996).

———. "Equal Opportunity and Genetic Intervention." *Social Philosophy and Policy* 12, no. 2 (Summer 1995): 105–35.

Bushnell, D. E., ed. *Nagging Questions*. Lanham, Md.: Rowman & Littlefield, 1995.

Campbell, Jane, and Mike Oliver. *Disability Politics: Understanding Our Past, Changing Our Future*. London: Routledge, 1996.

Canguilhem, G. *The Normal and the Pathological*. New York: Zone Books, 1989.

Carlis, Michael, and Scott McCabe. "Are There No Per Se Disabilities under the

Americans with Disabilities Act? The Fate of Asymptomatic HIV Disease," *Maryland Law Review* 57, no. 2 (1998): 558–614.

Carlson, Angela Licia. "Mindful Subjects: Classification and Cognitive Disability." Ph.D. diss., University of Toronto, Toronto, 1998.

Caws, Peter. "Panel Discussion on 'What Do We Owe People with Disabilities?' " *Mount Sinai Journal of Medicine* 62, no. 2 (1995): 116–23.

Chadwick, Ruth, ed. *The Encyclopedia of Applied Ethics.* San Diego: Academic Press, 1997.

Charlton, James. *Nothing about Us without Us.* Berkeley: University of California Press, 1998.

Chronicle Staff Report. "1 in 10 Americans Disabled, Study Says." *San Francisco Chronicle*, 17 September 1997, A 10.

Cohen, G. A. *Equality of What? On Welfare, Goods, and Capabilities:. The Quality of Life.* New York: Oxford University Press, 1993.

———. "On the Currency of Egalitarian Justice." *Ethics* 99 (July 1989): 906–44.

———. "Self-Ownership, World-Ownership, and Equality." In *Justice and Equality Here and Now*, ed. Frank Lucash. Ithaca, N.Y.: Cornell University Press, 1983.

———. "Self-Ownership, World Ownership, and Equality: Part II," *Social Philosophy and Policy* 3, no.2 (Spring 1986): 77–96.

Cohen, Marion Deutsche. *Dirty Details: The Days and Nights of a Well Spouse.* Philadelphia: Temple University Press, 1996.

Cohen, Sherill, and Nadine Taub, eds. *Reproductive Laws for the 1990s.* New York: Humana, 1988.

Cole, Daniel, and Carol Comer. "Rhetoric, Reality, and the Law of Unfunded Federal Mandates," *Stanford Law and Policy Review* 8, no. 2 (1997): 103–25.

Cole, Phillip. "Social Liberty and the Physically Disabled." *Journal of Applied Philosophy* 4, no. 1 (1987): 29–39.

Colker, Ruth. *The Law of Disability Discrimination: Cases and Materials.* Cincinnati, Ohio: Anderson, 1995.

Cooper, Jeremy, and Stuart Vernon. *Disability and the Law.* London: Atheneum, 1996.

Cottingham, John. "Rectificatory Justice." In *Encyclopedia of Ethics*, ed. Lawrence Becker and Charlotte Becker. New York: Garland, 1992.

Couser, G. Thomas. *Recovering Bodies: Illness, Disability, and Life Writing.* Madison: University of Wisconsin Press, 1997.

Cranor, Carl F., ed. *Are Genes Us? The Social Consequences of the New Genetics.* New Brunswick, N.J.: Rutgers University Press, 1994.

Crehan, Matthew. "The Disability-based Peremptory Challenge: Does It Validate Discrimination Against Blind Prospective Jurors?" *Northern Kentucky Law Review* 25, no. 3 (1998): 531–52.

Crenshaw, Kimberle. "Demarginalizing the Intersection of Race and Sex: A Black Feminist Critique of Antidiscrimination Doctrine, Feminist Theory, and Antiracist Politics." In *Living with Contradictions: Controversies in Feminist Social Ethics*, ed. Alison Jaggar. Boulder, Colo.: Westview, 1994.

Crocker, David. "Functioning and Capability: The Foundations of Sen's and Nussbaum's Development Ethic, Part 2." In *Women, Culture, and Development,* ed. Martha Nussbaum and Jonathan Glover. New York: Oxford University Press, 1995.

Crow, Liz. "Including All Our Lives: Renewing the Social Model of Disability." In *Exploring the Divide: Illness and Disability,* ed. Colin Barnes and Geoff Mercer. Leeds, U.K.: Disability Press, 1996.

Daniels, Norman. "Equality of What: Welfare, Resources, or Capabilities?" *Philosophy and Phenomenological Research* 50 (Fall 1990), suppl.

———. *Just Health Care.* Cambridge: Cambridge University Press, 1985.

———. "Justice and Health Care." In *Health Care Ethics: An Introduction,* ed. Donald Van DeVeer and Tom Regan. Philadelphia: Temple University Press, 1987.

———. "Mental Disabilities, Equal Opportunity, and the ADA." In *Mental Disorder, Work Disability and the Law,* ed. Richard Bonnie and John McNahan. Chicago: University of Chicago Press, 1997.

———."The Distribution of Scarce Medical Resources." In *The Human Genome Project and the Future of Health Care,* ed. Thomas Murray, Mark Rothstein, and Robert Murray. Bloomington: Indiana University Press, 1996.

Davis, Alison. "Women and Disabilities: Abortion and Liberation." *Disability, Handicap, and Society* 2, no. 3 (1987).

Davis, Dena. "Genetic Dilemmas and the Child's Right to an Open Future." *The Hastings Center Report* 27, no. 2 (March–April 1997): 7.

Davis, K., and A. Mullender, eds. "Key Issues in Disability: Rights or Charity, the Future of Welfare, Social Action." *Journal of the Centre for Social Action* 2, no. 1 (1994).

Davis, Lennard, ed. *The Disability Reader.* New York: Routledge, 1997.

———. *Enforcing Normalcy: Disability, Deafness and the Body.* London: Verso, 1995.

———. "The Linguistic Turf Battles over American Sign Language." *The Chronicle of Higher Education* 44, no. 39 (5 June 1998): A60.

———. *The Sense of Sign Language: Memoir of a Childhood with Deafness.* Urbana: University of Illinois Press, 1998.

Davis, Phillip, and John Bradley. "The Meaning of Normal." *Perspectives in Biology and Medicine* 40, no. 1 (Autumn 1996): 69–70.

De Roose, Frank. "Ethics and Marginal Cases: The Rights of the Mentally Handicapped." *Journal of Applied Philosophy* 8, no. 2 (1991): 87–95.

Deegan, Mary Jo, and Nancy A. Brooks. *Women and Disability: The Double Handicap.* New Brunswick, N.J.: Transaction, 1985.

DeJong, Gerben. *Independent Living & Disability Policy in the Netherlands: Three Models of Residential Care and Independent Living.* New York: World Rehabilitation Fund, 1984.

DeJong, Philip. "U.S. Disability from a European Perspective." In *Disability: Challenges for Social Insurance, Health Care Financing, & Labor Market Policy,* ed. Virginia Reno, Jerry Mashow, and Bill Gradison. Washington, D.C.: National Academy of Social Insurance, 1997.

DeLaGarza, Denise Verret. "Exploring the Web: Hispanic Women with Visual Impairments." In *Multicultural Women: Health, Disability, and Rehabilitation*, ed. Anita Leal-Idrogo, Judith Gonzales-Calvo, and Vickie Krenz. Dubuque, Iowa: Kendall/Hunt, 1996.

Despouv, L. *Human Rights and Disability*. New York: United Nations Economic and Social Council, 1991.

Devlieger, Patrick. "Why Disability? The Cultural Understanding of Physical Disability in an African Society." In *Disability and Culture*, ed. Benedicte Ingstadt and Susan Reynolds Whyte. Berkeley: University of California Press, 1995.

Diller, Matthew. "Dissonant Disability Policies: The Tensions between the Americans with Disabilities Act and Federal Disability Benefit Programs," *Texas Law Review* 76 (April 1998): 1003–82.

Donchin, Anne, and Laura Purdy, eds. *Embodying Bioethics: Feminist Advances*. Lanham, Md.: Rowman & Littlefield, 1998.

Donley, Carol, and Sheryl Buckley, eds. *The Tyranny of the Normal: An Anthology*. Kent, Ohio: Kent State University Press, 1996.

Dorgan, Charity Anne, ed. *Statistical Handbook of Working America*. Detroit, Mich.: Gale Research, 1995.

Doyle, Brian. *Disability Discrimination: The New Law*. London: Jordans, 1996.

Drimmer, Jonathan C. "Cripples, Overcomers, and Civil Rights: Tracing the Evolution of Federal Legislation and Social Policy for People with Disabilities." *UCLA Law Review* 40 (1993): 1341–1410.

Duster, Troy. *Backdoor to Eugenics*. New York: Routledge, 1990.

Dworkin, Ronald. "What Is Equality? Part 1: Equality of Resources." *Philosophy and Public Affairs* 10, no. 4 (1981): 283–345.

———. "What is Equality? Part 2: Equality of Resources." *Philosophy and Public Affairs* 10, no. 4 (1981).

———. "Will Clinton's Plan Be Fair?" *New York Review of Books*, 13 January 1994, 20–25.

Dwyer, Susan, and Joel Feinberg. *The Problem of Abortion*, 3d ed. Belmont, Calif.: Wadsworth, 1997.

Edwards, Steven D. "The Moral States of Intellectually Disabled Individuals." *Journal of Medicine and Philosophy* 22: 29–42.

Eiesland, Nancy L., and Rebecca S. Chopp. *The Disabled God: Toward a Liberatory Theology of Disability*. London: Abingdon, 1994.

Eiser, C. "Psychological Effects of Chronic Disease." *Journal of Clinical Psychology and Psychiatry* 31, no. 1 (1990): 85–98.

Elster, John, and John E. Roemer. *Interpersonal Comparisons of Well-Being*. Cambridge: Cambridge University Press, 1991.

Engelhardt, E. E., and D. D. Engelhardt, eds. *Ethics and Life: An Interdisciplinary Approach to Moral Problems*. Dubuque, Iowa: Brown, 1992.

Engelhardt, H. Tristram. *The Foundations of Bioethics*. New York: Oxford University Press, 1996.

Fine, Michelle, and Adrienne Asch, eds. *Women with Disabilities: Essays in Psychology, Culture, and Politics.* Philadelphia: Temple University Press, 1988.

Finkelstein, Vic. *Attitudes and Disabled People.* New York: World Rehabilitation Fund, 1980.

Fisher, Nancy L. ed. *Cultural and Ethnic Diversity: A Guide for Genetics Professionals.* Baltimore, Md.: Johns Hopkins University Press, 1996.

Fraser, Nancy. "From Redistribution to Recognition: Dilemmas of Justice in a 'Post-Socialist' Age." *New Left Review* 212 (1995): 68–93.

———. *Justice Interruptus: Critical Reflections on the "Postsocialist" Condition.* London: Routledge, 1997.

Fredrickson, George. "America's Caste System: Will It Change?" *New York Review of Books* 44, no. 16 (23 October 1997): 68–75.

Funk, Robert. "Disability Rights: From Caste to Class in the Context of Civil Rights." In *Images of the Disabled, Disabling Images,* ed. A. Gartner and T. Joe. New York: Praeger, 1987.

Galston, William. *Liberal Purposes: Goods, Virtues, and Diversity in the Liberal State.* New York: Cambridge University Press, 1991.

Gardner, R. J. M., and G. R. Sutherland. *Chromosome Abnormalities and Genetic Counseling.* New York: Oxford University Press, 1989.

Garland, Robert. *The Eye of the Beholder: Deformity and Disability in the Graeco-Roman World.* Ithaca, N.Y.: Cornell University Press, 1995.

Gartner, A., and T. Joe, eds. *Images of the Disabled, Disabling Images.* New York: Praeger, 1987.

Gates, Henry Louis, Jr. "Ethics and Ethnicity." *Bulletin of the American Academy of Arts and Sciences* 51, no. 1 (September/October 1997).

Gilligan, Carol. *In a Different Voice: Psychological Theory and Women's Development.* Cambridge, Mass.: Harvard University Press, 1982.

———. "Moral Orientation and Moral Development." In *Women and Moral Theory,* ed. Eva F. Kittay and Diana T. Meyers. Totowa, N.J.: Rowman & Allanheld, 1987.

Glover, Jonathan. "Future People, Disability, and Screening." In *Justice between Age Groups and Generations,* ed. P. Laslett and J. S. Fishkin. New Haven, Conn.: Yale University Press, 1992.

Goffman, Erving. *Stigma: Notes on the Maintenance of Spoiled Identity.* Englewood Cliffs, N.J.: Prentice Hall, 1963.

Goode, David, ed. *Quality of Life for Persons with Disabilities: International Perspectives and Issues.* Cambridge, Mass.: Brookline, 1994.

Gooding, Caroline. *Disabling Laws, Enabling Acts: Disability Rights in Britain and America.* London: Pluto, 1994.

Grady, Denise. "Studies of Schizophrenia Indicate Psychotherapy." *New York Times,* 20 January 1998, B17.

Griffin, James. *Well-Being: Its Meaning, Measurement, and Moral Importance.* Oxford: Oxford University Press, 1986.

Groce, Nora. *Everyone Spoke Sign Language Here: Hereditary Deafness on Martha's Vineyard.* Cambridge, Mass.: Harvard University Press, 1985.

Hacking, Ian. "The Looping Effects of Human Kinds." In *Contemporary Issues in Bioethics*, 4th ed., ed. T. Beauchamp and L. Walters. Belmont, Calif.: Wadsworth, 1994.

Hahn, Harlan. "Civil Rights for Disabled Americans." In *Images of the Disabled, Disabling Images*, ed. A. Gartner and T. Joe. New York: Praeger, 1987.

Hales, Gerald, ed. *Beyond Disability: Towards an Enabling Society*. London: Sage, 1996.

Hanna, William John, and Elizabeth Rogovsky. "On the Situation of African-American Women." *Journal of Applied Rehabilitation Counseling* 23, no. 4 (1992): 39–44.

———. "Women with Disabilities: Two Handicaps Plus." *Disability, Handicap & Society* 6, no. 1 (1991): 55–56.

Haraway, Donna. "Situated Knowledges: The Science Question in Feminism and the Privilege of Partial Perspective." *Feminist Studies* 14 (1988): 581–84.

Hardin, Russell. *Morality within the Limits of Reason*. Chicago: University of Chicago Press, 1988.

Harding, Sandra, ed. *Feminism and Methodology: Social Science Issues*. Bloomington: Indiana University Press, 1987.

Hartsock, Nancy C. M. "The Feminist Standpoint: Developing the Ground for a Specifically Feminist Historical Materialism." In *Feminism and Methodology: Social Science Issues*, ed. Sandra Harding. Bloomington: Indiana University Press, 1987.

Heller, Joseph. *Catch-22*. New York: Simon & Schuster, 1961.

Hillyer, Barbara. *Feminism and Disability*. Norman: University of Oklahoma Press, 1993.

Hirsch, Karen. "Raising Our Voices: Perspectives on the Book *Feminism and Disability*," *Resourceful Woman* (a newsletter published by the Health Resource Center for Women with Disabilities, Rehabilitation Institute of Chicago) 3, no. 1 (Winter 1994): 3.

Hopkins, Kevin. "Public Attitudes toward People with Disabilities." *Willing to Act*, Washington, D.C.: National Organization on Disability (September 1991): 7.

Howe, Kenneth R. "Educational Ethics, Social Justice and Children with Disabilities." In *Disability and the Dilemmas of Education and Justice*, ed. Carol Christensen and Fazal Rizvi. Buckingham, U.K.: Open University Press, 1996.

Howell, J. H., and W. F. Sale, eds. *Life Choices: A Hastings Center Introduction to Bioethics*. Baltimore, Md.: Georgetown University Press, 1995.

Hudson, Yeager, and Creighton Peden, eds. *The Social Power of Ideas*. Lewiston, N.Y.: Mellen, 1995.

Hull, K. T., ed. *Ethical Issues in the New Reproductive Technologies*. Belmont, Calif.: Wadsworth, 1990.

Ingstadt, Benedicte, and Susan Reynolds Whyte, eds. *Disability and Culture*. Berkeley: University of California Press, 1995.

Iserson, K. V., and Mary B. Mahowald. "Acute Care Research: Is It Ethical?" *Critical Care Medicine* 20, no. 7 (1992): 1032–37.

Israel, Jamie, Margaret Cunningham, Helen Thumann, and Kathleen Shaver Arnos. "Deaf Culture." In *Cultural and Ethnic Diversity: A Guide for Genetics Professionals*, ed. Nancy L. Fisher. Baltimore, Md.: Johns Hopkins University Press, 1996.

Jaggar, Alison M., "Caring as a Feminist Practice of Moral Reason." In *Justice and Care*, ed. Virginia Held. Boulder, Colo.: Westview, 1995.

———. *Feminist Politics and Human Nature*. Totowa, N.J.: Rowman & Allanheld, 1983.

———, ed. *Living with Contradictions: Controversies in Feminist Social Ethics*. Boulder, Colo.: Westview, 1994.

Jaggar, Alison M., and Paula Struhl. *Feminist Frameworks*. New York: McGraw-Hill, 1978.

Jaggar, Alison M., and Iris Marion Young, eds. *Blackwell's Companion to Feminist Philosophy*. Oxford: Blackwell's, 1998.

Janack, Marianne. "Standpoint Epistemology without the 'Standpoint'? An Examination of Epistemic Privilege and Epistemic Authority." *Hypatia: A Journal of Feminist Philosophy* 12, no. 2 (Spring 1997): 125–39.

Jencks, Christopher. "Whom Must We Treat Equally for Educational Opportunity to Be Equal?" *Ethics* 98 (1988): 518–20.

Johnson, William G., ed. special issue on "The Americans with Disabilities Act: Social Contract or Special Privilege." *Annals of the American Academy of Political and Social Science* 549 (January 1997).

Jones, Melinda, and Lee Ann Marks, eds. *Disability Divers(ability) and Legal Change*. The Hague: Kluwer Academic, 1999.

Jonsen, Albert R., and Stephen Toulmin. *The Abuse of Casuistry*. Berkeley: University of California Press, 1988.

Kallianes, Virginia, and Phyllis Rubenfeld. "Disabled Women and Reproductive Rights." *Disability & Society* 12, no. 2 (Spring 1997): 203–21.

Kane, R., and A. Caplan. *Ethical Conflicts in the Management of Home Care: The Case Manager's Dilemma*. New York: Springer, 1993.

Kaplan, Deborah. "Prenatal Screening and Diagnosis: The Impact on Persons with Disabilities." In *Women and Prenatal Testing: Facing the Challenges of Genetic Technology*, ed. Karen H. Rothenberg and Elizabeth J. Thomson. Columbus: Ohio State University Press, 1994.

Kass, Leon. "Implications of the Human Right to Life." In *Intervention and Reflection: Basic Issues in Medical Ethics*, ed. Ronald Munson. Belmont, Calif.: Wadsworth, 1983.

Katz, Irwin, R. Glenn Hass, and Joan Bailey. "Attitudinal Ambivalence and Behavior toward People with Disabilities." In *Attitudes toward Persons with Disabilities*, ed. Harold Yuker. New York: Springer, 1988.

Kavka, Gregory S. "Disability and the Right to Work." *Social Philosophy & Policy* 9, no. 1, 1992.

Keith, Lois. *What Happened to You? Writing by Disabled Women*. London: Women's Press, 1994.

Kelman, Mark. "Concepts of Discrimination in General Ability Job Testing." *Harvard Law Review* 104, no. 6 (April 1991): 1157–1248.

Kelman, Mark, and Gillian Lester. *Jumping the Queue: An Inquiry into the Legal Treatment of Students with Learning Disabilities.* Cambridge, Mass.: Harvard University Press, 1997.

Kemp, Evan. "Could You Please Die Now?" *Washington Post,* 5 January 1997.

Kent, Deborah. "Disabled Women: Portraits in Fiction and Drama." In *Images of the Disabled, Disabling Images,* ed. A. Gartner and T. Joe. New York: Praeger, 1987.

———. "In Search of Liberation." *Disabled USA* 1, no. 3 (1977).

Kessler, R. C. "Lifetime and 12-Month Prevalence of DSM-III-R Psychiatric Disorders from the National Comorbidity Survey." *Archives of General Psychiatry* 51 (1994): 8–19.

Kevles, Daniel. "Grounds for Breeding: The Amazing Persistence of Eugenics in Europe and North America." *Times Literary Supplement* 4944 (2 January 1998): 3–4.

———. *In the Name of Eugenics: Genetics and the Uses of Human Heredity.* New York: Knopf, 1985.

Kittay, Eva F. "Not My Way, Sesha, Your Way, Slowly: Maternal Thinking in the Raising of a Child with Profound Intellectual Disabilities." In *Mothering in the US Today,* ed. Julia Hanisberg and Sara Ruddick. New York: Beacon, 1998.

Kittay, Eva F., and Diana T. Meyers, eds. *Women and Moral Theory.* Totowa, N.J.: Rowman & Allanheld, 1987.

Klein, Bonnie. "We Are Who You Are: Feminism and Disability." *Ms* (November/ December 1992): 70–74.

Kleinfield, N. R. "Patient's Quest for Normal Life, at a Price," *New York Times,* 22 June 1997, A1, A15.

Kohlberg, Lawrence. *The Philosophy of Moral Development.* San Francisco: Harper & Row, 1981.

Kopelman, Loretta, and John C. Moskop, eds. *Ethics and Mental Retardation.* Dordrecht: Reidel, 1984.

Koppel, Christine. *Perspectives on Equality: Constructing a Relational Theory.* Oxford: Rowman & Littlefield, 1998.

Koppleman, Andrew. *Antidiscrimination Law and Social Equality.* New Haven, Conn.: Yale University Press, 1996.

Kuhse, Helga, and Peter Singer. *Should the Baby Live? The Problem of Handicapped Infants.* Oxford: Oxford University Press, 1985.

Kuusisto, Stephen. *Planet of the Blind.* New York: Dial, 1998.

Kymlicka, Will. *Liberalism, Community and Culture.* Oxford: Clarendon, 1991.

———. *The Rights of Minority Cultures.* Oxford: Oxford University Press, 1996.

Lamb, Brian, and Susan Layzell. *Disabled in Britain: A World Apart.* London: SCOPE, 1994.

Lane, Harlan. *The Mask of Benevolence: Disabling the Deaf Community.* New York: Vintage, 1993.

Lane, Harlan, Robert Hoffmeister, and Ben Bahan. *A Journey into the Deaf-World.* San Diego: Dawn Sign, 1996.

Leal-Idrogo, Anita, Judy Gonzalez-Calvo, and Vicki Krenz. *Multicultural Women: Health, Disability and Rehabilitation.* Dubuque, Iowa: Kendall/Hunt, 1996.

Lebowitz, Todd. "Evaluating Purely Reproductive Disorders under the Americans with Disabilities Act," *Michigan Law Review* 96, no. 3 (1997): 724–53.

Lempinen, Edward. "States Care of Disabled Assailed," *San Francisco Chronicle,* 26 February 1997, A1, A9.

Lester, M. A., A. Lemke, D. Levinson, and Mary B. Mahowald. "The Human Genome Project and Women: Cystic Fibrosis, a Case Study." *Journal of Women's Health* 4 (December 1995): 623–35.

Liggett, Helen. "Stars Are Not Born: An Interpretive Approach to the Politics of Disability." *Disability, Handicap & Society* 3, no. 3 (1988): 263–74.

Linton, Simi. *Claiming Disability: Knowledge and Identity.* New York: New York University Press, 1998.

Little, Jan. *If It Weren't for the Honor—I'd Rather Have Walked.* Cambridge, Mass.: Brookline, 1996.

Longsdale, Susan. *Women and Disability: The Experience of Physical Disability among Women.* New York: St. Martin's, 1990.

MacIntyre, Alasdair. *Rational Dependent Animals: Why Humans Need the Virtues.* Chicago: Open Court Press, forthcoming.

MacKinnon, Catharine A. "Feminism, Marxism, Method, and the State." In *Feminism and Methodology: Social Science Issues,* ed. Sandra Harding. Bloomington: Indiana University Press, 1987.

Macklin, Ruth, and Willard Gaylin. *Mental Retardation and Sterilization: A Problem of Competency and Paternalism.* New York: Plenum Press, 1981.

Magee, Bryan, and Martin Milligan. *On Blindness.* Oxford: Oxford University Press, 1995.

Mahowald, Mary B. "A Feminist in the Medical Academy: An Idealistic Pragmatist Account." In *Women in Medical Education,* ed. Delese Wear. New York: State University of New York Press, 1996: 47–58.

———. "A Roycean Pragmatic: Insights for Applied Philosophy." *Frontiers in American Philosophy, Vol. II,* ed. Robert Burch and Herman J. Saatkamp, Jr. College Station: Texas A&M Press, 1996: 267–76.

———. "Abortion and Equality." In *Abortion—Understanding Differences,* ed. S. Callahan and D. Callahan. New York: Plenum, 1984.

———. "Are Codes of Professional Ethics Ethical?" *Health Matrix* 2 (1984): 37–42.

———. "Baby Doe Committees: A Critical Evaluation." *Clinics in Perinatology* 15 (1988): 879–90.

———. "Beneficence, Autonomy and Paternalism." *Health Matrix* 3 (1985): 37–39.

———. "Care and Its Pitfalls." *In Ethical Dimensions of Pharmaceutical Care,* ed. Amy M. Haddad and Robert A. Buerki. New York: Haworth, 1996: 85–102.

————. "Embryos and Rights." In *The Bill of Rights: Bicentennial Reflections,* ed. Yeager Hudson and Creighton Peden. Lewiston, N.Y.: Mellen, 1993: 195–204.
————. "Ethical Considerations in Infertility." In *Infertility: A Comprehensive Text,* ed. Machelle M. Seibel. Stamford, Conn.: Appleton & Lange, 1997: 823–28.
————. "Ethical Decisions in Neonatal Intensive Care." In *Human Values in Critical Care Medicine,* ed. S.J. Youngner. New York: Praeger, 1986: 63–86.
————. "Ethical Dilemmas and the Disabled Infant." *Baby Doe Handbook,* Ohio Department of Human Services (1987): 47–52.
————. "Ethical Issues and Perspectives in Genetic Technologies: An Overview." *International Journal of Bioethics* 1 (1990): 156–64.
————. "Feminism and Medicine." *Journal of Social Philosophy* 18 (1987): 3–11.
————. "Gender Justice and Genetics." In *The Social Power of Ideas,* ed. Yeager Hudson and Creighton Peden. Lewiston, N.Y.: Mellen, 1995.
————. "Gender Justice in Genetics." *Women's Health Issues* 7, no. 4 (July/August 1997): 230–33.
————. "Genetic Technologies and Their Implications for Women." *University of Chicago Law School Roundtable* 3, no. 2 (1996): 439–63.
————. *Genetics, Women, and Equality.* Oxford: Oxford University Press, forthcoming.
————. "Hospital Ethics Committees: Diverse and Problematic." *Newsletter on Medicine and Philosophy of the American Philosophical Association* 88, no. 2 (1989): 88–94.
————. "Is There Life after *Roe v. Wade?*" In *Life Choices: A Hastings Center Introduction to Bioethics.* Baltimore, Md.: Georgetown University Press, 1995.
————. "Marx, Moral Judgement and Medical Ethics." In *Moral Theory and Moral Judgements in Medical Ethics,* ed. B. Brody. *Philosophy and Medicine* 32. The Hague: Kluwer Academic, 1988.
————. "Maternal/Fetal Conflict? Positions and Principles: Ethical Dilemmas in Obstetrics," *Clinical Obstetrics and Gynecology* 35, no. 4 (1992): 729–37.
————. "On Caring for Children." In *Birth to Death: Biology, Science, and Bioethics,* ed. David Thomasma and Tomi Kushner. Cambridge: Cambridge University Press, 1996.
————. "On Treatment of Myopia: Feminism, Standpoint Theory, and Bioethics." In *Feminism and Bioethics: Beyond Reproduction,* ed. Susan Wolf. New York: Oxford University Press, 1995.
————. "Person." In *Encyclopedia of Bioethics,* rev. ed., ed. T. Reich. New York: Simon & Schuster Macmillan, 1995.
————. "Possibilities for Moral Agency in Children." In *Freedom, Equality, and Social Change,* ed. Creighton Peden and J. Sterba. Lewiston, N.Y.: Mellen, 1989.
————. "Reproductive Genetics and Gender Justice." In *Women and Prenatal Testing: Facing the Challenges of Genetic Technology,* ed. Karen H. Rothenberg and Elizabeth J. Thompson. Columbus: Ohio State University, 1994.

————. "The Fetus: Ethical and Philosophical Issues." In *Encyclopedia of Bioethics,* rev. ed., ed. W.T. Reich. New York: Simon & Schuster Macmillan, 1995.

————. "The Human Genome Project and Women: Introduction and Overview," *Women's Health Issues* 4 (1997): 230–33.

————. "When a Mentally Ill Woman Refuses Abortion," *The Hastings Center Report* 15 (1985): 22–23.

————. "Women and Children First," *Medicine on the Midway* 47, no. 3 (Winter 1993/94): 6.

————. *Women and Children in Health Care: An Unequal Majority.* New York: Oxford University Press, 1993.

Mahowald, Mary B., Dana Levinson, and Christine Cassel. "The New Genetics and Women." *The Milbank Quarterly* 74, no. 2 (1996): 268–70.

Mahowald, Mary B., D. Schubert, and I. B. Gordon. "How One Ohio Hospital Resolved the DNR Question," *Ohio State Medical Journal* (1986): 382–85.

Mahowald, Mary B., J. Silver, and R. A. Ratcheson. "The Ethical Options in Transplanting Fetal Tissue," *The Hastings Center Report* 17 (1987): 9–15.

Mairs, Nancy. *Waist-High in the World.* Boston: Beacon Press, 1996.

Manning, Rita, and Rene Trujillo, eds. *Social Justice in a Diverse Society.* Menlo Park, Calif.: Mayfield, 1996.

Margolis, Joseph. "Applying Moral Theory to the Retarded." In *Ethics and Mental Retardation,* ed. L. Kopelman and J. C. Moskop. Dordrecht: Reidel, 1984.

Martin, D. "Disability Culture: Eager to Bite the Hands That Would Feed Them." *New York Times,* "Week in Review Section," 1 June 1997, 1.

Mashaw, Jerry. *Bureaucratic Justice: Managing Social Security Disability Claims.* New Haven, Conn.: Yale University Press, 1983.

McCullough, Laurence, and Tom L. Beauchamp. *Medical Ethics: The Moral Responsibilities of Physicians.* Englewood Cliffs, N.J.: Prentice Hall, 1984.

McDevitt, William. "Defining the Term 'Disability' under the Americans with Disabilities Act," *St. Thomas Law Review* 10, no. 2 (1998): 281–97.

McKibben, Bill. "What Only-Child Syndrome?" *New York Times Magazine* (3 May 1998): 48–49.

McMahan, Jeff. "Cognitive Disability, Misfortune, and Justice." *Philosophy and Public Affairs* 25, no. 1 (Winter 1996): 3–35.

McNeil, John M. "Americans with Disabilities 1994—Text", *Household Economic Studies, Current Population Report,* 70–61, //www.census.gov/hhs/www/disable/sipp/disab9495/asc9495.html.

Meekosha, Helen, and J. Pettman. "Beyond Category Politics," *Hecate* 17, no. 2 (1991): 75–92.

Miles, Mike. "Community, Individual or Information Development? Dilemmas of Concept and Culture in South Asian Disability Planning." *Disability & Society* 11, no. 4 (1996): 485–500.

————. "Disability and Afghan Reconstruction," *Disability, Handicap and Society* 5, no. 3 (1990): 257–69.

Miles, Rosalind. *A Women's History of the World.* London: Joseph, 1988.

Minow, Martha. *Making All the Difference: Inclusion, Exclusion and American Law.* Ithaca, N.Y.: Cornell University Press, 1990.

Miraie, E. D., and Mary B. Mahowald. "Withholding Nutrition from Seriously-Ill Newborn Infants: A Parent's Perspective," *Journal of Pediatrics* 113 (1988): 262–65.

Mitchell, David, and Sharon Snyder, eds. *The Body and Physical Difference.* Ann Arbor: University of Michigan Press, 1997.

Morris, Jenny. *Encounters with Strangers: Feminism and Disability.* London: Women's Press, 1996.

———. "Feminism and Disability," *Feminist Review* 43 (1993): 57–70.

———. *Independent Lives.* New York: Macmillan, 1993.

———. "Personal and Political: A Feminist Perspective on Researching Physical Disability." *Disability, Handicap and Society* 7, no. 2 (1992): 157–66.

———. *Pride against Prejudice: Transforming Attitudes to Disability.* Philadelphia: New Society, 1991.

———. "Tyrannies of Perfection." *The New Internationalist* (1 July 1992): 16–17.

Mosley, Albert G., and Nicholas Capaldi. *Affirmative Action: Social Justice or Unfair Preference?* Lanham, Md.: Rowman & Littlefield, 1996.

Murphy, Jeffrie. "Do the Retarded Have a Right Not to Be Eaten? A Rejoinder to Joseph Margolis." In *Ethics and Mental Retardation*, ed. L. Kopelman and J. C. Moskop, Dordrecht: Reidel, 1984.

Murphy, Robert F. *The Body Silent.* New York: Holt, 1987.

Nagel, Thomas. "Equality." In *Mortal Questions*, ed. Thomas Nagel. New York: Cambridge University Press, 1979.

———. *Equality and Partiality.* New York: Oxford University Press, 1991.

Nagler, Mark. *Perspectives on Disability: Text and Readings on Disability.* Palo Alto, Calif.: Health Markets Research, 1993.

Nicolaisen, Ida. "Persons and Nonpersons: Disability and Personhood among the Punan Bah of Central Borneo." In *Disability and Culture*, ed. Benedicte Ingstad and Susan Reynolds Whyte. Berkeley: University of California Press, 1995.

Noddings, Nel. *Caring: A Feminine Approach to Ethics and Moral Education.* Berkeley: University of California Press, 1984.

———. "Ethics from the Standpoint of Women." In *Theoretical Perspectives on Sexual Difference*, ed. Deborah L. Rhode. New Haven, Conn.: Yale University Press, 1990: 160–73.

Nora, Lois M., and Mary B. Mahowald. "Neural Fetal Tissue Transplants: Old and New Issues." *Zygon* 31, no. 4 (1996): 615–33.

Norden, Martin. *The Cinema of Isolation.* New Brunswick, N.J.: Rutgers University Press, 1994.

Nozick, Robert. *Anarchy, State, and Utopia.* Cambridge, Mass.: Harvard University Press, 1974.

Nussbaum, Martha C. "Aristotelian Social Democracy." In *Liberalism and the Human Good,* ed. R. B. Douglass, G. Mara, and H. Richardson. New York: Routledge, 1990.

———. "The Good as Discipline, the Good as Freedom." In *Ethics of Consumption: The Good Life Justice, and Global Stewardship*. Lanham, Md.: Rowman & Littlefield, 1998.

Nussbaum, Martha, and Amartya K. Sen, eds. *Women, Culture, and Development*. New York: Oxford University Press, 1995.

Oliver, Michael. "Defining Impairment and Disability: Issues at Stake." In *Exploring the Divide: Illness and Disability*, ed. Colin Barnes and Geoff Mercer. Leeds, U.K.: Disability Press, 1996.

———. "Disability and Dependency: A Creation of Industrialized Societies?" In *Disability and Dependency*, ed. Len Barton, London: Falmer, 1989.

———. *Disablement: A Sociological Approach*. New York: St. Martin's, 1990.

———. "The Integration Segregation Debate: Some Sociological Considerations." *British Journal of Sociology of Education* 6, no. 1 (1985).

———. *The Politics of Disablement: A Sociological Approach*. London: St. Martin's, 1990.

———. "Social Policy and Disability: Some Theoretical Issues." *Disability, Handicap and Society* 1, no. 1 (1986): 5–18.

———. *Understanding Disability: From Theory to Practice*. New York: St. Martin's, 1996.

Orentlicher, David. "Destructuring Disability—Rationing of Health Care and Discrimination." *Harvard Civil Rights and Civil Liberties Law Review* 31: 49–87.

Overall, Christine. *Ethics and Reproduction: A Feminist Analysis*. Boston: Allen & Unwin, 1987.

Parens, Eric, ed. *Enhancing Human Capacities: Conceptual Complexities and Ethical Implications*. Baltimore, Md.: Georgetown University Press, forthcoming.

Parfit, Derek. "Equality and Priority." *Ratio* 10 (n.s.) no. 3 (December 1997): 202–21.

Parks, Susan Hillier, and Marc Pilisuk. "Caregiver Burden: Gender and the Psychological Costs of Caregiving." *American Journal of Orthopsychiatry* 61 (1991): 501–9.

Parrot, H., ed. *Peirce and Value Theory: On Peircian Ethics and Aesthetics*. Philadelphia: Benjamins, 1993.

Pearce, Diana. "The Feminization of Poverty: Women, Work and Welfare." *Urban and Social Change Review* 11 (February 1978): 28–36.

Percy, Stephen L. *Disability, Civil Rights and Public Policy: The Politics of Implementation*. Tuscaloosa: University of Alabama Press, 1989.

Perlez, Jane. "Bitter Burden on Sarajevo: Invalids of War: A City with a Legacy of Tolerance Finds it Hard to Help the War Wounded." *New York Times*, 1 August 1996, A5.

Pernick, Martin S. *The Black Stork: Eugenics and the Death of "Defective" Babies in American Medicine and Motion Pictures Since 1915*. New York: Oxford University Press, 1996.

Pfeiffer, D. "Public Transit Access for Disabled Persons in the United States." *Disability, Handicap and Society* 5, no. 2 (1990): 153–66.

Pierre, Robert E. " For Parents of Disabled, Promise of a Respite in Maryland." *Washington Post*, 10 February 1998, 1.

Pinder, Ruth. "Integrating Models of Disability: a reply to Shakespeare and Watson," *Disability and Society* 12, no. 2 (1997): 307–10.

Pinet, G. *Is the Law Fair to the Disabled?* Copenhagen: World Health Organization, 1990.

Pogge, Thomas W. *Realizing Rawls*. Ithaca, N.Y.: Cornell University Press, 1989.

Pope, Andrew M., and Alvin R. Tarlov, eds. *Disability in America: Toward a National Agenda for Prevention*. Washington, D.C.: National Academy Press, 1991.

Post, Stephen G. "Women and Elderly Parents: Moral Controversy in an Aging Society." *Hypatia: A Journal of Feminist Philosophy* 5, no. 1 (Spring 1990).

Preston, Paul. *Mother Father Deaf: Living between Sound and Silence*. Cambridge, Mass.: Harvard University Press, 1994.

Priestly, Mark. "Commonality and Difference in the Movement: An 'Association of Blind Asians' in Leeds." *Disability & Society* 10, no. 2 (1995): 157–69.

Purdy, Laura. *Reproducing Persons: Issues in Feminist Bioethics*. Ithaca, N.Y.: Cornell University Press, 1996.

Randolph, Lillian, Bradley Seidman, and Thomas Pasko. *Physician Characteristics and Distribution in the U.S.* Chicago: American Medical Association, 1996.

Ravin, A., Mary B. Mahowald, and C. Stocking. "Genes or Gestation? Attitudes of Women and Men about Biological Ties to Children." *Journal of Women's Health* 6 (1997): 1–9.

Rawls, John. "Priority of the Rights and Ideas of the Good." In *Political Liberalism*. New York: Columbia University Press, 1996.

———. "Justice as Fairness: Political Not Metaphysical," *Philosophy and Public Affairs* 14 (1985): 223–51.

Reich, Warren. *Encyclopedia of Bioethics*. New York: Macmillan, 1995.

Rhode, Deborah L. *Theoretical Perspectives on Sexual Difference*. New Haven, Conn.: Yale University Press, 1990.

Rimer, Sara. "New Needs for Retirement Complexes' Oldest: New Needs for Retirement Communities in Trying to Serve the 'Oldest Old'." *New York Times*, 23 March 1998, A1, A14.

Rioux, Marcia. "Towards a Concept of Equality of Well-Being: Overcoming the Social and Legal Construction of Inequality." In *Disability Is Not Measles: New Research Paradigms*, ed. Marcia Rioux and Michael Bach. Ontario: L'Institut Roeher, 1994.

Rolland, John S. *Families, Illness, and Disability: An Integrative Treatment Model*. New York: Basic Books, 1994.

Rose-Ackerman, Susan. "Mental Retardation and Society: The Ethics and Politics of Normalization." *Ethics* 93 (1982): 81–101.

Rosen, Marvin, Gerald Clark, and Marvin Kivitz, eds. *The History of Mental Retardation: Collected Papers, Vol. I*. Baltimore, Md.: University Park Press, 1975.

Rosenberg, Alexander. "The Political Philosophy of Biological Endowments." *Social Philosophy and Policy* 5, no. 1 (1986): 2–31.

Rothenberg, Karen H., and Elizabeth J. Thomson, eds. *Women and Prenatal Testing: Facing the Challenges of Genetic Technology.* Columbus: Ohio State University Press, 1994.

Rothman, Barbara Katz. *The Tentative Pregnancy: How Amniocentesis Changes the Experience of Motherhood.* New York: Knopf, 1985.

Ruddick, Sara. *Maternal Thinking: Toward a Politics of Peace.* New York: Ballantine, 1989.

Saunders, Debra J. "Children Who Deserve to Die." *San Francisco Examiner,* 23 September 1997, A21.

Saxton, Marsha. "Disability Rights and Selective Abortion." In *Abortion Wars: A Half Century of Struggle, 1950–2000,* ed. Ricki Solinger. Berkeley: University of California Press, 1998.

———. "Prenatal Screening and Discriminatory Attitudes about Disability." *Gene WATCH* (January/February, 1987): 8–10.

Saxton, Marsha, and Florence Howe, eds. *With Wings: An Anthology of Literature by and about Women with Disabilities.* New York: Feminist Press at the City University of New York, 1987.

Scanlon, Thomas. "The Significance of Choice" in *Tanner Lectures on Human Values VIII,* ed. S. McMurrin. Salt Lake City: University of Utah Press, 1988.

Schneider, Joseph W. "Disability as Moral Experience: Epilepsy and Self in Routine Relationships." *Journal of Social Issues* 44, no. 1 (1988): 63–78.

Schuchman, Alan. "The Holy and the Handicapped: an Examination of the Different Applications of the Reasonable-Accommodation Clauses in Title VII and the ADA," *Indiana Law Journal* 73, no. 2 (1998): 746–63.

Scotch, Richard K. "Disability as the Basis for a Social Movement: Advocacy and the Politics of Definition." *Journal of Social Issues* 1 (1988): 159–72.

———. *From Good Will to Civil Rights: Transforming Federal Policy.* Philadelphia: Temple University Press, 1984.

———. "Politics and Policy in the History of the Disability Rights Movement." *The Millbank Quarterly* 67, no. 2 (1989): 380–401.

Scott, Robert. *The Making of Blind Men: A Study of Adult Socialization.* New York: Russell Sage Foundation, 1969.

Scott, Thayer C. "Disabled Woman, Alameda Depot Settle Bias Suit; 9 Years of Torment at Naval Station." *San Francisco Chronicle,* 27 November 1997, A25.

Segal, Jerome M. "Living at a High Economic Standard: A Functioning Analysis." In *Ethics of Consumption: The Good Life, Justice, and Global Stewardship.* Lanham, Md.: Rowman & Littlefield, 1998: 342–65.

Selingo, Jeffrey. "Boston U. Policy on Learning Disabilities Violated Federal Law, Judge Rules." *The Chronicle of Higher Education,* 18 August 1997. *Chronicle of Higher Education* Web site.

Sen, Amartya K. "Capability and Well-Being." In *Quality of Life,* ed. Martha Nussbaum and Amartya K. Sen. Oxford: Clarendon, 1993.

———. "Equality of What?" In *Tanner Lectures on Human Values,* ed. S. McMurrin. Salt Lake City: University of Utah Press, 1980.

———. *Inequality Reexamined.* Cambridge: Harvard University Press, 1995.
Sengupta, Somini. "Airline Wins a Bias Suit about Weight of Personnel." *New York Times,* 18 December 1997, A22.
Shakespeare, Tom. "Andre Gorz." In *Guide to Social and Political Theory,* ed. Stuart Sim. Harvester Wheatsheaf, 1997.
———. "Back to the Future: New Genetics and Disabled People." *Critical Social Policy* 44/45 (1995).
———. "Choices and Rights: Eugenics, Genetics and Disability Equity." *Disability & Society* (forthcoming issue).
———. "Coming Out and Coming Home." *Journal of Gay, Lesbian & Bisexual Identity* (forthcoming issue).
———. "Cultural Representation of Disabled People: Dustbins for Disavowal?" *Disability and Society* 9, no. 3 (1994).
———. "Disability, Identity and Difference." In *Exploring the Divide: Illness and Disability,* ed. Colin Barnes and Geoff Mercer. Leeds, U.K.: Disability Press, 1996.
———. "Disabled People's Self-Organization: A New Social Movement?" *Disability, Handicap and Society* 8, no. 3 (1993).
———. "Out on the Margins." *Disability Studies Quarterly* (forthcoming issue).
———. "Power and Prejudice: Issues of Gender, Sexuality and Disability." In *Disability and Society: Emerging Issues and Insights,* ed. Len Barton. London: Longmans, 1996.
———. "Redefining the Disability Problem." *Critical Public Health* 6, no. 2 (1995).
———. "Representations of Disabled People in Television Soap Operas." In *Framed: A Disability Media Reader,* ed. Chris Davies and Ann Pointon. BFI, 1997.
———. "Researching Disabled Sexuality." In *Doing Disability Research,* ed. Colin Barnes and Geoff Mercer. Leeds, U.K.: Disability Press, 1997.
———. "Rules of Engagement: Doing Disability Research." *Disability & Society* 10, no. 4 (1995).
———. "Social Constructionism as a Political Strategy." In *The Politics of Social Constructionism,* ed. Irving Velody and Robin Williams. London: Sage, forthcoming.
———. ed. *The Disabilities Studies Reader.* London: Cassell, 1998.
———. "What Is a Disabled Person?" In *Disability, Divers(ability) and Legal Change,* ed. Melinda Jones and Lee Ann Marks. The Hague: Kluwer Academic, 1999.
Shakespeare, Tom, Kath Gillespie-Sells, and Dominic Davies. *The Sexual Politics of Disability: Untold Desires.* London: Cassell, 1996.
Shakespeare, Tom, and Nicholas Watson. "Defending the Social Model." *Disability and Society* 12, no. 2 (1997): 293–300.
Shalit, Ruth. "Defining Disability Down." *The New Republic,* 25 August 1997, 17–22.

Shapiro, Joseph P. *No Pity: People with Disabilities Forging a New Civil Rights Movement.* New York: Times Books, 1994.

Sherwin, Susan. *No Longer Patient: Feminist Ethics and Health Care.* Philadelphia: Temple University Press, 1992.

Sidel, Ruth. *Women and Children Last.* New York: Penguin Viking, 1986.

Silvers, Anita. "A Fatal Attraction to Normalizing: Treating Disabilities as Deviations from 'Species Typical' Functioning." In *Enhancing Human Capacities: Conceptual Complexities and Ethical Implications,* ed. Eric Parens. Washington, D.C.: Georgetown University Press, forthcoming.

———. "Aging Fairly, Feminist and Disability Perspectives on Intergenerational Justice." In *Mother Time: Women, Aging and Ethics,* ed. Margaret Urban Walker. Lanham, Md.: Rowman & Littlefield, forthcoming.

———. "An Open Future: Exchange with Dena S. Davis." *The Hastings Center Report* 27, no. 5 (September/October 1997).

———. "Damaged Goods: Does Disability DisQALYfy People From Just Health Care?" *Mount Sinai Journal of Medicine* 62, no. 2 (1995): 102–11.

———. " 'Defective' Agents: Equality, Difference and the Tyranny of the Normal." *Journal of Social Philosophy*, 25th Anniversary Special Issue (1994): 154–75; anthologized in *Social Justice in a Diverse Society*, ed. Rita Manning and Rene Trujillo. Menlo Park, Calif.: Mayfield, 1996.

———. "Disability." In *Blackwell's Companion to Feminist Philosophy*, ed. Alison M. Jaggar and Iris Marion Young. Oxford: Blackwell's, 1998.

———. "Disability Rights." In *The Encyclopedia of Applied Ethics*, ed. Ruth Chadwick. San Diego: Academic Press, 1997.

———. "Don't Blame Impairment(s)." In *Bodies of Knowledge: Critical Perspectives on Disablement and Disabled Women*, ed. Shelley Tremain. Toronto: Women's Press, forthcoming.

———. "Double Consciousness, Triple Difference: Disability, Race, Gender and the Politics of Recognition." In *Disability Divers(ability) and Legal Change*, ed. Melinda Jones and Lee Ann Marks. The Hague: Kluwer Academic, 1999.

———. "From the Crooked Timber of Humanity, Beautiful Things Can Be Made." In *Beauty Matters*, ed. Peg Brand. Bloomington: Indiana University Press, forthcoming.

———. "How Can Women with Disabilities Countenance Feminist Bioethics?" In *Embodying Bioethics: Feminist Advances*, ed. Anne Donchin and Laura Purdy. Lanham, Md.: Rowman & Littlefield, 1998.

———. "(In)Equality, (Ab)normality, and the 'Americans with Disabilities' Act." *Journal of Medicine and Philosophy* 21 (1996): 209–24.

———. "On Not Iterating Women's Disabilities: A Crossover Perspective on Genetic Dilemmas." In *Embodying Bioethics: Feminist Advances*, ed. Anne Donchin and Laura Purdy. Lanham, Md.: Rowman & Littlefield, 1998.

———. "Protecting The Innocents from Physician-Assisted Suicide: Disability Discrimination and the Duty to Protect Otherwise Vulnerable Groups." In *Physician-Assisted Suicide: Extending the Debate*, ed. Margaret Battin, Rosamond Rhodes, and Anita Silvers. New York: Routledge, 1998.

————. "Reconciling Equality to Difference: Caring (f)or Justice for People with Disabilities." *Hypatia: A Journal of Feminist Philosophy* 10 (Special Issue on Feminist Ethics and Social Policy), ed. Patrice DiQuinzo and Iris Marion Young (Winter 1995), no. 1: 30–55.

————. "Reprising Women's Disability: Feminist Identity Strategy and Disability Rights." *Berkeley Women's Law Journal* 13 (June 1998): 81–116.

————. "The Politics of Disability," *San Francisco Chronicle*, 11 September 1996.

————. "Transforming the Culture: The Visibility of Disability in the Humanities." *Disability Studies Quarterly* 17, no. 1 (Winter 1997): 8–11.

Smith, Dorothy E. "Rethinking Standpoint Epistemology" What Is Strong Objectivity?" In *Feminist Epistemologies*, ed. Linda Alcoff and Elizabeth Potter. New York: Routledge, 1993.

————. "Women's Perspective as a Radical Critique of Sociology." In *Feminism and Methodology: Social Science Issues*, ed. Susan Harding. Bloomington: Indiana University Press, 1987.

Sober, Eliot. "Evolution, Population Thinking, and Essentialism." *Philosophy of Science* 47, (1980): 350–83.

Solinger, Ricki, ed. *Abortion Wars: A Half Century of Struggle, 1950–2000*. Berkeley: University of California Press, 1998: 374–93.

Spelman, Elizabeth. *Fruits of Sorrow: Framing Our Attention to Suffering*. Boston: Beacon, 1997.

Stein, Mark. "Rawls on Redistribution of the Disabled," *George Mason Law Review* 6, no. 4 (1998): 997–1012.

Stiker, Henri-Jacques. *Corps infirmes et societes*. Paris: Aubier Montage, 1982.

Strudler, Alan. "The Social Construction of Genetic Abnormality: Ethical Implications for Managerial Decisions in the Workplace." *Journal of Business Ethics* 13 (1994): 839–48.

Stuart, O. W. "Race and Disability: Just a Double Oppression?" *Disability, Handicap & Society* 7, no. 2 (1992): 177–88.

Stubbins, Joseph. "The Politics of Disability." In *Attitudes toward Persons With Disabilities*, ed. Harold Yuker. New York: Springer, 1988.

Sumner, L. W. "A Third Way." In *The Problem of Abortion*, ed. Susan Dwyer and Joel Feinberg. Belmont, Calif.: Wadsworth, 1997.

————. *Abortion and Moral Theory*. Princeton, N.J.: Princeton University Press, 1981.

Suzuki, David, and Peter Knudtson. *Genethics: The Clash between the New Genetics and Human Values*. Cambridge, Mass.: Harvard University Press, 1989.

Swain, J., Vic Finkelstein, Sally French, and Mike Oliver, eds. *Disabling Barriers— Enabling Environments*. London: Sage in Association with the Open University, 1993.

Swift, Adam. "Equality Matters." *The Times Literary Supplement* 17, no. 4959 (April 1998): 29.

Taylor, Charles, Amy Gutmann, Stephen Rockefeller, Michael Walzer, and Susan Wolf. *Multiculturalism and "The Politics of Recognition."* Princeton, N.J.: Princeton University Press, 1992.

tenBroek, Jacobus. "The Right to Live in the World: The Disabled in the Law of Torts." *California Law Review*, 54 (1966): 841–919.

Thomson, Rosemarie Garland. *Extraordinary Bodies: Figuring Physical Disability in American Culture and Literature*. New York: Columbia University Press, 1997.

Tong, Rosemarie. *Feminist Thought*. Boulder, Colo.: Westview, 1989.

Treischman, Roberta B. *Aging with a Disability*. New York: Demos, 1987.

Trent, James. *Inventing the Feeble Mind: A History of Mental Retardation in the United States*. Berkeley: University of California Press, 1994.

Tronto, Joan. "Beyond Gender Difference to a Theory of Care." *Signs* 12, no. 4 (Summer 1987): 644–61.

———. *Moral Boundaries: A Political Argument for an Ethic of Care*. New York: Routledge, 1993.

Tucker, Bonnie Poitras. "The ADA and Deaf Culture: Contrasting Precepts, Conflicting Results." *Annals of the American Academy of Political and Social Sciences* 551 (January 1997): 24–36.

Ubel, P., and Mary B. Mahowald. "Ethical and Legal Issues Regarding Living Donors." In *Encyclopedia of Bioethics*, ed. Warren T. Reich. New York: Simon & Schuster Macmillan, 1995.

United Nations. "Standard Rules on the Equalization of Opportunities for Persons with Disabilities." *G.A. res.* 48/96, 48 U.N. GAOR Supp. (No. 49) at 202, U.N. Doc. A/48/49 (1993).

U.S. Congress. *The Americans with Disabilities Act*, U.S. Public Law 10 (1990).

Van DeVeer, Donald, and Tom Regan, eds. *Health Care Ethics: An Introduction*. Philadelphia: Temple University Press, 1986.

Veatch, Robert. *The Foundation of Justice: Why the Retarded and the Rest of Us Have Claims to Equality*. Oxford: Oxford University Press, 1986.

Veille, J. C., Mary B. Mahowald, and M. Sivakoff. "Ethical Dilemmas in Fetal Echocardiography." *Obstetrics and Gynecology* 73, no. 5 (May 1989): 710–14.

Verne, Jules. *The Country of the Blind and Other Stories*. Freeport, N.Y.: Books for Libraries Press, 1971.

Wagner, Judith Welch. "The Antidiscrimination Model Reconsidered: Ensuring Equal Opportunity without Respect to Handicap under Section 504 of the Rehabilitation Act of 1973." *Cornell Law Review* 69: 40–516.

Walters, James W., ed. *Choosing Who's to Live: Ethics and Aging*. Urbana: University of Illinois Press, 1996.

Wasserman, David. "Behavioral Genetics." In *Encyclopedia of Biotechnology: Ethical, Legal and Policy Issues*, ed. Thomas Murray and Maxwell Mehlman. New York: Wiley, 1998/1999.

———. "Disabilities, Discrimination, and Fairness." *Report from the Institute for Philosophy and Public Policy* 13, nos. 1–2 (Winter/Spring 1993): 805–13.

———. "Forensic DNA Typing." In *A Companion to Genethics: Philosophy and the Genetic Revolution*, ed. Justine C. Burley and John Harris. Oxford: Blackwell, 1998.

———. "Impairment, Disadvantage, and Equality: A Reply to Anita Silvers." *Journal of Social Philosophy* 25, no. 3 (Winter 1994): 181–88.

———. "Let Them Eat Chances: Probability and Distributive Justice." *Economics & Philosophy* 12, no. 1 (April 1996).

———. "Public Funding for Science and Art: Censorship, Social Harm, and the Case of Genetic Research into Crime and Violence." In *Censorship and Silencing: Practices of Cultural Regulation*, ed. Robert Post. Santa Monica, Calif.: Getty Research Institute, 1998.

———. "Some Moral Issues in the Correction of Impairments." *Journal of Social Philosophy* 27, no. 2 (Fall 1996): 128–45.

———. "The Concept of Discrimination." In *Encyclopedia of Applied Ethics*, ed. Ruth Chadwick. San Diego: Academic Press, 1997.

Wasserman, David, and Robert Wachbroit, eds. *Genetics and Criminal Behavior: Methods, Meanings, and Morals.* New York: Cambridge University Press, 1998.

———. "Patient Autonomy and Value Neutrality in Nondirective Genetic Counseling." *Stanford Journal of Law and Social Policy* 6, no. 2 (1995).

———. "The Ethics, Law, and Technology of IVF, Surrogate Parentage, and Gamete Donation," *Clinics in Laboratory Medicine: Technology Applied to Problems of Human Reproduction* 12, no. 3 (September 1992): 429–48.

Wear, Delese, ed. *Women in Medical Education.* New York: State University of New York Press, 1996.

Wendell, Susan. *The Rejected Body: Feminist Philosophical Reflections on Disability.* London: Routledge, 1996.

———. "Toward a Feminist Theory of Disability." *Hypatia: A Journal of Feminist Philosophy* 4, no. 2 (Summer 1996): 104–24.

Wertz, Dorothy, and John Fletcher, eds. *Ethics and Human Genetics: A Cross-Cultural Perspective.* Berlin: Springer, 1989.

Wheeler, William. "Golf Cart Gives Disabled Athlete No Advantage." *New York Times,* 23 January 1998, A18.

Wilkes, Daniel. "Paternalism and the Mildly Retarded." *Philosophy and Public Affairs* 8, no. 4 (1979): 63–87.

Wilkinson, Richard G. *Unhealthy Societies: The Afflictions of Inequality.* New York: Routledge, 1996.

Williams, Donna. *Somebody Somewhere: Breaking Free From the World of Autism.* New York: Times Books, 1994.

Williams, Paul, and Bonnie Shoultz. *We Can Speak for Ourselves: Self-Advocacy by Mentally Handicapped People.* London: Souvenir, 1982.

Winant, Terry. "The Feminist Standpoint: A Matter of Language." *Hypatia: A Journal of Feminist Philosophy* 2 (Winter 1987): 1123–48.

Wolf, Susan, ed. *Feminism and Bioethics: Beyond Reproduction.* New York: Oxford University Press, 1995.

Wolfensberger, Wolf. "Human Services Policies: The Rhetoric vs. the Reality." In *Disability and Dependency*, ed. Len Barton. London: Falmer, 1989.

———. "The Origin and Nature of Our Institutional Models." In *Changing Pat-*

terns in Residential Services for the Mentally Retarded, ed. Robert Kugel and Ann Shearer. Washington, D.C.: President's Committee on Mental Retardation, 1976.

————. *The Principle of Normalization in Human Services*. Toronto: National Institute on Mental Retardation, 1972.

World Health Organization. *International Classification of Impairments, Disabilities, and Handicaps*. Geneva: World Health Organization, 1980.

Young, Iris Marion. "Asymmetrical Reciprocity: On Moral Respect, Wonder, and Enlarged Thought." *Constellations* 3, no. 3, 1997.

————. *Justice and the Politics of Difference*. Princeton, N.J.: Princeton University Press, 1990.

————. *Throwing Like a Girl and Other Essays in Feminist Philosophy and Social Theory*. Bloomington: Indiana University Press, 1990.

Youngner, S. J., ed. *Human Values in Critical Care Medicine*. New York: Praeger, 1986.

Youngner, S. J., M. Allen, E. T. Bartlett, H. F. Cascorbi, T. Hau, D. L. Jackson, B. J. Martin, and Mary B. Mahowald. "Psychosocial and Ethical Implications of Organ Retrieval." *New England Journal of Medicine* 313 (1985): 321–24.

Zola, Irving Kenneth. "Medicine as an Institution of Social Control." *Sociological Review* 20 (1972): 487–504.

————. *Missing Pieces: A Chronicle of Living with a Disability*. Philadelphia: Temple University Press, 1982.

Index

About the Authors

Anita Silvers is professor of philosophy at San Francisco State University and the author of more than fifty publications on ethics and bioethics, aesthetics, feminism, higher education, and public policy. She was the first recipient of the California Faculty Association's Human Rights Award for her leadership in opening higher education to people with disabilities.

David Wasserman is research scholar at the Institute for Philosophy and Public Policy, University of Maryland, who writes on philosophical issues occasioned by disability policy, the life sciences, and the law. He is a practicing attorney who represents clients with disabilities.

Mary B. Mahowald is professor at the Pritzker School of Medicine, University of Chicago. Her books on health care and feminist issues include *Women and Children in Health Care,* and her research on genetics has been supported by the National Institutes of Health and the Department of Energy.

Lawrence C. Becker is William R. Kenan, Jr., Professor in the Humanities (Philosophy) at the College of William and Mary. He is the author of a number of books, including *Property Rights* (1977), *Reciprocity* (1986), and *A New Stoicism* (1998), and is the editor, with Charlotte B. Becker, of the two-volume *Encyclopedia of Ethics* (1992).